COLORADO
LIVING AND WORKING IN THE ROCKIES

Denver is the capital of Colorado and the socioeconomic center of the Rocky Mountains. Photo by Bob Ashe, Stock Imagery

COLORADO
LIVING AND WORKING IN THE ROCKIES

JERRY RICHMOND

General Communications, Inc.
Denver, Colorado

For Judith,
My friend, muse, and spouse.

Credits:
General Communications, Inc., Publisher &
Staff for *COLORADO: Living and Working in the Rockies*
    Publishers: A. Emmet Stephenson Jr.
                 Terry Vitale
    Associate Publisher: Robert Zeis
    Executive Director: Joanna Reiver
    General Manager: Nancy Lippe
    Associate General Manager: Richard Haas
    Art Direction & Production: Carol Rush
    Sponsorship Director: Don Jansen
    Circulation Director: Susan E. Trask
    Business Manager: Bonnie Lipschitz
    Printer: W. A. Krueger Company, Joyce Yost
    Color Separations: American Color Corporation, Dan Popp
    Typesetting: Anderson Advertising Art, Andy Anderson
    Map Production: Image-Corp
    Map Design: Ken Hladek
    Editorial Assistant: Mary Ellen Kemp
    Cover Design & Production: Image-Corp

Colorado Association of Commerce & Industry
    Chairman of the Board 1985-86: N. Berne Hart
    Chairman of the Board 1986-87: Jeff Coors
    President: George Dibble
    Book Project Coordinator: Carol Beam

Library of Congress Cataloging in Publication Data

    Richmond, Jerry, 1936-
        Colorado: Living and Working in the Rockies

        Includes bibliography & index.
        1. Colorado—Modern life style and economy.
        Library of Congress Catalog Card Number
          86-081929 ISBN 0-939185-00-8

Copyright © 1986 by Jerry Richmond
    All rights reserved. Photo copyrights retained by contributing photographers. No parts of this book may be reproduced without permission in writing from the Publisher.
                General Communications, Inc.
                100 Garfield Street
                Denver, Colorado 80206

Contents

6	Foreword	
8	Introduction	
11	Chapter One	**A Highland of People and Resources** The Building of Colorado
31	Chapter Two	**Main Streets of Colorado** The Centers of Commerce
63	Chapter Three	**The Colorado Good Life** Community Institutions
85	Chapter Four	**Riches from the Mountains and Plains** Agribusiness, Mining, and Energy Development
107	Chapter Five	**Service Center for the Rockies** Pioneering the Information Age
131	Chapter Six	**Crossroads of the West** Transportation and Distribution
149	Chapter Seven	**People-Powered Industry** Manufacturing from Basics to High Tech
175	Chapter Eight	**Financing a Mile-High Empire** The Underwriters of Enterprise
193	Chapter Nine	**High-Altitude Recreation** A Mountain Land for Vacations, Arts, and Culture
213	Chapter Ten	**Managing for the Future** The Land and Its Uses
235	Chapter Eleven	**A Future Challenge** The Delicate Balance
250	Bibliography	
253	Index	

Foreword

"...to effectively present the Colorado business community to government and the public; promoting, supporting, and enhancing the economic climate of the state."

In assuming the important role as the voice of Colorado business, the Colorado Association of Commerce and Industry recognizes the tremendous potential for being the lead state in the Rocky Mountain region. Colorado is emerging as one of the top states in the country for investment.

Abundant natural resources, scenic beauty, and a strategic location is attracting educated and trained business, science, and arts professionals to Colorado. The state has an abundant supply of leaders, entrepreneurs, and other highly qualified individuals.

In order to capitalize upon its natural, produced and human resources, the state must follow a long-range plan to insure that it will remain economically viable and attractive for resource development. Business is working in cooperation with government, legislative, and executive branches at all levels to develop a plan that will address infrastructure needs vital to future economic development. Business and government are also working for an educational system to provide development opportunity for future generations and to attract the best minds in higher education.

As a growth state there remain exciting challenges. Colorado needs to continue careful review of its expenditures and revenue structure to insure a fair and equitable tax base while providing for the necessary development of water resources, transportation systems, capital projects, and education programs. The accomplishment of these goals will necessitate a long-term plan, not merely a year-to-year, crisis-to-crisis approach.

The Colorado Association of Commerce and Industry stands ready to provide the coordinated leadership through volunteers from all sectors of the economy. The Association was organized in 1965 as a broad-based, multi-goal organization representing Colorado's business, industry, commerce, and private enterprise. It represents the consolidation of efforts by two historic organizations—the Manufacturers Association of Colorado and the Colorado State Chamber of Commerce. As such it is the premier statewide business organization in Colorado, and provides a vehicle for representation of the large and small businesses of the state.

The Colorado Association of Commerce and Industry is an organization comprised of the many talents of diverse business leaderships through the volunteer structure. These volunteers are working vigorously through various councils, committees, and individual members to coalesce business and government planning toward insuring that Colorado remains economically viable today and tomorrow.

This strategy requires that Colorado maintain and enhance its competitiveness and overall business climate so that existing firms stay competitive, new firms find Colorado an attractive place to locate, and entrepreneurship thrives. Because of the new competition between states for jobs and business, Colorado must tell its story. It is not enough that the state offers some of the richest natural and man-made resources in the world. Young Coloradans desiring to remain and make their homes and careers in the state must be assured a stable and expanding base of opportunity. The economic health of all the

Author James Michener described the Pawnee Buttes near Raymer in his novel celebrating the centennial of Colorado. Photo by Arthur Bilsten, Stock Imagery

state's communities from the Eastern Plains, the Front Range, the mountain and valley areas, and the Western Slope depend upon the leadership of Colorado business and industry.

Colorado now enjoys a productive labor force and relatively high standards of living, yet it remains one of the most competitive in the United States. The state's modern capital equipment, fostered by a good investment climate, enhances this labor productivity. Reasonable taxation levels maintain the cost of capital at competitive levels, thereby fostering a healthy investment climate, and further enhancing productivity and development.

All these factors, coupled with the old-fashioned American work ethic and the state's bountiful natural resources, make Colorado an enviable place to live and work.

A book on contemporary life and work in Colorado, supported by full-color visual glimpses into all parts of the exciting state, is important in telling Colorado's story to others, and reminding Coloradans of their own blessings and responsibilities.

Such a book is COLORADO: *Living and Working in the Rockies*.

The Colorado Association of Commerce and Industry is pleased to have participated in making this book possible, and to provide its enthusiastic endorsement of the project undertaken by one of the state's outstanding publishers.

Introduction

GO WEST, YOUNG MAN.
—John B. L. Soule. Article in the *Terre Haute, Indiana, Express* [1851]

Horace Greeley, 19th century publisher of the *New York Tribune* and proponent of opportunities awaiting Americans on the western frontier, amplified that often quoted slogan which inspired the last great American migration:

". . .If you have no family or friends to aid you, and no prospect opened to you there, turn your face to the great West, and there build up a home and fortune," Greeley exhorted in an essay, "To Aspiring Young Men."

Colorado was the center of that western migration in the 1860s. More than 100 years later, the Nation is again looking to the West, as a new socioeconomic revolution unfolds for the 21st Century. And again, in the 1980s, Colorado is in the center of that movement.

A seer of change in these modern times, like Greeley more than a century ago, selects Colorado as one of the places where the new society is unfolding. John Naisbitt, in his bestseller *Megatrends*, specifically identifies Colorado as a place where the transition from "an industrial society to one based on the creation and distribution of information" is already happening.

In my visits to all parts of Colorado, and interviews with Coloradans from all life styles and vocations, one of Naisbitt's featured characteristics of this national social and economic transition seemed most apt.

"From a narrow either/or society with a limited range of personal choices, we are exploding into a free-wheeling multiple-option society," says Naisbitt in the introduction to his 1984 edition of *Megatrends*.

Colorado, coming from recent disappointments over the failure of the oil shale industry to develop in this decade and suffering its share of the nation's agriculture industry woes, is in a mood for change. Coloradans are conservatively optimistic and determined that they will build on an already substantial base of advanced technology to lead the way into the next century, now just a brief time in the future.

This book offers only a glimpse into life in modern Colorado, drawing on historic events that still influence the lifestyle and workplaces today and will probably affect the direction of the future. The documentation and the research material come from many sources, which are noted in the bibliography. In addition, trend material spanning the past several years has been drawn from numerous in-depth articles from Colorado's two leading newspapers, the *Denver Post* and the *Rocky Mountain News*.

Countless hours were provided to the author by individuals involved directly in the events shaping the economy today and tomorrow. Some of those individuals who took considerable time from their busy schedules are extended a note of appreciation in the Author's Acknowledgements, but these are by no means the only people who contributed. The managers of more than a score of local Colorado chambers of commerce, and volunteers working in economic development organizations for their towns and counties provided especially insightful information on the aspirations and challenges faced by their communities.

Sponsoring corporations and institutions of Colorado have provided the financial support to underwrite this presentation of modern Colorado. More importantly, their individual stories contribute a depth of understanding of how various entities form the social and

The lakes of Colorado offer pleasant contrast to the often stark beauty of the semi-arid region. Spring melting from nearby mountain snow packs provides water for the drier seasons. Photo by Ron Ruhoff, Stock Imagery

economic mosaic that is Colorado. These sponsors, whose organizations are reviewed on the profile pages in each chapter, are by no means the only noteworthy corporations or institutions in Colorado. They may not even be the largest, but they are representative. A special appreciation is extended to them for sharing their stories and assisting in the publication of this book.

The photography likewise is only representative of certain areas and topics in the state. All the great human and natural resources could not be pictorially presented. The publisher called on more than a score of Colorado's professional photographers, and screened more than 6,000 excellent images to select a representative depiction of living and working in modern Colorado.

Finally, the statistical representation of the sectors of the economy has been used to show the size of the work force, the relative magnitude, and the trends in the workplace. Numbers from the latest available sources have been rounded off to provide approximate scope of such factors as employment and value added to the economy. Special recognition is extended for the important and ongoing work of the Business/Economic Outlook Forums conducted each year by the College of Business Administration, the University of Colorado, and the Division of Commerce and Development, Colorado Department of Local Affairs. More than 60 key business, education, and government leaders, economists, and specialists contribute research to the Forum. Data shared from the Forum studies over the past decade was invaluable to the writing of this book.

The Author

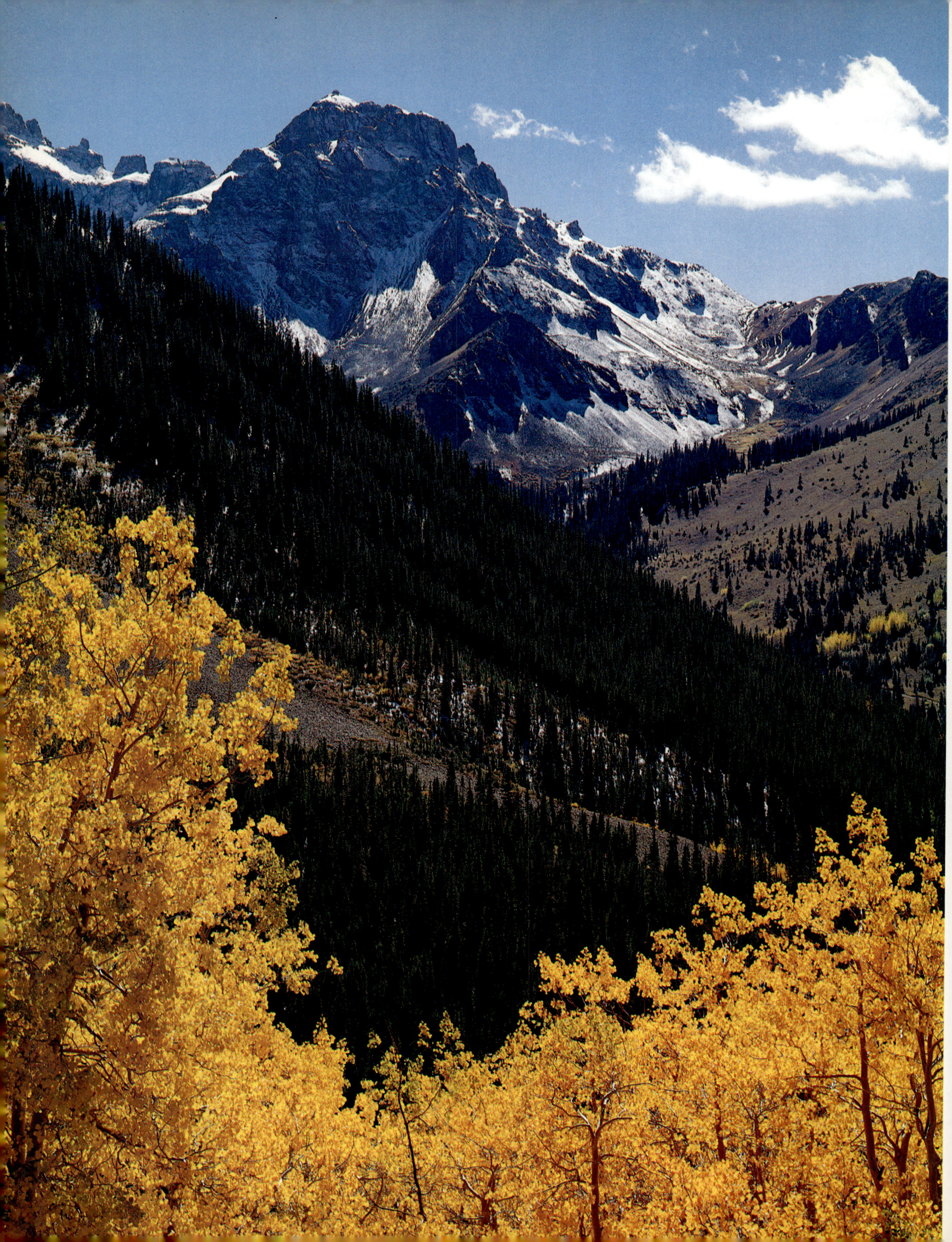

CHAPTER 1

A Highland of People and Resources
The Building of Colorado

Colorado is a state of alternatives. Some people are here seeking opportunity, and new frontier opportunities exist in a highly developed economy aiming straight and true toward the 21st Century.

Others are seeking escape from the fast-paced expectations of modern American society, and solitude among the high mountains, peaceful valleys, and endless plains is offered in abundance.

Colorado is a community where the space age mingles comfortably with vestiges of an earlier, rural way of life—where real astronauts rub elbows with real cowboys, and both respect and welcome the other's way of living and working.

Most of its 3,250,000 people live and work in super-modern urbanized areas. Eighty percent of the population is situated on the thin Front Range strip between Fort Collins-Greeley on the north and Colorado Springs-Pueblo on the south. The Denver Metropolitan Area in the center is home to 60 percent of the state's population, residing in five metropolitan counties.

But even the city and town residents seek refuge in the nearby mountain wilderness and resorts of the Rocky Mountains. In Colorado, almost everyone is an outdoors person, spending time in a year-round, natural and man-made treasure chest of recreational options. The remaining Coloradans, who have devised ways to live and work in the sparsely populated, forested mountains, sylvan valleys, and fruited plains that cover 90 percent of the state, are the envy of many resident weekenders and millions of out-of-staters who visit their highland Edens.

Colorado's topography is the highest in North America, averaging 6,800 feet above sea level. A semi-arid land described by early explorers as the "Great American Desert," Colorado waters the west with four of the major river systems in North America originating here.

The state is one of America's most important agriculture and mineral producing regions, and ranks among the leading high technology centers of the United States.

Coloradans are themselves a collection of people from different ethnic, regional, and social origins. Today's population is represented by families from every other state in the union, and many foreign lands. About 58 percent of the contemporary Coloradans were born in other states. Many of the native-born can trace a part of their ancestry to the earliest Spanish settlers on the North American continent. Colorado's opinion makers reflect this difference of origin, yet tolerance for the beliefs of others is an unwritten creed in Colorado.

Colorado's past and future are its present. If this duality of lifestyle appears to create a state of incongruency, it does not; because Coloradans are in harmony with, and actually cherish, the alternatives their unique place offers.

To understand the sweeping range of options in lifestyle and the economy of Colorado, it is necessary to look far back to its beginnings, because the present is very much a product of the past. What is happening in Colorado today, and what will happen within the state in the future, is not only tied to its relatively recent history of development, but also to its ancient prehistoric beginnings—the mountains.

The lifestyle and economy of Colorado are probably more directly linked to its natural

The Rocky Mountains are at their most splendid as they form the Continental Divide in Colorado. Photo by Ron Phillips, Phillips Photographics

Colorado's delicate state flower, the columbine, thrives in the shade of a mountain aspen grove. Photo by Tom McGill, Stockyard

resources than any other American state. Major parts of its historic industry base, which still survive if not thrive, are rooted in earth resources. Major parts of its new and future industry also rely on the aesthetics of its natural resources and the lifestyles they offer.

Colorado's first settlers came to exploit the minerals and stayed to reap wealth from the rich land. The modern descendants of those pioneers are here largely for similar reasons, with only the end-use of the land changing. The first hunters came to collect pelts from the animals in the mountains, and the miners followed to extract gold and silver. Today, Coloradan and visitor alike come to the mountains just to borrow a little of their majesty and beauty.

How the Mountains Came to Be

The highest point in Colorado is the 14,433-foot Mt. Elbert, and there are 53 other peaks over 14,000 feet above sea level. Colorado has most of the highest mountains in the United States, with 54 of the 87 mountains over 14,000 feet in altitude located in the Colorado Rockies. These mountains are a part of the longest mountain chain on earth including the Brooks Range in Alaska, the Canadian Rockies, and the Sierra Madre Oriental in Mexico. In all, 1,143 mountains in Colorado tower above the 10,000 foot or nearly two-mile-high mark.

Eons of mountain building, erosion, new mountain building and more erosion were required before these mountains reached their current rugged splendor. The process, according to geologists, began 2.5 billion years ago as continents were forming. Colorado's mountains began as bulges in the earth caused by pressures building up as continental shelves collided. As pressures built, cracks, faults, and upheavals formed mountains at stress points along the gigantic domed bulge.

Some of the newer mountains, particularly those in the San Juans in the southwest part of the state, were created by volcanic action, but most of the high Rockies rose gradually over hundreds of millions of years.

Rising from salty, silty primordial seas 250 to 600 million years ago, the first deposits of future minerals were formed from the earliest sea life in the Paleozoic Era, often called the age of fishes. Probably nothing lived on the new land for eons.

In the Mesozoic Era, the age of reptiles, there was land around the salt seas in the form of bogs, flood plains, and deltas at the bases of Colorado's ancestral mountains. Lush vegetation appeared over time and so did the dinosaurs. From 65 million to 240 million years ago, Colorado teemed with gigantic reptiles. The bones and solidified footprints of more than 70 kinds of dinosaurs have been unearthed in all parts of the state in valleys, on the mountainsides, and in the canyons.

The bones of the largest brontosaurus ever excavated on earth were found in the Canon City area. This giant herbivore, called the thunder lizard because it probably shook the earth when it walked, grew to 90 feet long and 14 feet high, weighing as much as 33 tons. The allosaurus, a mere 36 feet long, was a flesh eater, as big as a city bus. Other reptiles thriving in Colorado included the tyrannosaurus, a seven-ton carnivore that moved around on its hind legs, the diracadon, iguanodon, acrocanthosaurus, triceratops, ornithomimus, coelurid, and a tiny wading bird called ignotornis. They all joined the earlier shelled and soft-bodied sea life and prehistoric vegetation to help form some of the energy mineral deposits that 20th century man would search for so frantically ages later.

The seabeds and lush vegetation in huge

marshes were to become vast beds of coal. Almost the entire Western Slope of Colorado covers coal and oil shale deposits. Other large coal deposits underlie much of the Front Range from Colorado Springs to the Wyoming border, and rich seams are found in the Walsenburg-Trinidad area in southern Colorado, in the North Park area from Hot Sulphur Springs to Walden, in the Canon City-Florence area, and in South Park east of Fairplay.

In the mountains, breaking rifts brought up other minerals of future value to within reach of later exploiters. Lead, zinc, uranium, molybdenum, vanadium, tungsten, copper, tin, and other minerals from deep in the earth were forced upward with the rising mountains.

It was not until the Cenozoic Era, the age of mammals beginning about 65 million years ago, that anything like the present-day Colorado landscape began to emerge. That era marked the beginning of the building of the present Rockies, plains, valleys, mesas, and plateaus. Deposits of oil shale were formed in a 25,000-square-mile lake in western Colorado. As the main spine of the Rockies heaved upward along faults, volcanic activity created the San Juans and other mountains of southwestern Colorado.

Erosion of new mountains brought deposits of sand and gravel down from the rising heights as ancient rivers roared down from the newly forming highlands. Rich minerals were deposited in vast fans sloping off to the eastern plains, and in valleys along eroding riverways on the west of the mountains. Mesas, buttes, cuestas, and canyons were formed on the high plateau of the Western Slope.

Very gradually, a great bulge or uplift in the whole central western part of what was to become the United States rose to over 5,000 feet, as pressure from continental drift continued to bow the surface of the earth upward to form this high country. The land lurched higher by thousands of feet to form

Rocky Mountain National Park was one of the nation's first wilderness areas to be set aside for public use. Longs Peak is one of the most famous mountains in this Front Range park. Photo by Arthur Bilsten, Stock Imagery

The Rocky Mountains were formed millions of years ago to ultimately serve Colorado as sources for natural wealth and limitless recreation. Photo by Nathan Bilow

Colorado's high country becomes a frosted wonderland during winter. Photo by Nathan Bilow

the 14,000-foot mountains of today.

Another change had to occur before Colorado could sustain a thriving life of plants and animals similar to those surviving on earth today. The climates of prehistoric Colorado probably ranged from lush tropical periods to rainless droughts that lasted for entire epochs. At the peak of the last Ice Age some 18,000 years ago, Colorado's highlands were covered with ice. As ocean barriers between Asia and North America either froze or receded as the frozen ice cap consumed the water, some believe the first humans journeyed out of Asia onto the North American continent.

Gradually the Ice Age abated and the climate again mellowed, beginning a cycle that brought the region to today's four seasons. Although Colorado's climate is generally mild, some glaciers remain today in the high mountain valleys, carryovers from that Ice Age. Severe cold temperatures can still set national records in some of the mountain areas. But between the 5,000 to 6,000-foot elevations where most of the prehistoric animals lived, and where most of the present Colorado population resides, the weather was, and is, ideally suited for human enjoyment.

The mountains trap moisture from heavy snowfall during the winter and release it as precious water during the remaining seasons. Four great rivers of the West are formed by these snows. The Colorado River provides a major part of the water for parts of western Colorado, Utah, Arizona, and southern California. The Platte River, joined by the Cache la Poudre, flows east to provide cities and farmlands of Colorado and Nebraska with precious water supplies before joining the North Platte and becoming a part of the Missouri River system. The Arkansas River irrigates southern Colorado, flowing through Kansas and Oklahoma into the Mississippi River. And the Rio Grande, which irrigates New Mexico, becomes the international border between the United States and Mexico before flowing into the Gulf of Mexico.

Today Colorado is spared most of the worst winter storms that sweep out of the Arctic and western Canada, as they move east of this area onto the more exposed Great Plains. Much of the winter moisture comes on Pacific fronts that wring out against the high Rockies and leave the Eastern Plains and Western Slope fairly dry. Along the Front Range, Denver and Canon City enjoy a higher maximum winter temperature than any points of similar latitude from the Rockies to the Atlantic.

The earliest Coloradans developed one of the most sophisticated Native American societies before vanishing. Their mystery still awes millions of visitors at Mesa Verde National Park. Photo by James Blank, Stock Imagery

Occasional snows come to Colorado until about May, but usually last only a day or two before giving the land back to spring-like weather. Most communities in populated Colorado boast year-round golfing, because the snows at populated elevations do not stay on the ground for more than a few days even in the middle of winter. Some areas on the Western Slope enjoy sunshine more than 80 percent of the days, and Denver has almost as much sunshine as Los Angeles and Miami (both 73 percent), with 70 percent of the days sunny and bright. Sunny days along the Front Range exceed such temperate climes as Dallas/Fort Worth, 66 percent sunny; both New Orleans and Montgomery, 59 percent; Atlanta, 61 percent; and San Francisco, 69 percent.

Colorado is noted for its summers, which are dry and usually mild. While July and August temperatures may reach the 90s in the day, nights are cool. Autumn is the favorite season of many Coloradans and visitors, as it turns Colorado's famous aspen trees to shimmering gold.

After the Ice Age retreated from the plains back into the high mountains the mammal population emerged to dominate Colorado. Valleys and plains were the haunts of beasts almost as fearsome as the dinosaurs. Giant cave bears, wolves, and saber-toothed tigers preyed on mastodons, bison, prehistoric horse-like animals and camels pronghorn antelope and deer. Plants, animals and fish began to look more like the flora and fauna of today.

While the stage was being set over the millennia, it was not until around 20,000

Prehistoric artists left their work on cliffs near Craig, Colorado. The type animals they depicted abound in nearby mountains. Photo by Iris Photography

years ago that Colorado as it is known today really began to take shape. It took the most recent ice age, with its glaciers and frost, to perform the final sculpting. Glaciers moved, and shaved off mountain walls and cliff faces to expose valuable ores on the surface. Melting glaciers created rivers that brought down more mineral-rich soils to cover the fertile plains and valleys.

Edible shrubs, grasses and trees, and watering places were formed at elevations below the towering mountains to make a prehistoric Eden for an ever-widening variety of fish, birds, and mammals. As these creatures flourished to become the sole occupants for thousands of years, another creature was trudging toward Colorado. The first humans arrived—from whence no one is sure, and for what reasons, nobody can surmise.

The place was too good to pass up, and humans began to settle in Colorado. Even if these first human settlers had happened upon gold, which was already on the surface of the land around the site of such present towns as Central City, Idaho Springs, Cripple Creek, Leadville, Lake City or Creede, the discoveries would not have created much excitement. Silver deposits too, often mixed with lead and zinc, were already in place upon the arrival of the first people, but its later discovery at places such as Aspen, Central City, Creede, Gilman, Leadville, Silverton, and Lake City was likewise not the incentive attracting humans to the area in this prehistory time.

But the first Coloradans took no notice. Foraging and gathering for day-to-day survival was to be their most important pastime for several thousand years.

No one really agrees on the exact time the first people came along. The earliest human remains yet found on the North American Continent, the so-called Sandia man of northern New Mexico, are claimed to be about 20,000 years old. Charred wood, possibly from tools or campsites of an earlier so-called Old American, have been found in the High Plains of nearby Texas. These leavings of an early people predated the carbon-14 technique of dating back artifacts over 37,000 years. If such dating measures are correct, they place humans near Colorado along with wooly mammoths, mastodons, saber-toothed tigers, great ferocious cave bears, and dire wolves; as well as co-existent with ancient bison, antelope, deer, and other game that by then roamed the plains and valleys of Colorado in vast herds. It would also have put humans here in the Ice Age when the higher country was still covered with heavy glaciers.

The First Coloradans of Record

There are substantial records of the first real Colorado settlers. They left their houses and thousands of artifacts in testimony of their claim as the first citizens of record, and for modern Coloradans' enjoyment and amazement.

A people called the Anasazi, the Navajo Indian word for ancient ones, definitely settled large areas of southwestern Colorado as early as 2,000 B.C. University of Colorado anthropologists and archaeologists, working frantically in 1982-83 ahead of the McPhee Dam project on the Dolores River, identified almost 1,400 sites of Anasazi civilization. Rock chips, pottery, pithouses, and other human tracings have been dated back nearly 4,000 years.

The earliest fully developed civilization on the North American Continent evolved from these Colorado people in the famous Mesa Verde area and what is now the Mountain Ute Indian Reservation lands. At the time the Roman Empire was reaching its zenith in Europe, from around 100 to 200 A.D., a sophisticated culture was thriving in this part of Colorado. Elaborate stone cities were built

A young bull elk sports new antlers on his wade across a meadow stream. Elk herds flourish in Colorado high country. Photo by Mark H. Sims, Stockyard

Colorado's spectacular landscape was first inhabited by Native American Indians, whose history remains an important part of the state's heritage. Photo by Tom Stack, Tom Stack & Associates

in cliff walls and on mesa tops throughout this land.

By 450 A.D., when Rome was sacked by Vandals, plunging Europe into the Dark Ages, a Basket Maker people was cultivating vast acres of Colorado and trading with Indians as far away as the Pacific Ocean.

By 700 A.D. extensive permanent homes of wood, dried mud, and stone were built throughout this region. These early people introduced agriculture, raising corn, melons, and squash in the rich valleys. This civilization was of the longest duration of any yet established in what is now the United States. It lasted from 400 A.D. to around the middle of the 13th century—four times longer than the American civilization transplanted here by the Europeans has endured.

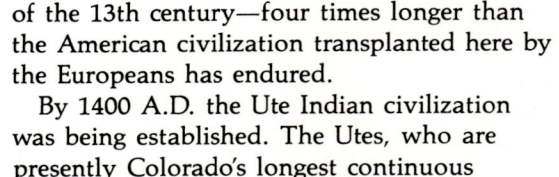

By 1400 A.D. the Ute Indian civilization was being established. The Utes, who are presently Colorado's longest continuous residents, may have hurried the disappearance of the cliff dwellers. They moved from the northern Rockies to claim these lands along with other parts of southern and western Colorado. The Utes were mountain people, probably held to the highlands by warlike Plains Indians who controlled the buffalo-covered prairies.

During this time, eastern and northeastern Colorado was the domain of the Arapaho, Cheyennes, Kiowa, Sioux, and Pawnee Indians. South and southeastern Colorado was controlled by the fierce Comanche, who are believed to have developed into a strong tribe in the prehistoric Rocky Mountains before migrating to the prairies. Parts of southern Colorado were controlled from time to time by the Apache people and the kindred Navajo.

On the Western Slope, the Colorado Utes had to contend with strong groups of Indians of the Shoshonean tribes, such as the Paiutes, Goshutes, Shoshones, and Bannocks. The Ute language is Uto-Aztecan.

Colorado's Utes roamed southwestern and western parts of the state from the time of the birth of Christ. They formed a powerful confederation and dominated this region at about the time that Columbus discovered the Americas. The Utes' confederation was comprised of seven bands. The Mouache band lived in southern Colorado and in New Mexico, near present day Santa Fe. The Capote band inhabited the San Luis Valley. The Weeminuche occupied the San Juan River valley. The Tabeguache (also known as the Uncompahgre) controlled the valleys of the Gunnison and Uncompahgre Rivers. The Grand River Utes (also called the Parianuc) lived along the Colorado River in Colorado and into Utah. The Yampa band controlled that river valley in northwestern Colorado, and the Uintah Utes controlled eastern Utah.

The Utes remain the only tribe concentrated in Colorado today, with only a tiny part of their once vast lands still under their control on the Ute Mountain Reservation, centered at Towoac, south of Cortez, and the southern Ute Reservation south of Durango and Pagosa Springs centered at Ignacio.

The Mouache and Capote Utes make up today's Southern Utes, and the Weeminuches are now called the Ute Mountain Utes. The remaining tribes, which once owned all of

Garden of the Gods frames Pikes Peak near Colorado Springs. The site is a favorite visitor attraction on the Front Range. Photo by Spencer Swanger, Tom Stack & Associates

western Colorado, were removed to reservations in Utah. Colorado's history was dominated by the Native American Indians until only 125 years ago when gold discovery brought hordes of European-Americans to seize the lands the Amerinds had ruled into antiquity.

The first Europeans to enter the state did not bring settlements, but were also gold-seekers.

As early as 1540 A.D., when Francisco Vasquez de Coronado led his conquistadors from Mexico to within a few miles of what is now the Colorado-New Mexico border, the search for gold was begun. Some historians believe the Spanish explorers actually might have crossed a corner of Colorado in their search for the fabled Cibola, reported to be Indian cities of gold similar to the Aztec cities in Mexico.

Whether they did or not, the expeditions began a historic series of events that played an important part in the development of Colorado until the present time. Santa Fe was settled by the Spanish and their Indian followers in 1640 A.D., about the time other Europeans were settling for the first time on the Eastern Seaboard. Spanish traders, explorers, and priests roamed the foothills of the Rockies all throughout the present site of Colorado. Farming communities were soon established in Colorado's San Luis Valley by the Hispanic descendants of these first colonists—200 years before Anglo-Americans ventured into the area.

These communities flourished through the 1800s and the territory they influenced under the flag of distant Spanish kings included parts of Colorado below the Arkansas River. Politics in Europe established the flag of France over a territory that was later to be known as the Louisiana Purchase, which included some of northern Colorado. But the French influence did not extend beyond an occasional fur-trapping expedition into the Colorado Rockies.

The Spanish and their descendants had introduced mobility into the region in the 1600s when the Indians acquired—by trade or raid—the first horses. The horse extended the power and the longevity of the Indians.

The American flag technically first appeared over parts of Colorado in 1803 when President Thomas Jefferson acquired the vast middle American wilderness from Napoleon. The first North Americans of record entered

Snow-fed mountain lakes abound in trout, and also provide some of Colorado's most beautiful vistas. Abandoned cabins offer proof that earlier settlers or miners tried to stake claims here. Photo by Arthur Bilsten, Stock Imagery

the region in 1806 when Captain Zebulon Pike and 16 soldiers were sent to map parts of what President Jefferson had purchased. When Pike's explorers reached the base of the mountain, which today bears his name, they guessed the height to be over 18,000 feet instead of its actual 14,110 feet above sea level. A later mapping expedition led by Major Stephen H. Long, for whom Long's Peak (near Estes Park) is named, was conducted in 1820. This exploration did not create much excitement since Major Long's party decided the area was a "great desert" blocked by impassable mountains.

The southern part of Colorado passed from Spanish ownership to Mexican territory in 1821, when Mexico won its independence from Spain. Trade routes from Missouri to Santa Fe were opened, and North American trappers began moving into the region. In 1828 Bent's Fort, a trapper station and trading post now restored, was established near present-day La Junta. Fort St. Vrain, down river from the present site of Fort Lupton, was settled by trappers and traders in 1838.

Texas had won independence from Mexico in 1836, and for a time claimed a section between the Arkansas and Rio Grande headwaters up the Continental Divide to U.S. territory in Wyoming. This section of the Republic of Texas includes what is now most of the ski resort areas in Colorado between Gunnison and Steamboat Springs. The Texans couldn't really occupy the area, and it was not until they began building ski resorts over 100 years later that they actually took some control. The area was ceded to the United States when Texas joined the Union in 1845.

The Mormons, who first settled Utah in 1847, laid claim to most of western Colorado as a part of their state of Deseret but only colonized the southwestern corner of Colorado.

In 1848, all of Colorado, as well as the present states of New Mexico, Arizona, and California, were wrested from the Republic of Mexico in the Treaty of Guadalupe Hidalgo, following a brief war. The entire region now containing Colorado was finally under the flag of the United States. Colorado's historians and amusement park developers could, if they so desired, also proclaim a "Six Flags Over Colorado," since during various times the flags of Spain, France, Mexico, the Republic of Texas, the Mormon State of Deseret, and the United States have flown over the land.

Even as a part of the United States, Colorado's Americanization was to be years in coming. The region was avoided because of its high mountains as pioneers poured west to California, Oregon, and Washington. Plains areas of the Dakotas, Nebraska, and Kansas were developed. Then John Fremont, a young explorer with a zeal for opening the West, was sent by the United States into Colorado in 1842, and the glowing reports written by his wife created the first favorable attention for the area. His guide was the famous Kit Carson. At that time Colorado was known as the Unorganized Territory.

Settlers, trappers, and traders began moving through, but not into, the area in larger numbers, setting the stage for the settlement to come. The dominant Indian tribes, the warlike Arapaho and Cheyenne on the eastern plains and the Utes in the mountains and western valleys, might have seen the handwriting on the wall had there been any walls. California became a state in 1850 while Colorado was still a wilderness. Colorado's first permanent town, San Luis, was not founded until 1851, when Hispanic farmers from the Santa Fe area moved permanently into the region.

In 1850, what is now Colorado was still divided into the Territories of Utah, Nebraska, Kansas, and New Mexico. Two events occurred in 1858 that began the momentum for the creation of Colorado. First, small traces of gold were discovered at the confluence of the Platte River and Cherry Creek. This site was to become Denver. The second important event leading to rapid settlement occurred when the spry wife of a goldseeker climbed Pikes Peak and wrote home about it.

Colorado historian Marshall Sprague thinks the letter home, which was widely publicized in the East, might have had as much to do with getting immigration started as the discovery of gold. Julia Archibald Holmes' climbing feat and subsequent announcement notified America that this nearby land was hospitable and waiting for the adventurous. Within a year after Mrs. Holmes' letter was reproduced in the Eastern press, some 50,000 Americans came to Colorado.

The Race to Civilization

There was not a great landrush, as when the Kansas and Missouri Territories were suddenly thrown open, but the great host of those who were to become the first perma-

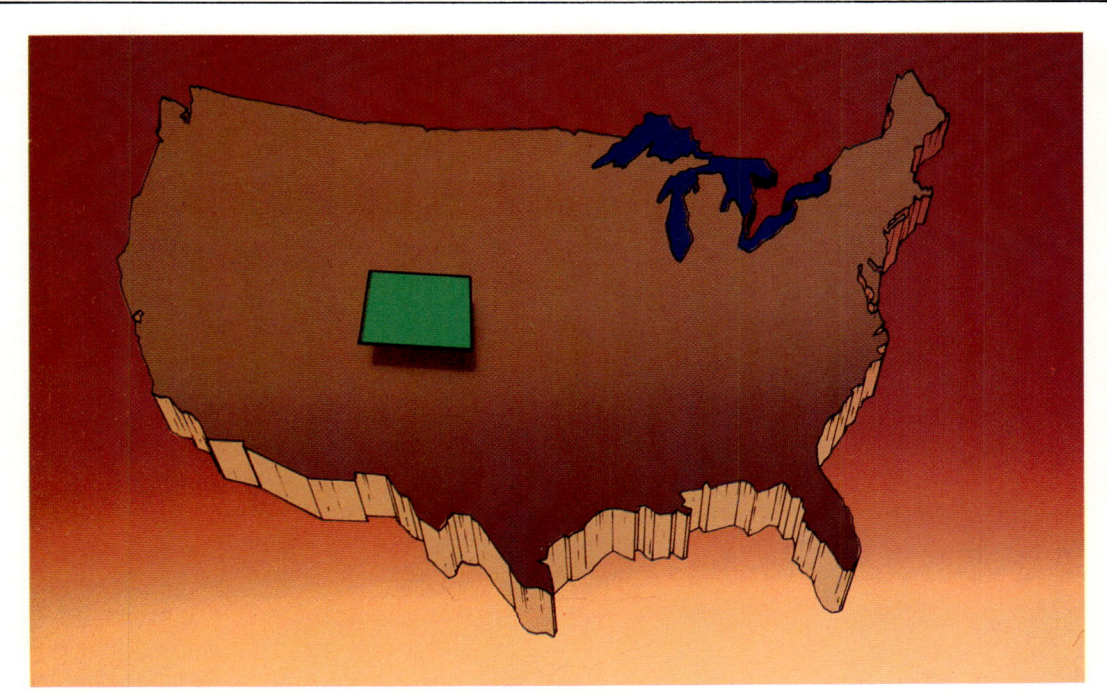

Colorado's Strategic Location—With outstanding transportation links to all parts of the nation via air, rail, and highway, Colorado's strategic location in the center of the rapidly growing western United States is a key factor in its promising future.

The harnessing of Colorado's bountiful water supply from mountain streams was important to progress in the state, and is vital to the future development. Photo by W.A. Hunt III, Phillips Photographics

Hawk chicks survey the grasslands of Colorado from a high aerie, undoubtedly expecting their next meal to arrive soon. Photo by W. Perry Conway, Tom Stack & Associates

nent American settlers came to Colorado in a steady and continuing stream after 1858. The first large numbers of immigrants came as gold prospectors, and moved into the mountains and valleys after stopping at the tiny village that was to become Denver. In 1859, it was the only real supply center the miners had before moving into the primitive gold fields nearby.

Then came those who would ultimately populate the region and join the miners in making Colorado a state. They came from all over the young United States, arriving from the U.S. frontier then established along the Missouri River and in Kansas. Some had sold everything "back East" and invested in wagons and goods to sell to the miners; they were the first entrepreneurs. Others carried all they owned on their backs and in hand-powered wheel barrows, walking to Colorado. The slogan "Pikes Peak or Bust" was the motto of this immigrating army of opportunity seekers.

Many were farmers, and brought families to settle permanently. And many who had started out to strike it rich in the goldfields returned to farming and the trades they had plied back home. The goldfields made only a few millionaires.

Finally, sufficient numbers of permanent settlers had arrived and stayed to justify the creation of the Territory of Colorado in 1861. However, with the nation entering the Civil War, little progress was made toward statehood or development of the region. A census of the Colorado territory in 1860 showed only 34,277 residents. Ten years later the census had hardly budged and reported 39,864 settlers in the whole territory.

Mining in the mountains went through several boom and bust cycles, as each new strike was made, exhausted, and rediscovered. During the mining periods of the late 1800s, gold and silver alternated as the most important discovery. Mining towns blossomed and faded. The more permanent town sites on the plains and in the foothills near the mountains—many of which started as agricultural colonies—were the principal survivors in the territory. Denver was always the leading town, and won a struggle with Golden to be named the territorial capital.

It was during this rough and often lawless period from 1859 until the mid-1860s, that one of the saddest pages in Colorado history was written. With the first great immigration into Colorado, the newcomers and the native residents—primarily the plains Indians including the Cheyenne and Arapaho, and the Utes in the mountains—frequently clashed. The tragic history of American settlement at

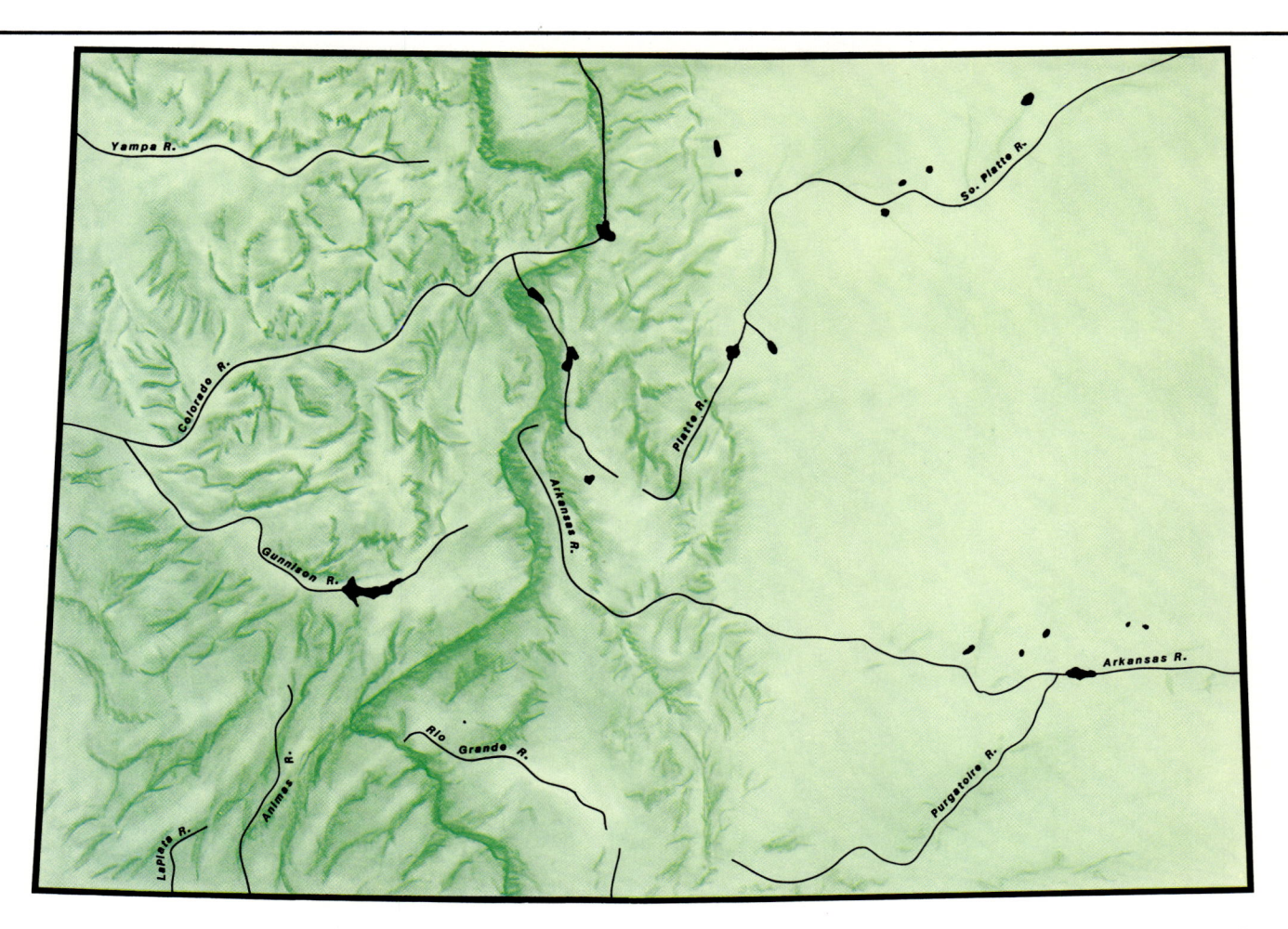

Colorado's Rocky Mountains—Nowhere in North America is the average elevation of a state or region higher than in Colorado. The Continental Divide, running north and south approximately through the center of the state, is no longer a barrier, but the source of unequaled opportunity for enjoyment and economic development.

the expense of the native Indians was repeated in Colorado time after time until the Indian nations were decimated, driven out of the Territory, or confined to what was then perceived to be worthless land areas. There were numerous battles between the new settlers and the Indian residents, but the extermination of the buffalo that had roamed Colorado and the Great Plains since the mountains had been formed millions of years before was the most devastating blow to the ancient Amerind culture. The buffalo was the primary source of their food, and the Plains Indians were gone from the state by 1867. Within another 15 years the Utes were forced from the mountains and valleys by one broken treaty after another. Their Ute treaty lands, which had included the western half of Colorado and over 30 million acres, were reduced to the present reservation land in southwestern Colorado consisting of about 757,000 acres.

The Census of 1870 showed only 17,583 persons employed in all occupations. In 1870 agriculture employed 6,462, the professions (medicine, law, education, etc.) 3,625, trade and transport 2,815, manufacturing 2,481 (which included blacksmiths, brick masons, carpenters, and sawmill operators), and mining 2,200.

Of the total population counted in 1870, 22,885 were United States citizens, 1,651 were citizens of Ireland, 1,493 English and Welsh, 556 British Americans (probably Canadians), 291 Scandanavians, 205 French, 184 Scots, 180 Italian, 161 other Europeans, and seven Chinese or Japanese. Blacks, many as freed slaves from Missouri, had come into the state since the earliest gold and silver discoveries, and Colorado's history is replete with records of the enterprises they established, political offices they filled, and other early accomplishments. With the above listing of U.S. citizens and foreign immigrants in the 1870 census totaling 30,349, another 9,515 persons were shown in the total census of 39,864. The census document did not explain this discrepancy, but that number could have represented

The Colorado big horn is a master of the steep Rocky Mountains and can be seen in ever-increasing numbers along the high peaks and cliffs. Photo by W. Perry Conway, Tom Stack & Associates

the Indian population of the state in that census year.

A phenomenal population explosion occurred within the next three years, and it propelled the population from 39,864 to 104,060 by 1873. Colorado had enjoyed its second gold boom in 1868 without much effect on the population. The almost instant growth could only have been caused by one event, and that was the coming of the railroads to the state.

After Denver was passed over for the main east-to-west coast line being built through an easier route in the Rockies at Cheyenne, a group of Colorado businessmen raised enough money to build a 100-mile spur line from Denver to join that trackage. At the same time the Kansas Pacific had moved from Kansas City into the developing western plains but had been halted at the Kansas line. Denver investors encouraged the line's builders to continue into Colorado and thus join the new Denver Pacific line under construction. On June 17, 1870 the Denver Pacific line was completed to Cheyenne, and two months later the Kansas Pacific reached Denver.

The future of development in the Territory of Colorado was assured, and its beginning was not long in coming. Once the rail linkage had been made to Colorado, connecting the region with the populated United States and the already booming West Coast, Colorado's first permanent boom began. This boom was to endure, because the people coming were not seeking gold and silver, but opportunity in every form of commerce and industry. They came to stay.

The coming of the railroads accomplished what several gold booms could not—the luring of permanent residents to Colorado. Not only the main line through Denver was important, but the unique Colorado narrow-gauge railroads completed the state's transportation system. The narrow-gauge lines, so-called because of the shorter width between rails, permitted smaller trains to travel around the sharp turns and narrow roadbeds of the Rocky Mountains. Within 20 years, more than 4,000 miles of narrow-gauge track was laid to mountain and farming communities throughout the state.

A special census in 1873 tells the story in a footnote:

Since the 1870 census, 40 new towns had been laid out, "some of them being already large and prosperous, with banks, newspapers, daily mails, churches, schools and other accompaniments of thrifty and intelligent communities. Among those are Colorado Springs with a population of over 1,200, Longmont 1,000, Las Animas 800, Caribou 650, Del Norte 800 and Granada 750."

That special census listed population in the already established cities of Colorado too, including Denver 20,000, Pueblo 4,000, Georgetown 3,500, Central 3,100, Trinidad 1,200, Golden 2,850, Greeley 1,500, Evans 1,200, Boulder 1,120, and Canon City 950.

If the railroads had provided the steam to begin the permanent immigration to Colorado, water was the catalyst needed for permanent economic development. Another event occurred at about the same time the railroads came. Horace Greeley, whose quote "Go West, young man" was more than idle advice, helped create one of many new farming colonies. The Union Colony, located at the town named in honor of Greeley, was founded in 1870. These agricultural colonists tapped into the nearby South Platte and Cache la Poudre Rivers, and constructed one of the first highland canal irrigation ditches. A 36-mile-long ditch irrigated the rich drylands, and started a program that is still administered by the U.S. Bureau of Reclamation for dryland irrigation.

Population growth finally justified the making of a new state. Colorado became the 38th state in the United States on July 1,

1876. Because it was admitted on the 100th anniversary of the nation, it came to be known as the Centennial State.

Soon, other agricultural colonies were thriving and bringing permanent population to the plains of Colorado. Irrigation by transshipping mountain water to the drylands created the communities of Longmont, Fort Collins, and Sterling. Mormon settlers in the San Luis Valley copied the process to create the towns of Manassa (later the birthplace of Jack Dempsey, the "Manassa Mauler") and Sanford. Communities along the Arkansas, such as Rocky Ford, now nationally noted for its Rocky Ford melons, soon followed the irrigation practices.

A substantial cattle industry also prospered on the more distant and as yet unfarmed eastern plains of Colorado. The great open ranching era began in the 1870s lasting nearly two decades. The old Goodnight-Loving Trail had moved Texas longhorns through the Colorado plains to railheads in Kansas and new ranches in Montana after the Civil War. Some of the cowboys and cattlemen later settled in Colorado to form their own vast ranching empires, but they were not to last long. Barbed wire and dryland farming closed down the open ranges in Colorado in the late 1880s. Sizable ranching operations remained, but behind fenced land owned by the cattlemen. Beef cattle raising in modern Colorado is the leading agribusiness income producer.

With the coming of the railroads and invention of modern irrigation, Colorado's many resources had been discovered. Between 1870 and 1880 population skyrocketed 387 percent to 194,327. It jumped 112 percent between 1880 and 1890, and passed the half-million level by 1900, when the census counted 539,000 Coloradans.

At the beginning of the 20th century, Colorado was largely an agriculture-mining state, but the commercial activities and manufacturing base had grown rapidly to support these natural resource industries. In 1910 half the population of the state, which had grown to just under 800,000, was urban (50.3 percent) and half rural (49.7 percent). While manufacturing expanded and a major industry based on farm and livestock products flourished for four decades, the state's population remained almost equally divided between the farms and the cities.

The last census prior to World War II

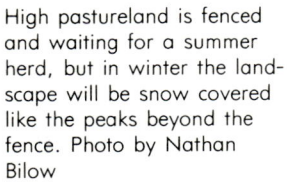

High pastureland is fenced and waiting for a summer herd, but in winter the landscape will be snow covered like the peaks beyond the fence. Photo by Nathan Bilow

A porcupine appears to be cuddly enough, but hikers beware. Common to most of the Colorado high country, the bristles have a bite too. Photo by Jeff Foott, Tom Stack & Associates

Beaver ponds, such as this one in Rocky Mountain National Park, attracted early trappers seeking the valuable pelts of the little builders. Today visitors seek a rare glimpse of the furry creatures at play. Photo by W.A. Hunt III, Phillips Photographics.

showed the state's 1,123,296 people were residing 52.6 percent in the cities and towns and 47.4 percent on the farms and ranches.

In 1940, 532,540 Coloradans lived on the farm. Most of the population of the West and South had been tied directly to the earth. But an era was coming to a close. Like so many other Americans, the young men and women of Colorado left the farms to serve their country in the battles and factories of World War II. When they returned to Colorado after the war, many did not return to the farm or ranch, but to the cities.

Tens of thousands of other Americans who had visited Colorado while training in the military camps situated throughout the state also discovered the vast beautiful land. They, too, would join the returning Coloradans in creating another great change in the state. Camp Hale near Leadville was created to train ski and mountain troops. Many of these specially trained soldiers returned to build the state's emerging ski and recreation industry.

Colorado's basic manufacturing industry and its farms and ranches had also been converted to higher production to support the war effort. New technology was introduced that would change the direction of all segments of the state's economy, and presage the modern industry of today.

The Modern Coloradans

By the first census after World War II, the state's total population had shown considerable growth, and the trend toward the urbanization of the state had begun. Between 1940 and 1950 the population had grown 28 percent from 1,122,196 to 1,325,089. In 1940 nearly half the Coloradans lived on the farm. By 1950 that percentage had declined to about 37 percent, and the trend for the future had been clearly established.

During the 1950s, particularly after Martin Marietta opened its first plant attracting satellite, space, and defense operations, the big changes began. Agriculture was also undergoing changes, with highly mechanized and larger farming operations being introduced. The machinery of war was turned back into plows, but the plows were super machines providing for mass agriculture production. The factories had been automated for greater production by the demands of the war.

Modern industry and business had discovered Colorado, and the population growth reflected these new jobs. From 1950 to 1960 an increase of 55 percent in the number of residents in the state heralded this industrialization. The population had increased to

Colorado is a land of great contrast from the magnificent mesas of Colorado National Monument near Grand Junction to the high peaks across the middle of the state, and down to the prairies on the east. Photo by James Blank, Stock Imagery

1,753,947. It surpassed two million a decade later in 1960, and has continued to grow at one of the nation's fastest rates.

The growth rate was 26 percent between 1960 and 1970, and 30 percent between 1970 and 1980 when the population was 2,908,375. Surpassing the three million population mark in 1982, Colorado's population stands at around 3,250,000 in 1986.

Colorado's growth rate was the seventh fastest in the nation from the mid-1970s to the mid-1980s, and most of that growth was created by newcomers arriving in the state. Most of the immigrants from other states were young adults, helping to keep the state's average age at a mature but youthful 29. A high percentage of the newcomers, like Coloradans already residing in the state, are well educated. Nearly 40 percent of the immigrating workers have college degrees. Colorado ranks first among the states in the proportion of persons 25 and over with four or more years of college.

Colorado boosters who worry that the state still has a rural image should not fear, because Colorado's population by 1980 was 80.6 percent urbanized; only 19.4 percent of the population of 2,889,964 lived in rural areas.

More significantly, of those 560,095 Coloradans living in unincorporated areas, only a fraction actually lived on farms. While the population of the state had soared since World War II, the farm population had shrunk from about a half million in 1940 to about 59,000 in 1980. At the same time the size of the average farm operation had grown from 833 acres to 1,403 acres by 1974. Farm production continued at record levels because of the continued mechanization and modernization of the farms.

Agriculture remains a major part of the economy. But in the three decades since shortly after the last World War, Colorado had also become an advanced manufacturing and high technology center in all areas of the economy, including business services.

In 1986, Coloradans on the job nearly exceeded the entire population of the state two

The fertile valleys offer some of Colorado's richest farm and ranchlands, providing grazing for sheep and cattle, and mineral-rich soils for planting. Photo by Nathan Bilow

decades before. The 1986 labor force of 1,769,000 was greater than the entire population of 1960. There are more Coloradans employed in the state's manufacturing sector—mostly high technology and advanced industry—than populated the entire state a century ago.

More important to the state of the state today, every sector of the economy shows greater employment and strength than it did just a decade ago—with the benchmark of employment soaring in nearly every sector except agriculture.

Despite the vagaries and cycles of boom-and-bust in some sectors of the economy, Colorado has obviously made a successful transition from the era of the smokestack industry to the new age of advanced technology.

Its enviable record of progress is clear when the decade from the mid-1970s to the mid-1980s is reviewed.

Total employment in the state rose by almost a quarter million jobs in the past five years, from 1,455,000 in 1981 to 1,667,500. Per capita income for Coloradans more than doubled between 1976 and 1986, up from $6,504 to $15,748 per year. Significantly, Colorado's per capita income was below the national average ten years ago, and by 1986 was well over $1,000 per annum above the national average of $14,612. This increase not only reflects the higher quality of jobs in Colorado, but also the state's advancing sophistication in the workplace.

During the decade the greatest growth occurred in the service industries sector from 196,500 in 1976 to 328,800 in 1986. This sector reflects the regional importance of Colorado to the other states in the Rocky Mountains and nearby Great Plains. Colorado is the personal and business service center for this region.

Even mining, which includes the energy extraction industry and all forms of mineral development, had a greater total employment in 1986 than in 1976, with 33,600 currently employed compared with 21,100 a decade ago. The other major natural resource industry, agriculture, was the only sector of Colorado's economy that had fewer jobs in 1986 than a decade earlier. Agriculture employment was about 34,400 in 1986, down from an average of 36,000 during the 1970s.

Strong and steady growth in the important manufacturing sector of the economy was shown in the increase of employment in the factories and plants of Colorado from 144,500 to 196,500 in the decade from 1970 to 1980. A closely-related sector, transportation and

A well-preserved country school and an early tractor remind modern Coloradans of their heritage on the land. Photo by Ron Ruhoff, Stock Imagery

public utilities, also showed steady growth from about 60,000 in 1976 to 88,500 a decade later.

Finance, insurance, and real estate employment climbed from 57,600 to 98,000 between 1976 and 1986. Long a leading center for federal regional offices, government employment in Colorado rose only slightly during that decade, from 219,500 in 1976 to 247,800 in 1986.

The decade since 1976 has been one of the periods of greatest capital improvement in the history of the state. Construction of residential units, office buildings, commercial and retail centers, and public facilities was fast-paced until after the mid-1980s. Even with a slow-down in construction due to some surplus in both residential and commercial buildings, construction employment was at record highs, up from 55,100 in 1976 to 87,900 in 1986.

The one sector of Colorado's economy that affects almost everyone in the state is trade, and that sector grew steadily with the other sectors of the economy from 249,000 in 1976 to 362,000 in 1986. Retailing is the one type of work found in every community of Colorado. While it is dependent on the health of every other sector, it is also basic to the support of all the other sectors upon which it relies. In looking at what makes up socio-economic Colorado today and tomorrow, this sector of the economy should be examined. In the next chapter on the modern geographical areas and political sub-divisions of Colorado, the Main Streets of this cross-section of America will also be reviewed. The cities and towns are the true heart of Colorado. Making the places they live compatible with the natural land is the Coloradan's greatest challenge.

Since entering the geographical area a relatively short time ago, man has brought significant change to the place now called Colorado. Some of the change has been good, and some not as good. Modern Coloradans, with a rich heritage based on these natural resources, are perhaps more aware of the human impact on their surroundings than many Americans. Their efforts to bring about a balance between progress and preservation is an important part of the story of modern Colorado.

29

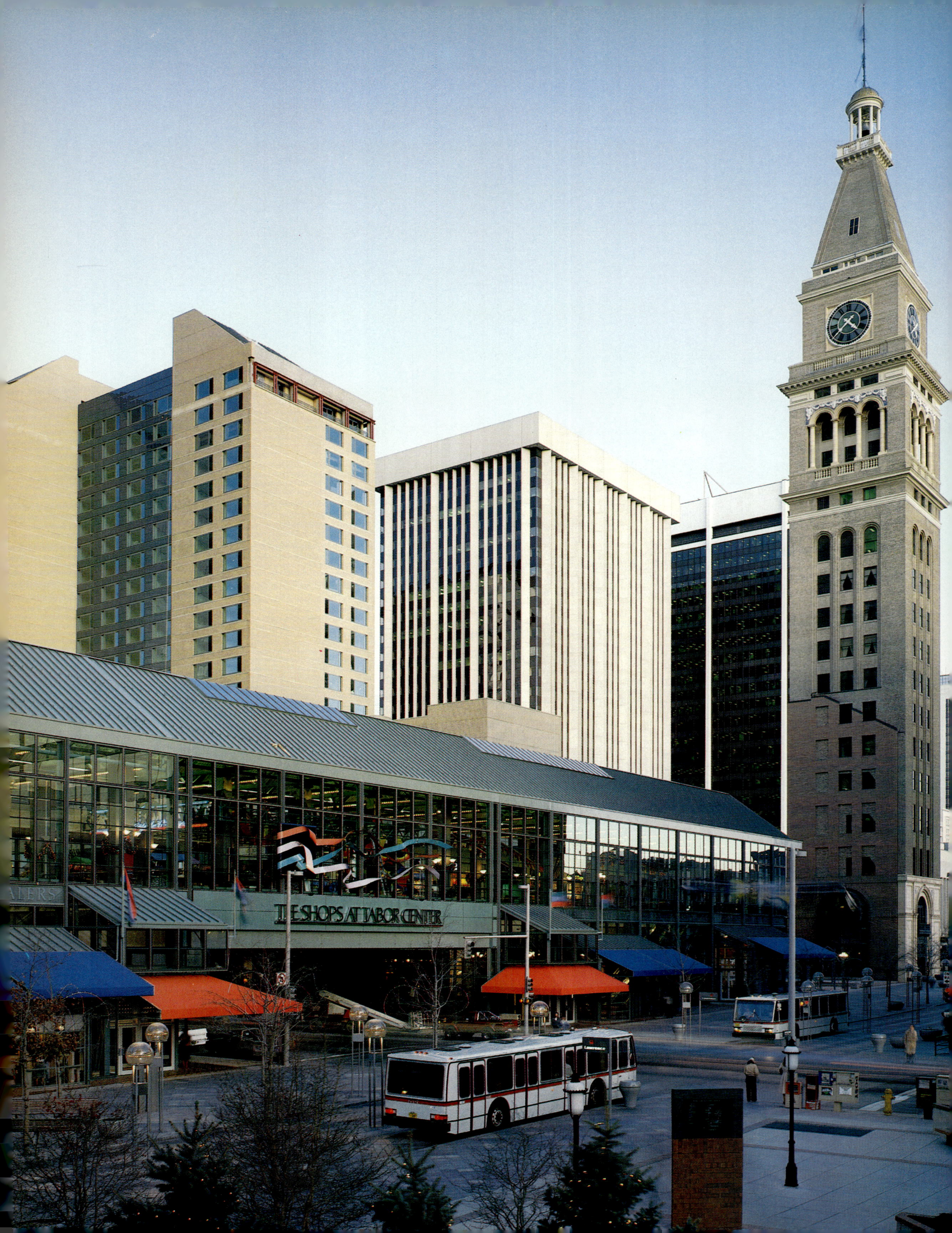
THE SHOPS AT TABOR CENTER

CHAPTER 2

Main Streets of Colorado
The Centers of Commerce

Every weekday morning, around 9 o'clock, an event occurs in the hamlets, villages, small towns, medium-size cities, and metropolitan centers of Colorado.

Men and women of all ages, ethnic groups, and social standing in more than 21,000 shops, stores, and shopping malls perform a single, time-tested ritual.

Each individual who performs this singular act makes an announcement to the world.

The ritual involves placing a small, but immensely important sign in a clearly visible spot in the front of a workplace. It simply states: "OPEN FOR BUSINESS".

This common little sign is like the sounding of reveille. It heralds another day of an awakened, vibrant economy in which Coloradans will again prove they are enterprising, determined, and here to work.

As the stores open in Colorado, all workplaces are opening—the offices, factories, laboratories, campuses, and support facilities. The merchant opening the little store is only symbolic of commerce; but the act is meaningful, since the ultimate destination for the products of all sectors of the economy is the marketplace.

Before taking a closer look at the important role the retail sector plays in the overall economy of Colorado, it is important to examine the characteristics of the sub-regions of the state. Each geographical sector of the state has its own unique set of economic activities, but the retail trade sector is the one common link found throughout the state. Therefore, this economic sector will be reviewed in more detail later in the chapter.

The economy of Colorado can be defined in many ways, but the trade territories and economic regions within the state offer the clearest picture of what Colorado is today.

Colorado has been the trade center for much of the Rocky Mountain and Plains States since early in its developmental history. The state is strategically located in the heart of a 13-state region, including the mountain states of New Mexico, Arizona, Utah, Nevada, Idaho, Wyoming, Montana, and the plains states of North and South Dakota, Nebraska, Kansas, and Oklahoma. Its primary, secondary, and tertiary influence, to a greater or lesser degree, extends to these states.

Colorado, which is the eighth largest state in the United States in geographical area, covers an area of 104,091 square miles. The state is approximately 300 miles wide from north to south and 400 miles across from east to west. The topography ranges from flat plains on the east to rolling foothills approaching the high mountains in the middle of the state. The Continental Divide traverses Colorado on a twisting line approximately through the middle of the state. This divide is literally a geographical wall running through the North American Continent. All waters flow east to the Atlantic and west to the Pacific (via the Gulf of Mexico) from each respective side of this line. It is along this spine of mountains that Colorado's chain of mountains rising over 14,000 feet above sea level stand as sentinels.

In the mountains and west the land features lush valleys shadowed by rocky peaks reaching above timberline where only Arctic-like plants grow. From 6,000 to 10,000 feet the mountainsides are heavily timbered. The Western Slope, a designated area west of the Continental Divide, offers a great variety of landscape from dormant volcanic mountains

Denver's 16th Street Mall, reserved for transit buses and pedestrians, has become the de facto "Main Street of the Rockies." Photo by Bob Ashe, Stock Imagery

31

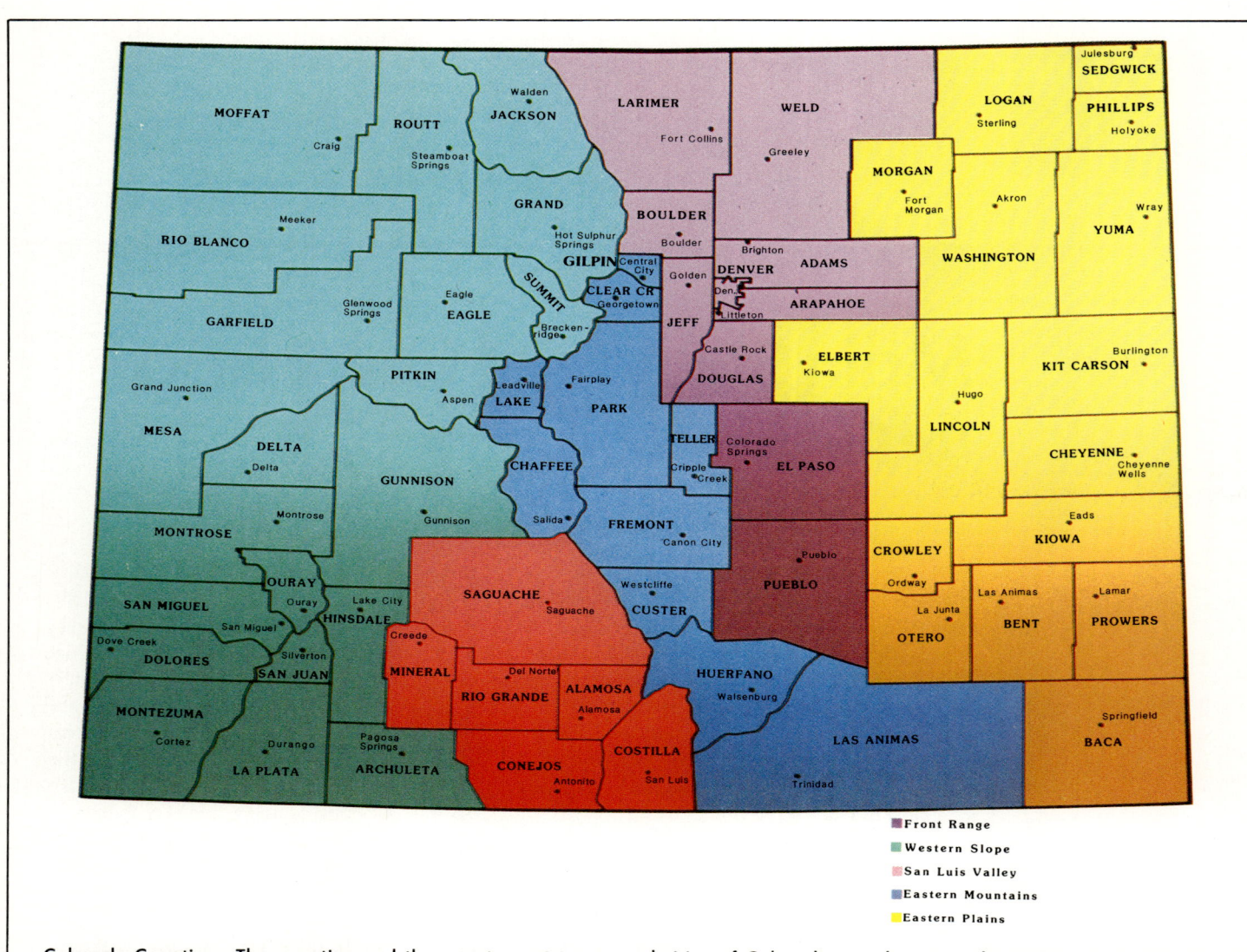

Colorado Counties—The counties and the county seat towns and cities of Colorado are shown on this map to assist in identifying places discussed in the book. In a few cases the county seat town is not the largest city in the county. Colorado's largest cities and towns are discussed in the text.

in the south to high mesas and deserts in the north.

To the east a vast sea of grassland and cultivated grainfields begin at an elevation of 3,350 feet in the Arkansas Valley and rise to the foothills of the mountains at an elevation of about 5,000 feet above sea level.

Of the state's 66,486,000 acres, more than one-third, or 23,919,000 acres, are owned by the federal government and administered by several agencies of the Departments of Agriculture, Interior, or Defense.

On the remaining 42.5 million acres not owned by the U.S. government, rapid urbanization of the land is occurring along the Front Range of the Rockies and in a few other areas of the state. In the past 20 years, land passing from rural to urban use has increased from 203,000 acres to 672,000 acres. More than 10 million acres remain in cropland, 24 million in non-improved rangeland, 4 million in forests, and 1.5 million in mining lands.

For planning and demographic purposes the state designated 13 planning and management regions in 1972. However, there are five distinct geographical/political sub-regions in the state that are often used to help delineate the economic and geographical areas. They also can be used to assist in understanding the lifestyle and workplace of the modern Coloradan.

Some regions share types of industry and sectors of the economy with all the other regions. Some are stronger in one sector of the economy than others. Some have a uniqueness not shared with the others because of natural or man-made resources, topographical features, and other factors. Colorado is a unified state; but there is regional pride, and on certain topics, such as water use, some degree of parochialism is often encountered.

Geographically, the five sub-regions of Colorado to be discussed here are named for their unique physical characteristics. They include, from east to west, the Eastern Plains, the Front Range, the Eastern Mountains, the San Luis Valley, and the Western Slope. The Western Slope will be further sub-divided because of the diversity of features of the land and the economy in that area of the state.

The Great Plains

Two important river systems, one in the northeastern part of the state and the other traversing southeastern Colorado, turn a vast prairie land of low rolling hills into one of America's most important agricultural areas. Within Colorado, an area of 27,000 square miles along the eastern border of the state, is a part of the huge Great Plains region of the United States known as "America's Breadbasket."

The vistas of open sky and seas of grass, or winter wheat in season, are the first views seen by many visitors to Colorado. A motorist entering the state from the east will begin to catch the first glimpse of the Rockies soon after crossing into the state from any point on the Eastern Plains. The terrain may feature either miles of flat plains or green river valleys surrounded by rich irrigated cropland. The flat open land is generally used for wheat production, while the fertile valleys may be dedicated to growing a great variety of crops.

The river systems responsible for watering this rich farming region are the South Platte, augmented by transmountain diversions of Colorado River basin water through the Colorado-Big Thompson Project; and the Arkansas River, augmented by Western Slope waters diverted under the mountains by the Fryingpan-Arkansas Project.

These waterways, which played such a large role in the development of the West, are even more important today, as modern agribusiness industries are formed to improve productivity from the farms. Along these rivers and other streams originating in the nearby mountains, cottonwood, pine, and willow trees break the routine of the grasslands. Before the pioneer farmers plowed it under for wheat crops, natural buffalo grass as tall as a man covered the whole region, feeding the giant natural herds. Estimates have been made that as many as 600 million bison once roamed the plains of Colorado and adjacent states during the zenith era of the vast herds. The rich soil, left from the roots of this grass sea and the minerals washing down from the mountains, is among

Colorado's Eastern Plains region shares the role of America's Breadbasket, producing an abundance of wheat and grain. Photo by Fred A. Luhman, Stock Imagery

PROFILE

Adams County Economic Development, Inc.
Transportation Boosts Economic Growth

The fast-growing communities of Adams County provide a balanced cosmopolitan environment of commercial, industrial, and residential features enhanced by a close proximity to Colorado's urban center in Denver and educational center in Boulder.

High-technology industries, served by one of Colorado's most comprehensive networks of highway, rail, and air transportation, complement a historic agribusiness to balance both the life style and economy of this region often called the "Greater Denver Metro North."

Adams County, with all or portions of nine of Colorado's leading cities located within its boundaries, is a 1,286-square-mile area extending from the foothills of the Rocky Mountains to the heartland of Great Plains. Its diversity of communities, businesses, industries, and services gives its citizens a broad choice of places to work and to live.

The county's economy mirrors practically every element that makes Colorado's economic base strong through diversification. Advanced technology and manufacturing, energy refining, mining, farming and ranching, retailing, services, and government all contribute to the jobs base that provides one of the highest employment rates in the state.

The largest communities in Adams County are those in the westernized urban area, including Arvada, Aurora, Brighton, Broomfield, Commerce City, Federal Heights, Northglenn, Thornton, and Westminster. Important farming centers located on the plains along Interstate 70 include Watkins, Bennett, and Strasburg.

In addition to five public school districts that consistently produce ACT scoring higher than the national average, Front Range Community College, located in Adams County, has the largest enrollment of full-time students of all the state's community colleges. The college offers industrial/technical training including on-location programs in cooperation with local business and industry.

No other geopolitical area in Colorado has a finer network of major highways serving both its individual and corporate citizens. Adams County is served directly by Interstate Highway 25 running north and south through Colorado, Interstate 70 running east and west across the state, Interstate 76 to Nebraska and the Midwest, and Interstates 225 and 270, and seven U.S. Highways.

This MetroNorth area also boasts excellent rail service, with major lines of the Atchison, Topeka and Santa Fe; Union Pacific; Burlington Northern; Denver and Rio Grande Western; Colorado and Southern; and Chicago, Rock Island and Pacific railroads providing direct rail links. About 40 major freight carriers have offices or terminals in Commerce City, one of Colorado's major truck transportation centers.

Because of its supporting infrastructure for business and industry, Adams County has attracted some of the area's largest and most advanced manufacturers. AT&T Information Systems is the county's largest private employer, with approximately 4,500 workers. Forty-six other private firms employ 100 or more persons, including these companies with more than 500 employees each: United Parcel Service, Sundstrand Aviation, Associated Grocers, Stanley Structures, Northwest Transport Service, and St. Anthony Hospital North.

New and expanding companies locating in the Adams County area are provided information and support services by the professional staff and volunteer business leaders working with Adams County Economic Development, Inc.(ACED), which is funded by the county, the municipalities, and the MetroNorth Chamber of Commerce. This economic development organization is a resource to business and industry, and can work with an individual company to match employment, physical plant, and support needs to services and facilities within the northern metropolitan area.

High-quality living in its rapidly growing communities remains important in Adams County even as this metropolitan area enjoys strong economic growth.

the best on earth for growing grain. Grains grown in this soil have the highest protein content of any in the world.

Agriculture, which has seen troubled times in America in the 1980s, is still the prime economic factor in the 16 counties comprising Colorado's Eastern Plains. Parts of Colorado's plains region are also rich in coal and oil deposits. Natural gas and oil wells actively produce side-by-side with grazing cattle and ripening crops.

The countryside changes with the seasons because of this agriculture-based economy. Rows of freshly turned springtime earth give way to miles of greening crops in early summer. By late summer wheat becomes a sea of golden waving grain, followed by what seems to be an army of harvesting machines moving methodically in columns across the plains.

A traveler can easily tell he is nearing the next town, miles before arriving. Two sights common to the communities of the plains are carefully planted trees, and various storage silos or grain elevators. Both, towering above the agricultural lands, provide a pleasing break in the prairie ocean, like islands on the horizon.

Diversification of the economy on the Eastern Plains, often based on manufacturing using crops raised in the area, has created more stability in this agricultural region than in some other farm areas of the nation. Manufacturing activity, some based on processing crops and livestock, has steadily increased in the cities and towns of the plains region. Incentives are offered for small to medium-sized industrial firms to locate operations in this region near the industrialized centers of the Front Range.

In an effort to diversify the economic base in the counties of the Eastern Plains, the communities have recently united for economic development efforts by forming the Colorado Plains Inc. This organization of volunteer community leaders is formulating plans to encourage the rapid diversification of local economies from their heavy dependence on agriculture.

There has been considerable diversification already—some based on agriculture and some totally unrelated. One of the state's newest major manufacturing plants is located at Lamar in the heart of wheat country, in the southeastern part of the state. That plant, Neoplan of West Germany, manufactures modern public transit buses and has delivered Colorado-assembled public transit vehicles to 50 U.S. cities. From apparel plants at Sterling to vegetable seed processing plants at Rocky Ford, the economy of the region is moving in new directions on the Colorado plains. The area has the advantage of space, excellent highways, and rail transportation for easy shipment of manufactured products. An available workforce from farming families trained and experienced in modern and mechanized farming operations has proven to be readily retrainable to perform skilled tasks in modern industrial operations.

The Eastern Plains region borders Nebraska to the north, Kansas to the east, and Oklahoma's Panhandle to the south.

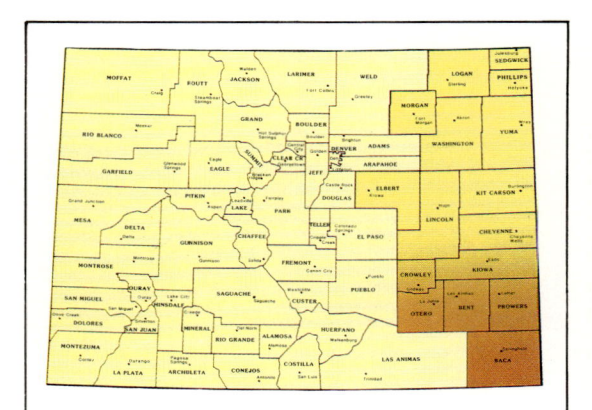

The Eastern Plains—Counties in this region lead the state in grain production, and in a diversified agribusiness economy. In recent years new types of manufacturing are locating in the region.

The highest concentration of population in this region is in the northern area along the South Platte River. Sterling, which is the government center for Logan County, is the leading supply center for that area. Other business centers and county seats and the counties they serve include Julesburg, Sedgwick County; Holyoke, Phillips County; Fort Morgan, Morgan County, and Brush, also in that county; Akron in Washington County; and Wray in Yuma County.

Principal seats of government and business in the central part of the Colorado Eastern Plains are Kiowa, Elbert County; Hugo, the county seat, and Limon, in Lincoln County; Burlington in Kit Carson County; Ordway, the county seat and site for the state's newest prison, in Crowley County; Cheyenne Wells, the county seat, and Kit Carson, in Cheyenne County; and Eads in Kiowa County.

In the southeastern part of this section, La Junta, the county seat of Otero County, is the largest business center. Rocky Ford, another major agribusiness center, is also located in Otero County. Las Animas is the business and government center for Bent County; Lamar for Prowers County; and Springfield for Baca County.

PROFILE

Colorado Division of Commerce and Development
A Diversified Economy Expanding to the Future

Colorado's Rockies form the background for a widely diversified economy from traditional agribusiness to advanced-technology industry of the future.

Colorado is at the crossroads of the modern economic expansion occurring in the western United States, but traces its role as the leading Rocky Mountain regional center of enterprise to the earliest frontier days.

A favorable business climate and strategic location serve new and expanding companies well, because the most important word for any business is "profitability." Colorado provides a diversity of environments that foster profitability for a wide variety of business endeavors.

Many Americans think of mountains when they think of Colorado. Certainly the tourist industry enjoys the benefits provided by the Colorado Rockies. The mountains are more than an asset to the recreational industries; they attract the modern manufacturing firms pioneering the technology revolution in America.

Since the founding pioneers came to the state, opportunities have abounded for economic growth and development. Today light manufacturing is finding Colorado's educated, work-oriented labor force and unique life style a major attraction. New businesses recognize the opportunities offered by the mountain life style, and the regional role long established for the state as a competitive edge for doing business.

A part of Colorado often overlooked, but with much to offer, is the non-metropolitan environment. Here, across the plains and in the valleys, extensive resources and a quiet life style present a special opportunity to the smaller company looking for a home. Excellent transportation services connect non-metropolitan areas with the rest of the state as well as the world.

A variety of businesses, from agribusiness to manufacturing, have already discovered the benefits of the state's low-cost labor and low taxes. In fact, the viability of this environment has made non-metropolitan Colorado impossible to overlook.

Metropolitan Colorado, including Denver and the Front Range cities of Pueblo, Colorado Springs, Boulder, Longmont, Loveland, Greeley, and Fort Collins, is experiencing significant growth in high technology. From gene splicing to teleports, fiber optics to technospace facilities, the future of America's new industry is being formed along Colorado's Front Range.

Major industrial developments, regional office centers, and large numbers of entrepreneurs are also finding metropolitan Colorado an ideal location.

When one examines the state's economy, a healthy diversity is readily evident. Colorado's individualized environments are proving profitable for high technology, major manufacturing, light industry, agricultural services, tourism, small businesses, and regional office centers. As Colorado continues to experience steady, quality growth, its economic base becomes even healthier.

Low personal and corporate income tax rates and a low average property tax rate, together with a high per capita income compared with the 49 other states, provide a favorable business climate. Fuel and electric energy costs are also low.

Educationally, Colorado leads the nation in the number of adults (23 percent) between 25 and 64 years of age having completed four or more years of college. Colorado is also a leader in the number of adults (87 percent) having completed high school.

Alexander Grant & Company places Colorado among the top 15 states in its "comparative business climate" ranking. A diversity of environments and life styles, together with a diverse economic base, provide any business—from entrepreneur to international corporation—with new opportunities for success.

The State of Colorado's Division of Commerce and Development works with new and expanding companies interested in Colorado's competitive position among other rapidly expanding western states. The Division's Office of Business Development maintains regional offices at strategic locations throughout the state, as well as in its Denver headquarters, to compile the latest data on communities and the assets they provide companies seeking the Colorado opportunity.

The state capital at Mile High Denver seems almost within reach of 14,000-foot Mount Evans. Few places in Colorado are removed from sight of the Rockies. Photo by David Williams

The Front Range

The plains rise gently from the eastern edge of Colorado for about 100 miles; then the terrain suddenly changes to the flanged foothills of the Rockies. The so-called Front Range is actually foothills or lower mountains of several ranges of the Rockies.

To the north, the Medicine Bow Mountain Range extends into Colorado from Wyoming. In the central Front Range, the foothills are the beginning mountains of the Gore Range, and to the south the Sangre de Cristo Mountain Range abuts the plains.

As a political boundary, the cities, towns, and counties of the Front Range encompass the largest part of the population of Colorado—more than 80 percent—in a relatively narrow strip of land extending from Fort Collins and Greeley in the north to Pueblo in the south. The middle section of this region includes the Denver-Boulder Standard Metropolitan Statistical Area (SMSA) consisting of six counties, and the two-county Colorado Springs SMSA. The U.S. Census Bureau designates an SMSA as a combination of metropolitan cities and counties that have certain economic and population characteristics in common.

However, this region is far from covered in pavement. Despite its heavy population and urbanization, the area is not now, nor likely to become, another megalopolis like Dallas-Fort Worth, Houston, Los Angeles County, or strips along the eastern seaboard. Development patterns and preservation efforts have almost assured that large areas will continue to be set aside for spacious greenbelts and open spaces between the major developments.

Many first-time visitors to the urbanized Front Range are also pleasantly surprised to find that wilderness mountain and prairie lands are only a few minutes drive from any point in even the most congested population centers, including Denver. Since the state's industrialization was relatively late in coming, most of the modern new factories and the industrial parks are surrounded by wide open spaces. Many of the newest plants, such as Eastman Kodak between Fort Collins and Greeley, were located in the middle of large tracts of natural land with farming pursuits continued as buffers. The state's largest single industrial employer, Martin Marietta, may have set the pace when it located huge facilities almost out of sight in the foothill canyons of south Jefferson County. When the Manville Corporation relocated its world headquarters to the Front Range, it built in the middle of a huge ranch, and set aside

37

PROFILE

Metro Denver South/Douglas County Economic Development Council
Centered in the New High Technology Corridor

Strategically situated in the heart of the urbanized Front Range, Douglas County is Colorado's most rapidly growing area, with projections of population growth exceeding 210 percent for the remainder of this decade.

A number of economic factors combine to make this scenic area, located between the high technology centers of Denver and Colorado Springs, the state's most actively developing region.

Leading the list might be the fact that Douglas County comprises some of the most beautiful geographic territory on the Front Range, and careful planning of its industrial parks and emerging residential communities is a powerful attraction to the sophisticated high technology companies moving operations to Colorado.

Despite its location near the midpoint of the Front Range sector, Douglas County had until the early 1980s remained largely an agricultural region. As a part of the Denver Metropolitan Statistical Area, its leaders often term the developing area Metro Denver South.

Douglas County is traversed by Interstate 25, the Rocky Mountain's main north and south highway belt and the economic corridor along which most of the rapid growth in a three-state area has occurred. As this county joins in the economic development of this region, local residents and developers are determined to retain the best features of the environment.

In the decade between 1970 and 1980 the county's population base expanded by nearly 200 percent. By the year 2000 population is expected to exceed 155,000, compared with a county population of 49,000 in 1986. A basic reason for this rapid population growth is the strong shift in the location of jobs for the technological centers in Denver's southern metropolitan area, and the extension of major industrial parks into Douglas County. From its county seat at Castle Rock the office parks in the Denver Technological Center are only 15 miles away, and 30 miles from the county seat to the south are located the northern business and aerospace parks of Colorado Springs.

Centered between Denver and Colorado Springs' technological and aerospace centers, Douglas County has a total of 540,000 acres. New office parks represent 6,500 acres which are strategically located to maximize quality use of this important land bridge.

From 1984 to 1986, more than 3.2 million square feet of modern light industrial and office park space was developed within Douglas County, and many of the top names in American industry located facilities or began development projects. By 1986, 92,000 acres of major development were underway, with 21 new communities under construction.

In 1985, Douglas County saw nearly $1 billion spent for development. In 1986 nearly three-quarters of a billion dollars in new construction was being invested in new housing structures, business structures, supportive infrastructure, and public buildings. Yet the area retains 70 percent of its agricultural and natural environmental charm in open space, public parks, and ranch land.

John Reardon, chief executive officer of the Economic Development Council, notes that the Denver/Colorado Springs development corridor, which is located mainly in Douglas County, will be tightly regulated through county-wide planning. This is to assure that economic development is balanced by environmental quality, both within the individual commercial projects and in the residential planned communities.

Located in the heart of the rapidly growing high-tech corridor, Douglas County maintains its natural environment for a high quality standard of community life.

Coloradans begin their love affair with the outdoors at a young age, and get their practice for the high country in the many urban parks to be found in every city, town and hamlet. Photo by Joel Silverman

wildlife preserves and open land.

Despite one of the nation's fastest growth rates in the number of new manufacturing plants, area leaders have succeeded in maintaining much of the natural environmental quality. The expanding industrial complex of high technology and advanced manufacturing locating within the Front Range area of Colorado is among America's most futuristic.

It was not necessarily foresight that caused Coloradans to preserve the natural beauty of their land, even within the emerging cities. They had the benefit of seeing the mistakes made elsewhere during a century and a half of industrial development. The limits of the fragile environment along this more than mile-high Front Range also dictate a more prudent way of developing the land.

Of course, some mistakes have been made. Almost every part of the urbanized Front Range is periodically vexed by air pollution problems created by automobile emmissions. But like the new era of economic development, nobody could have foreseen the adverse effect of carbon monoxide in thin mountain air until the car began arriving in great numbers after World War II.

All along this urbanized belt at the edge of the Great Plains, Coloradans live and work within sight of mountains that are snow-capped much of the year. Many live in the valleys or along the step-walled canyons that drop streams sharply out of the mountains to the plains below. Most mountain commuters are still only minutes from their offices and factories in the metropolitan areas. Others start their daily commutes after having breakfast with views from homes high on the sides and tops of the Front Range foothills.

The terrain rises sharply from the elevation of the plains at 5,000 to 6,000 feet. Some of the 14,000-foot mountains actually seem to abut the prairie. Long's Peak (towering above Boulder, Longmont, and Loveland), Mt. Evans (near Denver), and Pikes Peak (almost in the city limits of Colorado Springs), are all higher than 14,000 feet and clearly visible from downtown Denver.

This Front Range area encompasses about 17,000 square miles of varied terrain, where three out of four Coloradans make their livings and homes. Although highly urbanized, the parks and nature areas within this region contain deep, blue lakes, open meadows and valleys with wild flowers, and the beginning of the mountain pine, spruce, and aspen forests. Colorado's blue spruce grows wild on the mountains and as ornamental trees in the yards of the communities. The forests shelter deer, elk, small animals, and the birds that either live in the area year-round or rest on their migrations from the far north.

Every community in the region vies for the reputation of having the best parks. Denver even maintains huge nearby mountain parks outside the city limits. Most Front Range communities have restored historic sections where Victorian era villages provide a taste of the pioneer days. All have lovely, modern, landscaped neighborhoods where transplanted trees and manicured lawns extend the outdoors into the urbanized areas. In many of the towns and cities along the Front Range, deer still roam down out of the nearby foothills to irk the morning commuter and graze on the flower beds of the residents.

The 10 contiguous, urbanized counties of Colorado are commonly placed in the political boundaries designated as the Front Range. The county seats and the Front Range counties include Greeley, Weld County; Fort Collins, Larimer County; Boulder, Boulder County; Brighton, Adams County; Golden, Jefferson County; Denver, Denver County; Littleton, Arapahoe County; Castle Rock, Douglas County; Colorado Springs, El Paso County; and Pueblo, Pueblo County.

At the northern end of this area, two counties of the Front Range abut Wyoming. Like most of the cities in these counties, the major centers, such as Fort Collins in Larimer County, and Greeley in Weld County, are experi-

PROFILE

Greeley/Weld County Economic Development Action Partnership
Blending the Best of Agribusiness and High Technology

Blending the best of its agribusiness past with the high technology of the future has caused Weld County to emerge as a storybook example of successful development in Colorado.

While the county remains among the top four agriculture producers in the nation, it also has a notable reputation as an established center for advancing technology. Its future is pegged to both modern agricultural pursuits and futuristic manufacturing. Since 1983, 15 new firms have located in Weld County, adding 1,500 manufacturing jobs. Recently, the area's agribusiness giant, Monfort of Colorado, announced it was expanding again.

Although the county's new manufacturing firms are typically small in size, some of the nation's largest corporations have recently opened new plants in the area, most notably Hewlett Packard, Coors Golden Recycling and Coors Biotechnology, and Norwest Publishing. Weld County is home to the national or regional company headquarters of seven major corporations, including three firms on the Fortune 500 list.

The manufacturing workforce is highly skilled, with 45 percent engaged in advanced technology and 12 percent in electronics. Greeley and the other Weld County communities have no trouble attracting a skilled workforce because the countryside, which is located on the western edge of the great prairie land near the Rockies, offers the best of the Colorado climate and terrain.

Greeley, named for its famed patron Horace Greeley, is a cultural and educational center for northern Colorado. Its modern retail centers, attractive tree-lined neighborhoods, and supporting infrastructure make it a regional activity center serving a wider community that reaches across northeastern Colorado and into Wyoming, Nebraska, and Kansas.

The Greeley Philharmonic is the oldest west of the Mississippi River, entering its 77th year in 1986. The University of Northern Colorado Jazz Festival has become a national event with major performing groups in attendance. The UNC Jazz Vocal Ensemble was nominated for a Grammy in 1985, making it only the second university group ever to be so honored.

Climate might be considered a key factor in the Denver Broncos' choice of Greeley for its summer training camp, when that championship football team could pick practically any location in America.

Recreational opportunities abound in the region. Within an hour's drive are located the Denver Metropolitan Area, the top visitor attraction in Colorado—Rocky Mountain National Park, and four major universities with their attendant cultural and athletic events.

Island Grove Park, jointly operated by Greeley and Weld County, is home to the Independence Day Stampede, the largest July 4th rodeo event in the nation; as well as the unique Centennial Village, which offers a living history of the region's earliest settlement days.

Educational excellence is one of the major attributes of the area. College entrance examination scores from Weld County schools are higher, on an average, than national test results, and its largest school district is the pilot district in Colorado for a National Science Foundation grant to enhance science curriculum.

Weld County is home to the University of Northern Colorado. UNC's Business College has recently become the fastest growing segment of the university. Aims Community College offers vocational training through its two Weld County campuses, as well as specialized training for business and industry.

The Greeley/Weld County Economic Development Action Partnership, Inc. provides professional development assistance to businesses considering new or expanded facilities in Weld County, in a continuing effort to further enhance the quality of life and opportunity in the area.

Greeley in Weld County has maintained a strong agricultural economy as some of Colorado's largest high-tech firms have moved in to share the countryside.

encing rapid population growth. Population figures from the 1980 census may not reflect today's population, but will be used by demographers until the next official census in 1990.

Weld County, with its plains-like terrain, is one of the largest in land area and provides a true mix of industries from agriculture to high technology. Its county seat city of Greeley, which is also home to the University of Northern Colorado, is one of the most important commercial centers for the region and one of Colorado's five cities in the 50,000 to 100,000 population range. Other larger towns in Weld County are Evans City, Fort Lupton, Windsor, and Dacona.

Adjoining Weld County on the west is Larimer County, with its high-tech industries and university center at Fort Collins. Colorado State University, one of America's leading agribusiness institutions, is located here. The county begins on the east as a plains area, and rises to the peaks in Rocky Mountain National Park. In addition to Fort Collins, with a population of more than 65,000, the city of Loveland with over 30,000 residents, is another leading Colorado business center. One of the state's most important tourist cities—Estes Park, the gateway to the Rocky Mountain National Park—is located here, as well as the town of Berthoud.

Joining this county to the south is Colorado's higher education center, the University of Colorado, headquartered at Boulder. A city with a population exceeding 75,000, Boulder is located in the foothills with mountains towering above the bustling high-tech industrial and university center. The more densely populated urban area of the Front Range begins in Boulder County, with several larger cities and towns in the county. Longmont, with a population of over 40,000, and the community of Gunbarrel form an area of nearly continuous development east of Boulder.

Other larger towns in the county include Lafayette/Louisville, and a large part of the high-tech city of Broomfield. Smaller mountain towns of Lyons and Nederland are also in Boulder County.

Adams County, the fifth most populous in Colorado, is an area of Colorado where the contrasts of agriculture and development can best be pictured. The county, which frames the region's Stapleton International Airport on the north, features a great variety of advanced and basic industry in its cities, and extensive agricultural production on its eastern plains. Brighton is the government center, but larger cities and towns include Westminster, Wheat Ridge, Thornton, Northglenn, and Commerce City.

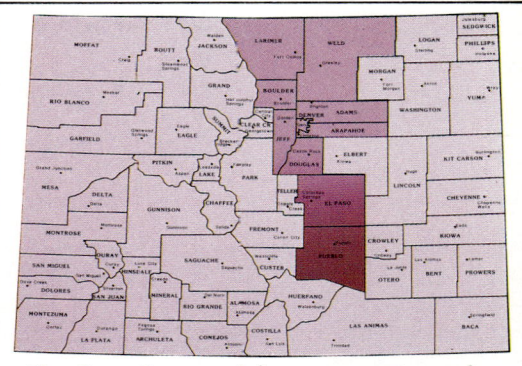

The Front Range—A large percentage of Colorado's total population live and work in these counties, where much of the industrial development has occurred, and where the largest cities are located.

Similar in terrain and mix of the modern industrial and the agricultural economy is Colorado's fourth most populated area—Arapahoe County. Arapahoe County is the seventh fastest growing county in the United States, according to studies conducted by New York-based Dunn and Bradstreet Corporation. The county reaches from the center of urbanization at Denver into the Eastern Plains, with its county seat at Littleton. Its largest city—and Colorado's fastest growing—is Aurora, with a population exceeding 158,000 in 1980. Other major cities and towns in Arapahoe County include Englewood, Southglenn, Cherry Hills Village, and Greenwood Village.

The city of Denver, which includes all of the county of Denver in its municipal borders, has the state's greatest concentration of population, with 492,365 residents counted in the 1980 census. In land area, it is one of the smallest counties in the state; but it is the business and financial, social and cultural, and government center not only for Colorado, but for the vast Rocky Mountain and nearby Great Plains states. Denver has held this important pivotal role in the development of the Rocky Mountain West throughout its history, and modern skyscrapers in the Central Business District office many of the national and multinational corporations of America.

Denver's 16th Street Mall, completed in the early 1980s at a cost of over $50 million, is truly the "Main Street of the Rockies." The heart of the city, whose skyscrapers have almost all been built since the early 1970s, is noted as one of the cleanest and most attractive major urban centers in the world. Visitors are often surprised to see a small army of street workers literally washing down

PROFILE

Broomfield Economic Development Council
New Town on the New Technology Frontier

Rocky Mountain Energy's headquarters blends into the natural environment and mountain backdrop offered by Broomfield to its growing list of firms.

Cities as new as the economic revolution that is making Colorado one of America's frontiers of opportunity have come to life in the high environment of the Rocky Mountains in the past few decades.

One of the best examples of the Colorado-style "new town"—spawned to a large extent by the technological and information age—is Broomfield, a thriving community nestled in the scenic foothills of the mountains and centrally located in the heart of the advanced industry belt of the Front Range. The freshness of this carefully planned new town is emphasized by the backdrop of the ancient mountains rising on the nearby horizon.

Situated between the state's university center at Boulder and its metropolitan center at Denver, Broomfield was incorporated in 1961 from a sleepy agricultural community and has become one of the region's most carefully designed cities.

Broomfield has developed an impressive social and cultural base within the community, to augment the fine arts activities of nearby Boulder and Denver. The city supports its own Broomfield Symphony, the Broomfield Chorus, and the Society for the Arts and Humanities, in addition to local school educational programs and a local school of dance. It also has the advantages of outstanding collegiate athletic events at the nearby University of Colorado, Colorado State University, and the University of Northern Colorado, as well as municipal youth leagues for youngsters in baseball, football, and soccer, and its high school and junior high athletic programs.

Local public schools, public and private recreational facilities, parks, and public service and safety provide the sound infrastructure attracting the upper-middle income professionals, executives, and technicians who largely comprise the Broomfield area labor force. New and expanding business and industry also find this total support package ideal for plant and office locations.

Executives and managers comprise 46 percent of the labor force, and sales and service personnel comprise 38 percent. The median age in the community is just over 28 years, and the median income is nearly $29,000, one of the highest in the country. The area population ranks second in the United States in percentage of high school graduates (53 percent), second highest in median years of advanced education completed (25 percent with one to three years of college education), and third in percentage of college graduates (22 percent).

High technology and light industry have found Broomfield's strategic location ideal for their operations—situated as it is on major highways and rail service, and close to both the Rocky Mountain region's principal commercial airport (Stapleton International) and one of the region's most modern executive airports (Jefferson County Airport).

Among the area's largest technically oriented employers are Rocky Mountain Energy Corporation (corporate headquarters for this Union Pacific subsidiary), Coors Components Inc. (electronics subsidiary of Adolph Coors Co.), AT&T Information Systems (high-tech telecommunications), Ball Aerospace Division (space and aeronautics), Storage Technology Corp. (computer technology), McData Corp. (data systems), Cord Laboratories (pharmaceuticals), Pentax Teknologies Inc. (advanced optics), and Rockwell International (nuclear and alternative energy).

One of the competitive factors in the attraction of high quality industry to the Broomfield community is its careful planning for properly zoned and fully serviced industrial areas. Broomfield currently offers some of the region's largest available and fully developed industrial parks. These include Atlas Industrial Park, Broomfield Industrial Park, Broomfield Park Centre, Depot Hill, Interlocken Business Park, Jeffco Airport Business Center, and Westech Business Park.

Detailed information relating to these new and expanding business opportunities and facilities is provided by the professional staff of the Broomfield Economic Development Corporation.

Coloradans preserve colorful reminders of the past amidst the bustle of a modern future. This old double-decker bus is used as a ticket outlet located on the most modern transitway mall in the West. Photo by Noel Sivertson, Stock Imagery

Front Range communities like Broomfield provide the best of all worlds with comfortable residential neighborhoods close to both mountains and jobs. Photo by Bill Snow

the central streets and sidewalks with soap and water.

Jefferson County, with its seat of government at Golden, is the headquarters for many of the state's federal regional offices and scientific laboratories. The county is the second most populous in Colorado.

Its foothill valleys and mesas, directly adjoining the mountains just east of Denver, provide the sites for large aerospace and advanced technology plants. The largest city is Lakewood, with a population of over 112,000, and several of Colorado's larger towns and cities are also located here, including parts of Wheat Ridge and Broomfield. Arvada, with a population exceeding 83,347, and Columbine, with over 21,000 residents, are two other municipalities within the county. Mountain communities of Evergreen, Morrison, and Conifer are popular commuting centers. Several other suburban communities are located in Jefferson County, the largest being Applewood, Edgewater, Sheridan, and the new town area at Ken Caryl, where Manville Corporation sited its world headquarters in the early 1970s.

Douglas County, south of the Denver Metropolitan Area, presently has the lowest population density of the metro area; but in recent years a score of major industrial, office park, and residential sub-divisions have been targeted for this picturesque, mountainous area. With its county seat at Castle Rock, this county lies directly in the path of new economic development between Denver and Colorado Springs on the Interstate 25 corridor. Emerging new towns in Douglas County are Parker, Mission Viejo, Larkspur, and Franktown. Sedalia, located in one of the most scenic parts of the metropolitan area, is another growing town in the Front Range community.

The Metropolitan Denver counties, including Adams, Arapahoe, Boulder, Denver, Douglas, and Jefferson, have been growing in population at a rate three times faster than the national average since the census of 1980. This metro-area population at mid-1980 was estimated to be about 1.8 million, and the growth rate was the 10th fastest in the United States, according to studies conducted by the Denver Regional Council of Governments.

The second largest and another of Colorado's fastest growing cities is Colorado Springs, county center for El Paso County. El Paso County is the third most populous county in the state. Colorado Springs, with a population of more than 214,000 in 1980, is host to additional large military populations at Fort Carson, the North American Aerospace Defense Command (NORAD) at Cheyenne Mountain, and the U.S. Air Force Academy. The Consolidated Space Operations Center (CSOC), which opened in Colorado Springs in 1985, is expected to make this city the Free World center for space exploration. The Pentagon has also chosen Falcon Air Force Station near Colorado Springs as the home for a futuristic computer center that will be used to train military specialists in new Strategic Defense Initiative (so-called Star Wars) tactics.

In the shadow of Colorado's best known mountain, Pikes Peak, El Paso County is also

PROFILE

Montrose Industrial Development Corp.
New Industries Discovering Western Slope

Montrose, Colorado has established an environment for business expansion, industrial relocation, and new business ventures by developing an infrastructure of land, location, transportation, utilities, and the supporting industrial base to make any company's move to Colorado a healthy one. The centrally located Colorado community offers new businesses and their employees an opportunity to enjoy unsurpassed quality of life.

These factors, plus the nearly limitless opportunities for recreation and scenic beauty that abound in the Montrose area, make this thriving Western Colorado city an attractive location that in recent years has continued to draw new and expanding businesses.

Montrose has successfully located at least one new industrial firm each year in the past several years, and the Montrose Industrial Development Corporation sees this pace continuing in the future.

Among the new plants locating since 1983 are Louisiana-Pacific's multimillion-dollar waferboard plant; the Best Manufacturing Company's modern plant for the fabrication of office and business signage, etched control panels for electronic equipment, decorative panels, and related informational products; Hauck Engineering, a precision-machining operation with a sister company making fishing equipment; and Tri-Sentry Chemical Company, a manufacturer of agricultural chemicals. A number of new retail and service companies have moved to Montrose or expanded operations, including Wal-Mart, Smith's Grocery, and City Market.

"Montrose offers an ideal place to live and raise a family," notes Giff Stoke, economic development manager for the City of Montrose, citing a pleasant climate with mild winters, a low crime rate, and some of the most beautiful scenery and best recreational areas in America. With a population of 9,600 and a county population of 26,000, Montrose offers the support facilities of a big city without the problems often related to high urban density. The community offers a well-educated work force at competitively lower wage scales because of a lower cost of living.

Some major employers are the Bureau of Reclamation Power Operations Center, Bureau of Land Management, local government, Colorado-Ute Electric Association, Russell Stover Candies, and Montrose Memorial Hospital.

Montrose is served by a jet-capable airport, assuring business and industry easy access to regional markets, and national and international markets through commercial air service connecting with Stapleton International Airport in Denver. Federal Express, UPS, and freight carriers such as the Denver and Rio Grande Railroad further provide the city's well-rounded transportation service.

The city's location in the immediate vicinity of some of Colorado's finest skiing, fishing, hunting, and boating country, is enhanced by close cooperation between the city and county governments, the Chamber of Commerce, and the Montrose Industrial Development Corporation (MID), a non-profit corporation comprised of local business leaders who assist new businesses in locating in the community. A unique reward program offers anyone up to $3,000 for providing a lead that results in a company moving to Montrose.

Established industrial parks at outstanding prices, and complete support facilities round out Montrose's competitive advantages as an important new economic development opportunity in Colorado.

Montrose, on the western edge of the Rockies, maintains the charm of an American hometown, while new industries join the community's corporate family.

one of the state's main tourist centers, with other communities such as Manitou Springs being the gateway to the central Rockies.

At the southern point of the urbanized area of the Front Range is Pueblo County, and the historically industrialized City of Pueblo. A transportation and heavy industry center, Pueblo is moving away from its historic role as a steel-making center for the western United States, as high technology industry moves into that area. East of Pueblo on the plains are important government facilities, including the U.S. Department of Transportation's high-speed test center for trains and rapid transit, and the Pueblo Ordinance Depot, a major military supply and storage center.

The Eastern Mountains

The spectacular mountains near the heavily populated Front Range provide a sudden and awesome contrast to the adjacent urbanized communities. It is in this 10-county region defined as the Eastern Mountains that much of Colorado's colorful mining history was made. Within a short drive of all the urban centers is a 13,316-square-mile region containing most of Colorado's 14,000-foot peaks, some of the state's most spectacular beauty, a vast amount of its non-energy mineral reserves, and yet the fewest number of people—about seven persons per square mile. The combined population of the 10 counties in this region is under 100 000 or less than any one of five of the cities on the neighboring Front Range.

But the population of this ruggedly beautiful region soars each summer, as tourists from all over the world come to visit its Victorian villages, reopened mines (some still extracting gold and silver and other minerals), guest ranches, and countless trout streams and lakes. The Coloradans fortunate enough to make their living in this area play host to those who wish they could.

It is a region of white-water mountain streams—crystal clear and dropping rapidly

Homes can be found nestled in the evergreens on the edges of the metropolitan areas, such as this development in Douglas County. Photo courtesy of Metro Denver South

45

PROFILE

Durango Industrial Development Foundation
Heartland of the Developing Southwest

With a year-round visitor industry already established in one of Colorado's most picturesque regions, Durango is diversifying its economy through a well-organized industrialization program. As the regional service center for the San Juan Mountains of southwestern Colorado, the community's infrastructure is already in place to accomplish its new goals.

Durango, the seat of government for La Plata County, has long been a visitor mecca because of its natural and man-made recreational features. Surrounded by 14,000-foot mountains providing some of the state's most awe-inspiring scenery and all-season outdoor recreation, its man-made attractions include the national treasure of prehistoric dwellings at nearby Mesa Verde.

Even though an estimated 60 percent of the local economy is supported by the visitors traveling to the area in both winter and summer, community leaders are actively seeking newcomers to come and stay.

"Despite the tens of thousands of visitors who come to enjoy the skiing, the mountains, the forests, and rivers, we feel that we are one of the most overlooked jewels in Colorado" says Bernard E. Anderson, professor of economics at Durango's Fort Lewis College and a consultant to the Durango Industrial Development Foundation. "We have a tremendous quality of life here, and we want to share it with target industries."

Durango's invitation to business and industry is backed by the Durango Industrial Development Foundation, which has packaged prime property and other local programs to provide new and expanding industry with all the start-up support required.

This cooperative effort was instrumental in raising the foundation's funding without state or federal support, and has succeeded in attracting a number of manufacturing and service establishments to its industrial park. The La Plata County area offers new companies a highly trained and educated labor force; an unusually strong cultural and fine arts base; outstanding educational institutions; one of the state's most varied recreational areas; and excellent support systems in health care, highway and air transportation, and public utilities.

The Durango area is rich in ancient heritage and history of the Old West, yet it is strategically located in the emerging industrial "new Southwest." A thriving cattle and agribusiness industry still flourishes along the area's mountain stream-fed seven river valleys. A land of sudden contrasts, the lush valleys (which include the site for the City of Durango) turn into the deserts of Arizona and New Mexico not far southwest of Durango. To the immediate west begin the canyons and high mesas of Utah.

The Durango Fine Arts Council sponsors many cultural events, festivals, and three theatre companies that perform throughout the year. Fort Lewis College, a fully accredited four-year state liberal arts college, and two modern full-service hospitals and numerous health centers serve the region.

Its temperate climate, located in valleys protected by the high mountains and in the moderate climes of southern Colorado, has attracted a large settlement of retired professionals who enjoy Durango's 310 days of annual sunshine.

Durango's community structure is well suited to support its citizens' goals for economic diversification and expansion of its industrial base.

Southwestern Colorado dons its bright autumn dress in the San Juan Mountains near the economic center at Durango. Photo by Bruce Conrad.

Early gold miners left their mark on the mountains, but nature has a way of reclaiming its own beauty. Ghost towns and old mines are favorite haunts of modern hikers. Photo by Gary R. Graf

to the thirsty plains below. Forests, high meadows, mountain valleys, and large natural parks form a vast wildlife preserve of rare flora and fauna. Its towns are remarkably preserved from the gold and silver boom eras; and the region, because of its nearness to the cities, is where most urban Coloradans locate their weekend homes and getaway chalets. Many of the hardier urbanites have permanent homes in these mountains and commute down the canyon roads.

To a majority of Coloradans who live in the cities nearby, this area provides the nearness to nature they treasure as one of the greatest assets of living and working in Colorado.

Two of the most historic and best preserved Victorian mining communities are located in the two counties closest to the Denver Metropolitan Area. Gilpin and Clear Creek Counties are where the first big gold rush to Colorado began, and where the yearly "visitor rush" produces revenues today. Central City, the county seat of Gilpin County, and Black Hawk, also in that county, were famed mining districts and remain famous visitor centers, only a few miles from Denver. Georgetown, the county seat of Clear Creek County, is a fully restored gold mining center; and Idaho Springs, the largest town in Clear Creek County, has also preserved its many Victorian homes and buildings.

No place in Colorado is more famous for mining than two-mile-high Leadville, the highest fully developed town in the United States and the county seat of Lake County. Nearby, another once-active mining center, Fairplay, now serves as the seat for the mountain-ringed Park County. This county is situated in a huge, highland meadow called South Park.

Adjoining the urbanized Colorado Springs area, and a part of that Standard Metropolitan Statistical Area, is Teller County. Its seat at Cripple Creek, another of Colorado's famous gold mining centers, offers one of the best examples of carefully restored historic buildings. Cripple Creek lies in the western shadow of Pikes Peak. A climb to the top of this peak inspired Katharine Lee Bates to write the words for "America the Beautiful" in 1893. Woodland Park in Teller County is an emerging business and industrial town.

Chaffee county, with its county seat at the historic railroad town of Salida, also includes Buena Vista, where one of the state's model correctional institutions is located. Salida is a main crossroads city, serving as a retailing and regional service center for the Sawatch Range and the Sangre de Cristo Mountain resort area.

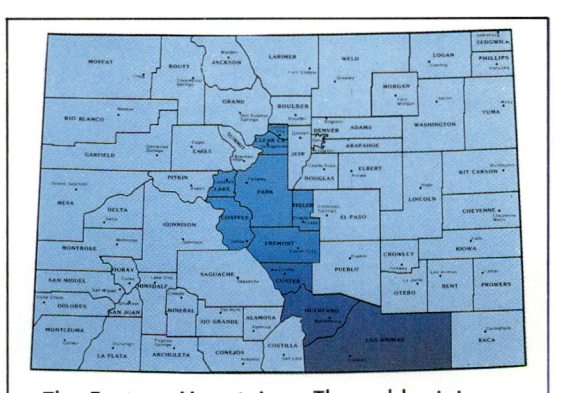

The Eastern Mountains—The gold mining that drew the first settlers to Colorado was, and is, conducted in this region. Also located here are many of the important winter and summer resorts.

The largest city in the Eastern Mountains region is Canon City, the seat for Fremont County. It is an active retailing and supply point for the mountain area, and the site of the state's central correctional institutions. Florence is the second largest town in Fremont County. Westcliffe is the seat for the high-mountain Custer County, and offers some of the state's best mountain fishing and recreational facilities.

The two counties at the southern point of the Eastern Mountains are also gateway cities to the southern mountain recreational areas of the Sangre de Cristos. Walsenburg is the county seat of Huerfano County and a sup-

47

PROFILE

City of Craig
Northwestern Center Set for New Industry

Situated in the scenic Yampa River Valley in Colorado's energy-rich northwest, the City of Craig has developed an infrastructure of man-made resources unequaled for a city its size. The water treatment facilities alone could accommodate a population triple its present size, and the community is the home site for one of the world's largest coal powered electricity generating plants.

Craig's historic location as the commercial center for northwest Colorado has made Craig a comfortable, family-oriented community with outstanding social, cultural, recreational, health, and educational facilities. Its people, from a heritage deeply rooted in developing the bountiful natural resources surrounding the community, are strongly committed to expanding the region's economy through modern industrial development.

Craig is also the host city for tens of thousands of visitors who annually come to the region to fish its streams, hunt big game in its nearby canyons and rolling low mountains, ski at nearby winter resorts, and venture back eons to view the traces of prehistoric animals at Dinosaur National Park.

The community has developed an extraordinary array of service and support businesses because of its historic role as a headquarters and supply center for a large mining, farming, and ranching region. It is the county seat of Moffat County, which has one of Colorado's most extensive reserves of coal, oil shale, oil, and natural gas. More than seven million tons of coal are produced annually; more than 220 wells yield nearly a half million barrels of oil and 17 million cubic feet of natural gas each year.

Much of the coal mined in the region goes directly to fire the giant electricity generators, such as the ultramodern $1.5 billion Craig Station operated by Colorado-Ute Electric Association, which serves vast regions of the Rocky Mountain West with power.

Craig is in the center of Colorado's northwestern cattle and sheep-ranching country. The ranches and farms in the immediate area produce lamb, wool, beef, wheat, and lumber. After the autumn crops are gathered, Craig area farmers and ranchers open their lands to large-game hunters from across the United States and foreign countries.

The community itself, with broad streets, tree-shaded parks, and open spaces, is home to about 11,000 Coloradans. Despite its relatively small geographical boundary, the city has set aside over 35 acres within the town for five city parks. Its modern water treatment facilities, with extensive water rights to draw from the major watershed of the nearby Yampa River, can presently accommodate a city and industry base of up to 32,000 people. Craig was one of the first western slope communities to comply with the standards for proper sewage treatment. Water and sewer rates are among the lowest in the country, and other utility rates are similarly low because Craig is surrounded by natural gas fields and huge electricity-generating stations.

Craig's schools are modern, both in curriculum and facilities. The high school was built in 1981, and the city leaders are in the process of developing vocational training programs to expand the available skill level of the area workforce. Training programs can be tailored for a new company locating in the community.

The modern Community Hospital and four private clinics serve the medical needs of the region, and Craig has an average of one physician for every 750 residents.

Located only 20 miles from Routt National Forest and less than 15 miles from two major reservoirs, Craig is noted for its outdoor recreational attractions in all seasons.

An economic activity center for northwestern Colorado, the City of Craig offers the best of the outdoors with a future of opportunity. Photo by Iris Photography

Nature's gigantic picture frame offers a view of the fertile San Luis Valley and the Sangre de Cristo peaks beyond. Photo by Hull & Kangas Photographers

ply center for the eastern parts of the San Luis Valley.

Trinidad, the seat for Las Animas County, is the port-of-entry to visitors arriving from New Mexico on Interstate 25 via Raton Pass. It is also an important business and commercial center for the Chuchara recreational area and the nearby southeastern plains agricultural area. Trinidad provides retail and business services to a part of northeastern New Mexico as well.

The San Luis Valley

The first section of Colorado to experience European influence was this high fertile basin that came to be known as the San Luis Valley. It is a 100-mile-long, 75-mile-wide farming region settled by farmers and ranchers from the 17th-century communities of northern New Mexico. The Spanish heritage introduced to Colorado by these early settlers provides a part of the rich culture still important today. More than 200,000 modern Coloradans with Spanish surnames can trace their ancestry to the founding families in this region.

Today the six counties of the San Luis Valley are among the most important agri-

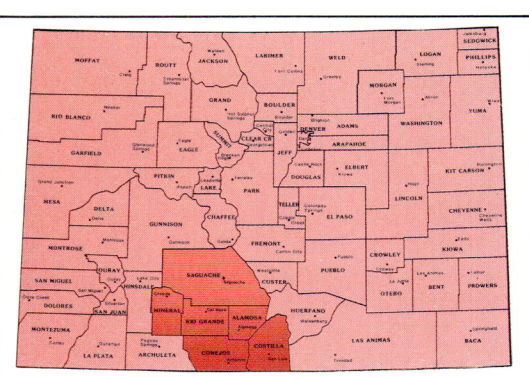

The San Luis Valley—Rich in history and culture, the counties in this high valley are striving to add diversified industry to their agribusiness economy.

cultural lands of the state; although modern industrial plants, both based on the agriculture in the area and not related to agribusiness are locating in its central cities of Alamosa, Monte Vista, and Del Norte. The area is one of America's most important potato producing regions, and the highland fields also produce barley, lettuce, and other cool-weather crops. It receives only about eight inches of moisture a year in the form of snow and rainfall, but is amply supplied water year-round from surrounding snow-

PROFILE

San Luis Valley Economic Development Council
High Valley Diversifies Its Economy

Rich in natural resources, recreational attractions, and Hispanic/Indian heritage, the highland San Luis Valley is poised to expand its economic base in step with Colorado's emerging economy.

Located in south central Colorado along the New Mexico border, the 100- by 75-mile fertile valley boasts the oldest permanent settlements in the state, and today offers one of the state's newest frontiers of opportunity. Historically agricultural, its diverse crops help to place the state in several leading farm produce rankings. But in more recent years the communities in the valley have been successfully diversifying the economy by capitalizing on some of the state's most scenic natural recreational areas and the finest year-round weather conditions.

The San Luis Valley region consists of Alamosa, Conejos, Costilla, Mineral, Rio Grande, and Saguache counties; and comprises the world's largest intermountain valley with an average elevation of 7,500 feet. Surrounded by towering mountain ranges with peaks on all sides ranging to 14,000 feet, the valley has been noted for its high-protein grain crops and its leading role as a potato-producing area. It is among Colorado's leading regions for production of brewing grade barley, as well as wheat, alfalfa, vegetables, and livestock.

The mountains serve as climate-controlling shields, providing moderate weather the year-round. And while precipitation averages only eight inches per year, a good supply of water on the valley floor is assured by the runoff of melting snow throughout the summer. The region provides the headwaters for one of North America's most important rivers, the Rio Grande. Snowfall is infrequent in the valley, but only a few miles from the western rim of the valley, famed Wolf Creek Pass gets 439 inches of snowfall in an average year.

The cities, towns, and farms of the San Luis Valley have the nation's highest per capita application of solar energy-assisted heating and cooling systems in the homes and businesses of the area.

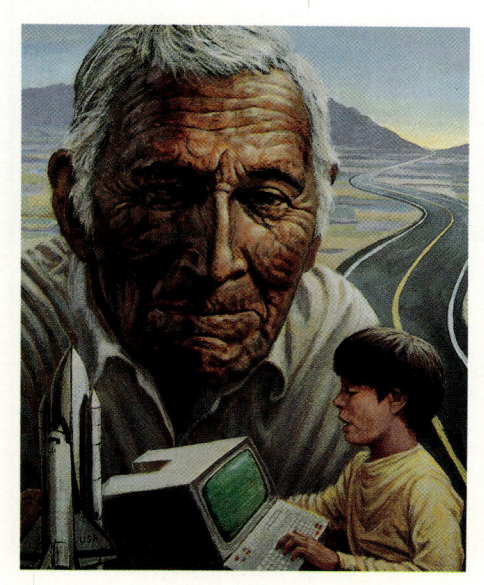

The San Luis Valley of Colorado is poised to enter the era of advanced industry by drawing on a rich cultural heritage and a skilled work force.

The San Luis Valley Economic Development Council, headquartered in Monte Vista, is actively assisting new and expanding companies in locating manufacturing and service-related facilities in the valley. Charles G. Gardner, president and chief executive officer of the Council, notes that the organization has a basic strategy to influence future economic activity in the Valley "without violating the existing life style, historical significance, environment, traditions, and culture of the area.

"We feel the economy can be successfully expanded without compromising the sensitive relationships between our citizens and the social, cultural, and educational dreams and expectations we share with other Coloradans," Gardner says.

The Valley offers a readily available labor force. Educational facilities, such as the modern Adams State College at Alamosa, work with new and expanding companies—whether in tourism, manufacturing, or service industries—to provide the types of skills a new company requires.

In 1986, under new Enterprise Zone legislation, the Valley made an application for designation as a trade zone on a six-county basis. The assembly of six contiguous counties into one such zone makes the Valley the largest single geographical area in Colorado to provide the investment incentives of an Enterprise Zone.

The Valley is especially ripe for economic expansion, since its infrastructure of support systems including educational, health, highway, air transport, and governmental services is in place. Pleasant county-seat towns and cities, combined with strategic location halfway between Denver and Albuquerque, and its close proximity to some of the Rocky Mountain's most noted recreation and visitor attractions, make the San Luis Valley one of the prime and yet-to-be-discovered areas in Colorado's rapidly developing industrial future. Local citizens are predicting that this region will become the state's next spotlighted area for economic development activity.

In addition to emphasizing a stronger role in Colorado's visitor industry, the agriculture-based economy offers opportunity for food-related industries to locate near the rich farmlands.

capped mountains in the Sangre de Cristos and San Juans.

Alamosa is the population center of the valley, and is also the commercial and service center with its college, medical facilities, and retail establishments. Alamosa is also the county seat of Alamosa County. Nearby is Del Norte, the county seat of Rio Grande County, where the Rio Grande River rises in the mountains. Monte Vista, another retail and supply center for the valley, and South Fork, a timber milling center, are also located in Rio Grande County.

The largest county in land area in the valley is Saguache, with its county seat also named Saguache. The farming supply town of Center is in the heart of the valley. Mineral County, which is in the mountains on the western edge of the valley, remains one of Colorado's leading mining districts, with its county seat at Creede.

Colorado's two oldest towns, Antonito and Costilla, are located on the New Mexico border. They serve as the seats of government and service centers for Conejos County and Costilla County, respectively.

In 1986, a renewed effort at diversification of the economy was being made in this high valley area under the direction of the San Luis Valley Regional Development and Planning Commission and the San Luis Valley Economic Development Council. The emphasis of this campaign was to provide additional jobs through the development of more advanced agriculture-related industry and to attract new types of non-agribusiness industry to the valley.

The Western Slope

Whatever images are conjured up by an out-of-stater when the name Colorado is mentioned are found in the vast region most often called the Western Slope. This 40,000-square-mile land, beginning along the Continental Divide and extending 200 miles across the western half of the state, indeed represents everyone's idea of Colorado. The Western Slope has majestic peaks, deep canyons, massive mesas, roaring white rivers, cattle ranches, coal fields, oil wells, and most of the world-class ski resorts in North America. It is Colorado River country, where that broad stream starts as trickles in snow fields and gains width as it plunges through canyons and orchard-covered valleys on its way to watering Arizona, southern California, and Mexico.

The vast Western Slope region includes 21 counties with a population sitting on some of the greatest energy reserves in North America. It is a region of such great contrasts

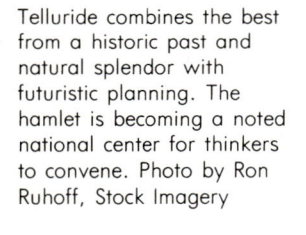

Telluride combines the best from a historic past and natural splendor with futuristic planning. The hamlet is becoming a noted national center for thinkers to convene. Photo by Ron Ruhoff, Stock Imagery

PROFILE

Denver Economic Development Agency
Leading the Way to New Horizons

The modern skyline of the mile-high capital city of Colorado mirrors the dynamic energy of the West as Denver serves the leading role as the financial, transportation and distribution, service, and social center of the vast Rocky Mountain Region.

Denver virtually hums with the activity of futuristic enterprises representing all sectors of the economy. It hosts the offices of regional federal government for most U.S. agencies, and hundreds of national and regional corporate headquarters. Its unequaled 16th Street pedestrian/transitway mall has become the "Main Street of the Rockies." Its adjacent 17th Street remains the "Wall Street of the West."

Yet the millions of visitors coming to Denver for meetings or vacations might be surprised to learn that the urban center's tree-lined neighborhoods and thousands of acres of garden-like parks provide a residential life quality second to none.

Urban revitalization, with emphasis equally focused on both renewal and preservation, is one of the newly formed Denver Economic Development Agency's top priorities. Not only are 10 historic business neighborhoods presently being refurbished almost in the shadows of the futurist skyscrapers, but the surrounding residential areas are constantly undergoing beautification to maintain Denver's vibrant intercity role as the region's capital.

Formed in January 1985, the city's Economic Development Agency established three challenging programs to assure the continued leadership position of Denver. Its Neighborhood Business Revitalization (NBR) program not only maintains Denver's reputation as one of the loveliest cities in America in which to live and work, but it supports the creation of new jobs through the expansion of small businesses. The city, working closely with neighborhood associations, is directly involved in this ongoing revitalization effort.

A second major thrust is the city's direct support of new and emerging companies. Specialists from both the private and public sectors provide expertise in every field of new business development and support. This program is scheduled for expansion with the opening of the Denver Entrepreneurial Growth Center near downtown early in 1987. That center will provide 82,000 square feet of space for small enterprises to locate on the site, and also will provide a professional outreach program. Designed as a "business incubator," it will bring the experts from all areas of business and government to focus on assuring the success of new companies.

A third major program of Denver's development agency is to inform business leaders across the nation of the excellent conditions existing for the location of headquarters operations. Competitive rates for office space make Denver one of the most attractive headquartering centers in the world.

Modern business development is further supported by four colleges and universities located in the city, and a strong city government with a bond rating described by one of its chief underwriters, Smith Barney, Harris Upham & Company, Inc., as excellent.

A key factor in the ability of a western U.S. city to continue to offer strong growth potential is its water supply. Denver, through its Water Department managed by the historic Denver Board of Water Commissioners, has assured an adequate supply well into the next century for the city and its neighbors participating in the Metropolitan Water Development Agreement.

Offering a high-quality life style, Denver is much more than the capital of the Rocky Mountain West. Photo courtesy of Denver Convention & Visitors Bureau.

Breckenridge has become a world-class ski resort, but a careful restoration program maintains the historic portion of the old town for the enjoyment of visitors and Coloradans alike. Photo by Ron Ruhoff, Stock Imagery

that demographers often further divide the Western Slope into four distinctively different geographical sub-regions.

The Western Slope is also paradoxical in nature due to a miscalculation on the part of developers in the late 1970s. While it is one of the least developed parts of Colorado, the infrastructure in many of its cities and towns is the most modern. Building on the false promises of an energy boom in the vast oil shale fields, some parts of the Western Slope have the most completely developed and surplus of modern community support facilities in all of Colorado. With new water and sewer treatment plants, schools, airports, housing, and public buildings in such places as Rangely, Rifle, Grand Junction, and Craig, it is modern beyond its current need. Yet the huge geographical region has a current population of less than 300,000.

It is not, as some say, Colorado's "best kept secret," because millions of tourists in all seasons visit this region for every form of outdoor recreation, and manufacturers are beginning to discover the advantages of locating in Western Slope communities.

While the cities on the Western Slope are not large compared to those in the urbanized Front Range, their historic location has made them complete centers for health, commerce, services, and local industry. Population centers such as Craig in the far northern part of the region, and Durango on the south, offer a far greater spectrum of services than other towns of their size, because they serve large regions in the state and in nearby states.

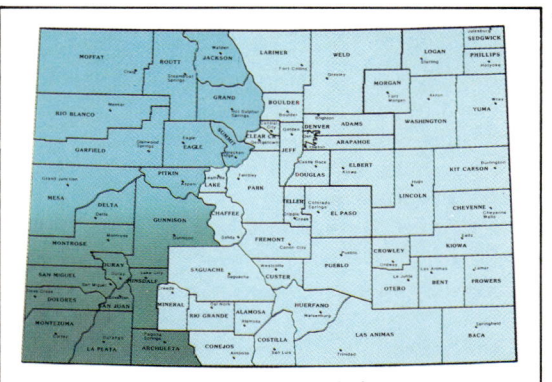

The Western Slope—West of the Continental Divide lies one of the most spectacular and geographically diversified regions in America.

The Western Slope abuts Wyoming on the north, Utah on the west, New Mexico on the southwest, and touches Arizona at the Four Corners area south of Cortez.

Its largest city is Grand Junction, which, together with the suburban towns of Palisade and Fruita, has a population of nearly 50,000. But like other supply centers in this sparsely populated region, Grand Junction offers amenities not commonly found in a small city. Grand Junction boasts one of Colorado's busiest and most modern commercial airports, large financial institutions, outstanding medical and health centers, an advanced college system, and major industrial parks served by interstate rail lines and the interstate highway network.

In a state where water limits often restrict the development of new business and in-

53

PROFILE

Tivoli Denver Center
Historic Brewery Becomes Leading Activity Center

The night sky over Denver lights up for the Tivoli, a unique new retail and entertainment facility for the Rockies. The center was built in a historic brewery.

A turn-of-the-century landmark has been turned into one of Colorado's most unique entertainment and retail centers, assuring that the historic old Tivoli Brewery in Denver is preserved for generations to come.

Coloradans have become noted for their dedication to conserving their colorful history by remodeling Victorian-era sections of town and retaining the elegance of those buildings while modernizing them for contemporary use. No better example of the success of this ambition can be found than at Tivoli Denver.

Late in 1985, more than 100 years after the original brewery was built by a pioneer immigrant, a 208,000-square-foot center near downtown Denver was opened to the public. Many sections of the seven-story former brewery were preserved and added space was constructed to maintain the atmosphere of the structure, which is on the National Register of Historic Places.

The new center, with shops and restaurants surrounding a three-story central atrium court, features several fine restaurants, specialty fashion stores, boutiques, and gift shops. The AMC theaters opening at Tivoli brought first-run American and European movies back to downtown Denver.

Tivoli Denver provides 90,000 square feet of restaurant and entertainment space, 95,000 square feet of retail space, and a 23,000-square-foot, 12-screen cinema complex. Its shops and restaurants were an immediate hit with Coloradans, and the renovated facility has become a popular community activity center.

Three trolley cars, operating seven days a week during regular hours when the shops, restaurants, and entertainment facilities are open, connect the Tivoli with the 16th Street Mall. Located adjacent to the Auraria Higher Education Campus, the center also offers easy downtown Denver parking for 700 cars.

Several restaurants in the Tivoli rapidly assumed roles among Denver's most popular, featuring live entertainment along with widely assorted menus. Dining reflects various cultures and tastes. The Tivoli's restaurants include Club Tivoli, with French cuisine; Kailua's Restaurant, with Hawaiian specialties; Rocky Rococo's Pan Style Pizza; the Viceroy India Restaurant, with exotic menus from the Orient; The Rattlesnake Club, a gourmet outing of unexpected meals; and Morton's of Chicago—rated by People magazine as the "best Steak House in North America." Small fast-food and snack stalls are conveniently scattered around the complex.

The retail shops and specialty stores bring another dimension to downtown Denver shopping. Apparel shops, shoe stores, accessory boutiques, gift and jewelry stores, a fashion eyewear shop, arts and crafts outlets, a sporting goods store, a book store, and other specialty stores opened on the first day.

The first structure on the site was known as Colorado Brewery, and was built by German immigrant Moritz Sigi. It was renamed Milwaukee Brewery by Max Melsheimer, who built the original seven-story tower to provide for a gravity-flow brewing operation.

The brewery was taken over by John Good in 1900, and renamed Tivoli Brewery after the famous gardens in Copenhagen. It remained a brewery through subsequent ownership, including that of brothers Carol and Joseph Occhiato, until 1969. The brewery was declared a Denver landmark in 1972 and entered in the national register.

The Tivoli Denver was created by the international development company Trizec Corporation Ltd., headquartered in Calgary, Canada. That company, which has extensive prime income producing properties in the United States, holds a property portfolio of more than $3.5 billion in assets. The Tivoli Denver property is operated by Trizec's wholly owned subsidiary, Ernest W. Hahn, Inc. of San Diego, and local management offices were built into the renovated structure at the old brewery. The company has 40 retail centers in the United States.

dustry requiring high-volume water use, the Western Slope has all the water and treatment facilities it requires for an immediate doubling in population. With more average annual rainfall than the eastern part of the state and the greatest snow-melt runoffs, the region battles with most of the West to keep its precious water resources available for the future expansion that is certain to come.

Water protectionists in the region say they don't mind watering the lawns of California for a few more years, as long as they can have the water rights returned later. A look at the high arid countryside would belie the abundance of water, because the region is on the beginning edge of the desert lands of the West.

Colorado's best-known ski resorts are located in the section of the Western Slope often called the Northern Mountains region. These counties include Routt, with Steamboat Springs at its seat of govenment and recreation; Pitkin, with Aspen as the seat of government and Snowmass Village as its second resort center; Summit County, with Breckenridge as its government and recreation center; and the other resort cities of Frisco, Dillon, and Keystone. Famous Vail is located in Eagle County, whose seat of government is the City of Eagle. Grand County, whose seat is Hot Sulphur Springs, includes the Winter Park ski and summer resort areas, and the City of Kremmling. The ranching and resort center at Walden is the county seat of Jackson County.

Adjacent to the wealthiest ski and mountain resort counties is an area known as the Plateau Region of Colorado. It consists of four counties with the world's richest known reserves of oil shale, a giant underground pool of undeveloped energy reserves covering almost 25,000 square miles of Colorado, and the adjoining corners of Utah and Wyoming. The region is a leading producer of coal, which fires the world's largest coal-generated electric plant and several other electric generating stations at Craig and nearby Hayden in Routt County. Craig is the county seat of Moffat County. Rio Blanco County, one of Colorado's leading energy counties, has its county seat at Meeker, and the oil center of Rangley is also located in this county. Garfield County, with the beautiful city of Glenwood Springs as its county seat, has also benefited from the construction boom with modern facilities in place.

Rifle, also located in Garfield County, is another business activity center benefitting from the construction boom in the late 1970s and early 1980s. Carbondale, a mountain town with an educational institution and several active "think tank" groups, is another Garfield County town.

Mesa County, with a broadly mixed economy based on energy, industrial plants, and business services, also remains a leading agricultural center. It serves the surrounding sheep and cattle ranching areas in the mesas and rugged valleys. The county seat at Grand Junction is in the heart of Colorado's fruit-orchard country, which begins along the Colorado River and extends into the next sub-region to the south.

The area known as the Black Canyon region is a leading agricultural land of cattle, sheep, fruit orchards, and new crops being introduced into Colorado such as broccoli and asparagus. This region also is the site for some of the larger emerging ski and summer resorts of Colorado.

With more than 50 peaks rising above 14,000 feet, Colorado is the loftiest state in the United States. Photo by McAllister of Denver

PROFILE

Fred Schmid Appliances
Tradition Kept Alive by Employee-Owners

One of the state's pioneering retail establishments grew from a small shop in the mining camps to become one of the largest independent appliance, television, and stereo dealers in the West. The chronicles of Fred Schmid—both the founder and the Company—is a story of opportunity and American free enterprise that abounded in the frontier West and still exists in Colorado today.

From its earliest days there was little predictability to the dramatic growth of Fred Schmid's enterprises in Colorado. In 1909, at the age of 17, Fredrick C. Schmid jumped ship in Boston and headed west.

He started his career in Colorado, barbering miners in the southwestern gold town of Silverton, and within a year had saved enough money to open his own small barber shop in Denver. A traveling salesman left six of the new-fangled inventions called "radios" at the barber shop. He sold them all in one week at a profit of $5 each, and Fredrick Schmid almost "accidentally" went into the appliance business.

Fred Schmid stores today sell more General Electric appliances than any independent dealer in the western United States, and the rise from a part-time dealership to the present multimillion-dollar operation is a tale of Old West magnitude. The founder continued to operate a barber shop throughout the years he built the chain, running from his shop to the store as priority called.

His example of hard work permeated the stores' operations, and as family members and employees grew up in the stores, the chain expanded. In 1984, the president who rose through the ranks from a $1-per-hour clerk, turned down multimillion-dollar offers for the appliance chain and deeded the store to the workers.

An Employee Stock Ownership Plan (ESOP) would turn over 100 percent of the stock to its employees, making the Fred Schmid ESOP the largest in Colorado and the West.

The chain's sales volumes continue to grow, and the philosophy remains that of barber-founder Fred Schmid.

"It's that little bit extra that counts," says Donald Andresen, who was named President and Chief Executive Officer after the turnover to employees. "It's not only quality, brand-name products, selection, and honest value, but extra customer service that helps a business prosper and grow. Today that is still our number one priority. We've just completed a new 14,000-square-foot service and parts center to support our Denver stores and we have six other service centers throughout Colorado.

"Also, we have just doubled the size of our new Denver warehouse and sales center," continues Andresen. "Add to this our own professional installation crews and our own high-tech installation specialists and that's what our customers have come to depend on."

Since the ESOP was initiated, the Fred Schmid sales volume continues to grow, because each employee, like the founder and the following generation of family and employees, now owns the business.

The Fred Schmid Company continues to grow with Colorado and neighboring states. Stores are located in the Denver Metropolitan Area, Colorado Springs, Boulder, Longmont, Fort Collins, Pueblo, Grand Junction, and most recently in Casper, Wyoming, and Billings, Montana.

The Company also operates appliance warehouses in Fort Collins, Colorado Springs, Grand Junction, and Denver.

The Company has a motto of "Ask Your Neighbor about Fred Schmid" In reality, it is more than a simple advertising slogan. It derives its meaning from the caring and concern of every Fred Schmid employee-owner. When customers deal with anyone at Fred Schmid's, they are dealing directly with an owner of the company.

Fred Schmid Appliances has grown with Colorado by providing modern merchandising choices to support the high-quality life style the citizens enjoy.

The Colorado moon competes with the night lights of Denver. The high altitude and thin, clear air makes the moon seem somehow larger. Photo by Nathan Bilow

In the Black Canyon region, Gunnison County, with its seat at Gunnison, is the site of the major new resort of Crested Butte. San Miguel County, with its seat at Telluride, is the site of the fully restored Telluride village resort and a second town being built atop the mountain. Both Gunnison and Telluride have modern new commercial airport runways, with Telluride's new port being the nation's highest commercial airport, at an altitude of 9,100 feet.

Delta County, with its seat at Delta, also includes the farming centers of Paonia, Cederedge, and Orchard City.

Montrose, the county seat of Montrose County, is a business center for the tourist and agriculture economy. Both Montrose County and Gunnison County are traversed by the spectacular Black Canyon of the Gunnison, for which the region is named. Montrose has been successful in attracting the attention of some excellent new manufacturing and business concerns, and conducts an aggressive campaign to let the business world know of its competitive community assets.

Dolores County, at the edge of the state, is a ranching and forestry area along the beautiful Dolores River, with its county seat at Dove Creek. Ouray and Hinsdale Counties are in the mountains, and both are still important mining as well as recreational centers. Hinsdale's county seat is at Lake City, and Ouray's county seat, also called Ouray, is recognized as one of the most picturesque Victorian villages in all of Colorado.

Colorado's most scenic mountain drive takes the motorist from Ouray to another mining and tourist center at Silverton, the county seat of San Juan County. Silverton is located in the sub-region called the San Juans, an area of spectacular dormant volcanic mountains in the southwestern part of the state. The region is in one of the state's most active gold and silver mining regions, and is also a popular winter and summer resort area.

Its principal city is Durango, the county seat of La Plata County. Durango is not only the supply center for this beautiful country, but an industrialized town with full business and service facilities. La Plata County also includes the town of Ignacio, the center of the Southern Ute Indian Reservation.

Near Durango is Colorado's southwestern corner county of Montezuma, and the famous Mesa Verde National Monument. Montezuma County's government and commercial center is located at Cortez. Two other commercial towns and tourist centers in the county are Mancos and Dolores. The Mountain Ute Indian Reservation is also located in Montezuma County with its headquarters at Towaoc.

Pagosa Springs, another popular winter and summer resort community, is also located in the San Juan region. This retailing community is the county seat for mineral rich Archuleta County.

57

PROFILE

Howard Lorton Galleries
Furnishing the Homes of the Rockies

For nearly six decades the Howard Lorton Galleries have been providing quality furniture to homes throughout the Rocky Mountain region. The Denver-based retail establishment, founded by Howard Lorton in 1927, is located in a showcase facility featuring five levels and covering a half-block on 12th Avenue between Lincoln and Broadway in downtown Denver. A 20,000-square-foot home furnishings store with complete interior design service was opened in Colorado Springs in 1979.

The family-owned furniture stores can truly claim to be "galleries," because the extensive in-stock selections of top names in quality furniture are displayed much like art in a museum-like atmosphere. During its 59 years of retail service to the region Howard Lorton Galleries has developed a distinguished reputation, not only for its stock, but for providing interior design service to homeowners in Colorado and neighboring states.

Influenced by the explosive growth of the Denver Metropolitan Area, Howard Lorton Galleries moved from its original location on Speer Boulevard, where it had served the community for more than a half century, to the extraordinary new showrooms it now occupies. William Lorton Cook, president of the firm and grandson of the founder, made the decision to build the spacious, gallery-like facility in Denver to accommodate the increased market demands. The new store was opened in 1982, with expanded in-stock capacity of famous international brands of furniture.

In 1986, further remodeling was undertaken to provide Colorado and Rocky Mountain region homeowners a complete Henredon Gallery—one of the finest of its kind in America.

An impressive selection from prestigious sources includes furniture from Baker, John Widdicomb, Statton, Kindel, Conant Ball, Hickory Chair, and Hekman. Fine lamps by Wildwood, Marbro, Chapman, Frederick Cooper, Knob Creek; rugs from Karastan and Customweave; and fabrics from such noted sources as Schumacher and Brunschwig & Fils are offered by the interior designers on Lorton's staff.

Howard Lorton Galleries is also well known for providing some of the most distinctive furnishings for executive offices throughout the region, with office furniture from Baker, Henredon, Kittinger, Councill Desks, and Sligh.

Howard Lorton Galleries in Denver and Colorado Springs has a staff of 20 designers, in keeping with the store's early decision to hire the first interior designer on the staff of a furniture retailer in this region.

Howard Lorton Galleries furnishes homes of Rocky Mountain families with a wide choice of the finest furniture. The company's showrooms are like art centers.

Many of Colorado's main streets, such as Telluride, have been preserved by modernization of Victorian Era buildings. Photo by Nathan Bilow

Shopping Center for the Rockies

While the cities, towns, villages, and resorts of Colorado offer a great variety of jobs and lifestyles, they all have one feature in common—the retail business.

Retail trade was discussed in the opening portion of this chapter as the one common denominator in the economy of Colorado. This sector of the economy is the second largest employer in the state. It ranks behind the service industry in numbers employed, but is much more broadly represented in all parts of the state. The service sector, while also found in most communities, is heavily concentrated in the Denver metropolitan area. Therefore, retailing and the wide number of lives it impacts is perhaps the most significant to the lifestyle of most Coloradans.

Colorado serves not only the supply and service needs of the citizens of the state, but because of the millions of visitors coming into the state in all seasons, its retail trade is a far greater economic factor than its population would warrant. The retail establishments, even in the smaller towns, are generally better stocked and more competitive than one would expect to find in an area with the low population densities of Colorado.

Retail employment has consistently enjoyed steady and long-term growth. In 1986, some 279,000 people were employed in retailing, with an annual payroll of nearly $4.5 billion. With a state and local sales tax, retail trade also provides considerable income for local and state government. Jobs in the retail sector have increased at a steady rate from 190,300 a decade ago to nearly 280,000 in 1986.

In Colorado the retail establishments are generally owner-operated, and comprised of small companies. More than 15,000 of the 21,000 retail establishments in the state employ fewer than 10 persons.

These retail establishments are located in the central business areas of towns across the state, where the "main street" is still very typically the heart of the community. Many of the smaller towns and cities have restored their central districts, and built "people" atmospheres around malls. Some have eliminated automobiles from surrounding blocks to enhance the main shopping street in the town.

Such malls have helped focus community activities back into the central part of the cities and towns. Notable pedestrian mall projects have been built in Denver, Boulder, Fort Collins, Grand Junction, and Aspen. Other types of redevelopment, such as central city parks, are helping to maintain the "main street" characteristics in Colorado cities.

PROFILE

May D&F Department Stores
Family Shopping Centers for Coloradans

Many of the pioneers who came to the Rocky Mountains with the gold booms stayed to build empires in businesses completely unrelated to the glamour of striking it rich. David May, a native of Germany, toiled only briefly in the mines before seizing one of the opportunities the newly opening West had to offer.

David May's enterprise and the giant national retail corporation he founded has been clothing Coloradans and other Americans for more than a hundred years.

The 11 Colorado department stores that still bear his name are part of one of America's largest and most successful retail operations. The May Department Stores Co., headquartered now in St. Louis, has 10 department store divisions. The May D&F Department Stores, in the Colorado division, still serve the state much as they did when David May opened his first store in Leadville in 1878; the difference is in the size and scope of operations.

There are seven May stores in the Denver metro area, two in Colorado Springs, and one each in Boulder and Fort Collins. The May tradition continues to expand in the state, with the newest May D&F Department Store opening in Westminster in 1986.

"Today, May D&F still is doing what David May did best, offering our customers the things they want and need most," says President Joseph S. Davis. "We will continue to grow with Colorado just as in its early history. We are a store with an eye to the future and the knowledge that Colorado people have made us what we are today."

The department stores currently employ more than 2,200 Coloradans—from the buyers who travel to international markets to the warehousemen in its huge central Denver distribution center. The department store chain provides complete merchandise departments for every clothing need for the whole family, as well as home furnishings, furniture, and housewares. It offers consumer services from personal shoppers to carpet cleaning, and provides an ever-broadening range of customer services in the retail industry.

The downtown Denver store, which was built in 1958 on Zeckendorf Plaza, is a retail landmark on one end of the 16th Street Mall. The name May D&F is derived from its founder's name, plus D&F for Daniels and Fisher, a historic Denver retailing firm acquired in 1957 by the May Company.

The modern May D&F chain is a part of the giant parent company, May Department Stores, which employ over 75,000 people in 42 states and in 12 offices overseas.

And it all started in Colorado, when a young German immigrant came West to seek the opportunity the new land had to offer. May, and his successors in the May D&F Department Stores, have been and remain major contributors to the Colorado story. Many of the fine arts, philanthropic, educational, and other humanitarian institutes in Colorado have been beneficiaries of May underwritings, and today's May D&F executives continue to serve on the boards of these organizations throughout the Colorado communities served by one of the state's premier retailers.

May D&F stores bring the families of Colorado a tradition of fine products. The department store chain was founded in Colorado to become a U.S. giant.

The architecture of modern Denver is the state's greatest contrast to the nearby irregular sculpture of Rocky Mountain peaks that frame the city's skyline. Photo by Joel Silverman

The mall project in downtown Denver, called the 16th Street Mall, is a one-mile long pedestrian busway on the main commercial street. A joint public and private endeavor, it has revitalized the downtown area in a metropolitan region boasting the biggest and best suburban shopping centers between Chicago and Los Angeles. The mall has directly caused the establishment of a major regional shopping district at the Lower Downtown Denver area. That district includes a new two-block complex of shops along 16th Street called the Shops at the Tabor. Across the street is a square-block of shops known as Writer Square. This complex joins the long-established Larimer Square shopping area, which was one of Colorado's first developments to restore turn-of-the-century buildings to full commercial use. Completing this district is the Tivoli Denver Center which opened in 1985, featuring the restoration of a historic old brewery into unique shops, restaurants, and amusement facilities. That development, a few blocks away from the Tabor-Larimer-Writer shopping area, was named the Tivoli Center after the brewery.

The outstanding shopping facilities are by no means limited to the larger cities. Resort areas have created some of the most imaginative shopping districts to be found anywhere. Breckenridge, Aspen, and Vail, international ski and recreation towns, are noted for their posh boutiques, fine jewelry and gift galleries, and shops featuring international merchandise selections. Catering to jet-setting visitors, and the rich and famous part-time residents, these and other small towns offer shopping facilities that would far exceed any expectations for towns their size.

Other small cities have also aggressively redeveloped shopping areas to compete for the buyer's dollar. Littleton's Riverfront Festival Center is an example of the numerous new retail and activity center projects in cities and towns across the state.

Neighborhood convenience centers, usually built around a supermarket, are situated in every town and suburban area with a population to provide a market.

The larger cities and large suburban areas of the metropolitan cities are served by huge regional shopping centers. Some of these centers become the heart of the emerging suburban communities making it hard to tell whether the big centers followed the population or created the communities. The centers attract shoppers from other states in the region as well as provide competitive shopping opportunities. They almost always center around one or more large department stores. In suburban cities of the Denver metropolitan area there are 14 large centers, each with between a quarter million to over one million square feet of retail space. The Denver Metropolitan Area is truly the "shopping center" for much of the Rockies.

The Colorado Springs metropolitan area has four major retailing centers in addition to a strong downtown area. Fort Collins has three big shopping centers in addition to its Central Business District, and Greeley has two in addition to its downtown area. Pueblo also has two large shopping centers to bolster its central retail district.

From the urbanized Front Range to the towns in the mountains and plains, the retail establishment provides the one economic common denominator found in all of Colorado.

The retailers provide the strong base that gives all Colorado cities and towns the spirit of community. And to support this sense of community, local institutions of education, health, public safety, and religion assure the higher standard of living enjoyed by Coloradans.

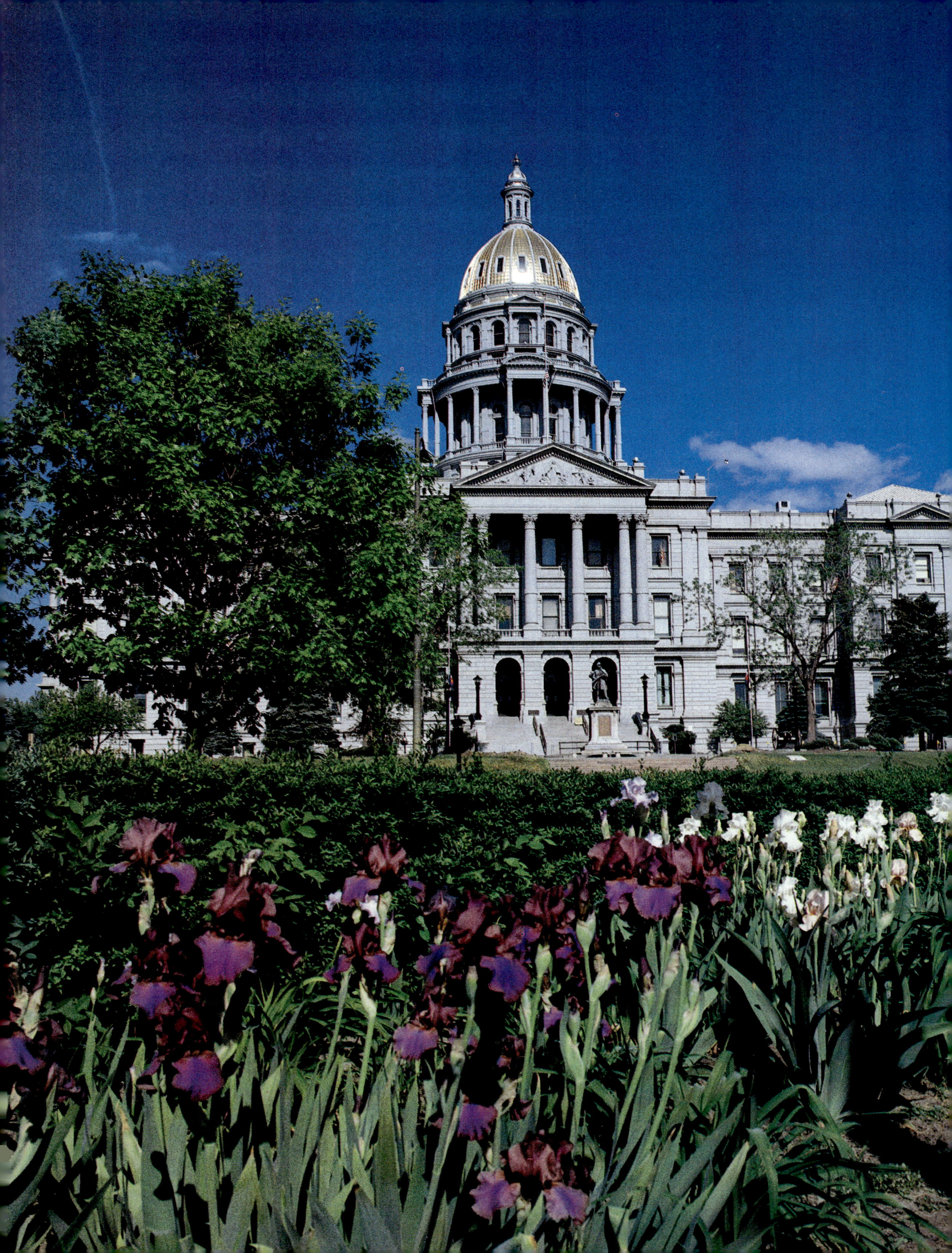

CHAPTER 3

The Colorado Good Life
Community Institutions

The natural environment of awe-inspiring mountains and pleasant valleys in Colorado provides an exceptional setting, but to achieve and maintain a high-quality lifestyle, the people-oriented institutions are essential to a good community environment.

The quality of Colorado's institutions of education, health, public services and safety, and social and welfare are as important to the good life in the cities, towns, and villages as the natural surroundings themselves.

Coloradans are challenged to match, with human effort, their bountiful resources, to assure that communities remain good "people places." Institutions of learning, health care and safety, and social services are not important just to provide a high standard of living, but they are also valuable to the economic well-being of the state.

Not only do they provide jobs and essential services for people within the communities, but both private and public institutions contribute directly to the success of a viable business and economic climate.

Public and private schools, universities and colleges, hospitals and health clinics, local and state government service agencies, police and fire departments, welfare agencies and philanthropic organizations, and churches all provide a broad base of professional people who contribute directly to the other sectors of the Colorado economy.

Of these community institutions perhaps none is more visible than the elementary and secondary school systems of the state.

Public Education

Colorado is a state of separate and individual public educational "systems." While there are basic standards, each system has its own individual program, since the philosophy of education in the state is based on local control. Each of the 185 school districts and the approximately 200 private schools designs its own curriculum for the particular needs of the local communities.

Within the 185 school districts there are 767 elementary schools, 125 junior high schools, 105 middle schools, and 176 high schools. In rural areas some schools combine junior and senior high facilities—there are 66 such arrangements. The smallest districts may house all programs in one facility. There are 14 such schools providing programs from kindergarten through the 12th grade.

In addition, the state's public school systems provide six adult education facilities, five alternative education schools, and eight special education schools. Fifteen vocational training schools at the high school level offer separate programs in technical education within the regular high schools.

There also are 130 private or parochial elementary schools, 23 private or parochial secondary schools, and 47 combined secondary private and parochial schools in Colorado. Most of these secondary schools are fully accredited by the Colorado Department of Education.

Certain basic courses are required for accreditation by the Colorado Department of Education for both public and private schools, but the state offers broad latitude to the local schools to develop innovative programs, within flexible guidelines. For that reason, many experimental and advanced teaching techniques can be found in Colorado schools. Programs pioneered in Colorado public and private schools have become national models for progressive education. Open classrooms, individualized instruction, team teaching, and flexible curricula at the local

The first gold for the dome of the Colorado capital building in Denver was contributed by early gold miners. Re-gilded every few years, the structure is a symbol of sound government in the state. Photo by James Blank, Stock Imagery

School buildings and educational programs are designed by the citizens in the communities they serve, with strong local voice in public education. The contrasts in buildings range from a solar application in a new suburban area, top, to a log schoolhouse in the historic mining center at Creede. Photos by Stewart M. Green, top, and Judith D. Morison

levels are designed to expand on the basic teaching of the "three Rs." This educational opportunity seems to have served the public well, since Colorado ranks in the top five states in the number of high school graduates who enroll in a college or university program after graduation.

The boundaries of the public school districts are not fixed according to county lines. Some encompass whole counties and others may overlap into adjoining counties. The size of the student population is as varied as the communities the districts serve. Some rural and mountain districts may have as few as 50 students, compared to the larger districts such as Denver with more than 70,000 students, and Jefferson County with a student population of nearly 76,000 in 1986.

School buildings often mirror their communities. Colorado school buildings in a rustic mining hamlet may consist of log timbers; an ultramodern design complete with an array of solar collectors for heating may match an advanced technology center.

Possibly because of the close local control of the public schools, many communities are fiercely proud of their schools. The local schools not only provide the educational needs of the students, but in many cases provide the main social and recreational focus for a community. During the football or basketball season the local teams not only carry the banner for their schools into statewide competition, but are the standard-bearers for their communities.

But of more serious concern to Coloradans is the responsibility they invest in their schools for preparing the state's young people for competition in the workplace.

A publication of the Governor's High-Tech Cabinet Council, entitled "Maintaining the Competitive Edge," describes public education's role in keeping the state competitive for new jobs:

"The attractiveness of an area is in good part determined by the quality of its schools. Any effort to retain or attract high-tech industry in Colorado must be coordinated with development of exemplary educational programs, beginning at the elementary and secondary levels."

In discussing Colorado's changing workplace, the study set the broad standards that the state's schools must meet to prepare its young people for jobs in the future, and to attract the type of new jobs the state is seeking. The standards include: (1) quality facilities, (2) measurable progress through standard achievement testing, (3) safe, well-disciplined environs, (4) rich curricula, both during and after school to condition both mind and body, (5) access to career information and counseling, and (6) exposure to developments in technology.

These standards are not just a wish list. Across the state, business and industry representatives are working with large and small public schools and colleges to develop a meaningful curriculum that combines basic education with the development of skills for the workplace.

One example is a non-profit foundation formed in Denver in 1985 to bring local businesses into partnership with the schools. Some 40 area business and industry leaders formed the initial task force, with an aim toward "linking the corporation with the classroom." Across the state major programs through such organizations as Junior Achievement, and in "on-the-job" training and direct counseling by business in programs sponsored by the Colorado Association of Commerce and Industry are becoming an increasingly important part of the state's public school curriculum development.

Colorado is second only to Alaska in the percentage of its population to graduate from high school. Nearly 79 percent of all Colorado residents over the age of 25 are high school graduates. The state leads the nation in the percentage of the adult population with four or more years of college. Of the 1.6 million Coloradans over the age of 25, more than 380,000 are college graduates. Twenty-three percent are college graduates, compared with a national average of 16 percent. Colorado is tied with Utah in the percentage of residents having attended at least one to three years of college, with 44 percent of the population in this category.

As in many parts of the nation, the slowing birthrate is causing a decline in grade-school enrollment in Colorado. Elementary enrollment between 1975 and 1982 declined by 4,000 students to 380,000, and high school enrollment during that same period dropped from 185,000 to 166,000. However, enrollment in the state's colleges and universities was up from 136,000 to 152,000 during the same period.

The public school workforce consisted of 55,300 persons in 1983, including administrators, teachers, and support personnel. The state invests about $1.7 billion annually in its schools, with much of the cost of education raised through local property tax. A total of more than 52 percent of the state's budget is spent on public and higher education.

The late 1970s and early 1980s saw tremendous growth in the use of advanced technology in teaching in the public and private schools. Microcomputers are now found in almost all public school facilities, and computer literacy is becoming a part of the curriculum in schools at all levels, from kindergarten through high school. The number of microcomputers being used in the public

Education is an essential ingredient in making the life style of Coloradans of the highest quality. This classroom in Broomfield is taking the "A-B-Cs" into the future. Photo by Bill Snow

From higher education to elementary school levels Coloradans enjoy a fine system to prepare their children for a challenging future. Photo by Bill Snow

65

PROFILE

Public Service Company of Colorado
Fueling Development and Progress

Harnessing the power to fuel the dynamic machines of Colorado industry and provide the high quality of life enjoyed by Coloradans has been the challenge of the state's largest utility company for more than 100 years.

Public Service Company of Colorado, which traces its beginnings to the early days of the new frontier in 1869, today provides dependable and inexpensive electricity and natural gas to approximately 75 percent of the state's people. The investor-owned company provides power to the companies and the families in a 20,000-square-mile area extending from the Wyoming to the New Mexico borders, and from Sterling in the northeast to Grand Junction on the Western Slope. Its service territory includes most of the Front Range area, including Metropolitan Denver.

Public Service Company has been serving this vital role in Colorado since its predecessor, Denver Gas Company, was incorporated in 1869. As the largest electricity and gas company in Colorado, Public Service is today an integral part of the current development that will see the state's population pass the 4 million level before the end of the century.

Public Service's capital investment in Colorado of well over $1 billion, assures all the energy needs will be met to sustain the expanding economy in the rapidly growing Front Range and in the diversifying base of the economy of the Western Slope.

Growth in electric operations during the remainder of this decade is expected to see residential connections increase from approximately 857,000 in 1986 to more than 928,000 by 1989. During that same period commercial electricity connections are expected to grow from about 113,000 in 1986 to more than 122,000 in 1989.

Natural gas service is also expected to grow dramatically. Major natural gas service to industrial connections provided by the company number almost 400 manufacturing plants.

Public Service Company generates electricity for Colorado from several primary sources including coal, natural gas, oil, and hydro power. Its primary source of energy for conversion to electricity is coal, because Colorado is situated in a region of abundant and easily accessible coal. The big Colorado utility has also developed the only nuclear generating station in the Rocky Mountains at its Fort St. Vrain plant.

Public Service Company, which formally came into being through mergers of predecessor companies from throughout the state in 1924, also owns several subsidiary energy companies. Most of its operation is in the most densely populated parts of the state, but its service also covers most of the mountain areas and extends into the San Luis Valley.

Public Service Company also owns Cheyenne Light, Fuel and Power Co., a public utility providing gas and electricity in Cheyenne, Wyoming. WestGas is a wholly owned subsidiary involved in the transmission of natural gas within Colorado. Fuelco, another wholly owned subsidiary is engaged in exploration, development, and production of natural gas and oil in Colorado, Montana, North Dakota, Texas, Utah, and Wyoming. Its subsidiary, Home Light and Power Co., is an electric company operating in the Greeley area.

The company's contribution to the economic welfare of the state is much broader than its role as a principal supplier of utilities. Throughout its history of service to the communities of Colorado, Public Service Company has been active in programs to develop and enhance the economies of the areas it serves. Representatives from the company's management work with local economic development organizations and chambers of commerce, and directly contribute expertise and financial assistance in support of community industrial development programs.

Public Service Company of Colorado is a leader in the state's plans to diversify its economy through attracting high-quality, advanced industry.

The institutions of higher learning provide a vital part of the community life in Colorado for both citizens and businesses of the state. Photo by Ron Ruhoff, Stock Imagery

schools increased tenfold in just three years, from 1980 to 1983. In addition to the use of microcomputers in training and education, the schools are also using videotape and videodisc equipment, combined with microcomputers. Public television programming, such as Denver's KRMA-TV Channel 6, is beamed directly into classrooms across the state.

The public schools also provide an extensive network of vocational training schools at the secondary, post-secondary, and adult level, as well as special programs for the disadvantaged and handicapped.

Ten schools, separate from the regular campus programs in the high schools, have been established specifically for job training, in addition to vocational programs in local district and community college systems.

These secondary level schools offer technical training in electronics, welding, drafting and design, machining, civil engineering, environmental control, industrial maintenance, the health disciplines, the building crafts, data processing, clerical and secretarial skills, bookkeeping, and other occupations. The state vocational programs also require that the student receive basic education in reading, writing, math, and science. They do not encourage Colorado young people to skip literacy and only learn a trade.

These schools are strategically located around the state to provide access to any youngster who wants or needs to learn a skill and enter the job market soon after high school graduation. Area vocational schools designated by the Colorado legislature include Aurora Technical Center (Aurora), Boulder Valley Technical Center (Boulder), Delta-Montrose Technical School (Delta), Emily Griffith Opportunity School (Denver), Larimer County Vocational Technical Center (Fort Collins), San Juan Basin Area Vocational School (Cortez), and San Luis Valley Area Vocational School (Alamosa).

Additionally, the state board of education has designated post high school vocational training at Arapahoe/Douglas Area Vocational School, Mesa College (Grand Junction), and Warren Occupational Center (Jefferson County). Vocational programs leading to associate certificates are also offered in district colleges and the state system of community colleges.

Higher Education

Colorado has established 21 area vocational schools and community colleges to serve the needs of employers seeking training programs for the development of new skills, and to serve the needs of employees and individuals planning to enter the workforce or upgrade their skills. These state institutions work directly with local employers and new employers in providing specific types of training to expand existing business and industry or to provide workers for new plants.

In recent years, new manufacturing plants locating in various parts of the state have been staffed by Colorado students trained for these specific jobs. Neoplan USA Corporation needed workers with special skills for its new assembly plant at Lamar, and 200 Coloradans received this special training while that plant was being constructed in 1980. When Russell Stover Candy planned a new Montrose plant, it required special skills in food preparation, and the vocational system provided the training for these workers prior to the plant opening. Miller Western Wear received similar training assistance for its Sterling garment factory, as did Aspen Skiwear in Lamar, and Gerry Division, Outdoor Sports Inc. in Alamosa. The Emily Griffith Opportunity School has ongoing programs to train skilled machinists for plants such as Sunstrand, which opened several new operations, including one in Grand Junction.

At the post-secondary level, colleges providing vocational programs as well as full programs in the liberal arts are also located

PROFILE

Blue Cross and Blue Shield of Colorado
Underwriting Better Health for Coloradans

A crisp, high-mountain climate, robust and active people, and exceptional medical facilities and professionals all contribute to Colorado's good state of health.

Blue Cross and Blue Shield of Colorado has been the state's leading health care insurer for more than half a century, and in the late 1980s remains a leader in innovative plans to meet modern health-care needs. Blue Cross and Blue Shield, which has diversified its programs for employer groups and individuals, is part of the mosaic making Colorado one of the nation's healthiest places to live and work.

The Colorado company, an autonomous, non-profit corporation, is a member of the international Blue Cross and Blue Shield organization that provides health and other insurance protection for millions of Americans. The company has diversified its programs to meet the changing needs of Coloradans by adding several services to basic health coverage, including a health maintenance organization (HMO), a preferred provider organization (PPO), and other packages designed to provide cost effective health care.

As the state's largest health benefits carrier, Blue Cross and Blue Shield of Colorado has joined business leaders, medical professionals, and individuals in instituting programs aimed at reducing the cost of medical care. Colorado has attained an enviable record in reducing costs through shortening the average length of a patient's hospital stay and other alternative cost-cutting incentives.

The company, in cooperation with employers, has pioneered wellness and fitness educational programs aimed at improving the health of Coloradans. It works closely with the management of large and small companies in Colorado to achieve meaningful cost-containment programs, reducing health insurance and medical expenses for both employers and their employees.

In helping businesses design benefit programs, Colorado Blue Cross and Blue Shield has developed a wide range of health, life, disability, and dental benefit packages. A number of health-care options, with a wide range of deductibles and coinsurances are available. Rocky Mountain Life Insurance Company, a wholly owned subsidiary of the company, provides complete life insurance and short- and long-term disability programs for businesses.

The company recently introduced a new dental option, featuring a prepaid plan that emphasizes preventive dental care. Under this plan, participating Colorado dentists are paid a fixed monthly fee for services, which makes the program more cost effective than previous plans available to employees.

Blue Cross and Blue Shield also assists Colorado companies in the development of work-site wellness programs and supplies information on community resources that can provide a variety of services to employees. Films, booklets, brochures, and posters are provided to employers at minimal cost so that employees can have access to information that helps them maintain healthful life styles.

Over 72 percent of Colorado's doctors are on contract with Blue Cross and Blue Shield and accept payment schedules for services provided in the company's plans. Group members using participating physicians have no additional out-of-pocket expense for services covered in the company's plans.

HMO Colorado, Inc. is part of a national network of HMOs developed by the Blue Cross and Blue Shield Plans. This health maintenance organization provides services to members through a designated clinic setting. Areas covered by the company's participating HMOs are being expanded to several parts of the state.

Blue Cross and Blue Shield of Colorado's preferred provider product, PRIME Health Plan, is the largest PPO in Colorado. PRIME uses a physician and hospital network and enables the company to offer businesses a new option for cost effective health care services. This newest program offers businesses a substantial savings on their health care premiums, while providing employees with a wide choice of providers.

Staff members from Blue Cross and Blue Shield of Colorado were active participants in the Governor's Task Force to study health care issues in Colorado. An evaluation of health care services and recommendations for ways to use services and streamline medical care are forthcoming from that task force study.

In other programs, top-level management from Blue Cross and Blue Shield chaired the Colorado Health Forum, a group of influential and concerned citizens who seek to make positive changes in the health care system. The Health Forum brings together all sectors of the health care community, to foster a greater awareness of the issues that must be addressed to assure continued progress in the state's health care industry.

Blue Cross and Blue Shield of Colorado also provides a number of services to businesses to make health care coverage a more efficient benefit to employee groups. Its modern processing capabilities are designed to meet the informational needs of a high technology society. The Colorado company annually processes more than 195,000 Blue Cross claims, paying more than $101 million in benefit dollars within the state. In addition, it processes Blue Shield claims, and Medicare Part A, Medicare Part B, and Medicare Supplemental Contracts.

"Blue Cross and Blue Shield of Colorado is in a position to offer the business community of this state a number of unique services—flexibility of product, quality of service, health promotion information, and cost containment programs," says Don Blanchard, president. "The businessman must shop prudently in today's market, and Blue Cross and Blue Shield of Colorado is providing a wide variety of programs for businesses and individual health care coverage."

The company, which continues to expand and change its programs to meet the changing medical scene in Colorado, believes that business must play a vital role in the kinds of benefits purchased for employees and in the incentives they give employees to become active participants in the health care system and in their own personal health.

"At Blue Cross and Blue Shield of Colorado, we are concerned about the future of health care in the state as well as the nation," says Jerome H. Lynch, chairman and CEO of Blue Cross and Blue Shield of Colorado. "Each year the cost of health care takes a greater cut of the Gross National Product, 10.6 percent today compared with 5.2 percent in 1960. Businesses have a large share in the health care bill.

"Because health care is such a complex and interdependent problem, it is important that all segments involved in the health care picture recognize the contribution that each can make in finding practical and viable solutions. We are actively enlisting the business community and all interested citizens to join with us in turning our attention to combatting health care costs in the state of Colorado and across the nation."

Blue Cross and Blue Shield of Colorado has been an innovator in developing health care programs to assure that Coloradans can better enjoy their state.

strategically around the state. College level vocational training for the Denver Metropolitan Area is available at Arapahoe Community College (Littleton), Community College of Aurora (Aurora), Community College of Denver (Auraria campus in downtown Denver), Front Range Community College (Westminster), and Red Rocks Community College (Golden).

On the Eastern Plains, vocational programs are provided by Morgan Community College (Fort Morgan), Lamar Community College (Lamar), Northeastern Junior College (Sterling), and Otero Junior College (La Junta).

Aims Community College at Greeley provides vocational programs for the northern part of the Front Range. Pikes Peak Community College at Colorado Springs, Pueblo Community College at Pueblo, and Trinidad State Junior College serve the southern part of the Front Range, with two-year college vocational programs.

Colorado Mountain College has three campuses to provide vocational as well as liberal arts programs. Its facilities are Spring Valley Campus at Glenwood Springs, Alpine Campus at Steamboat Springs, and Timberline Campus at Leadville. Colorado Northwestern Community College at Rangely provides industry support training in western Colorado, along with the vocational program at Mesa College in Grand Junction.

A unique higher education facility has been established in the downtown Denver area. The Auraria Higher Education Center provides a single campus with shared facilities, such as library and laboratories, for three types of advanced education programs. The campus, with an off-campus student body exceeding 30,000 students, is home to the Community College of Denver, Metropolitan State College, and the University of Colorado at Denver. Metropolitan State, the largest of the state's four-year colleges with an enrollment of about 15,000 students, also provides extensive continuing education opportunities. All programs of the three institutions on the Auraria campus, with some integration of courses, are heavily oriented toward business and advanced technology training.

Colorado's colleges and universities are also integrated into the lifestyle of the communities they serve. They provide far more than an abstract educational opportunity for young people within the regions they serve. They not only provide the advanced training for Colorado's graduating high school students, but all colleges and universities offer continuing educational opportunities targeted at the business and commercial needs of their communities. College and university activities often play a dominant economic, social, and cultural role in their communities.

The academic and professional staffs pro-

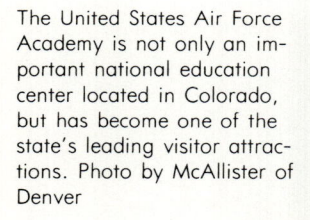

The United States Air Force Academy is not only an important national education center located in Colorado, but has become one of the state's leading visitor attractions. Photo by McAllister of Denver

Three universities and colleges share the innovative downtown Auraria Campus in Denver providing education and business support facilities. Photo by Joel Silverman

vide other assets to the community. An example of the important community service role of the college in community life is a recent contribution to the economic betterment of the San Luis Valley area made by the four-year college at Alamosa. Human resources within Adams State College were called upon to assist in the research and preparation of the San Luis Valley's Overall Economic Development Plan. Both professional staff and students of the college provided the research and community asset inventories used to write a comprehensive planning document. That document is being used extensively in the valley's efforts to diversify and expand its economy.

Many cases of similar direct contributions by the colleges and universities to the economic welfare of their communities could be cited in regions across the state.

Colorado's four-year colleges, most offering master's degree programs in select courses of study, are geographically located to provide easy access to serve local students as well as to provide continuing educational opportunities within easy commuting distances. Western State College at Gunnison provides full four-year bachelor's and master's degree programs. Because of its mountain location and outdoor recreational environment, it is a popular campus for out-of-state students, and had a 1985-86 enrollment of more than 2,700 students.

Mesa College at Grand Junction, with a 1985-86 enrollment of more than 3,600, offers four- and five-year baccalaureate degrees. Adams College, with a current enrollment of nearly 2,000, serves the San Luis Valley with programs through master's degrees. Fort Lewis College at Durango also offers four- and five-year baccalaureate degrees in 24 major courses. Its latest enrollment is more than 3,700.

Colorado is also the host state to many non-public higher education institutions, including both private and parochial colleges. Among the state's oldest and largest private higher education institutes is Regis College with a full-time enrollment of more than 3,000. Regis College's main campus is in Denver, and other campuses are located at Colorado Springs and Sterling. Loretto Heights College, also located in Denver, is another of the state's oldest institutions, with a current enrollment of over 700.

Other private and parochial colleges in the

PROFILE

Regis College
Building Educational Support for Enterprise

As Regis College observes its 100th year of providing higher educational service from its main 90-acre Denver campus in Colorado, its curriculum is designed to prepare students for the complex changes facing tomorrow's leaders as the 21st century approaches.

A private, coeducational, Jesuit institution of higher learning, Regis College has continued to exemplify the four-century old Jesuit tradition of providing educational excellence since its founding in 1877 in New Mexico. The main campus was opened in Denver in 1887, and has been expanded to offer adults accelerated degree completion programs in support of business at campuses in Colorado Springs, Sterling, and southeast Denver.

In addressing the changing needs of the state, Regis College in 1978 began career programs for adult students in Colorado Springs and later expanded to offer a Master's Degree Program in Business Administration (MBA). In 1979 both programs were started in Denver.

Regis College's impact on the higher educational needs of the Rocky Mountain region, with an enrollment of more than 5,200 students in undergraduate and graduate programs, is evidenced by its continued expansion. At a time when many private universities across the country are cutting programs and reducing enrollment, Regis College has continually grown in both.

The Regis Career Education Program (RECEP) offers bachelor degrees in business administration, technical management, and computer information systems to adults who have prior college and work experience. Over 100 Colorado businesses and professional organizations send their employees to RECEP.

In 1985 this popular program

Regis College has established a tradition of providing high quality education to Colorado. A graduating class prepares to begin new careers.

enrolled nearly 2,000 students in the Denver area, 737 in Colorado Springs, 34 in Sterling, over 300 in the Academy of Health Sciences, and 25 in the Health Records Information Management program. In addition, Regis enrolled 475 students in its MBA program, and 130 students in the fourth year of its Master of Arts in Adult Christian Community Development (MAACCD) program. The MAACCD program is unique in that there are only a few similar master's degrees offered in the world.

The RECEP curriculum is demanding. Students, who usually hold full-time jobs, must assume an intensive, accelerated academic program offering nine, five-week terms. The RECEP and MBA adjunct facility is comprised of 175 business professionals who have undergone an intensive selection process to determine if they are qualified to teach adults.

Regis College's high academic standards are also met by the professional tone of its four-year undergraduate faculty, with more than 85 percent of the full-time teachers holding a doctorate or equivalent degree in their field. This is one of the highest doctorate/faculty ratios in Colorado.

Another feature of this private college is its outstanding student-to-faculty ratio of 15-to-1. This close association between professor and student provides a tremendous amount of personal attention to the student's educational development.

The school has constantly expanded its program as the needs of the community changed. Today Regis offers degrees in 27 major programs, including preparation for professions in law, dentistry, and medicine. Its business programs are considered among the best in the region. In keeping with modern demands, graduates of Regis College have the computer proficiency that is needed to succeed in business and industry, even if they are not directly majoring in computer science.

The college also prepares its graduates to assume management and community leadership roles. The Regis College Leadership Program is designed to help students enhance their abilities to bring a positive influence to both corporate and community problems. This program evolves from the traditional Jesuit educational philosophy, which has historically stated that its institutions should "form leaders who will carry forth into their personal and professional lives a mission of service to others."

While the college stays centered on the liberal arts tradition, the faculty, programs, and community focus have expanded to help Colorado meet the challenges of its rapidly emerging technological future.

state and their approximate 1985-86 enrollment include Baptist Bible College, located in Broomfield, 149; Colorado College, Colorado Springs, 1,850; Colorado Christian College, Denver, 360; Colorado Technical College, Colorado Springs, 600; Denver Conservative Baptist Seminary, Denver, 544; The Iliff School of Theology, Denver, 377; Naropa Institute, Boulder, 300; Nazarene Bible College, Colorado Springs, 436; Parks College, Denver, 725; Saint Thomas Seminary, Denver, 116; and Yeshiva Toras Chaim Talmudical Seminary, Denver, 35.

Colorado Women's College, located in Denver, is now a part of the University of Denver system.

The state's largest private institution of higher education is the University of Denver, with a 1985-86 enrollment of more than 8,000 students. Located in Denver, the university was founded in 1864.

The United States Air Force Academy was established in 1954 and located at Colorado Springs. This federal service academy has an authorized student population of 4,417 cadets, attracting students from all 50 states.

Colorado's state university system, includng the University of Colorado with campuses at Boulder, Colorado Springs, and Denver; Colorado State University headquartered at Fort Collins; the University of Northern Colorado at Greeley; the University of Southern Colorado at Pueblo; and Colorado School of Mines at Golden, had a combined, full-time enrollment of almost 84,000 students in 1985-86.

Colorado School of Mines, located at Golden, is an internationally recognized natural resources development institute. Its current enrollment of nearly 3,000 includes students from Free World countries; and the school provides advanced training for many students from developing nations. Specializing in engineering, science, and mining, School of Mines offers a wide range of baccalaureate, master's and doctorate degrees.

Located at Greeley, the University of Northern Colorado has a full-time enrollment of nearly 10,000 students. UNC offers a wide range of liberal arts and sciences degrees including baccalaureate, master's, and doctorates.

The University of Southern Colorado at Pueblo, with a current enrollment of almost 5,000, provides bachelor's and master's degree programs.

Colorado State University, headquartered at Fort Collins, is one of the nation's leading agricultural and biotechnology institutes. CSU had a 1985-86 general enrollment of nearly 18,000 students, and about 500 advanced students enrolled in the college of professional veterinary medicine.

The huge University of Colorado system is headquartered at the Boulder campus, with a full-time enrollment of more than 22,000 students. CU's major courses cover the full spectrum of higher education from liberal arts to sciences at all degree levels.

The University of Colorado's second largest campus population is at its Denver facility, with approximately 11,000 students attending school on the Auraria Higher Education Cam-

Auraria Campus in the heart of Denver boasts one of the nation's largest student populations. While modern facilities are shared by three colleges and universities, the historic Ninth Street Parkway and other areas have been preserved. Photo by David Williams

PROFILE

Rocky Mountain News
Providing News and Information to Colorado

Even the earliest pioneers on the wilderness frontier of Colorado yearned for a sense of community with a vehicle to communicate their ideas and garner information.

Appropriately, those needs were served by one of Colorado's first businesses, which today remains the state's oldest business in continuous operation since the first permanent settlement was founded. The Rocky Mountain News, located in Denver since 1859, has grown with the state through "booms and busts" and has long served as a statewide daily newspaper.

Its growth in both service and circulation throughout Colorado was given vigorous impetus in the last decade when management of the national Scripps Howard Newspaper chain made heavy capital commitments to the Denver-based Rocky Mountain News.

Since 1972 more than $50 million has been spent for land and buildings, equipment, and construction. This huge expansion program, at a time when many national newspapers were cutting costs or curtailing publication altogether, culminated in the 1985 completion of the $14 million five-story addition to the News' business and editorial offices in downtown Denver.

The modern-day capital investment at the News was a calculated business investment in the future of Colorado, according to William W. Fletcher, president and general manager at the News.

"The business side of newspapering has become increasingly important to the communities served," Fletcher believes. "The newspaper is no longer only required to keep the citizenry informed on events affecting all aspects of living, but is the principal source of vital consumer information. The role of the Rocky Mountain News is essential to the entire business system—from retailing to the highest level of finance and investment."

The Rocky Mountain News organization has expanded its capacity to meet the needs of the metropolitan area and the state.

"Investments in people and capital facilities had to be made to assure the News a continued leadership position in a growing city and state," recalls Fletcher. "As a result, we were able to grow with the region."

Its role as a regional newspaper and its capacity to meet consumer demands has made it the ninth largest daily and Sunday paper in the United States in total advertising, ahead of such national dailies as the New York Times. It ranks fifth in the nation in classified advertising and tenth in retail advertising.

In an expansion period covering just a dozen years, the Rocky Mountain News built a combination newsprint warehouse and off-site printing facility on the Platte River, expanded its on-site press capacity from 14 to 48 printing units, constructed an on-site newsprint roll-handling and storage facility, and installed a computer-driven, automated newspaper bundle loading system.

During this same period the workforce, in all sections of the newspaper operation, was expanded from under 750 to more than 1,200 employees.

Evolving as the flagship newspaper of the Scripps Howard Newspaper chain, the Rocky Mountain News main offices in its newly completed complex provide Colorado with one of the nation's best equipped and most modern information centers.

These modern facilities are in keeping with the 127-year-old paper's tradition for innovation in the news field. Founded by pioneer western newspaper publisher William Newton Byers, the Rocky Mountain News was acquired by the Scripps Howard Newspaper chain in 1926.

Colorado's Rocky Mountain News expanded into modern new facilities in Denver from a historic position as the first newspaper and business in the state.

High technology extends to the traditional printing industry as Colorado becomes a key state in the new information age. Photo courtesy of American Web Offset

pus. The University of Colorado-Colorado Springs Campus has an enrollment of about 5,500 students.

Colorado's medical school at the University of Colorado Health Sciences Center in Denver provides graduate programs for physicians, dentists, and nurses. The medical school provides educational training for health service students from throughout the Rocky Mountain Region and other parts of the nation.

In addition to the public and private schools, colleges and universities, Colorado has a well-developed network of privately operated trade and technical schools developing skills in service trades, technical fields, and business support.

Education in all of Colorado's institutions of higher learning has in recent years become more closely tied to the changing economy of the state. The requirements for advanced technology skills in almost every sector of the economy are creating this closer relationship between education and commerce. Some of these emerging roles and interrelationships are discussed in subsequent chapters on specific sectors of the economy.

Information Resources

Colorado's privately owned newspapers, magazines, and radio and TV stations also play an important role in continuing education of the public as well as providing an important link to the rest of the nation, the world, and within their local communities. The need for the link is reciprocal, because as Colorado has become an increasingly important regional and national economic center, the demand for information about Colorado has grown. The Denver Metropolitan Area is the headquarters for correspondents from many national newspapers and magazines.

Colorado has 29 daily newspapers, of which 10 have Sunday editions. Combined paid daily newspaper circulation is more than one million in the state. In addition, community papers, publishing at least weekly, number 122, with six weekly newspaper chain publishers located in Colorado. The state is headquarters for a score of general interest and trade magazines.

Colorado's two large multi-state newspapers, the Denver Post and the Rocky Mountain News, not only provide news coverage and circulation in Colorado, but circulate widely throughout the Rocky Mountain region.

In addition to being the national headquarters for several of the top cable television companies in America, Colorado communities are well covered by local stations affiliated with ABC, CBS, NBC, and independent news networks. The Public Broadcasting System's major news program, The MacNeil-Lehrer News Hour, covers all news in the western United States from its news bureau in Denver.

Locally, Colorado has 12 full-service television stations, 53 FM radio stations and 72 AM radio stations—all providing news programming. Even in areas of the state where

PROFILE

Saint Joseph Hospital
Advanced Care with a Tradition of Caring

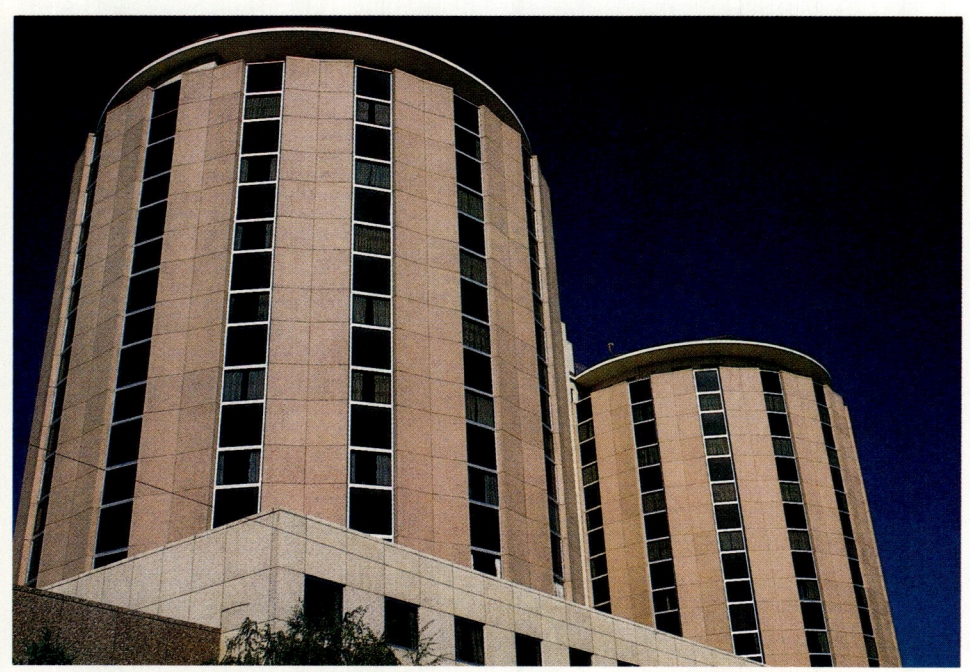

Saint Joseph Hospital delivers modern medical care with a tradition of caring for the residents of the state and region from its facilities in Denver.

Established by the Sisters of Charity of Leavenworth in 1873, Saint Joseph Hospital in Denver is recognized as one of the most modern regional care centers in the Rocky Mountain states. The hospital serves patients from throughout Colorado and the Rocky Mountain region with specialized diagnosis, general and acute care, and a wide range of rehabilitative and preventive health services.

Still owned and operated by the Sisters of Charity, the hospital is recognized for its excellence in delivery of medical and health care with highly cost-effective financial and administrative management.

With a staff of over 1,000 physicians representing all medical specialties, this private teaching hospital provides training for resident physicians in internal medicine, surgery, obstetrics and gynecology, family practice, emergency medicine, and dentistry.

A noted regional diagnostic center, Saint Joseph installed the state-of-the-art Magnetic Resonance Imaging system in 1986, which provides internal body images in color for the best resolution of any current diagnostic tool. This system was added to its diagnostic imaging technology which includes CT scanning, ultrasound, and a wide range of sophisticated cardiovascular, brain, spinal, lung, and other organ diagnostic equipment.

Saint Joseph Hospital's highly specialized surgical facilities provide all major surgical procedures including open heart, brain and nervous system, and reconstructive surgery in one of the most technologically advanced centers in the western United States. SurgiCare One, a convenient and cost-saving unit, provides certain types of surgery for patients whose conditions do not require overnight stays at the hospital.

The hospital's Women's Pavilion brings together some of the region's best facilities and staff specializing in the needs of women. About one in 10 Colorado babies are born here, including Colorado's first quintuplets in 1985 and two sets of quadruplets in recent years. Its intensive-care nursery is famous for providing facilities and physicians able to tend the needs of critically ill newborns.

The Cardiac Care Unit provides intensive-care nursing and round-the-clock bedside monitoring for heart attack patients. Cancer care at Saint Joseph Hospital combines the latest technology in medicine with support programs for cancer patients and their families.

The Orthopedic Unit is equipped for patients requiring surgical joint repair and replacement. Physical and occupational therapists are on hand to give follow-up care to return patients to normal activities as soon as possible.

The hospital provides one of the region's most up-to-date medical centers for eye, ear, nose, and throat surgery and treatment, and its neurological specialists are noted for diagnosis and treatment of brain, spine, and nervous system problems.

The hospital was recently honored by the American Hospital Association for its extensive patient education program aimed at helping patients and their families learn more about their diagnoses, treatments, and post-hospital health care. Outreach facilities are provided at other locations, including a new occupational medicine facility, and a sports medicine and health clinic in the new Greenwood Athletic Club.

Saint Joseph Hospital is a major resource to business and industry in the state, providing information and programs on current issues in occupational health and safety.

no local television station provides coverage, all communities, no matter how small, have access through cable or satellite connections to national and regional news programming.

In a State of Good Health

Colorado, because of its high altitude and thin mountain air, was perceived by early settlers to be a healthy place to live. Its mineral springs and spas added to that image. Today, Coloradans enjoy a healthy environment, and perhaps the emphasis placed on healthful outdoor activities such as hiking and jogging contributes to its reputation as a healthy place. Coloradans spend fewer days in the hospital than the average American, and spend 12 percent less on health care per person than the national average. Latest statistics on average length of hospital stays show the national average to be over seven days, while in Colorado the average stay in the hospital is less than six days. Nationally, the average per patient hospital bill is $2,492, and in Colorado the bill averages $2,289.

A recent study conducted by the Colorado Hospital Association indicated that hospital occupancy rates and length of stay were both declining in Colorado. In 1984, 45.2 percent of hospital admissions and 31.3 percent of the inpatient days were for newborn delivery and care, not for treatment of illness.

Colorado's natural environment has always made it a popular state for health professionals to set up practice, and the state has a higher ratio of doctors and dentists to general population than the national average. In the mid-1980s, Colorado had nearly 6,000 practicing physicians and 2,000 practicing dentists. Doctors per 100,000 population numbered 195, compared to the national ratio of 185 per 100,000 population. There are 64 dentists per 100,000 Coloradans, compared with a national average of 55 per 100,000.

The medical facilities in Colorado, even in the smaller cities and towns, are exceptionally modern. In 1986, Colorado had 107 hospitals, including 84 general and acute-care facilities. Other hospital facilities in the state include seven psychiatric, six federal, three rehabilitation, two research, two regional centers, and one each of alcohol treatment, podiatric, and state penal hospitals.

The majority of Colorado general hospitals, 48, are private, not-for-profit facilities, with 32 operated by counties or special hospital districts. The state's hospitals have over 15,000 beds for general and acute-care patients. Most of these general hospitals, 41, have fewer than 50 beds, and are strategically

Medical services in Colorado are as modern as any in the nation, and the state's health professionals serve the entire region. Even industry gets into the process by manufacturing such items as this X-Ray film. Photo courtesy of Kodak Colorado

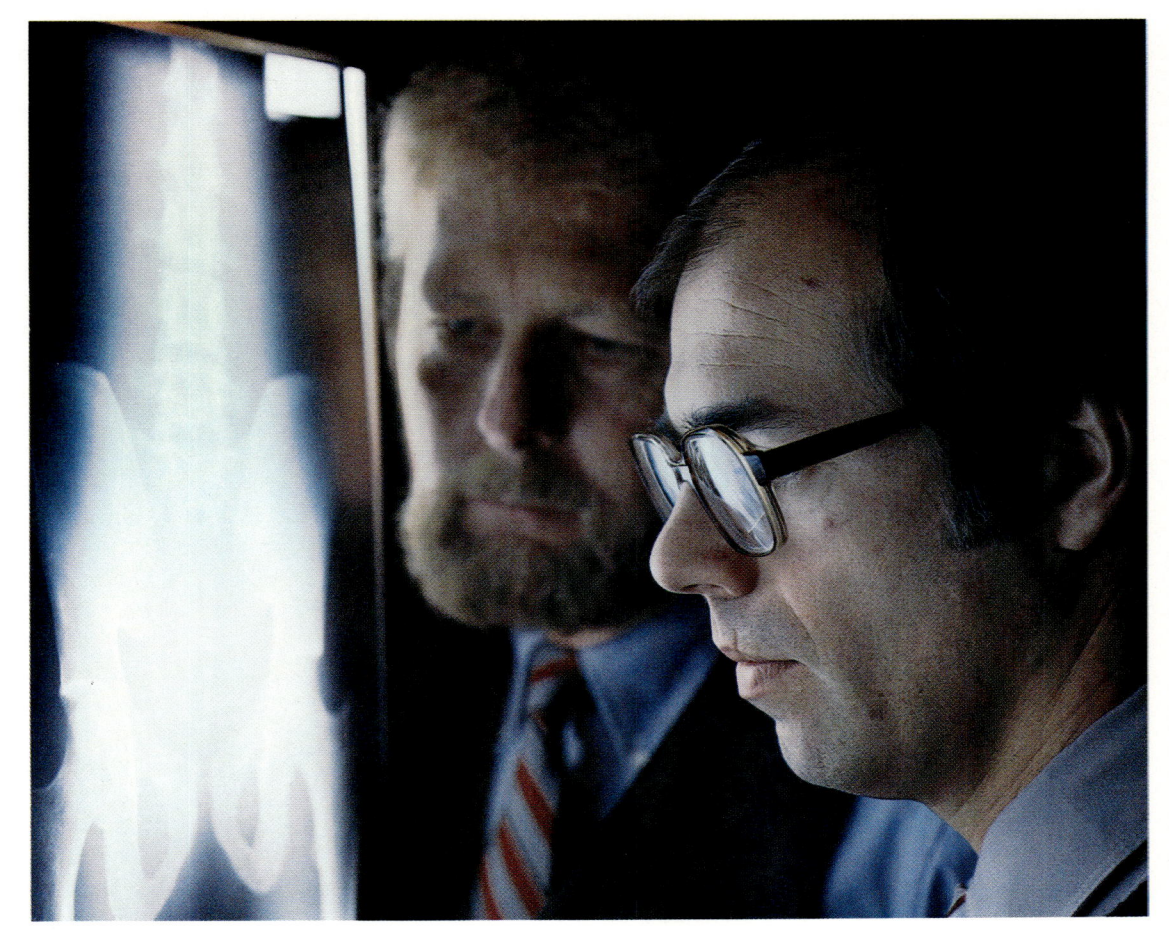

PROFILE

Penrose Hospitals
Medical Care for Colorado's Space Age

Since the early days when Colorado was reputed to have the healthiest climate in the nation, the state's health care has been consistently upgraded by one of its most advanced medical centers.

The Penrose Hospitals, which serve the Pikes Peak region, are today as advanced as the high technology community they serve along the southern Front Range. Their healthcare programs, advanced facilities, and staff of medical professionals offer Colorado Springs and the surrounding communities an excellence in family and individual care.

Operated by the Sisters of Charity of Cincinnati, Ohio, this facility of hospitals and special medical centers brings a historic tradition of gentle, personal concern to the best in modern medicine.

"The concerned and compassionate attention given by all the people who care for patients at The Penrose Hospitals, and the response to that care by those who are sick or injured, creates the common bond which makes Penrose one of the state's leading providers of health care," states Sister Myra James, president.

The Pikes Peak regional center consists of a two-hospital complex representing 460 beds and a staff of 2,000 physicans and medical support personnel.

With the rich history of providing medical service since the earliest days of development in Colorado, the Penrose Hospitals are in every medical sense modern in programs, facilities, and technology.

Programs range from complete acute-care services to full chronic rehabilitation centers for alcohol treatment, Alzheimer support, birth and maternity services, cancer treatment and research, complete cardiac care, rehabilitation programs, and advanced trauma aid.

Penrose's new $23.5 million ambulatory care center was added to its main facility in 1984 to broaden the already extensive list of basic and specialized hospital services. That center is designed to keep Coloradans out of the hospital by offering time- and cost-efficient medical programs to prevent overnight stays whenever possible.

Another of the major facilities provided as a resource to Colorado by The Penrose Hospitals is the Eleanor Capron Rehabilitation Center, the largest and most comprehensive facility of its type in southern Colorado. That center provides pediatric and adult rehabilitation for brain injury, stroke, arthritis, limb amputation, burns, back injury, psychological disorders, and other impairments.

From emergency care and open heart programs, to patient and family educational programs, the coronary units at Penrose provide excellence in medicine to the large southern Colorado region it serves.

At the Women's Life Center, Penrose also offers an extensive specialized program through its family-centered Birth Center Service. Located at Penrose Community Hospital, an 88-bed home-atmosphere facility, the Birth Center provides family-centered care through pregnancy, labor and delivery, and during the nurturing of newborns and new mothers.

Penrose's Riegel Center and Brockhurst Ranch Youth Recovery Center provide modern medical and therapy programs for alcohol and drug treatment for both adults and adolescents.

Penrose Cancer Hospital is the only community hospital in the region to be granted a National Cancer Institute contract for a cancer communication network and cancer information service. This program links Penrose to 18 major comprehensive cancer centers to share the latest information in diagnostics, treatment, and research.

The Penrose Hospitals provide the total community health support required to match the rapidly advancing technological future in this region of Colorado. And the Sisters of Charity still maintain the tradition of compassionate care that they brought to their first Colorado hospital almost a century ago.

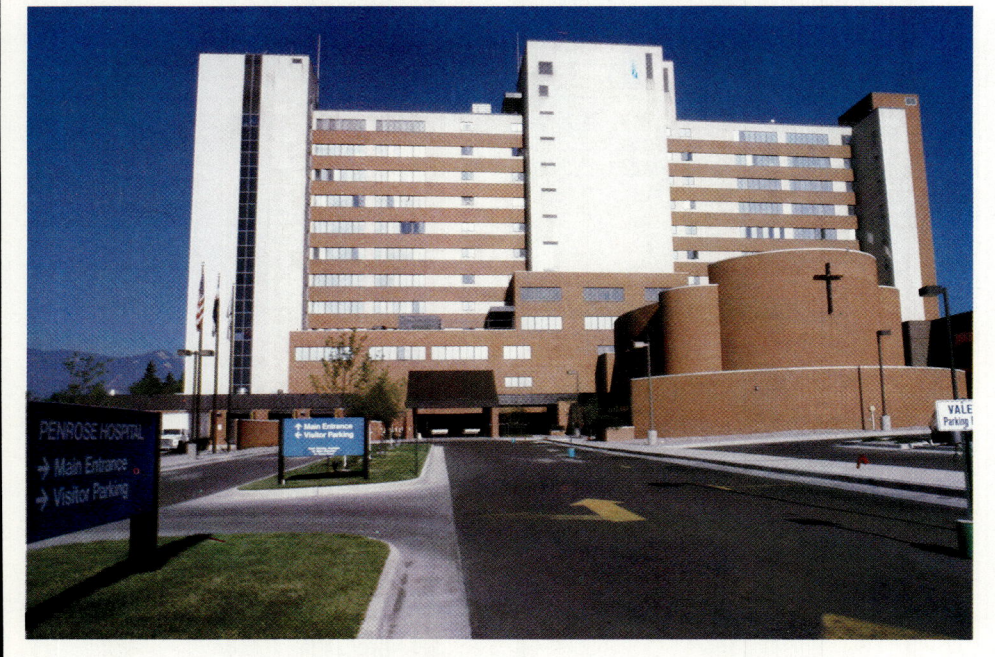

Penrose Hospital offers advanced health care facilities and staff to match the aerospace future emerging in the Colorado Springs/Pikes Peak region.

Caring is a part of the life style of Coloradans. With more and more seniors choosing to retire in Colorado, special attention is given their needs. Photo courtesy of Penrose Hospitals

located in communities across the state. In all, 61 communities of Colorado have full-service hospitals, even if some are in the small category. Only six of the state's hospitals are large, 500-plus bed facilities; and 47 are medium-size general hospitals with between 100 and 500 beds. Twenty-three Colorado hospitals have between 50 and 100 beds.

The Colorado Department of Institutions also operates two mental health facilities for inpatients, and contracts for local community services on an outpatient basis with 23 mental health clinics around the state. It operates state-owned residential centers for the developmentally disabled, and contracts for additional residential and day care centers.

In addition, Colorado has 160 privately owned nursing homes with more than 25 beds each. These homes provide more than 17,000 beds in state inspected facilities for senior citizens.

Colorado, with strong Health Maintenance Organizations (HMOs) and Preferred Provider Organizations (PPOs), has experienced a sizable savings in the cost of medical care in recent years. As national health care costs have continued to rise sharply, doctors, hospital administrators, insurers, and employers have launched new programs to slow the rising cost of health care in Colorado. Their efforts seem to be producing results.

Hospital care inflation rates slowed dramatically in the state between 1983, when they were up 18.6 percent and 1984, when they were up 5.4 percent. Actual hospital admissions also declined in that period, from 407,577 in 1983 to 381,303 the following year. Length of inpatient stays in Colorado hospitals decreased by nearly 14 percent, from over 2,400,000 patient days to 2,100,000.

The Colorado Hospital Association believes this trend is permanent, and represents major progress in solving a problem of national concern.

"New methods of paying for care for Medicare and other patients, incentives by business and insurers to encourage cost-effective use of health care by employees, and an increasing emphasis on wellness have brought about dramatic changes in how hospitals are used," notes the Colorado Association's annual report for 1985.

With excellent health care facilities available in most of the smaller cities and towns in Colorado, Denver provides support services in more advanced medical technology. In emergency cases, several of the large regional medical centers are within quick reach via helicopter ambulance services operating from Denver.

Denver has 22 regional hospitals, general and acute care hospitals, and specialty medical centers. An example of the regional role that Colorado plays in providing health care to the Rockies is one of the nation's most advanced medical centers for children. Children's Hospital at Denver serves a 500,000-square-mile area of mid-America with the most advanced equipment and some of the best-trained specialists available anywhere in the world. Infant emergency cases are flown to this huge regional center from as far away as Canada, Texas, and Minnesota, as well as the Rocky Mountain states.

The teaching and research center at the University of Colorado Health Sciences Center is also one of the most advanced facilities in the western United States. Fitzsimons Army Medical Center, a military center located in Aurora, also serves the entire western region. And National Jewish Center for Immunology and Respiratory Medicine, located in Denver, is a world center for those areas of special medical care and research. Denver's other major hospitals provide a degree of medical care that assures support for the smaller hospitals and clinics of the state and region.

Health care also is a major employment sector of the state's economy, with more than 75,000 Coloradans employed in medical-related professions.

PROFILE

Waste Management, Inc.
Keeping Colorado's Environment Clean

Bringing the best of technology and research to bear on one of modern society's most difficult problems—the safe disposal of the waste by-products of progress—is a daily challenge accepted by Waste Management, Inc. in Colorado as well as in its areas of operations around the world.

Communities in Colorado—the metropolitan Front Range, the mountain resorts, and the Western Slope—are the beneficiaries of expert services of one of the world's most experienced and environmentally advanced waste handling companies. The international Waste Management, Inc. is among the world's leading experts in solid waste, chemical waste, chemical-nuclear waste, and toxic wastes disposal.

Waste Management of North America, the largest division of Waste Management, Inc., is addressing the solid waste disposal problems of nearly 500 U.S. communities in nearly every state, and in a number of Canadian communities, including disposal work in the Denver Metro Area, Colorado Springs, Fort Collins, and Summit County. In addition, affiliated disposal companies in Waste Management Partners are serving more than 50 other markets in 24 states, including Colorado.

Waste Management, Inc. also tackles the more difficult tasks of managing toxic, chemical, and nuclear waste through its subsidiaries, Chemical Waste Management and Chem-Nuclear Systems. The company operates in Australia, the Middle East, Europe, Asia, and South America through its subsidiary Waste Management International.

With a strong commitment to environmental protection, the company's disposal facilities are closely and continually monitored by the corporate Environmental Management Department staff. Emphasis is placed on protecting groundwater and on strict compliance with applicable laws and regulations to ensure that wastes accepted by the company facilities are safely disposed and contained.

Waste Management, Inc. maintains what is believed to be the largest private groundwater monitoring system in the United States. Groundwater samples are collected quarterly from each of the more than 3,000 monitoring points at company facilities nationwide, and subjected to rigorous analysis. The data is maintained on a computerized system for constant comparative analysis.

The company also has established strict policies—far exceeding federal and state regulations—on control of its own landfill operations, and is working with a number of cities and industries to develop waste-to-energy systems for the future.

To develop even better and safer methods of controlling municipal and industrial wastes, the company is a major financial supporter of The Environmental Institute for Waste Management Studies independently administered by the University of Alabama. Company research programs, particularly in the areas of better management for toxic and chemical wastes, are often called upon by federal and state environmental specialists; and Waste Management, Inc. provides expert environmentalists and waste managers to state and federal agencies to assist in drafting control regulations to meet the growing needs of waste disposal.

Waste Management subsidiary operations in Colorado also include Aurora Disposal, Colorado Springs Landfill, Denver/Arapahoe Disposal Site, Downhill Pickup, U.S. Disposal Systems, Waste Management of Colorado Springs, and Waste Management of Northern Colorado. In a state such as Colorado, where the maintenance of a clean and healthy environment is essential to future development, Waste Management, Inc. provides a vital service to the communities and their citizens.

Maintaining the high quality environment of Colorado amidst rapid development is a challenge accepted by Waste Management and its affiliates.

The majesty of the mountains inspire Coloradans to a strong commitment to their chosen faith. All denominations and creeds are represented in the state. Photo by James Blank, Stock Imagery

Private Humanitarian Agencies

In the related social services field there are more than 950 non-government agencies in the state employing over 12,000 workers. Philanthropic organizations in the state number more than 220, and in 1983 had assets totaling nearly a half billion dollars.

The state's communities are strong supporters of local welfare and helping agencies, and United Way or United Fund organizations are found in every major community of the state. Churches also are important in the life of the communities, with more than a third of the population adhering to the Christian and Jewish faiths, and most affiliated with local religious organizations. A census report in 1980 listed 1,052,000 Coloradans as adherents of the Christian faith and 42,000 of the Jewish faith. Membership in Christian churches is about equally divided between Roman Catholics and 100 Protestant denominations. The largest of the Protestant denominations in Colorado are the United Methodist Conference, the United Presbyterian Synod, the Southern Baptist Conference, and the Latter Day Saints.

Public Services

Local and state agencies of the government provide many of the support services that Coloradans have come to demand in keeping their cities, towns, and counties attractive and safe. These government agencies also are among the largest employers when all public jobs are considered, employing more than 195,000 in 1986, with a payroll of nearly $4 billion. Combined with the federal agencies located in Colorado, which include more than 51,000 additional jobs, the public service payroll in the state is well over $5 billion annually.

Colorado's constitution requires a balanced budget, and limits annual expenditure increases to a maximum of seven percent. The state legislature, with 35 senators and 65 house members, broadly represents a mixture of Democrats, Republicans, and Independents. The voters send some lawyers to the state legislature, but just as often the representatives will be from the professions, business, agriculture, education, and other career fields.

The governorship in modern times has been held by both Democrats and Republicans, and the U.S. Congressional seats are also regularly filled by both parties.

Local politics are rarely drawn along party lines, with mayors, councilmen, and commissioners most often selected on issues rather than party affiliation.

Colorado's police and fire protection is under the local direction of the communities, except for the state's highway patrol, which reports to the Department of Highways at the state level. In 1983, the state had 11,100 police and firemen guarding the public safety. In some of the rural counties, where budget constraints prevent large standing police agencies, Coloradans have formed citizen organizations, which can be called upon to assist paid sheriffs' deputies during peak visitor seasons. These special deputy organizations consist of volunteers who are given extensive law enforcement training, but provide their own uniforms and equipment and work on shifts without pay.

Because of Colorado's mountain terrain and large numbers of often inexperienced moun-

PROFILE

Colorado-Ute Electric Association
Bringing Energy to Emerging Cities

Colorado-Ute provides the electricity to power economic development in a vast area of the state. Its big generating plants are among the largest in the West.

Colorado-Ute Electric Association Inc. began generating and transmitting electrical energy in 1959 to meet the energy requirements of people living in rural Colorado.

To provide themselves with a reliable and economic source of power, rural residents formed rural electric associations. Four REAs in southwestern Colorado were the first customers of Colorado-Ute, which was formed in 1941 as a wholesale supplier of electricity.

Today, the Montrose-based association serves 14 member distribution cooperatives, which provide electric service to about 187,000 customers, or a population of about 600,000. These cooperatives, governed by consumer-elected representatives, provide service in 48 of the state's 63 counties, representing more than one-half of the land area in Colorado.

One generating source Colorado-Ute uses to meet these needs is Craig Station, a three-unit, coal-fired power plant located near the northwestern Colorado town of Craig. The plant is the largest electric generating station in Colorado, with a total generating capacity of nearly 1,250 megawatts.

Colorado-Ute has another coal-fired generating station about 20 miles east of Craig near Hayden, Colorado. Hayden Station, which has a total capacity of 446 megawatts, also is a major generating source for Colorado-Ute. Its first power plant, Nucla Station, went on line in 1959.

Colorado-Ute's coal-fired plants are located either adjacent to or near major Colorado low-sulfur coal fields. This abundant natural resource provides a steady, cost-effective fuel supply for the plants.

Wisely using the state's natural resources, while maintaining the ecological balance, has been a long-time goal of Colorado-Ute. The association is dedicated to preserving the high quality of Colorado's environment. Reclamation projects at surface mines meet or exceed high ecological standards, and great care is given to the protection of wildlife.

Colorado-Ute also is involved in studying other energy sources such as solar power, and owns three small hydroelectric stations, which were acquired from Western Colorado Power Company in 1975. In all, Colorado-Ute's assets total more than $1 billion.

Colorado-Ute transmits electricity over more than 1,400 miles of transmission line, and the power is delivered to member cooperatives through 44 substations. The cooperatives distribute the bulk of this energy to their consumers in Colorado. Some co-ops also serve limited sections of Utah, Wyoming, and New Mexico.

Cooperatives based on the central and northern Western Slope that buy electricity from Colorado-Ute are: Delta-Montrose Electric Association (Delta), Grand Valley Rural Power Lines (Grand Junction), White River Electric Association (Meeker), and Yampa Valley Electric Association (Steamboat Springs).

In southwestern Colorado the association's members are: Empire Electric Association (Cortez), La Plata Electric Association (Durango), and San Miguel Power Association (Nucla). In the central mountains Colorado-Ute serves Gunnison County Electric Association (Gunnison), Holy Cross Electric Association (Glenwood Springs), and Sangre de Cristo Electric Association (Buena Vista).

In the San Luis Valley, Colorado-Ute serves San Luis Valley Rural Electric Cooperative (Monte Vista). The San Isabel Electric Association, based in Pueblo, serves a portion of the Front Range, as does Sedalia-based Intermountain Rural Electric Association. Southeast Colorado Power Association, with headquarters at La Junta, serves a large section of the southeastern plains with Colorado-Ute-generated electricity.

Forest fires in the Rockies call forth experts from throughout Colorado and the mountain region to preserve the wilderness. Photo by Patricia Barry Levy, Stockyard

tain visitors, another type of special volunteer organization provides public safety assistance. There are seven well organized and highly trained teams, certified by the Mountain Rescue Association, on 24-hour call in the mountain communities. Like the special deputies, these teams provide their own equipment and are trained in first aid, mountain climbing, winter survival, and mountain life-saving techniques. They participate under the direction of professional public safety officials in search and rescue operations.

Volunteers staff the mountain rescue teams providing quick response to save lives. Fortunately, in this case, practice makes perfect. Photo by Howard M. Paul, courtesy of Alpine Rescue Team

Coloradans generally demand strict enforcement of criminal laws and laws pertaining to the public safety. The state recently adopted one of the nation's toughest drunk-driving laws, and in recent years has passed increasingly stiff sentencing laws for criminal violations. Mandatory sentences to be served in correctional and rehabilitation institutes have caused the state and county governments to invest in more jail facilities in recent years. The state currently operates 10 correctional facilities, with six located at Canon City, and one each at Buena Vista, Rifle, Delta, and Golden. A new medium-security facility is scheduled for completion at Ordway in 1987.

The state is divided into local county courts and 22 judicial districts, with district courts located in geographic centers over Colorado. Of the approximately 100,000 suits filed each year, most are civil cases, with only about 17,000 criminal cases. The state's appeals court and supreme court are located in Denver.

At all levels, Colorado government is closely tied to the community, and is designed to be responsive to the people. In the early days of development, the first county governments were formed for the primary purpose of locating the administrative functions, such as recording mining claims and farm land deeds, near the settlers. This practice has been extended into modern times, with local citizens participating directly—not only in the election process, but in advisory roles when matters of government affect their communities.

The support functions of education, health care, and public safety are primary instruments to assure a high quality of life in the cities, towns, and rural areas of Colorado. But in the final analysis, the lifestyle of the communities is most directly dependent on the economy. Coloradans, with a historically strong work ethic, support the good life with a strong and diverse economy. In the mid-1980s the average Colorado worker ranked as the 11th highest paid in the nation, with an average annual paycheck of $18,774.

The nearly 88,000 businesses of the state, in reality, form the nuclei for the high quality of life in the communities. No single type of business or industry dominates, but each sector of the economy is integral to the whole. Just as the cities and towns, large and small, are equally important to the whole community known as Colorado, the places of living and working are closely related to the natural environment enjoyed in the state. Business and industry also benefit from the bountiful natural landscape and resources.

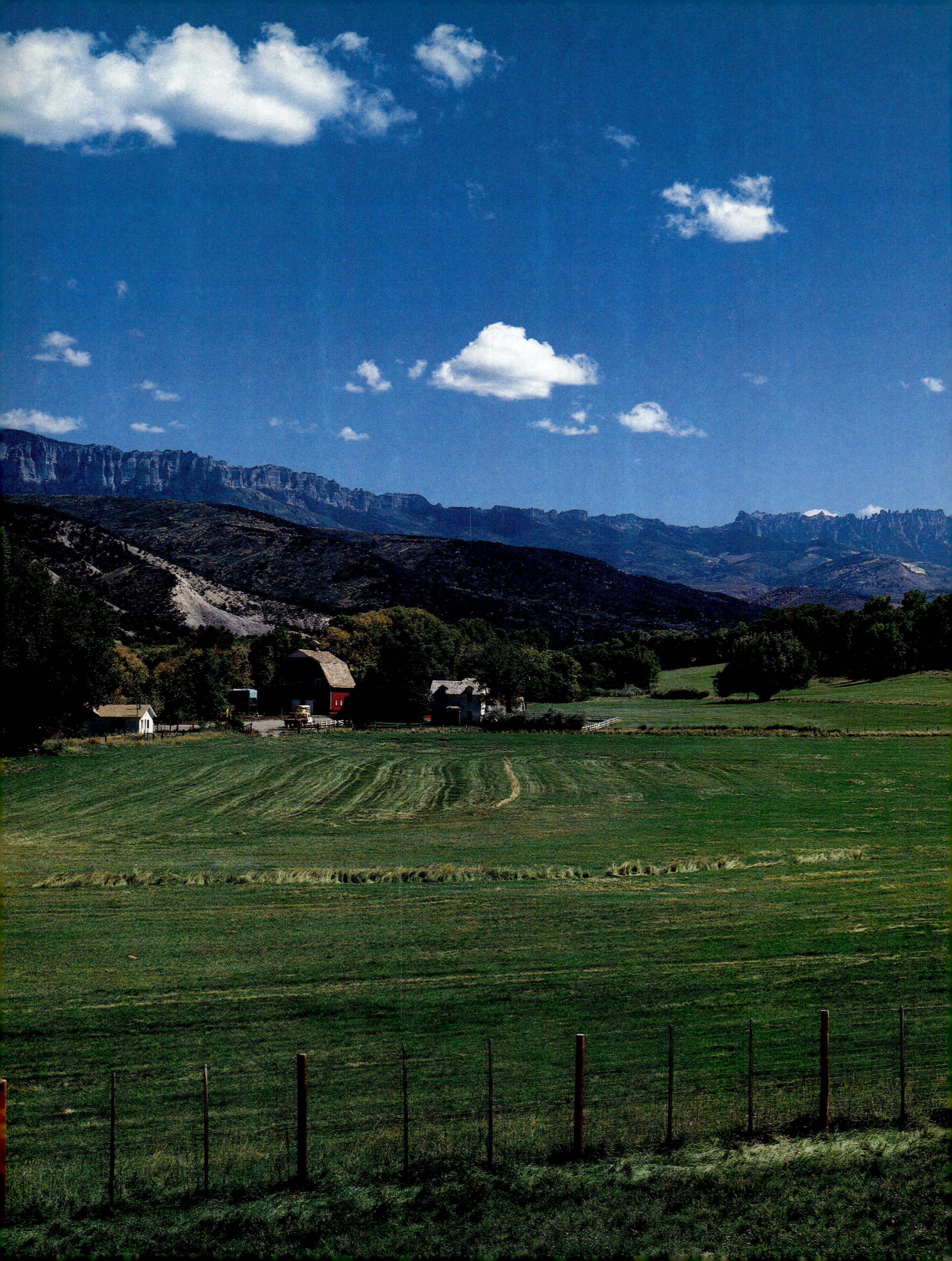

CHAPTER 4

Riches from the Mountains and Plains
Agribusiness, Mining, and Energy Development

The roots of modern lifestyle are deeply embedded in the Colorado earth. No person anywhere in the state, regardless of occupation, is more than minutes away from the great outdoors and the natural resource base.

Few jobs are far removed, directly or indirectly, from a foundation in agribusiness, mining, or energy development; and even those that are—such as high technology—thrive in an environment surrounded by reminders of the plains and mountains industry base. Many of the new companies in both manufacturing and service industries are drawn to Colorado by the magnetism of the mountains and their ability to attract the type of people required for advanced management and technology jobs.

Not only has natural resource development provided the basis for most of the other sectors of the economy, but it can be safely said that the very "booms and busts" in the earth-related industries gave early impetus to the diversification that has created Colorado's dynamic modern economy today.

Agriculture and agribusiness support activities are still the most visible and among the leading economic sectors of the Colorado economy. Mining—and its modern successor, energy development—was a primary factor in the pioneering of the Colorado frontier, and the impetus for its latest major economic expansion. Even the earliest, and some of the more lasting, manufacturing development was tied to supplying the needs of the agricultural-mining population. The machinery manufacturing industry, for example, was an outgrowth of the early forges developed to supply the mines and farms.

Agriculture and mineral development have left a profound heritage and established a strong work ethic that pervades nearly every aspect of modern work life in Colorado. Major manufacturers have located in Colorado because of this work ethic, and giant industrial plants hum in technological sophistication alongside grazing cattle and ripening wheat.

Private and public sector services that first located in the Rocky Mountains' center state of Colorado to serve these early industries have grown and expanded to provide services to emerging new industries.

The natural resources from the mountains and plains remain the staple asset of the entire economy.

But there is a significant difference in the natural resource industries of today and yesterday. Colorado, through its higher education system, is leading the world in scientific and technological advances in both agricultural and mineral development. The primary college and university systems contributing to these technological advances in the natural resource industries are Colorado State University in the agribusiness arena and Colorado School of Mines in the various fields of mineral development. Both Colorado schools have international reputations for their pioneering programs to bring high technology to the natural resource industries they serve.

The Changing Menu

Colorado historically has been one of the important food-producing regions of the North American continent. Despite some recent problems endemic to all U.S. agriculture, Colorado remains a major producer of crops and livestock for both the domestic and

The high altitude ranches and farms in Colorado continue to place the state among the nation's agribusiness leaders. Photo by Ron Phillips, Phillips Photographics

Mountain meadows produce some of the finest beef in the world. Colorado ranks 11th in the production of cattle and calves. Photo by Nathan Bilow

foreign markets. The state ranks 16th in the nation in total agricultural production. The principal change in the agriculture-based sector of the economy in the late 1980s is a vigorous effort on the part of both private and public agencies to enhance the Colorado agricultural economy through "value added" programs. Major efforts have been launched, since the general downturns in the farm economy after the boom years of the late 1970s and early 1980s, to process and manufacture local agriculture products, rather than depend on competing in the marketplace with unprocessed, bulk products. One example is the development of a fruit juice industry in the orchard country on the Western Slope where fruits once shipped in bulk are now processed and shipped with the upgraded value added. Farm and ranch organizations have also targeted agriculture markets with new types of crops and new uses for livestock and poultry. In the San Luis Valley vast acreage that was once dedicated to winter wheat and barley production has been converted to the growing of new types of potatoes developed especially to suit that area's climate and soil conditions.

The modernization of entire agricultural systems is not a rapid process. Such factors as foreign competition, declining exports due to the strength of the U.S. dollar, falling land prices, low commodity prices, increased farm debt, and lower farm equity plague many sectors of the Colorado agriculture economy, just as they threaten the foundation of all U.S. agriculture. Peculiar local problems, such as the decline of the historic sugar beet industry, further exacerbate the problems in Colorado.

Because of the historic and present role of agriculture in the state's economy, finding successful solutions to these problems is critical to the overall welfare of Coloradans in all sectors of the economy. Colorado has more than 35 million acres of land dedicated to agriculture, valued at more than $15 billion. While there are 27,000 operating farms in the state, farm population has declined steadily from 143,000 in 1960 to 59,000 in the latest U.S. Census. The size of farm operations has grown steadily during that time, and today more than 1,600 Colorado farms and ranches have sales exceeding a quarter million dollars a year. Indications are that actual farm values are once again on the increase and the size of the farms in acreage is growing. Colorado's average farm covers nearly 1,300 acres, compared to a national average of 437 acres per farm. These trends are caused by the increasing mechanization of the farm, and transition from the family farm to the corporate farm.

Agriculture, because of technology and mechanization, does not employ a sizable number in the population, but it accounts for one of the largest sectors of the economy in producing cash receipts. About 48,000 farm workers are hired seasonally, in addition to the ownership labor operating the farms and ranches. Total cash receipts of nearly $3.3 billion annually in the mid-1980s compares to just over $2 billion annually a decade ago, a gain of more than 30 percent. Agriculture income of $3.3 billion is comparable to the state's tourism income of about $4 billion annually.

Livestock production accounts for nearly two-thirds of the cash receipts at about $2 billion annually, and wheat and other crops of all types make up the balance. Government agriculture subsidy payments in 1986 were estimated at about $120 million. Agriculture products are among the state's chief foreign exports, averaging more than $620 million annually during the mid-1980s. Wheat and feed grains, amounting to over half the exports, are the crops hardest hit by the strength of the U.S. dollar. Meat exports to foreign markets have actually grown steadily over the past decade.

Colorado ranks high among other states in a number of different products from farming and ranching. Production of barley, beans, potatoes, sorghum, sugar beets, and wheat ranks among the top 10 states. Colorado is the second largest producing state for storage onions, the seventh in carrots, fifth in lettuce, and ninth in sweet corn (for human consumption). Colorado ranks seventh in the production of tart cherries and sixth in pears.

Cattle Upon a Thousand Hills

In livestock production the state ranks even higher in many major sectors. Colorado is first in the number of sheep and lambs on feed (being fattened in feed lots), and fourth in cattle on feed, feeder cattle marketing, and in overall production of sheep and lambs.

In 1985 there were a total of 3 million cattle and calves on Colorado farms and ranches, of which a million head were on feed. The previous year, 2.25 million fattened cattle were marketed from feedlots. In addition, the state's dairy herds total about 75,000 head, producing about 950 million pounds of milk a year.

With the exception of the City and County of Denver, where no rangeland exists, and mountainous San Juan County, cattle are raised in every one of Colorado's counties. Ranching is the biggest income generator in several areas of the state.

The cattle center of Colorado is Weld County, where over a half million head are raised. Giant feedlots in the Greeley area prepare cattle for the world marketplace, and a high technology industry has grown around livestock fattening in that area. Five other Colorado counties had more than 100,000 head of cattle in the 1985 inventory, including Yuma, Prowers, Morgan, Logan, and Kit Carson Counties. The inventory value of cattle in Colorado was placed at $1.32 billion in 1985.

In 1986, Monfort of Colorado expanded its workforce in the largest cattle-processing plant in the region. The Greeley operation will employ more than 2,700 workers. In addition, Monfort announced it would increase production from 780,000 head to 1.4 million cattle slaughtered annually.

Semi-arid mountain slopes and valleys of Colorado are ideally suited for sheep and lamb raising, and make Colorado a national leader in this segment of the agriculture industry. The value of sheep in Colorado in 1985 was about $41 million. The state's sheep stock has ranged as high as a half million head during the 1980s, and wool production in 1984 was about 6.7 million pounds. Most sheep and lamb production in Colorado is conducted on the Western Slope. Moffat County in the northwest corner of the state, with Craig as its main supply center, is the leading sheep-producing area. The adjacent counties of Routt and Rio Blanco, along with Montrose and San Miguel in the southwest are also leading centers for sheep, lamb, and wool production.

Hog and pig production is not as extensive

Colorado leads the nation in sheep and lamb feedlot operations, and is fourth in the nation in the total number of sheep and lamb production. Photo by Nathan Bilow

PROFILE

Adolph Coors Company
Tradition and Technology Opens Worldwide Markets

No personal story better tells of the opportunities that awaited Colorado's pioneers a century ago than that of the young, orphaned Prussian immigrant who worked his way across the Atlantic and half the North American continent to become the founder of Adolph Coors Company. Four generations later, his grandsons and great-grandsons continue to build on that pioneer brewer's dreams, expanding product lines and marketing capabilities with the same spirit of dedication and set of values that marked the course so long ago.

Adolph Coors was 25 when he arrived in Golden in 1872, not riding the new train west, but working on the railroad. He owned his brewery one year later.

The Coors headquarters and primary brewery site, after four generations of family ownership, is today the largest single brewing facility and the largest aluminum can manufacturing plant in America. Coors is the nation's fifth largest beer producer. The company ranks high in Fortune 500's top American corporations and, with its subsidiary operations, employs nearly 10,000 workers. The payroll alone, mostly issued in Colorado, exceeds a quarter billion dollars annually. From the tiny initial brewery built at Golden to make beer, Coors has expanded to 45 states where, in 1985, they sold almost 15 billion barrels of product.

The opportunities found on the old frontier apparently are still available on Colorado's new space-age frontier, and Adolph Coors Company is proving it. Today, in 1986, Coors has diversified into 22 separate companies representing food, energy, and many new high-technology industries. The brewery is still the mainstay of the Coors operation and, until 1985, all its beverage products were made in the giant plant at Golden. For the first time, a second facility will be making Coors beer.

Coors has built a name in the American brewing industry from origins in early Colorado. The company is also noted for its concern for the environment.

Called the Shenandoah Brewery, it is under construction in the Blue Ridge Mountains of Virginia. More than 600 distributorships (five company-owned) across the United States sell five labels of the famous Colorado-made beer, including Coors, the flagship brand; Coors Light, the low-calorie brand; George Killian's Irish Red, an ale; Herman Joseph's, a super-premium, long-aged brand; and Coors Extra Gold, a fuller-bodied, more robust beer currently being tested in seven markets. Adolph Coors Company is a diversified family. Most of the subsidiaries were formed as direct support companies to the main brewing product line, or because opportunities for new products were created by the brewing and bottling processes of the parent company. One example is Golden Recycle Company, which opened a high-tech plant in Fort Lupton in 1982. In 1959, Coors pioneered the use of the aluminum can in the beverage industry, leading the way for the rest of the beverage industry, and setting the stage for America's first major environmental industry—recycling of used beverage cans. In 1970 Coors launched its recycling program, and in 1980 opened its subsidiary recycling company. The company now, through such programs as Cash for Cans, actually recycles more aluminum than it puts into the marketplace. Its recycling mill at Fort Lupton not only processes aluminum for the company's use, but sells the high-quality aluminum sheet stock to other manufacturers. Coors' mills, manufacturing plants, and other operations are located in all parts of Colorado, and expansion continues within the state, across the nation, and in foreign countries. Coors' largest operation, aside from the brewery, is Coors Porcelain Company, which has three manufacturing plants in Colorado, one in California, and subsidiaries in Arkansas, Colorado, Oklahoma, Oregon, Brazil, and the United Kingdom. Coors Porcelain is one of the largest producers of technical ceramics and is the sole supplier of chemical porcelain used in the United States, Canada, and Mexico.

Coors' glass bottling plant is located in Wheat Ridge, and a paper converting plant is located in Boulder. Grain elevators in support of large agricultural operations are located at Delta, Longmont, and Monte Vista; there's a grain processing facility in Johnstown, Colorado; as well as elevators in Arkansas, Idaho, Montana, and Wyoming. A large food processing plant is located in Greeley.

As one of the nation's largest beverage and food manufacturers, Coors employs state-of-the-art high technology in its manufacturing processes. Many of its innovations have broad applications in other industries, and a sweeping range of subsidiary companies have capitalized on this high-tech know-how.

"At Coors, we pride ourselves in

being a technological leader," says Chairman William K. Coors. "Some of the most advanced industrial equipment in the world has been pioneered at our brewery, based on our philosophy that where technology does not exist we will create it in order to meet the demands of the future."

Coors Container Manufacturing created the industry's first all-aluminum, two-piece cans, and its glass division is the only glass plant in existence that has an operating, all-electric powered furnace producing amber glass.

Coors Biomedical Company produces products for dental restorative work. In 1985 Coors BioTech Products Company was formed to use the brewer's expertise in fermentation for the development of new microbiology products. This new high-tech company located in Johnstown, Colorado, opened laboratories at Fort Collins to be close to some of the nation's leading microbiology research being done at the Colorado State University center.

The Colorado company, which is one of the state's leading employers, operates its own refrigerated trucking fleet through Coors Transportation Company. Since 1977, Coors Food Products Company at Greeley has become a leader in the agribusiness industry. It operates a subsidiary rice mill in Arkansas, in addition to manufacturing food and agriculture products from its Colorado plant.

Coors Energy Company is both an energy buyer and seller, providing much of the coal and natural gas for its own operations from fields on the Western Slope, and northeastern Colorado and Utah. It operates its own pipeline, too, and sells petroleum products not used in Coors plants.

Advantage Health Systems is a Coors company that develops health and safety tests and services for its own work force and for more than 300 companies at 1,800 locations nationwide.

"But there is more to doing business than producing a quality product in the most technologically efficient way," says Chairman Coors. "Our goal is to be a responsible corporate citizen by setting positive examples which demonstrate industry can live in harmony with its surroundings."

Coors has a Regulatory Affairs Department that not only assures its plants meet or exceed established environmental standards, but also designs pollution-control devices and procedures for the future. Its water and air pollution equipment employs advanced technology methods, and its recycling of aluminum and byproducts has created new products divisions.

The company operates two of the most technologically sound wastewater treatment plants in the nation, and has been an industrial pacesetter in wastewater management. One plant converts water and spent grains from the brewing process into a protein-rich cattle feed supplement. The other plant treats all non-brewery water generated by Coors plants and also treats waste water for the City of Golden. Solids generated at this plant are aerobically digested and used as soil conditioners and low-grade fertilizers.

By products from both these treatment plants are distributed for use as Colorado agriculture products.

An extensive in-house recycling program has enabled Coors to reuse such materials as spent machine oil, and the company has in recent years reduced its wastes by 94 percent.

An elaborate air pollution control system, specifically tailored to Coors' manufacturing plants, has made the company's facilities one of the cleanest coal-burning factories in America. In the fall of 1982, the company ran an underground steam line more than half a mile to provide less expensive heat to the Colorado School of Mines.

In addition to providing more than a million dollars a year to philanthropic, educational, and cultural institutions and programs through direct grants, Coors has pioneered two economic development programs to assist minorities in entering the business and employment mainstream. Coors launched the two five-year programs in 1984 with combined investments of $675 million.

Adolph Coors may have proved that everything was possible through hard work on the American frontier over a century ago, but it's the modern and diversified Adolph Coors Company and succeeding generations of the Coors family that keep the promise of opportunity alive for thousands of Coloradans today.

Bill Coors has stated it this way: "The cornerstone of our operations continues to be the dedication and consistently superior performance of our employees."

Adolph Coors Company operates one of the world's largest brewing plants at Golden, and other facilities for food processing and high tech in Colorado.

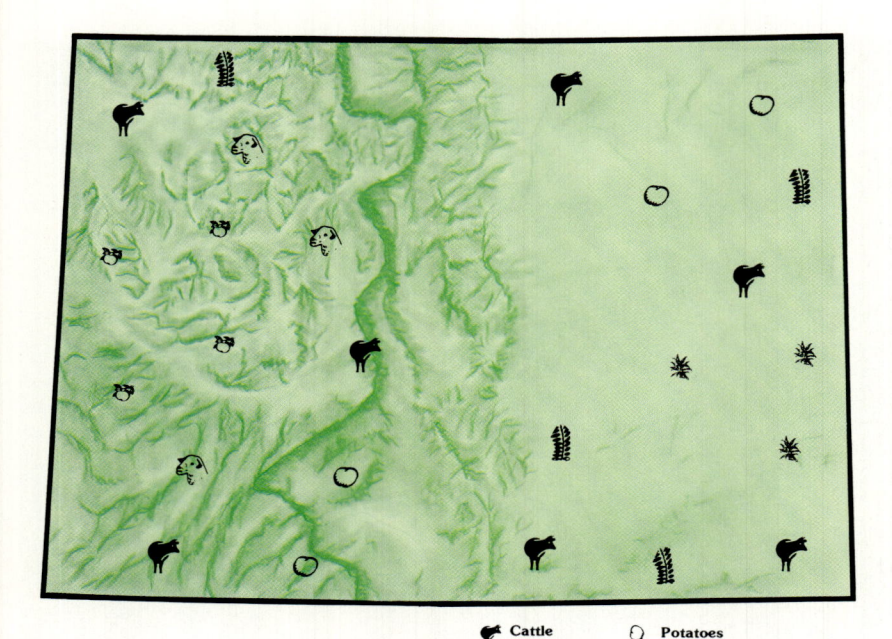

Agriculture in Colorado—The state's agricultural diversity includes grain crops, potatoes, fruit, vegetables, cattle, and sheep. Agriculture will remain one of the most important parts of the state's economy, even as high-tech and aerospace industries expand.

Some of the finest breeding stock in America is raised on the high mountain ranges of Colorado. Photo by Nathan Bilow

in Colorado as in some midwestern states, but accounts for a significant farm income. Inventory value of hogs and pigs in 1985 was about $17.5 million. This segment of the industry is highly technical, with most production in modern feeding centers in Morgan, Weld, Logan, Yuma, and Adams Counties.

Likewise, chicken and egg production is not a leading part of the Colorado agriculture industry, but does provide a sizable farm income. Colorado laying flocks produce about 640 million eggs annually.

Raising livestock, with all the glamour of the Old West it conjures up, is still a picturesque part of Colorado's heritage. A traveler in any part of the state is likely to see fine herds of cattle and sheep grazing in fields of high grass. In the autumn, many narrow mountain roads are jammed by working cowboys bringing herds down from high pasture to winter pasture. While pickups and jeeps do a lot of the work, the old standby is still the horse in most parts of Colorado. Horseback herding by Colorado cowboys is a reward of the business. The historic love of the horse has developed a nationally recognized Quarter Horse industry in the state, and thoroughbred racing also supports a sizable horse breeding industry. Horse breeding and horse raising is no longer considered an agricultural pursuit. Horses are primarily raised for recreational purposes. The latest inventory of horses and ponies in the state included about 71,000 head, with annual sales of about $11 million.

Western Colorado is dotted with the lonely shepherd wagons brought here before the turn of the century. Their single smokestacks can still be found pouring out smoke from an evening meal amidst flocks of bleating sheep.

But the livestock business is a modern industry, and modern methods of fattening livestock take over when calves, lambs, pigs, chickens, or turkeys pass the earliest stages of life. Giant operations, like Monfort of Colorado, are truly agribusiness industries. Monfort, one of the largest public corporations in Colorado, operates the largest feedlot in the world and the third largest beef processing plant in the United States—both near Greeley. Colorado meat is processed and sold, not only across the United States, but around the world.

Other industrial value is added from manufacturing and processing hides, skins, fats, oils, and grease from the livestock industry.

And Colorado turkey is not only a leading Thanksgiving dinner product, but a year-round packaged product. The state produces

A phalanx of reapers crosses a Colorado wheat field during harvest time. Colorado is the sixth ranked American wheat-producing state. Photo by Iris Photography

over 50,000 tons of turkey annually. Dairies operate just like factories, with modern assembly lines. Colorado livestock raisers annually export to foreign countries almost $70 million in hides and skins, and $40 million in fats and oils. In the export of specialty agriculture products there has been a 100 percent increase since the early 1970s. Colorado meat exports to foreign markets amounted to about $45 million in 1986.

The World's Breadbasket

Wheat production leads the impressive list of field crops, which place Colorado among a group of states called the "breadbasket of the world." High yields in modern times have led to surpluses which in themselves have caused severe storage problems and contributed to the financial difficulties in the nation's agriculture industry. The rich plains and valleys of Colorado produce some of the world's most nutritious grains. Colorado wheat contains 12 percent or more protein, and is a highly favored world export, amounting to about $200 million annually.

"Bumper" crops have been common during most of the 1980s, with the 1985-86 winter wheat crop exceeding 134 million bushels. The state produces two seasonal crops—winter wheat and spring wheat. The winter and spring wheat crops are designated for the season in which they are planted, with both crops harvested in late summer and early autumn. By far the larger crop is winter wheat. It is grown and harvested on almost 3.5 million acres in literally every county of Colorado except Denver and two of the highest mountain counties.

Most of the winter wheat crop is raised on the eastern plains. Based on 1984 reports, the leading counties and approximate annual production include: Kit Carson (over 13 million bushels), Washington (over 13 million), Yuma (nearly 9 million), Weld (nearly 8.5 million), and Kiowa (8.4 million).

Sixteen other Colorado counties produce more than a half million bushels of winter wheat each year, including Adams (7.8 million), Arapahoe (1.3 million), Baca (4.7 million), Bent (528,000), Cheyenne (5.3 million), Dolores (777,000), Elbert (2 million), Larimer (791,000), Lincoln (6.8 million), Logan (6.8 million), Moffat (754,000), Morgan (3.1 million), Phillips (4.7 million), Prowers (5.6 million), and Sedgwick (3.5 million).

Spring wheat is a major crop in northwest Colorado and in the San Luis Valley in southern Colorado. Almost 5 million bushels of spring wheat are harvested each year in Rio Grande, Alamosa, Saguache, Conejos, and Costilla Counties in the San Luis Valley. Moffat County in northwestern Colorado is the fifth largest producer of spring wheat.

While irrigation is important to some field crops, contrary to common belief, winter wheat is largely produced without irrigation.

Barley, corn, and potatoes are increasingly important cash crops in the state. A newspaper headline in 1985 lamented the Colorado bumper crop in corn, reading: "Bad News, Corn Crop Huge." The more than 100 million bushels of corn produced each year in Colorado are primarily used in the livestock feed industry, and off years in cattle production

91

PROFILE

King Soopers, Inc.
Bringing the Best of Agriculture to Coloradans

King Soopers has continued to modernize its supermarkets to bring the widest possible selection of foods and merchandise to the families of Colorado.

Bringing agricultural produce from the land to the modern marketplace in a competitive environment has been the challenge of one of the West's largest and most diversified supermarket chains, since its founding by one innovative Coloradan almost 40 years ago.

King Soopers, Inc., with modern supermarket facilities throughout the Denver Metropolitan Area and along the Front Range, has grown from its first store of 3,000 square feet in 1947 to its modern stores of the 1980s, averaging more than 60,000 square feet of space.

Now affiliation with the national Kroger chain, modernization in merchandising, and expanded selection of products has not changed the operating philosophy of founder Lloyd King. The company is still community oriented and maintains strong customer relationships. Its slogan over the years has remained, "Our People Make the Difference."

King Soopers was merged with the Dillon Companies of Hutchinson, Kansas in 1957, but remained under the direct management of its founder. The acquisition by Kroger did not change this local management and held advantages for both companies.

Jim Baldwin, King Soopers president and CEO, follows the same merchandising traditions and policies toward the customer and community involvement as did the founder, and Ray Rose, who was president from 1972 to 1979. The most evident change has been in response to the customer's need for a complete merchandise center, and the rapid expansion in both size and number of King Soopers.

While the larger-store format is due in some part to the accessibility of foods and products of different brands, today's modern Colorado life styles command a different type of supermarket. Most of the newest King Soopers stores are from 58,000 to 60,000 square feet in merchandise and production area, and this larger grocery center provides the customers with one-stop shopping convenience for the widest range of items.

King Soopers offers fresh seafood departments, full-service specialty meat shops, floral departments, video departments, expanded and upgraded bakery departments, and European delicatessens with professional chefs. All the stores now have enlarged areas devoted to frozen foods, general merchandise, health and beauty, and specialty produce. More space in the stores has been given to imported food, live plants, natural foods, pharmacies, greeting cards and gifts, and the bakeries.

In 1968, in a consumer-oriented move, King Soopers closed their stores, covered the windows, marked down all prices, and reopened with the announcement that the chain had "gone discount." Prices and gross profit margins were drastically cut, trading stamps were eliminated, and a renewed emphasis was placed on maintaining quality of products and service. That merchandising move placed King Soopers among the low-price leaders in the grocery business, and the policy has remained a strong part of the marketing strategy of the growing chain.

King Soopers has long been active in community betterment projects in all of the parts of the Front Range where its stores are located. Management takes an active role in the volunteer organizations and chambers of commerce in the state. And the chain has been a leader in the retail community in the initiation of environmental programs.

It provides community service to philanthropic groups by offering donated advertising space on shopping bags, receipt tapes, and space in its own advertising programs. King Soopers developed the first in-store recycling program in the nation, redeeming aluminum cans, glass bottles, and plastic soft drink containers. It recently became the first supermarket in the nation to institute an in-store newspaper recycling program. In 1985 the chain was named Colorado Recycler of the Year for "meritorious efforts that have contributed to the success of recycling in Colorado."

have a direct effect on corn prices. In recent years, a number of Colorado farmers have developed major sweet corn crops for an expanding food market. The leading corn producing counties are Yuma, Weld, Morgan, Phillips, and Kit Carson.

A substantial barley crop, exceeding 20 million bushels a year, largely for the brewing industry, is raised in the state. Leading producers of barley are located in the San Luis Valley counties of Saguache, Alamosa, Rio Grande, Conejos, Costilla, and in Weld County in northeast Colorado. Each of these produces more than a million bushels annually.

The San Luis Valley counties, along with Washington County in the northeast, are also the leading producers of oats. The state produces nearly three million bushels of oats each year. Over 16 million bushels of sorghum grain are produced in Colorado with the biggest crops in Baca, Prowers, Kiowa, Kit Carson, and Cheyenne counties in eastern Colorado.

Other than wheat exports, Colorado feed and grain-product exports to foreign countries amounted to over $170 million in 1986.

Fruits and Vegetables for the U.S. Table

Colorado is seldom thought of as a leading producer of dry beans for human use, but it ranks sixth in the nation, producing almost 3 million hundred weight. Leading bean counties are Weld, Yuma, Morgan, and Kit Carson in northeastern Colorado, and Dolores County in southwestern Colorado.

When the public thinks of potatoes, Idaho most often comes to mind. But Colorado has increasingly become a major potato producing state. Intensive efforts are under way in the San Luis Valley to develop a potato processing industry to freeze its outstanding crop for shipment to new markets. Acreage and production of potato farming are rapidly increasing in Colorado, primarily in the San Luis Valley and in select areas of the northeastern plains. Acreage planted in potatoes in 1980 was about 43,000, compared with about 65,000 in 1985. Production increased from about 12.5 million hundred weight to more than 20 million over that five-year period. The leading counties now producing potatoes, including several new varieties developed in Colorado, are Alamosa, Conejos, Costilla, Morgan, Rio Grande, Saguache, and Weld.

Orchards cover the valleys of western Colorado, producing apples, peaches, pears, and cherries for a rapidly growing whole fruit, fruit juice, and wine industry. The major fruit-growing areas of the state are Delta, Fremont, Mesa, Montezuma, and Montrose counties, with nearly 600 commercial orchards in that region. Substantial rebuilding of orchards is under way, and in 1985, more

Colorado's fruited plains, including some of the best melons and pumpkins grown in America, are a part of America's breadbasket.
Photo by Steven Samuelson

PROFILE

Miller International, Inc.
Modern Industry Built on Tradition of the West

If one company could be singled out as representative of Colorado's economic evolution—from its pioneering days of mining and agriculture to the modern era of an economy built on retailing, marketing, manufacturing, and wholesaling—it might well be Miller International.

Formed in 1923 to supply farmers, stockmen, and miners with hard-wearing, long-lasting clothing, saddlery, and tack that fit the rugged western life, the privately held, family corporation is today one of Colorado's leading retailers, manufacturers, distributors, and wholesalers.

Miller International is made up of three divisions: the locally well-known retail division, Miller Stockman, and two manufacturing divisions, Miller Western Wear and The Prior Company. The corporation's international operations are conducted from headquarters at 8500 Zuni Street in Denver. While its many lines of merchandise remain true to the company's original calling, Miller International also makes and markets fashion lines popular around the world.

The company's founder, Philip Miller, actually may be the father of the now world-popular "western shirt." While attending a silent Tom Mix movie, Miller noticed that the cowboy hero was wearing a regular dress shirt. He went back to his shop and created a unique cowboy shirt, launching a product line that is the company's hallmark today and an item that is identified with the American West in markets around the world.

Today the firm's two manufacturing arms operate five of its six manufacturing plants within the state of Colorado. These factories make western shirts, outerwear, and fashion jeans for men, women, and children. The western wear and fashion products manufactured in Colorado are marketed throughout the world.

Miller Stockman's catalog is a colorful reminder of Colorado's western heritage as the international company expands to new frontiers of the future.

Its first retail outlet store, Miller Stockman, was opened in 1951 and has expanded to 28 outlets, including 24 Miller Stockman stores and four Rocky Mountain Shoe Company stores. Rapid expansion of the retail operation began in 1969 and has been continued under the company's current administration, headed by President Marvin Levy.

Rocky Mountain Shoe Company specializes in lines of walking and hiking shoes to fit the high demand created by Colorado's outdoor life. Twelve of the Miller Stockman stores and three of the shoe company stores are located in Colorado at Denver, Boulder, Longmont, Fort Collins, Greeley, Colorado Springs, and Grand Junction. Other retail outlets are located in California and Nevada.

The evolution of Miller International parallels the history of development in Colorado. Founder Philip Miller came West in 1919 as a traveling hat salesman, and discovered a "retail gold mine" in supplying other clothing requirements for the farmers, ranchers, and miners of the state. Four years later, along with two employees, he incorporated Miller Hat Company. From that time the company has expanded under family ownership, with his son Benjamin K. Miller becoming president in 1961. When both the founder and his son died in 1972, a nephew, Seymour Simmons Jr., assumed the presidency in 1973. Simmons continues today as president of Miller International.

During his early years traveling to sell the new products of the Denver-based company, Philip Miller developed the company's Stockman-Farmer Supply Company catalog. Initially, the catalog served a utilitarian purpose, offering hats, tack, and saddlery—the staples of Colorado living in that era. The catalog marketing expanded over the years to its present important role in Miller Stockman's outreach to families worldwide.

Miller's first manufacturing operations began in western shirts, with a factory opening in Denver in 1949. With the manufacturing plant, Miller Western Wear also expanded its wholesale and distribution operations. Along with The Prior Company, the manufacturing operations have continued to expand both in product lines and distribution markets. The Miller Western Wear manufacturing arm is run by President Marv Debber. The Prior Company, a 100-year-old company that built its business on the production of work jeans, is a leading manufacturer of ladies' and girls' fashion jeans. George Hattori is president of The Prior Company.

Like the state's economy, the company's activities and product lines have grown and diversified. But both maintain roots deep in the agricultural and mining heritage of modern Colorado.

The high, dry climate on Colorado's Western Slope, combined with abundant water from such rivers as the Colorado, has made the region one of the most important fruit producers in America. Photo by Judith Morison

than 40,000 new fruit trees were planted in Mesa County and the Grand Junction area alone.

In 1985 Colorado produced about 60 million pounds of apples, and 13 million pounds of peaches. But the state's pear and sweet cherry crops can be measured in tons with nearly 4,550 tons of pears and almost 250 tons of sweet cherries. A smaller tart cherry crop in the state produces between a half million and 1.5 million pounds of this fruit each year. The state's fruit industry produces, in commercial quantity, six varieties of standard apples, and seven types of dwarf apples; 15 varieties of peaches, three varieties of pears, and four types of sweet and tart cherries. Colorado fruit accounts for well over half the nearly $60 million in fruits and vegetables exported from Colorado to foreign countries each year.

Commercial flower growing is also a sizable industry in Colorado, with the state providing a large share of U.S. carnations. Colorado ranks as the second largest producer of carnations and the fifth largest producer of roses for the floral wholesale industry. A moderate industry also exists in the growing of ornamental trees.

Despite its vast forests, commercial logging has not been a major industry in Colorado in recent years. A lumber milling industry exists in southern Colorado, but most logging for cash is presently for home firewood. Colorado has over 11 million acres of commercial timberland, with estimated reserves of 54,941 million board feet of saw timber.

Other Cash Crops

With depressed prices in the wheat and grain industry, more and more Colorado farmers are looking at alternative vegetable markets. Colorado farmers harvest nearly 300,000 tons of fresh-market and process vegetables annually, with a value of approximately $65 million. The leading vegetable cash crop is dry onions, and Colorado ranks third in the nation in their production. Sizable fresh vegetable markets exist in sweet corn, iceberg lettuce, tomatoes, carrots, cabbage, and melons. The state is famous for its Rocky Ford cantaloupes, and in 1985 shipped a half million boxes, in addition to an estimated 100,000 boxes sold along roadsides.

Onion growing represents 71 percent of both the tonnage and value of production, with an annual crop value of over $45 million. Lettuce is the second cash crop, with farmers producing around 800,000 hundred weight for a value exceeding $10 million. The

PROFILE

Robinson Dairy, Inc.
Better Produce from Advancing Technology

Products from Colorado's agricultural heritage have been processed for the consumer for five generations of the Robinson family in ever-expanding dairy facilities located across the state.

This agribusiness industry has grown from a family farm settled in 1885, in an area of frontier Colorado which was to become Lakewood. The dairy company now serves Colorado and Wyoming communities from Denver to the Western Slope and from Pueblo to Cheyenne. Milk, the basic product, is just about the only ingredient in the family-owned business that has remained the same.

Expanding the operation from a horse-and-wagon, door-to-door service before the turn of the century, Robinson Dairy, Inc. today is a modern processing concern, employing advanced equipment that could only be described as "high technology" food manufacturing.

Computerized equipment governs every stage of the manufacturing process for a score of milk-derived products delivered to grocery outlets in more than half of Colorado. Robinson Dairy is also a major supplier of dairy products to vending machine companies, hotels, hospitals, airlines, and school cafeterias.

Many of the quality-controlled items from the Robinson Dairy, such as several types of milk, cream, and butter, have been on the Robinson's order list for over a century. Robinson's modern menu of more than 25 products—including yogurts, dips, ice creams and ices, and milk-based specialty foods—evolved as consumer demands changed and food processing technology developed.

Quality of product is a family tradition, and the automated processing facilities assure a high degree of accuracy at each step, from the making of milk products to packaging, inventory control, shelf-life regulation, and delivery.

The family tradition of bringing fine dairy products to the tables of Coloradans is carried on by Edward A. Robinson (left) and Richard L. Robinson.

And the method of delivery, in a fleet of refrigerated trucks equipped with computerized data for inventory and routing, has also advanced far beyond the early days when customers were served by dipper to pail, from a wagon-hauled vat of fresh milk.

The first Robinson dairy farm was established in 1885 by Louis Robinson, who immigrated from Europe to the new American frontier. The farm was located in a rural area close by the new town of Denver, so milk deliveries could be made while the products were fresh. Of course, that original farm area is now in the heart of Colorado's largest metropolitan area. The milking barn has been replaced by modern processing facilities in Denver, and sales and warehousing branches at Colorado Springs and Silverthorne. The refrigerated delivery truck has assured the same product freshness as the first-day delivery, but expanded the territory to hundreds of miles from the dairy.

Robinson Dairy, which purchases its raw milk "fresh daily" from regional dairy farms, is a leading member of Colorado's agribusiness support system. As one of the major food processors and distributors in Colorado, the family-owned company has supported Colorado's agriculture economy for more than 100 years.

This tradition continued when Sam Robinson started the dairy company, which was ultimately to carry the family name. He had worked with his father and uncle in Colorado dairies until opening his own company. For a time after selling his company, then called Gold Seal, Sam worked as sales manager for that company. But the family again started their own company, and the present generation of Robinson dairymen joined the operation in 1950.

Today, Richard Robinson serves as chairman and chief executive officer, and Edward Robinson serves as president, treasurer, and chief operating officer for the company.

The Robinson dairy family has long maintained another tradition in Colorado, beyond direct participation in the day-to-day operations of their food processing plant. The family-run business is a leading Colorado industry in community development and community betterment programs. In keeping with the pace set by their grandfather and great-grandfathers, the Robinsons are found serving on boards and committees promoting economic development, medical and health care improvement, and cultural improvements in the communities of Colorado.

As a member of the state's industrial family, they are also actively involved in programs to assure that environmental quality and economic development are a balanced part of the future of Colorado.

carrot and sweet corn crops each year are valued at more than $3.5 million each, and the nearly 15,000 tons of Colorado tomatoes processed in the state are valued at more than $1.5 million annually.

A new vegetable crop has been introduced into the state on the Western Slope. The Uncompahgre Valley farmers introduced broccoli to the state's vegetable menu in 1985 and, despite early problems with management of a new crop, expect to build this sought-after vegetable into a significant revenue producer in coming years.

The vegetable industry is becoming so important to the agricultural industry that the Colorado Department of Agriculture and Denver's KCNC NewsCenter 4 published a new buyers' directory in 1985. This guide listed 97 major roadside farmers' markets across the state, and scores of "U-Pick" farms and orchards. The publication also featured 50 pages of locations where the public can buy directly from the farm.

Colorado State University works closely with the state's farmers and ranchers developing new crops and improving existing crops. The Fort Collins-based school also works with the Colorado Department of Agriculture in developing new and expanded markets. The worldwide grain surplus has led to intensified efforts to find new crops, and many exotic experiments for high-yield, high-cash crops are conducted by agronomists from the university and the industry. In the future, such strange names as amaranth, stevia, rapeseed, and quinoa may be added to the crops of Colorado.

In Fort Morgan, a $6 million investment was made in 1985 for a new processing plant to produce sunflower seed oil. That plant may also process soybean oil and sesame oil in the future, creating new cash crops in the state.

Since 1888, CSU has operated the vital Colorado Agricultural Experiment Station program, with 11 research centers conducting studies, scientific investigations, and experiments to improve and expand production of the state's farms and ranches. CSU's Agriculture Research Centers are located at Akron, Center, Cortez, Austin, Grand Junction, Fruita, Gunnison, Rocky Ford, Springfield, and Walsh. Greenhouse and field research programs are conducted by scientists from 32 departments in seven other state and local colleges.

CSU's nationally recognized College of Veterinary Medicine, located near the campus in modern, new classroom-clinical facilities at Fort Collins, is a full veterinary teaching hospital. It is also one of the country's leading centers for biomedical and biotechnical research. Research projects beginning in the laboratories at CSU often find their way into the marketplace, vastly improving the health and productivity of American livestock. Likewise, research programs at CSU's College of Forestry and Natural Resources are improving the timberlands and forests of the United States and Canada. Its programs are vital to the timber industry and the recreational forestry program.

The economic impact of the agricultural industry on the state is also important in the service and manufacturing sectors. There are 32 major regional and national agribusiness associations with headquarters in Colorado.

Dryland farming techniques were pioneered in Colorado before the turn of the century. Irrigation systems utilizing mountain snow melt has turned the plains into gardens. Photos by Sally Brown, Stock Imagery

Deep-rock mining is still producing gold from mines such as this operation near historic Cripple Creek. Photo by Tom Stack, Tom Stack & Associates

Approximately 350 manufacturing and processing plants in the state are directly tied to the farm and livestock industry. In addition, more than 5,000 jobs in the state provide non-government agricultural services, and almost 2,000 jobs are provided in veterinarian and animal services.

The variety of farm-related processing plants in the state seem endless. Meat and poultry packing plants and processors, dairies, bakeries, tanneries, tallow rendering plants, honey bottlers, genetic engineering companies, graineries and mills, seed packagers, fresh and frozen food processors, canners, bottlers, brewers, picklers and sauce manufacturers, pasta plants, tea and herb factories, fertilizer and feed producers, and specialty food manufacturers are operating in the major cities, farm belts, and small towns of Colorado.

Agriculture is still today, and promises to remain, one of the largest and most important sectors of the Colorado economy.

Mining the Resources

The second segment of the natural resources industry of Colorado with its basis in products from the earth is the mining, mineral, and energy development industry. Historically, it is hard to determine which came first in Colorado's development. While the first Europeans came into the region seeking gold as early as the 1500s, the first permanent settlers in the valleys of Colorado did not follow until the early 1800s and were Spanish agricultural colonists. The gold seekers came in the mid-1800s, and the permanent Anglo settlers soon followed, to farm the land and establish the beginning of the agricultural economy.

Mineral development and agriculture have developed side by side into the present day.

World economic pressures are felt in the mining and energy development industries in Colorado, just as they are in the agricultural industries. Nevertheless, Colorado's modern economy is closely tied to metals and mineral mining, coal production, oil and gas production and exploration, and the development of synthetic fuels and renewable sources of energy. In 1986 the state produced about 15 million short tons of coal, about 29 million barrels of crude oil, and 361 billion cubic feet of natural gas. The value of these energy minerals to the state's economy has been radically diminished by the recent world pricing events. Individuals and government entities in Colorado lost an estimated $43 million in royalty revenue from declining oil prices in 1986 alone.

The state's mines lead the nation in production of molybdenum and vanadium. The state ranks second in production of feldspar, pyrites, carbon dioxide, and tungsten, and fourth in the production of gold and silver. Colorado is tied with Montana as the 13th largest oil producing state, and is a major producer of coal.

In 1983-84 there were nearly 3,000 establishments involved in mining and mineral production in the state, with a value added to the economy exceeding $3.7 billion annually. Most of the mining and mineral extraction operations in the state are small, with only about 400 of the nearly 3,000 operations employing more than 20 workers.

Despite the downturns in the mining and mineral development industries, the state is rich in a heritage of mining and mineral development. The industry remains as historically significant as it is economically important in modern Colorado. It promises new "booms" in the future as it has periodically throughout the history of the state.

In 1986, employment in mining and energy production dropped to approximately 33,600 from a high level in 1981 of 43,000. Declines in production in coal, molybdenum, and oil and gas were blamed on a number of world economic factors. Weakness in this sector of the economy in Colorado is also being experienced by the other natural resource producing states of the West.

World surpluses in petroleum have the same negative effect on this segment of the economy as America's wheat surpluses have had on the farm economy. Higher costs of producing Colorado coal, attributed to the rugged terrain in the coal producing areas and distance to transport mined coal to markets, have done much to slow production of the state's huge reserves. Large inventories and foreign competition have slowed Colorado's metal mining industry in recent years.

Employment in the Colorado mineral industries in 1986 included approximately 5,600 metal mineral miners, 4,300 coal and nonmetal miners, and 23,700 oil and gas workers. The world oil glut threatened to reduce that number even further.

The glitter of gold and silver, while no longer the major economic factor in the mineral industry of Colorado, still excites the imagination of many of the residents and visitors to the state. In fact, only about 500 miners are still employed in digging the precious metal from its hiding places in the mountains. And any miner will affirm that there's still more "gold in them Colorado hills" than has ever been taken out.

During the gold boom years from 1858 to 1910, with periodic ups and downs, 23 million ounces of gold were reportedly taken from Colorado mines and streams. In 1980, only about 42,000 ounces of gold were mined, for a production valued at just over $21 million. Silver production that year was valued at $45.8 million. Considering that the state's total annual mineral production value is around $3 billion, gold and silver are not the mineral leaders that once brought the "boomers" to Colorado.

But many Colorado dreams still center on these fabled precious metals, and occasionally the state's interest is perked by announcements of new strikes or rumors of new "mother lodes" awaiting the lucky prospector—who will most likely be a geologist in Colorado's modern mine fields.

One such announcement in 1985 involved a rumor of a big silver discovery near Creede in southern Colorado. A silver discovery was said to have been made that was twice the size of the 1859 Comstock Lode in Sierra Nevada, the richest lode in American history. Published reports caused a brief flurry of excitement and stocks soared on Wall Street as in the heydays of Colorado mining. If those rumors are confirmed, such a find would be worth more than $4.6 billion, according to the published rumor. And Colorado mining could expect to see yet another "boom." It is almost certain that such big strikes will occur, because the U.S. Bureau of Mines estimates there are still millions of ounces of gold and silver in large undiscovered lodes and small deposits throughout the Rocky Mountains.

Gold and silver mining both showed improvements in more recent years, and in 1984 the state produced more than 92,000 troy ounces of gold valued at nearly $35 million. Silver production was at more than a ton, valued at $16.5 million. Metal mining employment rose by about 100 jobs between 1985 and 1986. Listening to anyone around the mining communities, it is not hard to believe that if the price of gold could just get to $1,000 an ounce, there would be "another gold boom in Colorado." That boom does not seem likely in the short term with gold prices ranging between $290 and $350 an ounce during 1986.

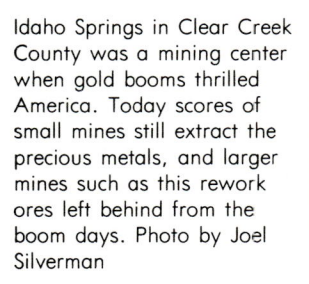

Idaho Springs in Clear Creek County was a mining center when gold booms thrilled America. Today scores of small mines still extract the precious metals, and larger mines such as this rework ores left behind from the boom days. Photo by Joel Silverman

PROFILE

Ultimate Foods Inc.
Enterprise Opens New Lines in Colorado

Using the same principles of enterprise applied by Colorado's pioneer businessmen, a venturesome graduate educational counseling student seized an opportunity to turn a part-time kitchen industry into a multimillion-dollar, multistate food distribution company.

Ultimate Foods Inc. was founded in 1974 because Alan Y. Strom identified a need in the changing Colorado marketplace, and in just over a decade he has turned that opportunity from a $300 investment into a thriving business with annual sales exceeding $6 million. The need was for "upscale" frozen food products, and the lead item was an especially sought-after East Coast gourmet ice cream called Haagen-Dazs. While the original gourmet item is still the best-seller in the company's extensive line of products, the company is now recognized as a national leader in the small, but growing group of frozen specialty-food distributors.

"Timing was good, Colorado was maturing as a cross-section of America with a young, relatively well-educated population," recalls Strom. "The desire for unique, better quality products was apparent."

And Strom believes that while the Colorado marketplace now expects more sophistication than it required a decade ago, the opportunities for a repeat of his company's success still abound.

"It can still be done," says Strom. "The opportunities are still there for those who can identify the right products. The region is still expanding and the economy is dynamic."

His own business, headquartered at office and warehouse facilities in Denver, has followed that guideline in opening new markets for ice cream, frozen foods, dry specialty foods, and dozens of new high-quality items. As sales trends continue upward, Ultimate Foods projects annual sales in excess of $10 million within the next two to three years, and Strom has purchased a large site in an airport industrial and warehouse district for the construction of a new ultra-modern warehouse. The new facility will have state-of-the-art freezer storage and custom-designed space for warehousing the frozen and dry products in his ever-expanding line.

Strom also attributes some of Ultimate Foods' success to a return to basic business practices of servicing the customer, and paying attention to old fashioned management principles.

"We fully expect to double our size without losing the aspect of the personal touch," says Strom. "Our customers give us advice, and we take their direction gladly. The day I, or any of my work force, become unreachable is the day we have no business being in business."

Today Ultimate Foods Inc. serves all the major communities of Colorado where specialty foods outlets are available in supermarkets, gourmet foods stores, fancy grocers, restaurants, hotels, cheese shops, delis, ice cream dipping stores, and military installations. He also distributes in parts of five contiguous states, and has promoted the name recognition of Haagen-Dazs ice cream in Colorado to a degree second only to its native state of New York.

From distributing the exotic New York ice cream out of a 15-foot freezer in his kitchen to a multi-million-dollar distributorship serving more than 1,200 accounts, Strom and Ultimate Foods are proving that opportunity, when joined by hard work and old-style management, still abounds in Colorado.

Better ideas still find a receptive audience in Colorado, as Alan Y. Strom discovered when he opened the western markets for gourmet food products.

Coal to fire the engines of industry and develop ample supplies of electricity is found in abundance in many parts of the state. Photo by W.A. Hunt III, Phillips Photographics

But for the time being, some of the most valuable minerals extracted in Colorado—other than the huge reserves of molybdenum—are sand and gravel worth $88 million in 1980; and lesser, but still valuable, yields exceeding a million dollars each year in limestone, building stone, and simple clay. Colorado also produces substantial commercial quantities of dolomite, volcanic scoria, gypsum, peat moss, perlite, and other non metals. Other metals mined commercially include copper, iron, cadmium, and tin.

The biggest mining industry in modern times has been molybdenum, a mineral used to harden steel. In the early 1980s this mined product was reaching levels of a half billion dollars annually. Colorado has the greatest reserves of "moly" in accessible areas known to exist on earth. But troubles in the steel industry have caused a cutback in production of that valuable mineral in recent years. In 1984, production value dropped to around $51 million. Whole mountains of "moly" await development.

Coal Reserves Abound

Like "moly," vast reserves of coal cover huge areas of Colorado, and coal mining has its roots in the early history of the state. Coal production peaked in the state in 1981, when nearly 20 million short tons were produced in Colorado mines. Production in 1986 was estimated to be down to 15 million short tons, and there were fewer than 3,000 coal miners working in the state that year. The heaviest production of coal is in Moffat and Routt Counties in northwestern Colorado, and mines there directly supply the huge coal-fired electricity generating plants nearby. Coal is also mined in commercial quantities in Archuleta, Delta, Fremont, Garfield, Gunnison, Huerfano, Jackson, La Plata, Las Animas, Mesa, Pitkin, Rio Blanco, and Weld Counties. There are about 65 operating coal mines in Colorado.

The Colorado coal industry is impacted by a number of pressures, and the decline in production is primarily caused by price competition. Colorado coal is losing markets to eastern and central U.S. competitors partially because of the distances it must be shipped after mining. Most of the mining in Colorado is close-to-surface strip mining, which requires heavy investment in rehabilitation of the terrains after operations are completed. However, in many cases the reclamation work done in the mining area leaves the surface in better condition for use as pasture and grassland, because top soil is replaced and enriched with fertilizer.

The glut of oil has also slowed the development of Colorado and other western U.S. coal reserves. This worldwide oil glut continues to cause problems in Colorado's largest natural resource industry—oil and gas production.

Oil and Gas Production

Colorado's oil and gas industry is not new. Oil was being produced in the Canon City area as early as 1862. Several producing fields are located in the state, including the Denver-Julesburg basin covering most of the northeastern and eastern sector of the state,

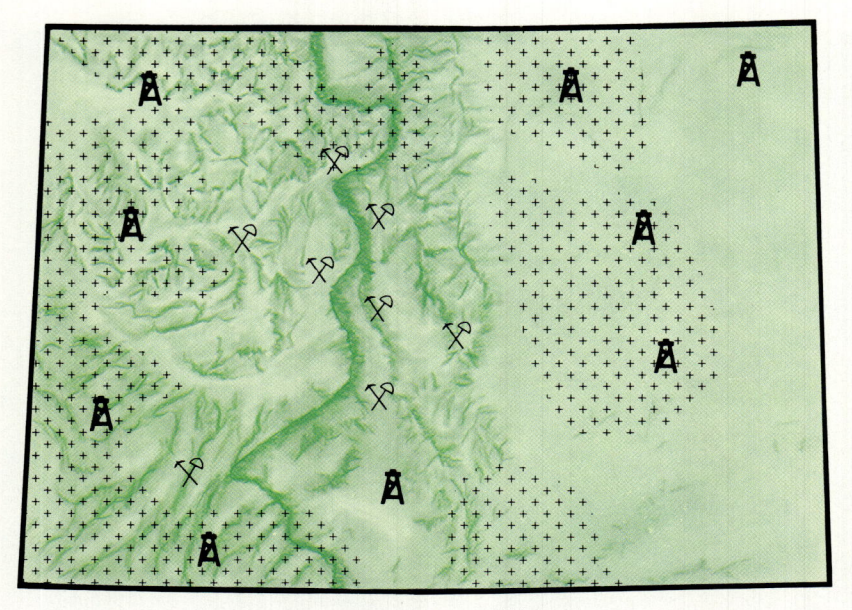

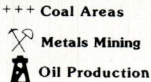

Mineral Resources of Colorado—The state is blessed with rich deposits of many types of commercial metals, including gold and silver; and energy deposits of coal, oil shale, oil, and natural gas promise to make mining a key part of the foreseeable future.

+++ Coal Areas
⛏ Metals Mining
🛢 Oil Production

the Sand Wash Basin and Piceance Basin in western Colorado, portions of the Paradox Basin extending into southwestern Colorado from Utah, and the San Juan Basin crossing into the southern part of the state from New Mexico. The San Luis and Raton Basins in the southern mountains, and the North and South Parks Basins in central Colorado also have small fields.

In the mid-1980s, some of the most extensive drilling operations in the oil industry's history were conducted, despite a general slump in the business. The third best year in Colorado oil drilling history was recorded in 1984, up 16 percent from the previous year, according to the Petroleum Information Corporation. Production in 1985 was more than 30 million barrels of crude, about the same level as the good years of 1981 and 1982, but well below the boom production years of the late 1970s. However, because of the decline in crude prices brought about by the world oil glut, production was expected to drop below 29 million barrels of crude in 1986, and drastic reductions in oil prices in the year caused further concern in the industry that production would continue to decline.

Natural gas production, on the other hand, continued to reach new high levels in 1985 and 1986, exceeding 350 billion cubic feet annually.

Employment in oil and gas extraction also was dropping each year, and exploration activities slowed as world oil prices declined.

Oil and gas production is spread throughout the state, with 38 of the 63 counties in Colorado reporting production of oil and gas in 1986. Until January 1984 the largest producing counties and their approximate cumulative production since drilling began have been: Adams, 43 million barrels (Bbls) of oil, 237 million cubic feet (Mcf) of natural gas; Jackson, 14 million Bbls oil, 670 Mcf gas; Kiowa, 11 million Bbls oil, 37 Mcf gas; La Plata, 1 million Bbls oil, 874 Mcf gas; Larimer, 16 million Bbls oil, 26 Mcf gas; Logan, 103 million Bbls oil, 199 Mcf gas; Moffat, 57 million Bbls oil, 600 Mcf gas; Morgan, 88 million Bbls oil, 192 Mcf gas; Rio Blanco, 761 million Bbls oil, 1.2 billion cubic feet of natural gas; Washington, 134 million Bbls oil, 70 Mcf gas; and Weld County, 86 million barrels of oil, and 590 million cubic feet of natural gas.

While many of the major oil companies have operations in Colorado, much of the drilling activity is conducted by independents. Some of the so-called independents headquartered in Colorado are large companies with international operations. Colorado has more than 1,000 oil companies with headquarters in the state. Their operations are not restricted to the state, but are extensive in the major fields of the Rockies and throughout Canada. Some of the Colorado companies have operations in such faraway fields as the North Sea and Asia.

Oilmen, by the very nature of their risky business, are a hardy breed and weather boom and bust cycles, dry holes, and gushers with the same stoic attitude. Practically any experienced oil hand will readily predict the return of the energy industry on a boom-size scale to Colorado and the energy rich Rockies.

A leading Denver-based economist, Tucker Hart Adams, observed during the downturn in the oil business in 1984, that "while 142 oil companies went out of business that year, 128 opened their doors."

In 1985, Colorado's deepest well was drilled to a depth of almost 24,000 feet. The well, drilled primarily for natural gas by Celsius Energy Corporation in Moffat County, was 4,190 feet deeper than the previous deep hole. That well went down 19,710 feet and was drilled in 1968 in Rio Blanco County by Mobil Corporation. Spokesmen for the Celsius company said the lower cost of drilling encouraged the Utah-owned company to drill that deep.

But with the continued decline in the price of oil and natural gas, deep-well drilling is not common in Colorado. Even normal drilling activities are likely to be curtailed in the

Wheat ripens as an oil well pumps in Weld County, where sectors of the economy often work together. Photo by W.A. Hunt III, Phillips Photographics

Colorado has become an energy center for the West, and despite some downturns in the industry in the mid-1980s, has a destiny tied to supplying America's needs in the future. Photo by Steve Ogden, Tom Stack & Associates

state, as elsewhere, until the prices once again stabilize. But when they do, Colorado oil explorers and producers can again be expected to rush to the challenge of the next energy boom era—which they all know is coming in just a matter of time.

Another energy industry in Colorado's future, which has seen bust days in recent years, is the research and development of synfuels—primarily the mammoth Colorado reserves of oil shale. The booms and busts in the oil shale industry have largely been on paper and dependant more upon grantsmanship than geology, because most of the activity has been in the R&D sector. Despite millions of dollars spent in research and experimental refinery operations, no commercial fuel has been produced from oil shale to date, and with the world energy glut and low prices this industry is not likely to be developed until the next century. But reserves are in the Colorado ground in astonishing amounts.

Colorado is estimated to have the equivalent of more than 900 billion barrels of oil locked in its known oil shale reserves. Colorado, Utah, and Wyoming have the largest known reserves of oil shale, with about 25,000 square miles of the mineral underlying these states. Colorado's reserves are the richest and thickest, with about 80 percent of the known high-grade reserves located in the Piceance Creek Basin of Garfield, Mesa, and Rio Blanco Counties.

Since the Arab oil embargo of the early 1970s, the Nation has focused attention on methods of recovering this vast energy resource. A number of companies actually started large-scale operations to build plants to extract oil from the rock-like mineral, and several limited R&D projects continue. At one point the U.S. Synthetic Fuels Corporation, a federally funded program to encourage private companies to develop this energy source, had funding exceeding $7 billion. The federal program was killed by Congress late in 1985, but some funds were already allocated to continue one Colorado project near the heart of the oil shale country at Parachute. A suit to block the payment of the $500 million already allocated to Union Oil Company for the Parachute project was filed against the now defunct U.S. Synthetic Fuels Corporation. So even the continuation of that R&D project is now in question.

That this vast reserve oil shale resource will someday be developed to meet the Nation's energy needs is not questioned. But communities on the Western Slope, which have on several occasions geared up for new energy booms, are not planning on any boosts to their economies in the near future.

The same skepticism prevails when other Colorado energy-related research projects involving renewable energy are discussed.

The nation's preeminent renewable energy research facility, the Solar Energy Research Institute at Golden, opened in July 1977 with high expectations to lead the world into a near-term solar future free of dependency on fossil fuels. While that institution today continues research into photovoltaics, alcohol fuels, biomass energy, thermal energy, and other technologies, its programs are projected for use in a more distant future when the oil

PROFILE

San Luis Valley Potato Administrative Committee
New Markets for Colorado Agribusiness

Americans from South Carolina on the Atlantic to California on the Pacific frequently enjoy a bit of Colorado without even knowing it. A little-known fact about the highland state is that it ranks among the top producers of high-quality potatoes, and this distinction comes largely from the efforts of farmers in the San Luis Valley to produce a better staple for the American table.

Colorado consistently ranks high among the ten leaders in the United States in potato production, and the 8,000-square-mile San Luis Valley can stand alone as the seventh leading spud producing area in the nation.

With 95 percent of the Valley's potato crop being shipped into the fresh markets of the south, southwest, and western United States, San Luis Valley potatoes hold the fourth leading position in that important market.

Even though potatoes have been grown in the Valley since the historic days of the first Spanish settlement of the Valley and formed an important part of the diet of miners later coming to the state, it has taken the development of modern agribusiness research and market management to bring this important cash crop to its leading position in Colorado's agricultural economy.

The growing importance of this major Colorado crop is attributed to the development of three varieties of the nation's highest quality potatoes by the Colorado State University researchers headquartered in the Valley, and marketing innovations by the San Luis Valley Potato Administrative Committee.

Five San Luis Valley counties are reaping the harvest of years of research and development to produce three distinctive Colorado potato types. These counties, situated in one of America's most ideal potato-growing climes, are Rio Grande, Alamosa, Saguache, Conejos, and Costilla.

The 56,000 acres dedicated to potato growing on the floor of the Valley are situated at elevations ranging from 7,000 to 8,000 feet above sea level. While the Valley itself receives less than seven inches of moisture in the form of snow and rain annually, its inexhaustible subsurface water table and drainage from snowmelt provide the irrigation to make it one of the West's most important crop-producing areas.

The Centennial Russet was developed in the valley and named in 1976 in honor of the state's 100th anniversary. This thick-skinned Colorado product is noted for its excellent shape, durability, and longer storage life. It is now the primary potato grown in the Valley. The second potato developed by the CSU Research Center is the round, red Sangre, named for the nearby mountain range; and the third potato grown for shipment is the Russet Burbank, which is also grown in other U.S. potato-growing regions.

The ideal conditions for growing potatoes, plus the assurance that crops will be virtually free of destruction by common insects due to colder temperatures of the high altitude, make the Valley a prime location for consideration of expanding agribusiness industries built around the Colorado potato. Modern processing opportunities of the expandable crop by the frozen food and prepackaged foods industry have yet to be tapped, but the Valley leaders are actively seeking development of this new market opportunity.

"Commercial agriculture is the heart and soul of the San Luis Valley, and our good location for the strongly emerging markets of the West and Southwest places us in an ideal situation for solid expansion of the agribusiness industry," notes Wayne D. Thompson, manager of the San Luis Valley Potato Administrative Committee. He points out that the Valley's Potato Committee, along with newly organized economic development organizations, will actively work with food process manufacturers to establish new or expanded industrial plants.

The modern communities within the Valley, along with an excellent and trained labor supply, provide the support needed for just such economic expansion of the historic agriculture industry of the San Luis Valley.

New crops, such as the famed San Luis Valley potato, keep the farm tradition alive in Colorado. The valley is one of the state's richest farming regions.

The world's premier research institute into alternative energy sources of the future is located at Golden where the Solar Energy Research Institute is headquartered. Photo by McAllister of Denver

glut is consumed. Other evolving factors of concern, such as the growing evidence that fossil fuels may be damaging the environment and the atmosphere, might move up some of the development timetables for the work being conducted at SERI. Despite deep cuts in the federally funded program, some of the world's most knowledgeable renewable energy scientists are still working on long-term, high-risk R&D on solar technologies that private industry cannot be expected to undertake.

On a more immediate basis, another of the world's leading energy institutions is turning out energy and mineral development specialists who are working on projects throughout the Free World and most emerging Third World nations. The Colorado School of Mines, also located in Golden, is recognized as a leading institution in advanced management and technology development for exploration, extraction, and refinement of minerals. The state institution, which is the second oldest institute in the United States devoted to minerals and energy engineering, is not only a world teaching facility, but a major resource to the development of the mineral and energy rich Rocky Mountain region.

Its curriculum not only includes basic and master's degrees in geology, mining, mathematics, metallurgy, physics, geophysics, and petroleum and chemical engineering, but it offers 10 Ph.D. programs in high technologies of mineral resources. Its research facilities include an Advanced Materials Institute, Center for Wave Phenomena, Center for Welding Research, Earth Mechanics Institute, Industrial Ecology Institute, and others. Its campus provides facilities for, and the school has research grams in cooperation with the U.S. Geological Survey: Branch of Earthquake Tectonics and Risks, and the Branch of Global Seismology. The National Earthquake Information Service, which is the world's watchdog for earthquake disaster, is located nearby.

While development of both agricultural and mineral resources in Colorado was the basis for the first American settlement of the region, and has provided the economic foundation on which it has grown, the natural resources have provided something more.

Perhaps the greater economic legacy from the good earth in both areas of agriculture and mineral development is only now being realized at the end of the 20th century. Both these basic industries provided the catalyst for the huge service-related economy strongly emerging in Colorado.

Despite the economic problems in the transitional agriculture, mining, and energy industries, much of the Nation's natural and real wealth remains undeveloped in the Rocky Mountain States. Vast coal reserves, enough oil shale to provide the energy needs of the nation far into the future, and some of the world's great untapped natural gas reserves extending from New Mexico to Canada, guarantee the energy self-sufficiency of the Nation and her Allies in any future crisis. The Great Plains, extending from Texas to Canada across Oklahoma, Kansas, Wyoming, Montana, and the Dakotas, produce far greater yields of the highest protein grains and pasturage than any area on earth.

Even as Colorado cities and towns see the emergence of a high technology/aerospace industry, their role as service centers to the region's basic natural resource industries grows more important.

The importance of the natural resource industries and the riches from the Colorado earth cannot be diminished by any temporary economic problems on the farms and in the mines. It could well be argued that just as it all began in agriculture and mining, the key to the long-term future is still held in the natural resources with which Colorado is so amply blessed.

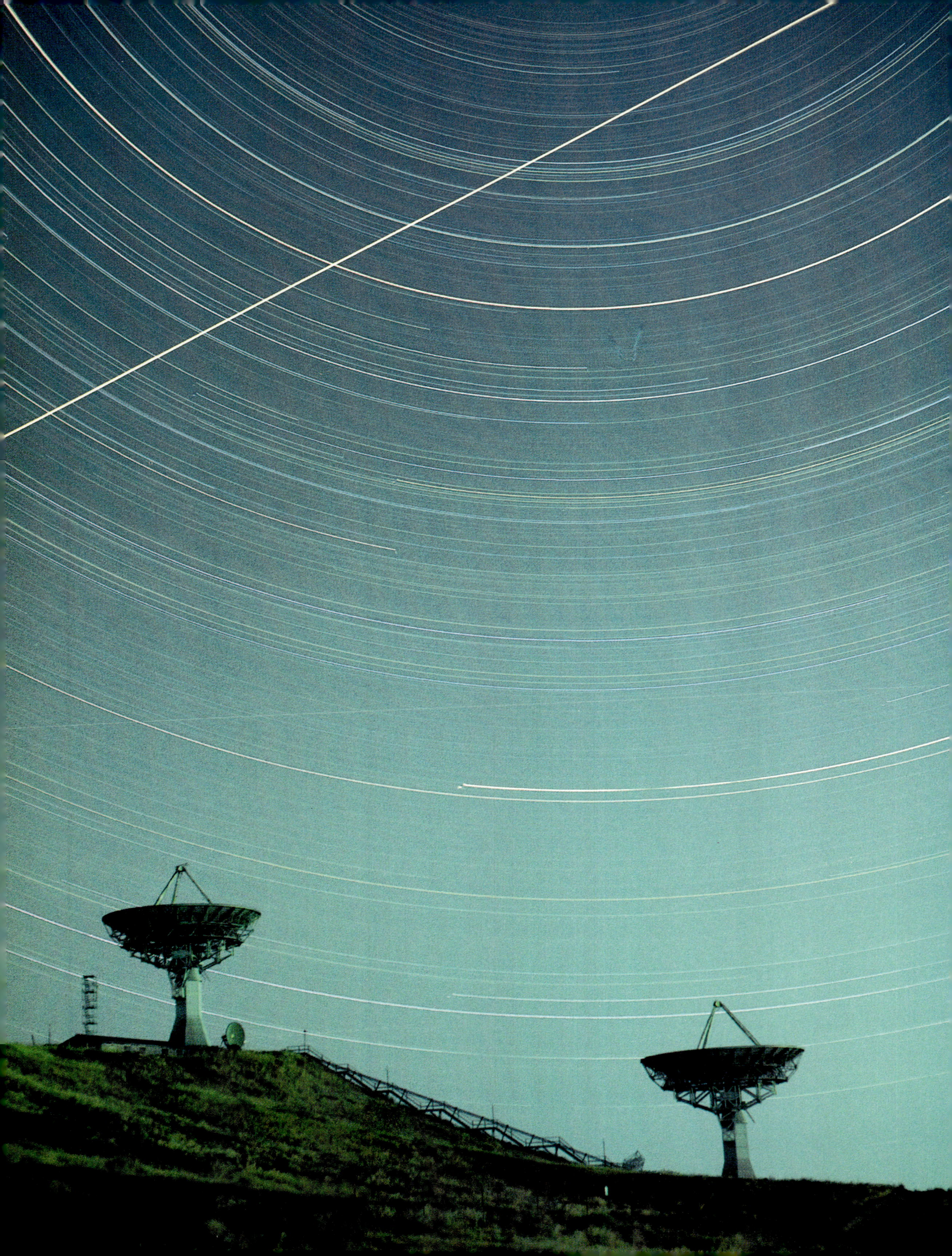

CHAPTER 5

Service Center for the Rockies
Pioneering the Information Age

Seeds for one of the most important economic sectors of the Colorado economy were sewn in the past by development of the natural resources of the mountains and plains.

A service industry responding to the business-support needs of the 13-state Rocky Mountain and Great Plains region has emerged and continues to grow in Colorado. The complex mosaic of service and support institutions centered in the six counties of the Denver metropolitan area—and to a growing extent in such regional centers as Colorado Springs, Grand Junction, Pueblo, Fort Collins-Greeley, and Durango-Cortez—is comprised of both public and private sector elements. Many were first put in place to service the vast federal lands and the agricultural, mining, and energy industries of the Rocky Mountain West.

Multistate, regional services such as federal and state government programs, higher education, transportation and distribution networking, wholesale activities, medical and health specialization, engineering and architectural services, management and marketing services, accounting business, employee benefits, financial and corporate legal services have long been centered in Colorado, providing support for the entire region.

More recently, the headquartering of national and international corporations and associations, the consolidation of information services and telecommunications, and intensified foreign trade and investment efforts have accelerated the growth of the service sector of Colorado's economy.

The payroll in the service sectors of the economy—including government, utilities, communications, and the traditional sectors of lodging, health care, personal services, and the professions and business services—far exceeds any other sector of the economy. The service industries are estimated to employ some 329,000 persons. Federal, state, and local governments in Colorado employ about 248,000 more. Communications industries employ about 26,700, and the utilities about 13,000. In addition, the printing industry, which is usually considered to be a manufacturing industry, but which provides most of its products in support of business and government, employs about 22,000.

The service sectors of the economy have continued to be the strongest growth area in Colorado's economy; and despite federal reductions-in-force and state belt-tightening, government jobs remain a fairly stable part of the overall employment picture. Business and professional services continue to expand, and service industry employment is increasing at a steady pace. The growth rate has slowed after very substantial increases experienced during the earlier 1980s, in support of the headquartering activities in the state.

This headquartering role or centralization of multi-state services is not a new socio-economic function for Colorado's cities, but it increasingly becomes a stronger part of the economy. In fact, Colorado was already positioned to become one of America's new service-center states even before the trend toward an "information society" was identified by such forecasters as John Naisbitt.

Even before the turn of the century, Denver and several cities across the state assumed important regional service roles, primarily because of the location of railroad transportation hubs. Military and federal government headquartering came a bit later, and in more

Colorado is leading the way to the stars in the new information age. The state is the service center for the Rockies. Christopher Roger, Stock Imagery

PROFILE

Arthur Andersen & Company
World Team with Commitment to Colorado

Arthur Andersen & Company, the largest public accounting and consulting firm in the world, established its Denver office over 30 years ago.

Serving several states throughout the Rocky Mountains as the region's largest public accounting firm, Arthur Andersen provides accounting, tax, audit, and information systems consulting expertise to century-old industries and emerging companies alike.

The organizational structure of Arthur Andersen & Co. is unlike that of other major accounting firms, and the difference in the structure is meaningful to multicity and multinational clients.

The company explains its difference thusly: "Supporting a one-firm concept, we maintain uniform professional standards, follow consistent practice procedures, and provide standardized training for all personnel worldwide.

"No other firm is structured to give clients this kind of assurance and confidence," the company says. "A further advantage of our organizational structure is our total control and responsibility for each client at the Denver office level. Regardless of a client company's size, a designated Denver office engagement partner has the overall responsibility for services to that client."

That partner directs and coordinates the work of a client service team that might include Arthur Andersen & Co. personnel in literally scores of locations. This supports and strengthens communications with client-company management. The result is superior service, provided responsibly and professionally.

Arthur Andersen's regional success results from the broad range of professional expertise housed in the Denver office. A diverse client base, in terms of industry and size, as well as consulting requirements has been developed and maintained. Practice areas of particular strength include natural resources, banking, real estate, cable television, telecommunications, health care, manufacturing, high technology, government, and education. Within these industries, Arthur Andersen professionals are prepared to address strategic issues and information systems planning for small businesses as well as Fortune 500 companies. Recommendations and results are tailored to client specifications and goals.

Creating competitive opportunities and advantages for clients has caused Arthur Andersen to greatly expand the meaning of full service. The traditional strengths of accounting, audit, and tax are now complemented by complete business support functions such as detailed business analysis; financial budgeting and forecasting; management information systems design, planning, and installation; capital funding; and income and estate planning.

The Denver office has a professional staff of 290, making it one of the largest of Arthur Andersen's 176 offices in 44 countries. The personnel represents a broad spectrum of talent and training in addition to accounting. This additional expertise includes law, engineering, liberal arts, business, and other disciplines. Community development and charitable support have always been focal points for those in the Denver office.

Arthur Andersen's one-firm concept, combined with the professional and personal strengths of the Denver office, assures present and future clients consistently high quality service, and an overall commitment to excellence.

The leading accounting firm of Arthur Andersen brings top professionals like Richard H. Kristinik, Robert L. Scott, and Bruce L. Arfmann to a client's service.

The spires of local and state government symbolize the importance of the public sector in the economy of Colorado. Photo by Nathan Bilow

recent years the energy boom brought scores of corporate regional and national headquarters into the state. This headquartering fueled commercial building construction and contributed to a large-scale upgrading of public facilities such as water treatment and disposal plants, schools, airports, local government buildings, and schools in cities and towns all across the state. In many communities the most lasting contribution of the energy boom of the late 1970s and early 1980s was the greatest improvement of facilities the communities had seen in the modern history of Colorado.

Another lasting contribution was the establishment of a solid business infrastructure of services that came to support the energy companies and have stayed to support other sectors of the economy. Direct business support firms in computer and data processing, building maintenance, telecommunications, marketing and sales training, equipment leasing, public relations and advertising, printing and graphic arts, audio-visual production, employee and personnel services, legal and accounting, engineering and design, and a host of others are now firmly established in Colorado. These service companies not only provide support for clients within the state and region, but export their skills throughout the western United States.

Government, the Service Pacesetter

From a small cadre of federal regional offices primarily administering the affairs of the forest, mineral, and agriculture services of government, a significant federal headquartering move into Colorado began in the late 1930s and early 1940s. Federal regional offices serving a dozen or more mountain, plains,

109

PROFILE

Coopers & Lybrand
Professionalism Enhances Service Center Reputation

Colorado's role as the business service center for the Rocky Mountain Region has been enhanced by such long-established professional firms as Coopers & Lybrand, an international public accounting firm which has broadened services to match the needs of the changing economy.

Established in 1963, Coopers & Lybrand's Denver office has grown with the region during more than two decades, when both growth and diversity have been the hallmarks of the region's economy.

The firm was founded in Philadelphia in 1898 as an accounting practice and has expanded to 94 offices, including the Denver office. Coopers & Lybrand has 12,000 partners and staff members throughout the United States, with a total of 33,000 employees in 100 countries. As an international accounting and consulting firm, it ranks in the "Big Eight" of its field.

In 1986, Coopers & Lybrand is still primarily involved in accounting, auditing and taxation services, but its scope has also expanded with the changing times.

The Denver office provides management consulting services, merger and acquisition services, compensation and benefit consulting services, and an ever-widening professional service system. It can also offer its clients computer systems design and implementation, financial and business litigation consulting, and telecommunications consulting.

A typical service package offered by Coopers & Lybrand under its Emerging Business Service group might include: financial statement services (audit, review, compilation), financial planning, evaluation of budgets, forecasts and plans, cash management advice, development and evaluation of systems and procedures, preparation of corporate and individual tax returns, development of executive and employee compensation packages, and design and implementation of data processing systems.

Coopers & Lybrand continues to diversify its professional services to keep pace with the growing needs of the western economy, and its 200-member Denver staff is encouraged to develop innovative approaches to serving its clients.

"Our philosophy, simply, is that we believe our strength lies in our people," says Kurt Caulson, managing partner of the Denver office. "We encourage individual initiative and creativity, and we do not attempt to impose one personality on our staff. Our strength comes from their vitality and diversity. Our emphasis on personal growth has produced professionals who are known in the business community for their involvement and personal attention to the unique requirements of each client."

Caulson says Coopers & Lybrand has seen a great evolution in the Colorado economy over the past 25 years that the firm has served in this region.

"We've seen the state's business climate evolve from a fairly static mineral/agriculture base to a diverse and sophisticated economy of intense competition," the veteran accounting partner says. "The competition is everywhere, in every sector of the economy, from tourism to technology. It's healthy, because it assures a constant infusion of new ideas to stimulate the economy."

Coopers & Lybrand brings an expert staff of professionals to serve the accounting needs of large and small businesses throughout the mountain region.

The telecommunications era is dawning and Coloradans, who have long served as the communications professionals for the region, greet the new age with expertise and innovation. Photo by Douglas Stewart, Stock Imagery

and western states are consolidated in Colorado today, providing a federal civilian employment nearly 52,000 jobs. In addition, more than 43,000 military men and women are stationed at the major military bases and military service centers in the state.

Large concentrations of federal civilian employment representing the broadest spectrum of federal regional headquarters to be found outside of Washington D.C. are located in Denver, Lakewood-Golden, Colorado Springs, Fort Collins-Greeley, Aurora, Pueblo, Boulder, and Grand Junction. Denver has more than 15,000 federal employees headquartered in the city; Jefferson County follows with almost 10,000, and El Paso County with nearly 9,000. Other counties with a federal employment exceeding 1,000 are Adams, Arapahoe, Boulder, Larimer-Weld, Mesa, and Pueblo.

A number of other Colorado communities provide facilities for major federal service operations. Some of these federal services and the towns outside the metropolitan areas where they are located include: U.S. Department of Agriculture/U.S. Forest Service—Leadville, Salida, Canon City, Springfield, Fairplay, Limon, La Junta, and Alamosa; Social Security Administration—Canon City, Durango, Glenwood Springs, La Junta, Montrose, and Trinidad; Geological Survey—Durango and Meeker; Bureau of Land Management—Canon City, Craig, and Montrose; National Park Service—La Junta, Montrose, Fruita, Gunnison, Dinosaur, Florissant, Mosca, Mesa Verde, and Estes Park; Bureau of Reclamation—Loveland; Immigration and Naturalization Service—Alamosa; and Federal Aviation Administration—Longmont, Akron, Eagle, La Junta, Aspen, Cortez, Glenwood Springs, Parker, and Trinidad.

Dozens of Army, Air Force, Navy, Marine, and Coast Guard recruiting stations and reserve centers are located in cities and towns across the state. Three major active military stations are also located in Colorado, including the U.S. Army's huge Fort Carson complex between Colorado Springs and Pueblo; the U.S. Air Force's world payroll headquarters at the Air Force North American Aerospace Defense Command (NORAD), the Air Force Academy, and Peterson Air Force Base at Colorado Springs.

Local Government Payrolls

State and local government in Colorado provide a core of services both to the citizens living and working in the region, and in support of business and economic development. There are a total of 1,544 various agencies of government in the state, of which 63 are county government bodies, 267 are municipal governments, and 185 are public school districts. Colorado's state and local government agencies employ nearly 196,000 persons.

The largest body of government agencies, numbering more than 1,000, are the so-called "special districts" or silent governments, providing specific services. Such special services

PROFILE

U S WEST
Blazing the Trails in the New Information Era

Colorado is a trail blazer in the high technology information age.

In 1983 the state was chosen as home for U S WEST Inc., one of the largest diversified telecommunications companies in the world.

U S WEST owns Mountain Bell, Northwestern Bell, Pacific Northwest Bell, and a dozen other information-related companies.

"Nobody knows the trails better," the company's ads proclaim. And its Bell companies have more than 100 years experience to back up the claim.

But the company's vision today is of new horizons.

U S WEST's Bell companies are investing more than $1.5 billion a year in new technology. And its diversified companies are staking claims in such growing national markets as information systems, directory publishing, mobile telephone systems, financial services, real estate, and more.

The company's optimism is rooted in the West itself, and in a strategy emphasizing growth and competition.

The region served by the Bell companies of U S West includes the majority of 14 states. It stretches from Washington and Oregon in the Pacific Northwest to Minnesota on the Great Lakes, and from Canada to Mexico.

In the heart of it all is Colorado, where the company found the combination of ingredients it sought for a headquarters.

Demographers forecast 41 percent growth in the 14-state region by the end of this century, certainly one of the fastest growing regions in the nation. Company officials also cite the area's proximity to the Pacific Basin, the fastest growing region in the world, not only in population but also in the development of technology and natural resources.

The U S WEST companies employ some 65,000 men and women in the 14 states, where they are the major provider of telephone services. But they are not stopping with basic telephone services.

In 1985, U S WEST created a major new company: U S WEST Information Systems, which markets communication systems and services to businesses coast-to-coast. The company designs, sells, installs, maintains, and modernizes business communication systems including telephones, PBXs, computer terminals, modems, and other equipment. Like the parent company, Information Systems is headquartered in Englewood.

Another U S WEST company is Denver-based LANDMARK Publishing, one of the nation's largest publishers of telephone directories and city directories. LANDMARK's largest subsidiary is U S WEST Direct, of Aurora, which publishes telephone directories for the Bell companies of U S WEST. In 1985, LANDMARK acquired Lomar/Johnson/Directory Publishing Co. of Loveland, one of the nation's largest independent publishers of telephone directories and city directories. The firm publishes 480 directories in 42 states.

Another fast-growing business is cellular communications, which places clear, reliable phone service in cars, buses, boats, oil rigs, and even briefcases. And U S WEST is there, via NewVector Communications of Seattle. Among the first dozen cities to receive NewVector services are two in Colorado—Denver and Colorado Springs. NewVector also is building a system in the Gulf of Mexico and will custom-build systems all over the world.

Other units of U S WEST, all based in Colorado include:

• U S WEST Financial Services, which provides equipment leasing and sales financing for customers of the U S WEST companies, as well as to other companies. Financial Services has offices in several major U.S. cities and manages over a quarter of a billion dollars in receivables.

• BetaWest Properties, which develops and owns commercial real estate for the U S WEST companies and for other companies nationwide.

• U S WEST International, which is exploring business opportunities overseas.

• U S WEST Material Resources, which manages purchasing for the U S WEST companies.

• U S WEST Corporate Communications, which provides long distance services and other communications needs of the U S WEST companies.

• Strategic Marketing, a headquarters organization which monitors the marketplace and provides marketing direction for all the U S WEST companies.

• U S WEST Advanced Technologies, which selects and oversees the development of hardware and software for all the U S WEST communications companies.

Most of these fast-growing Colorado companies have moved from the drawing board to the marketplace since 1983. But all are expected to contribute significantly to the growth of U S WEST—and of Colorado—during the years ahead.

PROFILE

A.S. Hansen, Inc.
Innovation in Employee Benefits and Compensation

Since the days when a "pension plan" was a gold watch at the end of a long career, employee benefits have evolved and changed to meet the needs of a modernized society.

A.S. Hansen, Inc., one of the largest benefits and compensation consulting firms in the United States, has proven that sophisticated advances in the service industry are as vital to the economy as technological breakthroughs. The company serves Colorado and the Rocky Mountain states with the largest professional staff specializing in employee benefit and compensation programs in the region.

The Hansen expertise is important to modern employers—large or small—that have sizable investments in skilled and highly trained or professional employees. Hansen has been a pacesetter in the development of innovative employee benefit packages to encourage the retention of valued manpower for business, industry, and government.

A.S. Hansen, Inc. began operations in 1930 as a proprietary firm specializing in pension consulting and actuarial services. The Denver regional office was opened in 1961, to bring important employee benefit and compensation consulting services to public and private sector employers in the Rocky Mountain area. In the past two decades, the company has continually expanded in both scope of services and specialists available to its growing client base. Its professional, on-site staff of 50 now offers the region vital support services in every phase of the constantly changing benefit and compensation field.

"With so many of the retirement, compensation, health care and other benefit programs subject to changing tax laws and legislation, it is essential

Hansen consultants help public and private sector employers design benefit plans, manage costs, and keep current with changing legislation.

for employers of Colorado and this region to have close access to our consulting professionals," says R. Paul Schrader, Hansen's regional vice president in Denver. "This is a sophisticated professional market. Colorado business and government want their service available locally and not performed long-distance from Dallas, New York, or the West Coast."

The Hansen organization, now employing 650 of the nation's leading professionals in the field, is a full-service international firm headquartered in Chicago, Illinois, with 19 other offices across the country, including New York, Los Angeles, Atlanta, and Dallas. International offices are located in Toronto, London, and Paris. Full service is provided in the Denver office, which includes staff professionals in accounting, actuarial science, business administration, compensation/benefits, communication, data processing, finance, law, and mathematics.

Hansen serves as consultants to employers of all sizes and types, working with them to design and implement total compensation programs. The firm provides the full range of services which enable clients to attract and retain the type of employees they need. Increased competition for skilled and professional employees, changing laws and regulations, and new corporate goals have directed Hansen's services into other related areas in human resources management. These include investment services, compensation systems, employee communications, health care plan design and cost containment, specialized surveys, and administrative services.

"The entire field of employee benefits is undergoing tremendous change, as the cost to employers of providing these benefits continues to escalate," says V. Benjamin Haas, managing principal of the Denver office. "For example, we are currently seeing a strong trend toward flexible compensation programs, which allow employees to tailor benefits to fit their needs. The revolution in health care is causing most companies to redesign their plans, to incorporate cost-containment and cost-sharing features."

Hansen's consulting tone matches the modern Colorado economic frontier served from their Denver offices.

"Hansen has been here for a quarter century, and our commitment is to Colorado and the region," says Schrader. "Like Colorado itself, the Hansen staff is bright, aggressive, dynamic, and diversified."

And like the evolving modern role of Colorado in the Rockies, Hansen is typical of the service-oriented business rapidly assuming a lead position among the more historic industries.

Public safety becomes a key part of the high quality of life in Colorado. The state's local lawmen are among the best trained in America. Photo by Nathan Bilow

as fire protection in unincorporated areas, water and sewage treatment, solid waste disposal, parks and natural resource protection, housing, and economic or community development are provided by the special groups of government. Many are quite small with a single purpose; but others, such as the giant Regional Transportation District, and some of the large water boards and sewage treatment districts, are substantial.

Major employment sectors in state and local government include more than 55,300 in local schools, almost 16,000 in hospitals and health facilities, about 7,500 in streets and highway departments, nearly 12,000 in police and fire departments, and almost 4,000 in public welfare agencies.

While these agencies administer the public needs from education to housing criminals, there are several agencies of both local and state government which provide direct economic development support to the local cities and the state. Many actually generate private sector jobs through development and product marketing activities. The Colorado Department of Agriculture, for example, has an active marketing program, which vigorously sells products of the state's large agricultural community in both U.S. and international markets.

Another Colorado agency directly working with business and the consumer is the Department of Regulatory Agencies, which regulates and licenses most of the professions and trades.

The largest of the state business development agencies is the Department of Local Affairs, with strong programs in business development, foreign trade, industrial training, and direct services to assist local communities in their transitions from weak economies to new business bases.

That department's Division of Commerce & Development actively markets Colorado as a business location in competitive programs with other states. It organizes foreign trade missions to increase Colorado product exporting, and provides countless support services in economic research and development that individual industries could not be reasonably expected to perform. Its foreign trade office, with direct links to the U.S. Department of Commerce, serves as a clearinghouse for Colorado products throughout the world.

A unique office within that department, the Colorado Motion Picture and Television Commission, is a direct revenue producer. Since the movie and television promotion program was organized in 1969, more than $100 million has been spent in Colorado by production companies coming into the state to make feature films, television shows, and commercials.

The effectiveness of this agency's work was demonstrated one summer day in 1985, at Loveland Pass west of Georgetown, when three American automobile companies simultaneously had production crews on the pass filming new car commercials.

Colorado was the first state in the United

PROFILE

Denver Merchandise Mart
Fashion and Trade Center of the Rockies

A fashion center located in the heart of the rugged Rocky Mountains might seem an unusual concept to anyone not familiar with the role that the Denver Merchandise Mart has played in putting Colorado on the world's fashion and merchandising maps.

In only two decades the Denver trade show center has helped focus the attention of leading clothing, jewelry, and gift manufacturers on Colorado. The Denver Merchandise Mart is the largest trade center and hosts the largest market events between Dallas and Chicago and the West Coast.

The Denver Merchandise Mart, covering more than 40 acres at 451 East 58th Avenue, adjacent to Interstate Highway 25, has been successful in bringing a growing number of manufacturers' representatives to service the entire Rocky Mountain region from its Colorado location. Six hundred representatives of national and international merchandise labels with more than 1,000 employees now occupy the permanent showrooms of the big market center.

Merchandise is shown by manufacturers' representatives on four tiers of permanent showrooms, ranging from 200 to 6,500 square feet each. The permanent showrooms are conveniently located by types of merchandise to make the buyers' visits more efficient.

Showrooms surround the skylit area called the Terrace Gardens. The first two floors are primarily gifts, gourmet items, decorative accessories, and jewelry showrooms. The third and fourth floors feature apparel and western wear, boots and shoes, and sporting goods.

Buyers from Montana to New Mexico, Kansas to Utah, the Dakotas and Nebraska, flock to the showrooms and the big special market events hosted by the Merchandise Mart.

When the big shows come, the Denver Merchandise Mart has some of the best facilities located anywhere in the western United States to stage anything from an intimate private fashion show, complete with models on runways, to seated banquets for several thousand and exhibit booths for hundreds of vendors. The merchandising service center provides parking for over 3,000 vehicles. A 165-room lodge, the Inn at the Mart, is connected by a breezeway to the main facility for the convenience of buyers and exhibitors.

The number of showrooms has doubled since the Mart was opened in 1965, and the representation of major manufacturers has likewise increased over the two decades. The

The Denver Merchandise Mart has expanded its facilities in its lead role as the retail support center of the Rockies has grown.

region served by the center covers about one-third of the geographical United States, and buyers find the facility is a one-stop marketing center tailor-made for their wholesale shopping trips to Colorado. Some of its bigger shows attract buyers from throughout the nation.

One feature, which has made the merchandise center a popular stop for the bigger shows and "market season premiers," is the Denver Merchandise Mart's ability to stage large functions simultaneously. The center can host a 3,000-seat banquet in one of its facilities while a major show with hundreds of exhibits is staged in an adjoining room.

The Mart has grown from one building with 345,000 square feet to a complex encompassing 840,000 square feet since its opening in 1965. In 1973 a 120,000-square-foot exhibit hall, the Exposition Building, was opened and in 1986 the completion of the 65,000-square-foot Mart Pavilion brought to three the number of modern halls available for big shows.

The original building, which houses the Terrace Gardens and the central exhibit area, is capped by a massive, four-story-high skylight and provides 12,500 square feet of open space used for exhibits or dinner dances. The Terrace Gardens can accommodate up to 1,000 people for cocktail parties or seat up to 800 for dinner. It works as an adjunct to the huge Expo hall when exhibitors/buyers need two functions.

The major exhibit buildings are served directly by dock facilities providing easy access for exhibitors to load and unload from off-street parking areas.

The Denver Merchandise Mart also maintains a full-service staff of professional merchandising and exhibit specialists who assist the manufacturers' representatives and buyers attending the shows. A full-time reception staff, with security screening at all entrances, assures the privacy of the shows. Only buyers, who are badged by security, are allowed to enter the various exhibit areas. Retailers who regularly order

Buyers from throughout the West focus on the latest fashions and wares at shows hosted at Denver. The Mart has made Colorado a regional merchandise center.

from the permanent showrooms or attend the shows are given permanent identification badges. Once an exhibit is set up, the Mart provides 24-hour security and electronic surveillance.

In advance of the shows, staff members prepare buyers' guides and advertising and promotional material, and work with associations for pre-show mailings. The staff also assists in the production of fashion shows, helping to locate models, and can provide construction crews to build special exhibit props or renovate showrooms.

When not booked for trade shows, the Denver Merchandise Mart is also available to companies and organizations for large functions and events, offering complete in-house catering and bar facilities. Annual meetings, graduation ceremonies, banquets, indoor scouting exhibitions, public shows industrial shows, and numerous other events are staged at the Mart.

The addition of the new $5 million Pavilion in 1986 expanded the capacity of the business service center, providing space for 340 exhibit booths or a seating capacity for more than 4,000 persons.

Because of the Denver Merchandise Mart's location, Colorado has become the home of more than 100 annual trade shows introducing new merchandise to buyers coming into the state from throughout the Rocky Mountain and Central Plains states. Its location can also be attributed to helping make Colorado the western wear capital of the world. The Denver International Western Apparel and Equipment Show, held at the Mart the weekend before the National Western Stock Show and Rodeo at the nearby Denver Coliseum, is the largest western apparel show conducted anywhere in the world.

Darrell R. Hare, general manager of the Denver Merchandise Mart and past president of the World Association of Merchandise Marts, sees the Mart complex as a valuable resource to Colorado:

"The successful growth of the Denver Merchandise Mart through our many acquisitions and expansions has proven that the region's buyers look to Denver and Colorado as the wholesale and distribution center for the Rocky Mountain West. This role will grow in importance, since we are located in the heart of the fastest growing part of America, and we will continue to expand as the needs of this area increase in the future."

Sophisticated financial services are provided by Colorado's banks and other financial institutions. Photo courtesy of Central Bancorporation

States to create a film commission, and the relatively small investment has paid big dividends to the private sector. Combined with the natural beauty of the region, the international promotional program is expected to generate about $25 million in direct income to audio/video supply companies, other industry suppliers, retailers, motels and hotels, and in direct wages. Because of this activity, Colorado has established a substantial new business in supplying the film industry. A secondary effect has been the widespread publicity of the beauty of the state in every media from big screen movies to TV commercials.

All or parts of some notable film productions have been created in Colorado in recent years. Numbered among them are *How the West Was Won*, *Butch Cassidy and the Sundance Kid*, *Across the Wide Missouri*, *Around the World in 80 Days*, *True Grit*, *Cat Ballou*, *In Cold Blood*, *American Flyer*, and 121 other feature films or full length documentaries.

It is appropriate that Colorado has become one of the best-filmed states in America, because the movie industry might be said to have had its start in the state. A film company featuring Tom Mix was headquartered in Canon City in 1912, and Durango had its own Hollywood-style production company from 1915 to around 1920. But Hollywood soon seized the opportunity, and now sends crews back to the state for a lot of filming. Perhaps the situation could have been reversed if the state had developed its film commission earlier.

Federal, state, and local government in Colorado provides a major level of support service, not only to the citizens of the state, but throughout the region. And government is business in the state. The fact that government is big business in Colorado is easily demonstrated by its annual wages and salaries. All government in Colorado has a yearly payroll exceeding $5 billion.

Closely akin to government, but with a broader-based and more direct support role for business service, has been higher education in Colorado. The network of higher educational facilities—universities, public and private colleges, community colleges, and business and trade schools—has played a vital role in making Colorado the service center for the region.

Two of the largest Colorado universities—the University of Colorado and the University of Denver—have targeted a large percentage of their programs to support business in the state and the region. Private colleges, such as Regis, with campuses in Denver and Colorado Springs, also provide business support programs.

The University of Colorado, with four campuses comprising 16 schools and colleges, is also one the largest employers in the state, with a payroll of 15,500 full- and part-time jobs. It is a billion-dollar industry in its own right, and brings more than $300 million annually into the economy for out-of-state sources.

CU's programs in support of high technology manufacturing and medicine will be reviewed in other chapters, but its direct support to business and commerce of the region is also substantial. Its main campus at Boulder, and campuses at Denver's Auraria Higher Education Center and Colorado Springs offer more than business-related curricula. The facilities and the faculty and students are vital resources to the business community of Colorado.

Beyond the comprehensive business education programs on the three campuses offered by the Graduate School of Business Administration and the College of Business and Administration, these facilities provide the main economic data resource for the state's business planners. CU provides the brainpower for the important annual Business Outlook Conference, co-sponsored by the state's Division of Commerce and Development, and used extensively in development decisions in all sectors of the economy.

For existing business, CU provides an Executive MBA program for continuing education, with the average age of the upwardly mobile, high-achiever in the classes being 38 years. The university also offers clinics designed by business, industry, and government to meet special needs of the economic community. Starting with a base in its excellent mathematics program, a special program referred to as "realities of real-world problem solving" was designed to meet specific needs in the rapidly changing world of business and technology. This program has included special clinics on manpower planning and employment of the future, mathematics of portfolio planning and analysis, and supercomputing and robotics. An offshoot of the program is the development of a Computational Mathematics Institute planned for the Denver campus to meet needs of the near future, such as supercomputing, environmental science, and computer science.

Like the specific business support programs offered at the University of Colorado, the University of Denver's College of Business Administration implements its educational program with applied special projects to underwrite the changing needs in various sectors of the region's economy.

Each year 100 internships provide business graduate students and undergraduates work experience in the business community, and DU's Small Business Institute is one of the region's primary training centers for the next generation of business managers. The business college at the university provides ongoing research programs such as the Finance Research Group and the Center for Business and Economic Forecasting. Economic forecasting for the entire Rocky Mountain Region is provided for both government and business decision makers and offers access to the highly sophisticated data resources developed at the center. The school works directly with area business entities in developing course work through its Center for Management Development in such fields as communications, marketing, management development, financial management, computer literacy, and other outreach programs required by businesses. A unique Weekend College was developed to offer undergraduate degrees to women in business, and an Urban Observatory program was designed to solve community problems in the changing society of the region.

The University of Denver Law School reaches the business community through special programs involving business law, taxation, and the other legal support systems needed by commerce and industry.

The university's Denver Research Institute, the Center for Studies in Public Communications, the Graduate School of Social Work, and the Graduate School of International Studies all design their programs around emerging needs in the changing public and private sectors of the economy.

If government and higher education demonstrated that Colorado was a good place to

Colorado provides the facilities, the skilled people power, and the support systems to serve many segments of the regional economy. A western-wear fashion show is held for buyers from across the nation. Photo courtesy of Denver Merchandise Mart

PROFILE

The Summit Group, Inc.
Retaining Colorado's Human Resources

Of the various resources of Colorado, more and more corporate and institutional employers are identifying the state's skilled and motivated workers as the most important.

With the employee thus identified as a key factor in the increasingly competitive national and international marketplace, a unique human resource management company is striving to assure that Colorado retains its best workers.

The Summit Group, Inc., founded in 1981 with a primary mission of assisting companies and individuals in all areas of human resource management, has grown from a Denver-based company to a national and even international consulting service. Their attention to the needs of the employer and the employee during times when layoffs are necessary has not only softened the impact of unemployment, but has positioned thousands of workers back into the work force.

The Summit Group, with a staff of nine service professionals and 27 in its temporary service pool (Summit Staffing), concentrates its expertise in three major human resource areas: (1) corporate outplacement, (2) individual career continuation programs, and (3) human resource management.

Small and medium-size firms, as well as some of the Rocky Mountain Region's largest companies, have retained the Summit Group when cuts in work force were created due to fluctuations in the region's dynamic economy.

The Summit Group works closely with corporate management and internal personnel managers to make layoffs or reductions-in-force less painful to the company.

At the time a reduction-in-force is first anticipated, the group of experts moves rapidly into the client organization to provide a complete program aimed at getting the employees back to work. In many cases jobs can be waiting before the termination.

"Career displacement is one of the most complex and often traumatic experiences a family can face," notes William E. Mason, Summit Group's president. "We see people who are competent and who, for no reason of their own, are faced with the loss of a career position, disruption of family, and all the related serious personal and professional problems. This person may be a brilliant professional or technician, but have no idea how to begin the search for a new position. We tell this person the day he is terminated that he has a 'new job', and that job is finding a job.'"

Summit Group's programs are more sophisticated than those of placement or search organizations. All the basic support systems, from resumes to target interviews, are provided; but The Summit Group goes further to provide support in retraining (in the case of job obsolescence), and in personal counseling in the myriad details of career change. The group stays with the client for a year after the initial contact, even if a new job is found immediately. Recently, The Summit Group has expanded its corporate outplacement services to provide similar service to individual professionals and managers.

"Colorado is a state that has historically drawn the best and most skilled people," says Mason. "Some sectors of the economy are in transition, and a dynamic economy is always subject to vagaries. We feel that one of our real services to Colorado business and the motivated Colorado employees is to make sure these valuable people remain here. We do not want to see an exodus of this resource. After all, our people and our skilled managerial and technical work force really are among the state's finest assets."

The Summit Group, a leading-edge human resource firm, is rapidly becoming another important asset to the businesses and institutions of Colorado.

The Summit Group has developed a lead role in Colorado's service industry by helping to keep the state's valued human resources fully employed.

The world is getting the message from Colorado. A leading state in the development of telecommunications systems, microwave is used to remove the barriers once posed by the high Rockies. Photo by Gary Milburn, Tom Stack & Associates

centralize services, private enterprise did not lag in capitalizing on the advantages of the prime location and its supporting systems.

An Exploding Service Industry

Business and professional services operating out of Colorado provide every type of modern support needed for the mountain and plains states, with a combined population of about 20 million people. The region is one of America's fastest growing, and the growth in Colorado's service industry sector is keeping pace.

Centralization in Colorado of the computer and data processing, telecommunications, and information gathering and handling services for the 13 states in the region has provided a great impetus to growth in the business services of the state, because most modern business and economic development support services now rely heavily on these communications services. The advent of the so-called "information age" was nowhere more dramatic than in the emerging energy-rich mountain region, because the new technologies brought down the last great development barriers created by the region's vast distances.

This change was apparent even before the full extent of the computer and telecommunication revolution was clear. One of America's fastest growing industries, cable television, literally had its birth in the region.

While more densely populated centers of the Nation had the luxury of competitive television stations representing all networks, a void existed in the Rocky Mountain Region in areas outside the very largest cities. Pioneers of the cable industry saw this void as a profit potential; and not only the first, but some of today's largest cable and satellite operations had their beginnings in Colorado. Three of the

PROFILE

American Color Corporation
Expanding Communications Horizons

Graphic colors help communicate, and American Color is providing the service that is making Colorado the telecommunications center of the Rockies.

The rapidly expanding role of Colorado as the communications center for the Rocky Mountain West has seen the introduction of sophisticated graphics techniques in the American printing industry, and American Color Corporation has become a strong part of this growing sector of the economy.

Founded in 1975 in Phoenix by Doug Brazell, American Color now has 10 plants located in six states, with an eleventh plant opening in 1986. The company has become a leader in the pre-press color service business in the Rocky Mountain and western states; and provides color separations and related services to printers, advertising agencies, publishers and catalog businesses on a nationwide basis. The company has been heavily involved with the lithographic process, but expanded into the gravure marketplace in 1981. Its rapid growth continues to be linked to the lithographic and gravure printing processes. In recent years the use of color illustrations in all types of publications has greatly expanded.

American Color Corporation's manufacturing plants are modern and its personnel skilled in the leading edge processes of state-of-the-art, high-tech electronic equipment. Its staff is augmented by special management and technical talent a job may require.

Transportation is a key to the fast-paced graphics industry, and American Color's plants are situated within minutes of major airport facilities, such as Stapleton International in Denver. Its management system, with working plant managers at each plant location, permits projects to be moved from plant to plant to take advantage of specific time requirements and special production facilities. Identical materials and process methods are used at all plants so the interchange of work in process can be effected smoothly and efficiently.

With a sales force of 34 full-time technical and service-oriented graphics specialists from diverse backgrounds, the company offers its clients flexibility when specific expertise is needed to solve a client's color process problems.

American Color has established a close working relationship with its customers, the customers' clients, and the trade associations representing all links in the printing industry chain. Personnel from American Color conduct audio-visual technical training programs and seminars to update their clients. To assist printers, the company's sales force and outside consulting specialists hold seminars, sponsored by American Color Corporation, on how to sell innovative new printing color processes to their customers.

Management personnel from American Color are actively involved, either on committees or as board members, on 10 graphic arts national trade associations. The ongoing education and development of key personnel from the company assures that American Color continuously upgrades its own capabilities in the rapidly advancing technology of the color printing industry.

With a growing base of customers across the nation and accounts in nearly every state, American Color provides its services to every section of the printing and publications industry.

American Color's application of high technology in the color separation and pre-press processing field, combined with emphasis on advanced training and retention of its craftsmen, has earned the company an important role in Colorado's growing position as a leading center in the emerging communications and information age.

top U.S. cable companies are headquartered in Colorado, including Tele-Communications, American Televison and Communications Corporation, and United Cable Television. Four others with Colorado headquarters are in the nation's top 100 cable systems.

The efficiency and speed of communication brought about by computerization of business, and the subsequent technology advancements in business telecommunications have been another boon to business development in the huge region. With its headquartering support system already in place, Colorado became the obvious choice for the service centers in those industries.

Denver and its neighboring metropolitan counties were the first to capitalize on the fledgling high-tech innovations; but increasingly, this growth industry has found that other regional activity centers in the state offer similar advantages. Business services alone employ more than 70,000 Coloradans, and the number of service-oriented businesses exceed even the number of retailing establishments in most major cities in the state. The majority of these service establishments provide direct support for government, manufacturing, and the natural resource development industries located throughout the multistate area.

Denver has the largest number of service firms (6,600), because it is the recognized socioeconomic capital of the region as well as the capital city of the state. Government-business services are closely tied. Arapahoe County, with its giant office parks and the headquartering centers in Aurora, Englewood, and Littleton, has nearly 3,000 firms in the service industries sector; and Colorado Springs, which is emerging as a national aerospace center, is close behind with over 2,600 service firms.

Other Front Range business support and service centers with between 1,000 and 2,000 service firms each include, Adams County, Boulder County, and Jefferson County.

The geographical location of other cities in Colorado and their historic roles in providing support to agriculture and energy industries is also causing the relatively new "service industry boom" to spread over the state. Grand Junction, as a primary service center for Colorado's Western Slope, and parts of Utah and Wyoming, has more than 800 firms listed in the service industry category. Fort Collins and Greeley provide similar service support to northeastern Colorado and portions of Wyoming and Nebraska, and have more than 2,000 firms listed in the service category.

In the southwestern part of the state in the Durango-Cortez area, service is provided to the Four Corners area of Colorado-New Mexico-Arizona-Utah by nearly 500 companies in the business of supplying services. And Pueblo, with over 800 service-type firms, provides similar support to a large section of southern Colorado and into northern New Mexico. There are a number of other Colorado cities with a substantial number of business service firms offering similar capacity for their section of the state, including Montrose-Delta, Glenwood Springs, Aspen, Breckenridge, La Junta-Rocky Ford-Las Animas, and the Fort Morgan-Sterling area.

Serving the financial and professional needs in the age of telecommunications still requires the personal touch. Photo courtesy of United Banks

PROFILE

AT&T
Introducing the New Telecommunications Era

With a tradition firmly based in history, the communications pioneering AT&T continues to play a leading role in making the information age a reality. As one of the state's largest employers, AT&T today is launching a sizable part of its international effort to "universalize" this new high technology information era.

AT&T operates highly diversified telecommunications programs, including manufacturing and service functions, at scores of locations throughout Colorado. AT&T employs nearly 9,000 Coloradans with a state payroll exceeding $400 million.

As a part of the international AT&T corporation, which employs approximately 337,000 people worldwide, several of AT&T's major operations are located in Colorado. Many of its Colorado-based functions serve a vast area of the Rocky Mountain West, and states beyond this region.

While the company has a large part of its operations headquartered in the several cities within the Denver Metropolitan Region, it also has important functions in almost every section of the state. Regional headquarters for AT&T Network Systems, the largest single supplier of telecommunications equipment in the world, is located in Aurora. This regional center serves U S West, the Bell operating companies, and subsidiaries by providing sales, customer services, specialized engineering, and installation services for a 14-state region.

AT&T Communications & Information Systems in Denver provides domestic and international long distance services, and other special services to business and residential users. In addition, this unit develops, manufactures, sells, and services a full range of telecommunications and computer products and services in the movement and management of information.

The Information Systems Laboratories in Denver provide much of the research and development of AT&T's large business systems, and the Regional Network Operations Center in Denver is one of seven regional centers monitoring AT&T's entire network throughout the country.

Two operator assistance facilities are located in Denver and another facility is located in Colorado Springs providing assistance to residence and business customers.

Marketing and sales offices are located conveniently throughout the state, as well as 15 AT&T Phone Centers. The Residence Business Office is located in Denver.

The National Customer Support Center in Denver provides technical support for new business products on a nationwide, round-the-clock basis. The Customer Programming Services Center is one of 10 facilities nationwide offering customized software design, applications support, technical consulting, and on-site customer training. A regional governmental relations office is also located in Denver.

An AT&T Technical Education Center in Golden is the regional advanced technical and managerial training center for service employees, and a National Training Center in Aurora provides a strong curriculum of product, sales, and management training for sales and marketing personnel.

AT&T's Corporate Data Center, located in Aurora, is the largest single first-class mailing facility in the United States handling all Information Systems billings for residence customers in 27 states.

The big company is more than just big business in Colorado. AT&T's employees are active in civic and cultural organizations, and its contributions to health, education, social action, and cultural programs in Colorado exceed a half million dollars annually.

AT&T Executive Conference Center allows customers to try the company's various telecommunications and computer equipment. Photo by Joel Grimes Photography

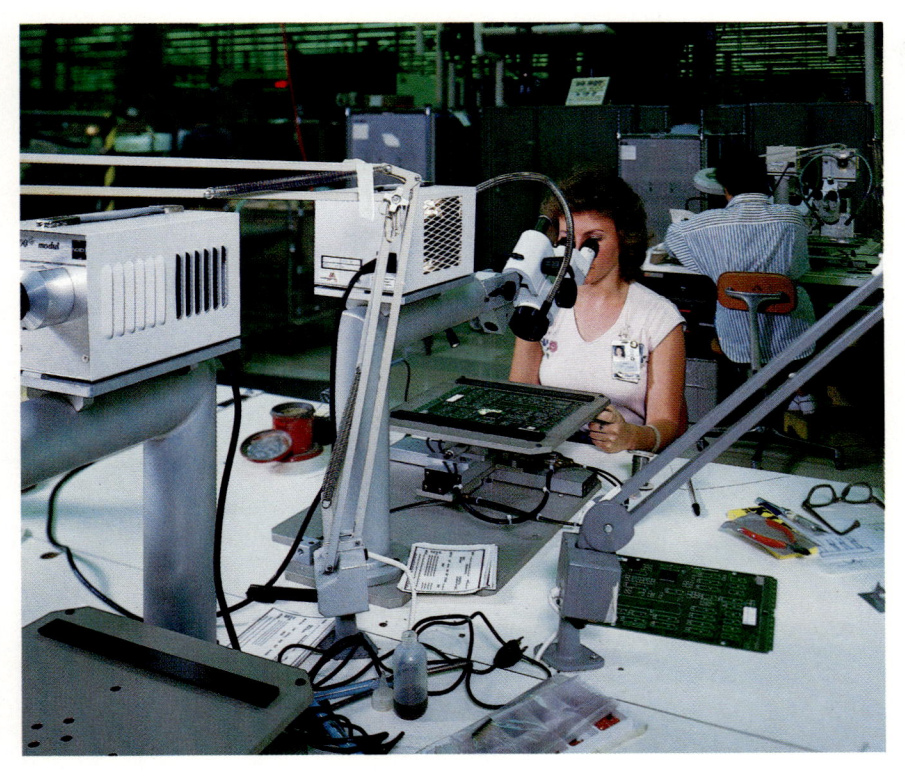

Accuracy is so critical in this AT&T facility that the work must be done under a microscope. Photo courtesy of AT&T

The types of business support services cover a wide variety of economic sectors. The visitor industry, transportation, health care industry, banking and finance, and real estate are all service-related industries, but because of their size and impact on the Colorado economy they are covered in more detail in other chapters.

Employment totals and numbers of service establishments in the state also include personal services firms providing support facilities such as laundries, personal grooming, automobile, and household repairs. But of primary importance to the overall economic development in the state are those firms providing direct support to business and industrial sectors of the economy, both within Colorado and to other states looking to Colorado for these services.

Direct business services, such as advertising, computer and data processing, telecommunications, legal and personnel services, and others, account for the largest single sector of the service-related employment.

Colorado businesses are notably "small business" in character, with about 90 percent of all private enterprise employment in the state in firms with fewer than 100 employees. For this reason the businesses in Colorado and throughout the Rocky Mountain region depend heavily on the availability of solid support from the business service consultants and professionals in the major activity centers of the state. Few companies can afford their own in-house public relations and advertising, legal, information handling and data processing, or personnel training and employee benefits departments. They look to an exceptionally sophisticated cadre of professional consultants in these specialized fields.

Because of this opportunity, Colorado has evolved into a business service center for the Rocky Mountain and Plains States with a degree of professionalism and talents one would expect to find only in areas with much greater population densities. Another reason the state is able to attract the needed skills is the high quality of life offered such professionals by the natural amenities in Colorado.

Public relations and advertising agencies headquartered in several Colorado cities service accounts throughout the region with account executives and creative support staffs, many of whom have worked for some of America's leading New York, Chicago, or Los Angeles agencies. In addition to those agencies that are regional offices for national and international companies, most smaller firms are associated with networks spanning the country. There are nearly 200 advertising firms in Colorado offering services in print, radio, television, and outdoor advertising. A network of approximately 225 firms provides the commercial photographers, photo finishers, graphic artists, product packaging and labeling specialists, and direct-mailing handlers required to support the advertising industry. Colorado also has one of the largest printing industries for any state its size in the country, with more than 900 printing and publishing firms located in cities and towns across the state.

National publications, radio, television, and other advertising media also focus efforts to cover the entire Rocky Mountain and Plains Region from sales offices located in the Denver Metropolitan Area. The national BusinessWire news service has its regional headquarters in Denver, linking business and industry of the region with all major national business news outlets and financial services.

In addition, the state offers nearly 850 professional firms providing management and administrative consulting, economic and social research, and specialized personnel consulting services.

Personnel training and search firms, secretarial services, employee benefits, compensation planning and consulting services, and a host of management and support services, are provided in this sector of the economy. Blueprinting and photocopying, and other technical and highly specialized business services are available in most of Colorado's activity centers.

PROFILE

General Communications, Inc.
Setting a Pace in the Communications Era

Colorado is frequently cited as a bellwether state for economic trends in the emerging information age, and a Denver-based group of publications is setting the pace for the modern role of the print media in this new era.

General Communications, Inc., founded in 1978 to publish a weekly business newspaper, has expanded to one of the Rocky Mountain Region's most prestigious magazine publishing companies. Its *Denver Magazine*, *Denver Business*, *Vail Magazine*, and *Development Sales Catalog* are serving to inform, educate, and entertain Coloradans with a combined statewide and regional circulation approaching 80,000 and a readership of over 250,000.

Growing rapidly with Colorado's role as the communication center for the Rockies, General Communications, Inc. has been cited three years in a row in *Inc. Magazine's* annual selection of the 500 Fastest Growing Private Companies in the United States.

Publisher A. Emmet Stephenson Jr. has assembled a staff of editorial, marketing, graphic arts, and publication management professionals that consistently earn for the publications the highest national and regional awards for editorial and artistic excellence.

The flagship magazine of the publications group is *Denver Magazine*, which serves a primary audience in the metropolitan Denver area. A full-color contemporary magazine, *Denver Magazine* provides in-depth looks into the area's government, politics, sports, entertainment, and changing social scene. It also contains humor, art, and dining columns, all of which inform readers how best to enjoy the good life in the Mile High City.

Denver Magazine has been honored with Maggie Awards for editorial and artistic excellence, the White Award (city and regional competition), as well as Starwards for editorial and photographic achievement.

Denver Business Magazine, also a full-color monthly publication, is rapidly becoming one of the leading information sources for the dynamic Colorado business and financial community. It is the magazine for the regional executive and financially sophisticated investor, reaching a readership with an annual household income of $149,500. Editorially, it covers the business scene of the Rocky Mountains, from in-depth information on economic trends to inside looks at individual companies. The magazine has also won numerous awards for editorial and artistic excellence, including awards from the Association of Area Business Publications, and Starwards for general excellence.

Vail Magazine is the oldest and most prestigious magazine serving Colorado's premier ski resort. The magazine's editorial coverage has grown with the Vail Valley to cover the new Beaver Creek area, and now enjoys a circulation of 30,000. *Vail Magazine* has one of the highest demographic profiles of any magazine in the United States.

Development Sales Catalog is the leading printed data base publication serving the residential development industry. Hand delivered to every realtor in Metropolitan Denver, the catalog has become the essential reference book for realtors who market new homes.

General Communications, Inc. goes beyond reporting on life and business in the Rockies. As a community-based publications group, the magazines support and participate in the communities they serve, sponsoring or co-sponsoring such events as the Colorado Harvard Business School Club of Business Statesman Dinner, Take Stock In Denver Art, Colorado Cream Music and Arts Festival, Douglas County Development Awards, Vail Institute Bluegrass Festival & Balloon Race, World Forum at Vail, and seminars to realtors on selling new homes. General Communications people are active officers, directors, and committee members of numerous community and civic organizations.

The General Communications publications group provides an expanding communications service, as Colorado leads the Rocky Mountain West into the new information era.

Keeping the public informed of the dynamic economy and events of the Rockies is a challenge accepted by the magazines published by General Communications.

Denver is also the regional legal center for the Federal District Courts, and with the state and local courts and the corporate headquartering for the mineral industry, the legal services sector of the company likewise serves the multistate area. Nearly 2,000 Colorado firms provide legal services in the state, employing almost 10,000 people. For the same reasons, the accounting, auditing, and bookkeeping services provided in the state serve a larger region than just the Colorado economy, with more than 1,000 accounting firms in Colorado. The unusually large number of accounting firms for a state this size is due to the regional focus of business support services located in the state.

Telecommunications Closes the Distance

One of the reasons business service activities have successfully centered operations in Colorado to service a vast area of over 1.2 million square miles in territory (larger in geographical size than all of Western Europe), has been the extraordinary technological advancements in the telecommunications and computer industries. The advancement in communications and information technology has contributed directly to the "new boom" of the 1980s—the boom in business service industries.

The communications sector of the state's economy is the largest single employer among the utilities, with nearly 27,000 workers in Colorado. This large base is due to headquartering of the major telephone and long-distance service companies that cover the large western states area.

Voice communications remains the principal service provided in support of business, manufacturing, and commerce of the region. Increasingly important to Colorado's role as the support center for the region are the other types of information and data processing, data storage, and data transfer now being developed by the revolutionary telecommunications industry.

Denver Business magazine, in a special report on the leading position Colorado is taking in this relatively new industry, summed up the emerging role of telecommunications: "Not since the Industrial Revolution of the 19th century have the winds of change blown so strong, altering human endeavor with every gale. Telecommunications is more than a buzzword for the 1980s; it is perhaps the simple herald of an age where technological advancement is limited only by the imagination."

Not only has this technological revolution altered a great part of the manufacturing character of Colorado, but it has placed Colorado on the leading edge of the new Information Age. Colorado, already the region's catalyst for the cable television industry, was a direct beneficiary of the deregulation of the nation's telephone industry. AT&T spun-off one of its largest regions to the Colorado-based U S West, which is parent to the

Telecommunications development projects centered in Colorado are effecting changes in the way the nation does business. Photo courtesy of AT&T

PROFILE

Image-Corp
Graphics Technology Enters New Era

In this new information age the competition for delivery of memorable messages becomes greater, and a Denver-based company is combining the latest advances in graphics technology with the best from the artist's creativity to make lasting impressions.

Image-Corp, an innovative graphics design firm that specializes in the design of special effects for print, slides, film, and video, was founded in 1982 by two young graphic arts experts who recognized the importance of bringing the advertising trade into the new age of information.

David Hoffman, a commercial artist by training, and Steve Samuelson, a professional photographer, created the new design studio on the concept that "Technology is a natural extension of an artist's creativity."

Image-Corp, which was developed around the latest technology being introduced into the field of graphic arts, has grown to a million dollar a year design business since its inception. Its leap to success in the highly competitive field of advertising design is attributed by its founders to two words: "high technology."

The young artists-entrepreneurs invested heavily in computers and sophisticated optical printing equipment to make photographic transparencies. They can turn actual photography into surrealist events that can catch the attention of the reader/viewer amidst any field of competing messages. With the in-house capability to combine the work of artists, photographers, and designers through computer enhancement or restructuring, Image-Corp considers themselves to be "designers for modern industry." The company serves clients in the widest range of products and services, and its client list of more than 200 local, national, and international firms spans practically every sector of the economy.

New methods of using art and technology are providing the company's clients better access to the public whether in introducing products to the marketplace or in communicating important information.

An example of the challenges the company will accept is the artwork on the dust jacket of this book. A design representative of all the elements of Colorado, including the industry of the cities and towns, the recreation and solitude of the mountains, the history and agribusiness of the plains, and the splendor of the skies, seemed impossible to accomplish in any one photograph. Image-Corp combined these elements into one photographic illustration using sophisticated technology in place of the paint brush.

Image-Corp has more than its growth record and impressive client list to attest to the success of its concepts in combining graphic arts and high technology. In 1985 the company won international recognition for a three-projector slide show at the prestigious Photo-Kena in West Germany. Its "best of show" award came in competition with photographers and filmmakers from around the world.

As a group constantly exploring the new forms of technology available to the artists, Image-Corp offers its clients the leading edge in graphics techniques to solve their communications problems. Using print, slide, or video media, the company applies high-tech concepts in every media as well as offering wide capability through creative concepts in existing graphics forms. Image-Corp slide presentations, including a variety of formats, offer an outstanding communications vehicle for a company's internal and external communications needs. In the print media, Image-Corp also has been awarded recognition for its creative design programs, and at present is involved in such futuristic print graphics work as holography, a three-dimensional art form created with laser beams.

Combining art and high technology, Image-Corp is a leading graphics firm helping to establish Colorado as a telecommunications center for the Rockies.

There is nothing complicated about the information age when challenges are tackled by the skilled professionals in the Colorado work force. Colorado is one of the nation's leading locations for advanced telecommunications. Photo courtesy of U S West

Fiber optics are connecting the present with the future in telecommunications. Colorado has become an international center for the information age. Photo courtesy of U S West

largest and one of the strongest telephone service regions in America. MCI, one of the major long-distance service companies emerging after the split-up of the telephone system, also opted to headquarter its largest region in Colorado.

The advancements matching computer and telephone have finally closed the distance gap in the big western states, and all lines lead to the urbanized centers of Colorado. New technology such as faster and higher capacity transmission via lightwave systems using laser-generated light pulses now transmit voice, data, facsimile, and video communications through hair-thin fibers. Greater computer storage using optical disks is creating whole new business information systems never before affordable.

And Colorado firms are second to none in the world in quickly capitalizing on such technologies. An example was noted by international marketing and systems consultant John McIntosh, writing in *Colorado Computing* magazine in a 1986 edition: "Colorado is the center of one of the world's most exciting new technologies—optical disk." Six of the country's eight optical disk drive manufacturers are located in either Boulder or Colorado Springs. The magazine notes that the entire 70 volumes of the Encyclopedia Britannica can fit on one compact disk that currently holds 45 minutes of music.

In another new technological development, Mountain Bell, which is installing the "lightwave systems" for transmission, points to the increasing capacity for moving information. A company publication notes, "The entire contents of Webster's Third New International Dictionary—all 2,700 pages—could be transmitted over a single fiber in less than two seconds."

And these examples are only the tip of the telecommunications iceberg, with other technological services such as voice mail, electronic mail, satellite communications, "smart" phones, cellular mobile phones, voice and data transmission mixing, and a vast array of new computer and telephone services almost daily extending Colorado's role as a service center into new geographical areas and more types of business.

While Colorado is a leading manufacturing center with its share of computer and communications whiz kids manning its industries, the state is also a gathering place for the consulting know-how so vital to apply the new technology to practical use.

With the rapid advancements in communications technology, the importance to Colorado's fastest growing sector of the economy—the business service industries—has not begun to be measured.

But one of the primary reasons Colorado has become the service center for the region, and its cities and towns provide this vital regionwide service function, is rooted in a historic sector of the economy dating to the very earliest settlement of the region. Transportation provided Colorado with the first network for a modern and rapidly growing service industry, even when the region was little more than a mining-agriculture frontier in the mid-19th century.

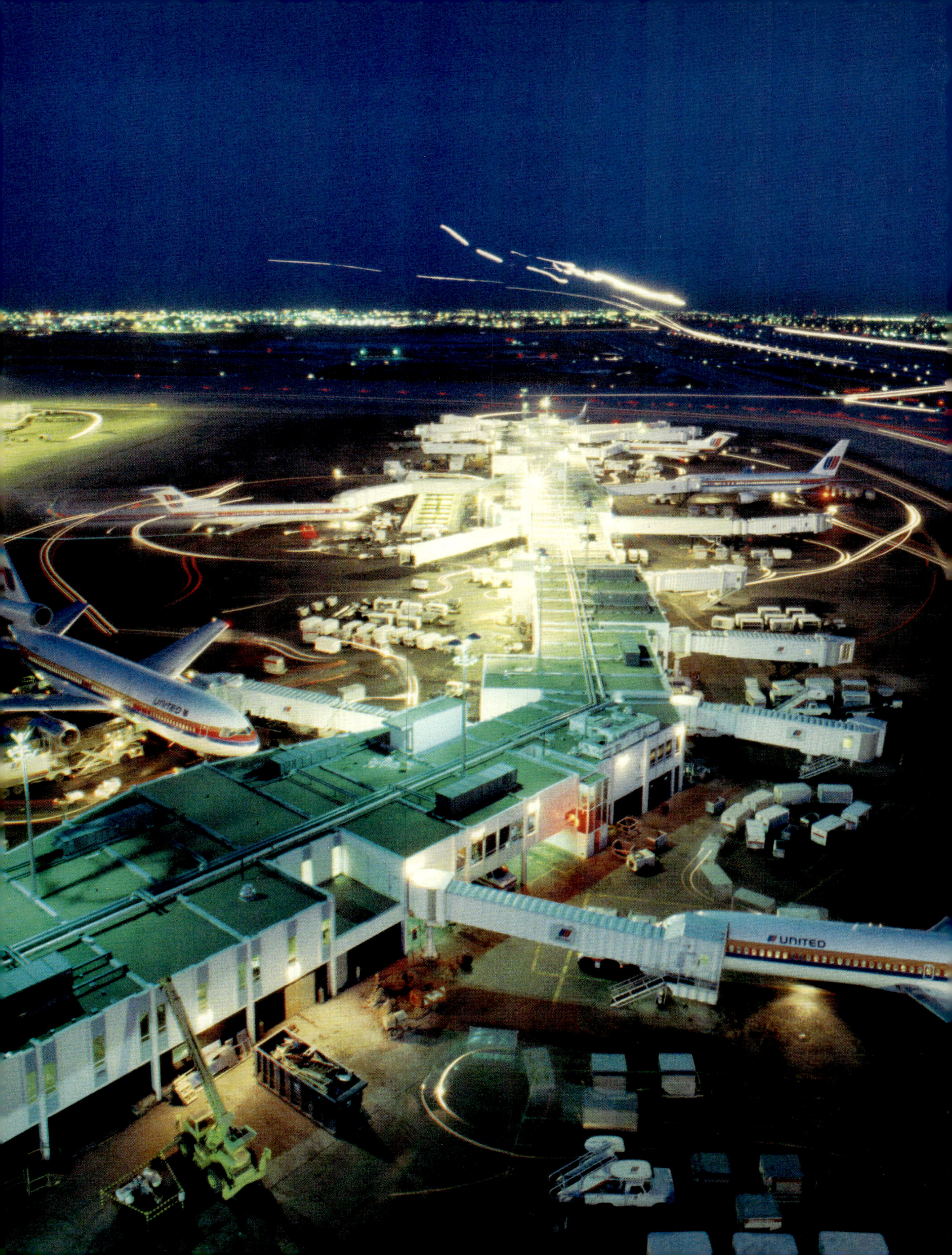
UNITED
UNITED

CHAPTER 6

Crossroads of the West
Transportation and Distribution

Colorado's strategic central location in the heart of the fastest growing sector of the United States, combined with a modern network of highways, rail lines, and airports, makes it the undisputed "crossroads of America's future."

The state's long expanse of plains and rugged spine of high mountains were once seen as barriers to development. It was only when transportation was brought to the land that the bountiful resources of Colorado began to open one of America's last great frontiers of opportunity.

Because of the difficulty in carving the roads and rail beds in the Rocky Mountains, transportation has never been taken for granted in Colorado. No single asset in the state is more essential to the health of the economy than transportation; and transportation is the subject of some of the state's greatest ongoing controversies.

Transportation in all its forms—highway, rail, and air—is literally the lifeline of every major sector of the modern economy. Air service and good roads are crucial to Colorado's gigantic tourism business. The rails and roads are imperative to the success of manufacturing and natural resource industries of agribusiness and mineral development. The major cities of Colorado providing the service and business support to the multistate region could not fulfill this role without efficient travel corridors to their service areas.

Employment in the various operating sectors of the state's transportation industry is sizable, estimated to be about 49,000 in 1986. While this is by no measure one of the larger employment sectors, it is one of the most important, because of the dependency of the whole economy on modern transportation.

Railroad transportation employs the fewest, with about 5,000 workers, and trucking and distribution the largest number in the transportation sector, at almost 20,000. Air transportation employs over 17,000 and is a growing employment area. All other types of non-government transportation employ about 7,200.

Despite some notable financial problems in continuing to provide an ever upgraded transportation system, Colorado's air, highway, and rail systems are the most modern in the Rocky Mountain region. Roads are higher and considerably more expensive to build. The major international airport at Denver, as well as local airports, are sophisticated in navigational equipment and runways. Its five Class 1 railroads and numerous smaller lines have been modernized, and remain the heavy workhorses of the farms, mines, and ranches, as well as some types of manufacturing.

As a result of the emphasis on good transportation, Colorado cities are the distribution centers and the wholesale outlets for much of the Rocky Mountain region and a good part of the adjoining plains states.

Rails Opened the West

Since Colorado's transportation story began with the railroads, this important segment of the state's mobility picture should be examined first. While railroads have lost their dominant role and much of the glamour of the era when they were "the only way to go," they remain very much alive and vital to the state's economy. Colorado cities, including Denver, Glenwood Springs, and Grand Junction, are still served by passenger rail via AMTRAK's east-west line connecting the U.S.

Stapleton International Airport is the transportation center for the Rocky Mountain West, and a hub of national and international flights. Photo by Margaret DeLuca, Peripheral Vision

The railroads of Colorado helped open the region to commerce and industry, and remain the backbone of heavy transportation. Photo by Joel Silverman

midwest to west coast cities.

But the real modern rail story in Colorado is related to its freight service.

Railroads brought Colorado up to speed with the rest of the developing West when cross-country lines joined in Denver in 1870. The great Transcontinental railroad had bypassed Colorado for an easier crossing of the Rockies west of Cheyenne, Wyoming. Even then the importance of transportation was apparent to community leaders, and local money was raised to build a 100-mile line from Denver to join Colorado with the nation's main line.

Within two decades more than 4,000 miles of narrow-gauge line was laid within Colorado. Almost every city or town in Colorado, except those new towns built since World War II, can trace the beginning of its growth to the day the railroad came to town. Except for a few rugged trails into the mining and timber camps, the mountain communities came to life when the narrow gauge arrived, because roads into the mountains were few. Even the spas, which became the resorts, depended on the rails. The state's first tourist attractions were mineral springs, discovered along the narrow gauge lines to the gold and silver mines, and the first tourists arrived by train.

When highways did begin to arrive, rail transportation lagged for a time. But in recent years, with such impetus as the energy boom in the 1970s and deregulation of rate structures, railroading in Colorado is experiencing a healthy comeback. The major railroads invested heavily in improving lines and equipment to meet the demands for coal hauling, and to compete favorably for the largest share of grain hauled from Colorado farms to ports for world marketing. World economic conditions in the energy and agriculture industries have slowed the resurgence of the railroad industry; but freed from restrictive regulation, the railroads are regaining their role in the state's economic picture.

Colorado shippers today enjoy three-day rail service to any major port city on the west coast, and a maximum of six-day service to the east coast. Two-day service to Dallas and Chicago is available.

While Denver is the main rail hub in the state, no major commercial area in the state is without rail service either from the Class 1 carriers or smaller railroads. Class 1 lines, the major interstate rail companies, also have major yard facilities at Grand Junction, Pueblo, Colorado Springs, and La Junta.

The Denver and Rio Grande Western Railroad, headquartered in Denver, is Colorado's home railroad, operating on about 1,140 miles of active line, plus additional trackage for switching, siding, and loading within the state. The Denver and Rio Grande serves Denver and Colorado Springs with tracks south to Pueblo and Trinidad, and west to the San Luis Valley. It serves western Colorado to Salt Lake City via the Royal Gorge from central Colorado, and via the Moffat Tunnel under the Rockies from Denver. The D&RG is a major coal hauler, and also hauls more than 2,000 cars a year each in petroleum, stone, and farm products.

The Union Pacific operates three main lines across Colorado, with 591 miles of main road and another 220 miles of rails in turnouts and yards. It operates the line from Denver to Cheyenne where westbound connections are made, and a line to Julesburg for eastern connections. A third direct route connects Colorado to Kansas City. Union Pacific is a major hauler of farm products, meat, and coal.

Burlington Northern is another of the Class 1 railroads serving Colorado, with a vital transportation role in the agriculture, food, and food processing industries. It operates 607 miles of Colorado main line, with service from Cheyenne through Fort Collins, Denver, and Colorado Springs to New Mexico and Texas. The Burlington Northern operates another major service from Denver to Chicago.

Pueblo is the hub for rail service in the southern part of the state. The Atchison, Topeka and Santa Fe, which operates nearly 500 miles of main line in Colorado, serves points both east and west. The Santa Fe is a major carrier of Colorado farm products and mineral ores.

The Missouri Pacific's western terminal is in Pueblo, with about 140 miles of main line, primarily serving the agriculture industry.

Colorado also has several smaller railroads operating to serve special transportation needs. The Cadillac & Lake City Railroad operates about 60 miles of track on an old section of Rock Island line hauling grain from the Limon area. The Colorado & Eastern operates on short trackage into eastern Colorado from Colorado Springs. Another short line, hauling grain in eastern Colorado, is the Kyle Line.

The Colorado & Wyoming is a specialty line primarily hauling coal in the Trinidad and Pueblo area for steel mill operations at C.F.&I.

The Great Western Railway Co., which at one time hauled only sugar beets from agriculture centers in Boulder, Weld, and Larimer Counties, was forced to diversify or close down when the Colorado sugar industry declined in the early 1980s. The little railroad with 56 miles of line wouldn't say die. Today it operates at a "small profit" hauling lumber, fertilizer, and a variety of other freight between Longmont, Loveland, and Eaton. Efforts to revitalize the sugar beet industry of Colorado could see this small line boom once again.

Colorado has another kind of railroad that is growing in popularity. The historic narrow-gauge lines of the 19th century are still running with larger passenger ridership than ever before. But the passengers are tourists, and the trips are to catch a view of Colorado wilderness unlike any vistas available from the highways.

The most popular of the tourist narrow-gauge railroads is the Durango-to-Silverton line, which covers 44 miles of some of Colorado's most spectacular mountain country. In the summer this little railroad is booked by reservation only. Not far away, in southern Colorado, is the Cumbres & Toltec Scenic Railway running from Antonito to Chama, New Mexico. Other tourist narrow-gauge trains still operating include the Georgetown

The railroads move the raw and refined natural resources of Colorado to markets across the nation and to ports for transshipment around the world. Photo by Joel Silverman

PROFILE

The Bench Advertising Company
Service to Transportation and Communities

When a private, for-profit company can also provide a valuable public service everyone is a winner, and a growing young Colorado company is making this public/private partnership a reality in the field of transportation service.

Bench Advertising Company provides more than 4,500 courtesy benches at municipal bus stops throughout the Denver Metropolitan Area and not only provides the convenience to public transit patrons but pays the cities it serves for the privilege. In exchange the company sells space on the bench backs to advertisers.

Beginning in his garage in 1978, Bench Ad President Rodger H. Pfeiffenberger found a formula for success that has not only grown into a profitable business, but saves the taxpayers of the region millions of dollars.

"You might say, it's a chance to literally support my community and my neighbors," quips Pfeiffenberger.

The business, which was joined by Rodger's engineer father Andrew in 1981, has steadily grown since its inception. Rodger states that the opportunity for the two to work together greatly expanded his vision for the company.

The company now provides the benches at bus stops in most of the metropolitan area cities and towns.

Bench-Ad contributes not only the service, which is avidly supported by the bus-using public, but pays tens of thousands of dollars each year in permit fees to the cities. The big dollar benefit to the public comes in the form of pure public service, because Bench-Ad not only constructs the concrete and wood seats but has a field team working five days a week to maintain the benches and the surrounding bus stop areas. Periodic inspections are made by Bench-Ad personnel to clean the seats and pick up around the sites. The company maintains several trucks, equipped with antifreeze and water spraying devices, and a full-time cleanup crew just to assure the sites are properly maintained. The crew not only repaints the benches, but mows and weeds around the sites in the summer.

The value of the service to the bus riders, particularly the elderly who are heavily dependent on public transit service, is incalculable. Pfeiffenberger, who serves as a volunteer on the Regional Transportation District's Transportation for the Elderly Committee, has a file cabinet filled with requests and testimonial letters in support of this public/private arrangement. Recently a citizens' group representing elderly residents who reside or use services in downtown Denver asked that benches be added in the Central Business District. City regulations forbid advertising on public right-of-way in the core city, but Bench-Ad surveyed the areas of need and installed the seats at its own expense with no hope of recovering its costs through advertising revenues.

"There was a need, and we felt it had to be met, in spite of the cost to the company," notes Pfeiffenberger. The company also provides advertising for community-wide humanitarian causes, and Pfeiffenberger philosophizes that such efforts are the firm's corporate citizenship responsibility.

When Rodger, with the help of his wife, began the operation in his garage, hand-mixing the concrete for the supports, sawing the lumber for the seats and backs, designing and having the advertising messages painted by hand, he had identified a business opportunity. But the pride of accomplishment for the growing company, which now employs over a dozen full-time personnel, was the fact that it was a business that could help others. Bench Advertising Company is a Colorado business that is community-oriented, and at the same time makes a profit in the best spirit of entrepreneurship.

Private-sector service to public transportation is offered by Bench-Ad in the Denver metro area, eliminating the high cost of waiting areas for taxpayers.

Amtrak serves Colorado from Chicago to several West Coast cities. The train trips through Glenwood Canyon are among the most scenic journeys in North America. Photo by Patricia E. Lucy, Stock Imagery

Loop Railroad, the Cripple Creek-Victor Narrow Gauge Railroad, and the Colorado Central Narrow Gauge Railway at Central City.

More modern tramways also serve tourists in summer months, including the Manitou Scenic Incline Railway, the Pikes Peak Cog Railway, and the Royal Gorge Scenic Railway. Dozens of aerial trams, many used to carry skiers up the slopes in winter, are open to tourists during the summer months, and are located at resort areas throughout the mountains.

The primary U.S. Department of Transportation rail test facility, located 25 miles east of Pueblo, offers testimony that the rail industry is far from a thing of the past. The Transportation Test Center, a 52-square-mile research and development facility, tests prototype rail systems for both freight and passenger travel. United States and Canadian railroads, public transit companies and agencies use the center for the development of new equipment and safety testing. The center has large-scale testing facilities unmatched in the Free World, and the rail transit equipment of the future is being designed and tested in this modern complex. It is managed by the Association of American Railroads.

Lanes in the Sky

Air service is as important to the future course of economic development in Colorado as the rail systems were to the founding pioneers.

In 1986, Colorado's airports and the commercial air carriers serving them booked approximately 32.4 million passenger trips. At that rate of travel every man, woman, and child in Colorado would have made 10 paid air trips per year. But the passengers are actually using Colorado air facilities from throughout the Rocky Mountain region, because the state—and particularly its principal international airport at Denver—is the air transportation hub for the inner-western United States.

Stapleton International Airport at Denver, which is served by 24 commercial airlines, accounts for most of the air travel, with about 29 million passengers using that facility each year. The airport is rated as the sixth busiest in the United States and the seventh busiest in the world. Stapleton is the only airport in North America that supports hub operations for three major airlines—United, Continental, and Frontier airlines. These three alone account for 424 departures each day.

Denver links the western United States through its modern Stapleton International Airport. An even bigger air center is being built for the future. Photo by Stewart M. Green

Stapleton International Airport, already the sixth busiest in the world, is the air hub of the vast Rocky Mountain region. The control tower is key to the efficient and safe regional service. Photo by Margaret L. DeLuca, Peripheral Vision

In addition, Stapleton is served by Air Midwest, American, Aspen, Braniff, Centennial, Delta, Eastern, Mexicana, Northwest Orient, Ozark, People Express, Piedmont, Pride, Republic, Rocky Mountain, Southwest, Trans-Colorado, Trans World, US Air, and Western.

Stapleton is not only the largest airport with the most service in the Rocky Mountain states, but one of the most important airports in the world. It truly is an international air-crossroad facility, and critical to the modern role Colorado plays as a headquarters center. With its approximately 29 million annual passengers, the big facility, seven miles from downtown Denver, is projected to carry twice that number of passengers before a new airport can be built. The present airport, which is expanded to near capacity on about 5,000 acres, is scheduled to be moved to a new 15,000-acre facility by 1995. That planned facility is further discussed in Chapter 11, "A Future Challenge."

To meet the needs of the present-day expansion in air transportation, which is growing in Colorado at a rate of 10 percent per year, $225 million was spent on improvements at Stapleton in the mid-1980s. This airport improvement program provided expansion of concourses, terminal areas, freight areas, baggage handling areas, and other support facilities.

While it is certainly the aviation hub of Colorado and the multistate region, Stapleton is not the only major commercial airport in

Doppler Radar to make the nation's airways safer is being field tested in Colorado. Photo by McAllister of Denver

Colorado. Other smaller airports with regularly scheduled interstate commercial service include Colorado Springs, Grand Junction, Pueblo, Gunnison (winter service only in 1986), and newer ports at Vail and Telluride. Additionally, regular commercial air service is provided at Alamosa, Aspen, Cortez, Durango, Lamar, Montrose, and Steamboat Springs-Craig (Hayden Airport).

Colorado has 219 airports with 88 fields open for public use. In 1980 Colorado was rated ninth among the states in the number of general aviation aircraft, with more than 4,500 registered. In addition to the regularly scheduled major and regional airlines serving Colorado, there are 45 call-and-demand air carriers with operations available in 77 cities and towns in Colorado.

The growth in popularity of skiing in Colorado is also creating a new emphasis on aviation. Commercial air carriers in the mid-1980s opened new interstate service direct to Colorado ski areas from Chicago, Dallas, Albuquerque, Phoenix, and Los Angeles. Gunnison's airport runway is scheduled to be expanded to 10,000 feet, and the airport is already receiving direct winter flights to serve the Crested Butte ski area provided by American Airlines from Dallas, Los Angeles, and Chicago. A new airport at Telluride was built primarily to match improvements at the existing ski area and a second Telluride ski area opened in 1985-86.

Grand Junction's modernized Walker Field is now advertising on the West Coast the advantages of flying the regular service provided to that city for easy access to all central Colorado ski areas and nearby Purgatory and Powderhorn. Sardy Field in Aspen remains one of the busiest ski airports in America, but is also a busy hub of commercial and executive aviation throughout the year. It is served by both Rocky Mountain and Aspen Airways all year, and Aspen is attracting winter direct service from Dallas and Houston. Yampa Valley Airport at Hayden serving Steamboat Springs resorts and year-round business activity in Steamboat and nearby Craig has winter flights from Dallas using Aspen Airways. Mesa Airlines provides winter service to Durango, and American West Airlines reported that its success with flights from Phoenix to Durango and Grand Junction would prompt it to expand service to other Colorado airports near ski areas in coming seasons.

As the deregulated airline industry continues changing to accommodate new demands and more competitive rate structures, impacts are felt in Colorado because of

PROFILE

Frontier Airlines
A History of Contributions to Colorado Transportation

Commercial aviation is pioneering the new frontier of the West just as the coming of the railroads opened the West to development a century ago, and much of Colorado's role as the air center of the Rockies was cemented by an airline company founded in the state.

As Frontier Airlines becomes a part of Colorado's transportation history, its role in helping to make Stapleton International the undisputed commercial aviation hub of the vast Rocky Mountain Region and western central United States should be recorded. A review of the history of Frontier is a chronology of the growth of commercial aviation in Colorado over the past 40 years.

The latest chapter in the aviation history of Colorado was written in July 1986, when United Airlines offered to acquire and absorb Frontier Airlines, bringing the combined Colorado aviation work force of the two airlines to 11,000. Because of the importance of aviation to the future development of Colorado and the Rocky Mountain states, it is appropriate that the merger would make an aviation company one of the largest single employers in Colorado and the 13-state Rocky Mountain Region.

The importance of aviation to the modern development of commerce and industry in Colorado can be traced to the immediate post-World War II period, and Frontier Airlines' predecessor was launched during that dawning of commercial aviation in the region in 1946. Denver-based Monarch Air Lines began service in November 1946, linking Denver with Durango via Colorado Springs, Pueblo, Canon City, and Monte Vista/Alamosa. The fleet consisted of five DC-3 aircraft, with a capacity of 21 passengers each. Unpressurized cabins required the new mountain airline to fly its planes around some of Colorado's tallest peaks, rather than over them.

In 1950, Monarch Air Lines merged with Arizona Airways of Phoenix and Challenger Airlines of Salt Lake City to form Frontier Airlines, and the regional carrier took its first step toward becoming a truly national airline. Frontier Airlines was serving

Soaring over the Colorado's Rockies, Frontier helped lower the mountain barrier to transportation as the new West opened to a high-tech future.

40 cities in seven states from Montana to the Mexican border. Within five more years Frontier had expanded to 28 additional cities, and by its 10th anniversary in 1956 was carrying over 1.5 million passengers a year.

Commercial aviation was becoming a major factor in the development of Colorado because of the sudden changes in the economy of the state. During 1956 such events as the opening of Martin Marietta's new aerospace plant were creating a new demand for fast and reliable air service between Denver and its soon-to-emerge new national marketplace.

Marking its 20th anniversary in 1966, Frontier Airlines became the first regional airline to introduce Boeing 727 tri-jets, seating 99 passengers and greatly expanding aviation service to the cities and towns of the Rocky Mountain Region. The following year, Frontier broke out of the regional airline category with the acquisition of Central Airlines of Fort Worth. Its routes then extended to 14 states, and by 1968 Frontier was an all-jet airline.

The 1970s saw commercial aviation soar into one of the most important industries of the Rocky Mountains, and Frontier assisted at every stage of this growth, through its commitment to extended service at Stapleton International Airport. When airlines were deregulated in 1984, Frontier was serving 89 cities in 20 states, Canada, and Mexico, and by the end of the 1970s Frontier had expanded its U.S. service and added more international service to cities in Canada and Mexico.

Celebrating its 35th anniversary in 1981, Frontier Airlines had become one of the big three carriers—along with United Airlines, which would ultimately bid to acquire Frontier—that were to make Stapleton International Airport one of the top commercial air centers in the world. In that first full year of the decade of the 1980s, Frontier boarded 4.9 million passengers, bringing its historical total of passengers served since its founding in 1946 to more than 61 million passengers.

The dramatic growth of commercial aviation during the decade of the 1980s propelled Stapleton International Airport to a position of sixth busiest airport in the nation by the mid-1980s. In later 1985, Frontier became a wholly owned subsidiary of People Express Inc. Frontier, with its expanding services and passenger boardings, along with a score of other lines serving the busy Stapleton center, was providing the kind of air service required by the high-tech industry emerging in the state, but deregulation and other industry problems were dramatically changing the scene for numerous air carriers.

Frontier lead the way in aviation for the West from its headquarters in Colorado. Passengers are served aboard People Express, which bought Frontier.

In less than two score years from 1946 to 1986, when Frontier was to observe its 40th anniversary, commercial aviation had come of age in Colorado not only as a major industry unto itself, but as one of the most important services to the development of the whole economy. The colorful history of airlines is in fact an important part of the modern history of Colorado, and definitely a vital part of its future. Frontier's permanent place in this history and its contribution to the future cannot be forgotten. The importance of its historic role in establishing air service will not be diminished.

Stapleton International Airport, and its new facility planned for the late 1990s, would be only so much concrete without the dedication of the airline industry to providing the safe, convenient, and economically viable service the region needs. Even the construction costs of the airports in the region, while underwritten by revenue bonds and federal funds, actually are paid for by the airlines and the passengers they serve. Commercial aviation is not only vital to the entire economic infrastructure of the region because of its service support, but as a deregulated free enterprise transportation system that contributes most of the revenue to provide the public facilities used by the industry.

Denver serves the national and international air transportation needs for most of the 13 Rocky Mountain and Plains States.

Because the major airlines have a tradition of high quality service to the Colorado and Rocky Mountain Region, air passenger increases, expansion of service, new transportation products, and continued support for the business and individual passenger are assured. The aviation future of Colorado and the Rockies also is assured by the commitment of the airline industry leaders and their thousands of employees.

Commercial aviation in 1986 and the future is the cornerstone of economic progress just as passenger rail service opened Colorado to settlement in the 1870s.

the high level of dependancy on air transportation. The local air services are also subject to the changes.

Colorado's regional air carriers are important to the state's transportation needs, and air passenger service within the state continues at a growing pace. Rocky Mountain Airways and Aspen Airways, both founded in Colorado and headquartered in Denver, each carry more than a half-million passengers a year. Both local airlines have been rated in the top 15 of the 175 regional carriers in the United States by the Regional Airline Association in Washington, D.C.

Trans-Colorado, which was founded in Gunnison and is now headquartered in Colorado Springs, is a rapidly growing regional carrier with annual passenger counts exceeding 120,000.

These regional carriers are bringing more air service to Colorado cities and towns, which are building and improving airport facilities as demands for the faster service grow.

Because of the region-wide nature of business centered in Colorado, executive and general aviation is important to all the major towns and cities in the state. One of the state's busiest is Centennial Airport, operated by Arapahoe County. That major facility, which was rated as the fifth busiest executive aviation port in America in the early 1980s, has nearly 1,000 aircraft based there. Its importance as an international business airport was noted in 1985 when the U.S. Customs Service agreed to provide inspection service at the bustling terminal. The airport completed nearly $3 million in a major expansion in 1985, constructing a 150-foot-high airport control tower and runway improvements.

Another major general aviation center for the Front Range is Jefferson County Airport, with more than 500 aircraft based at the airport. In addition to these major executive airports, and those airports with commercial service as well as centers for executive aviation, large executive aviation operations are conducted at airports located in Craig, Fort Collins, Sterling, Eagle, Leadville, Salida, and Canon City.

Air transportation has become an increasingly important part of the future of emerging cities in Colorado. Good aviation service is critical to the state's economic future in high technology manufacturing and to its expanding role as the service center of the region. And rail transportation will always be important in a region playing a leading role as one of the nation's agricultural, mineral, and energy resource centers.

But Colorado roads and highways are the state's real day-to-day lifelines, with this transportation network supplying the support for most sectors of the economy, the livelihood for its people, and the greatest access to all the things that contribute to the quality of life in the state. No man-made resource is more critical, and at the same time controversial, than Colorado roads. Those who would continue the orderly development of the state's resources work hardest for the development and maintenance of good roads. Those who would halt growth often seek to do so by stopping the roads.

The High Highways

In Colorado it can truly be said that in most cases "getting there is half the fun," because its highways and roads are the highest and offer some of the most spectacular vistas in America. With more than $2 billion invested in its highways and roads, Colorado virtually depends on these arteries for its existence. Just driving the highways and roads of Colorado can be a vacation experience; because, with the exception of relatively short stretches on the eastern plains of the state, the motorist is never denied the sight of truly breathtaking mountainscapes. The motorist will find few long stretches of Colorado roads, U.S. highways, or interstate highways without the "scenic overlook" pullouts built into the system just for viewing.

The state has 25 road and highway locations with points over 10,000 feet in altitude. It boasts the highest automobile road in the world—Mt. Evans State Road 5 at 14,264 feet. An automobile road also winds to the top of Pikes Peak at 14,110 feet. In the Rocky Mountain National Park the Trailridge Road west of Estes Park on U.S. 34 climbs to

Because of the vastness of the region, considerable business is transacted via executive aviation, and Colorado's network of airports puts the executive traveler in close distance to the marketplaces. Photo by Joel Silverman

Colorado's back roads and mountain trails are invitations to scenic wonders awaiting motorists. Photo by Ron Phillips, Phillips Photographics

12,183 feet. One of the most spectacular drives is over Independence Pass, at 12,095 feet, on Colorado 82 between Aspen and Leadville. All these roads are closed in winter by many feet of snow. But from any of these, and more than a score of others, views of mountains marching off in all directions below the high highways await the motorist.

Most of the high passes, which are actually the low points on the Continental Divide, are open year-round. Numerous major highways cross the Rocky Mountains in Colorado, including I-70, U.S. 6, 24, 34, 40, 50, 160, and 285. The passes bear names like Slumgullion, Lizard Head, Rabbit Ears, Muddy Pass, Wolf Creek, and Monarch; and each has a story of its own etched in the pioneering history of the gold and silver rushes.

The story of Colorado roads and road builders is as colorful as the history of the state. Colorado's first highway, after the well-worn trails of the buffalo and the Indians, was the Santa Fe Trail, blazed in 1821 across southeastern Colorado from Missouri to the region's first settlements in northern New Mexico. The modern traveler can virtually drive along much of that original route, which runs through modern-day La Junta.

Other modern routes in Colorado also follow old wagon train roads, miners' trails, former narrow-gauge railroad beds, and even buffalo migration routes. Many of the original mountain roads were built by Colorado convicts working in road gangs before federal highway funding became available, with its restrictions against using penal labor.

One of the most spectacular of all the roads in Colorado, called the Million Dollar Highway even when it was built in 1874, runs between Ouray and Silverton. It was so named not only because of the high cost of chipping it out of the solid rock walls of the mountains it traverses, but because the gravel on the surface was said to consist of fairly high-grade gold ore.

But a million-dollar road in Colorado is not unusual. Many stretches of mountain road cost more than a million dollars a mile.

Coloradans are accused, perhaps unfairly, of having a manic love affair with their automobiles. Denver is often wrongly cited as having the highest per capita automobile ownership in America, equal to auto-congested parts of California. But in a state where almost no transit options exist, automobile ownership is far more a necessity than an affair of the heart. Even in the larger cities, such as Denver, where bus service is offered, the widely dispersed residential and job centers make bus transit marginally useful at best. Public transportation provided ex-

Colorado becomes a crossroad as east-west and Mexico-to-Canada interstate highways converge at Denver. Photo by Jason Winter

clusively by buses works well in communities such as Aspen, where good service along the few fixed routes, can be used as an alternative to the car. Timely and regular bus service between cities in the state is even more scarce than within the cities. So the automobile in Colorado, as in most western states, is far from a luxury.

Even without any really viable public transit option, Coloradans are not the greatest per capita car owners in the land. At 588 cars per 1,000 population, Colorado per capita car ownership trails behind Connecticut, Florida, New Hampshire, New Jersey, and neighboring Wyoming.

When the automobile came to Colorado, it created impacts that have never stopped changing the very style of life. While the first cars were purchased by the very wealthy as novelties, the first Coloradans who really discovered the great advantages of the automobile were the farmers on the expansive eastern plains. Many of them even built their own roads to town, and most maintained stretches for the counties as a routine part of their chores.

In 1910 the state officially got into the road-building business, and 1,643.5 miles of primary roadway was authorized. Today there are nearly 10,000 miles of state highways, not including U.S. and interstate highways, or country roads and city streets.

The first roads were from Denver to Golden, Fort Collins via Denver and Colorado Springs to Pueblo, Pueblo via La Junta to the Kansas line, Denver via Fort Morgan to the Nebraska line, Colorado Springs via Buena Vista, Leadville, and Grand Junction to the Utah line, Grand Junction via Montrose and Durango to the New Mexico line, Walsenburg via Alamosa and Durango to the Utah line, and Buena Vista via Poncha Pass and Sedalia to Palmer Lake. One route from Durango over the Continental Divide to the San Luis Valley had to traverse the infamous Wolf Creek Pass, which has been the subject of song and verse even into the present time. Started in 1915, it was only in the early 1980s that a really modern and adequate road was completed over the 10,850-foot-high Wolf Creek on U.S. Highway 160.

It wasn't until 1922 that the federal government began assisting the state and counties in building roads. Colorado, its counties and municipalities, had already built more than 6,000 miles of roads, but few were surfaced. The federal program would only pay for seven percent of the roads open to public use in the state. There were about 48,000 miles of all types of roads, and the U.S. Bureau of Public Roads agreed to fund about 3,500 miles of highway.

Many of the state's roads were "oiled," but the first paved or concrete covered road in Colorado, built in 1921, only ran from Denver to Littleton.

The U.S. highways, many being improvements on existing state roads, were given names befitting the picturesque countryside they traversed. The main highway across Colorado from Cheyenne, Wyoming to Raton, New Mexico covering the state's Front Range, was called "The Great North and South Highway." In western Colorado, there was the Grand Valley and Hot Springs Scenic Route. Across southern Colorado there was the Rainbow Highway. Another long-forgotten name was the O.L.D. Route (Omaha, Lincoln, Denver). As highway building picked up steam, the colorful names were dropped for the numbering system used today.

A few entrepreneurs built toll roads and bridges before the turn of the century. The

Transportation in Colorado—Because of the once seemingly impassable mountains, Coloradans have concentrated on building an outstanding network of air, highway, and rail transportation for the movement of people and goods.

first of the early toll roads was built across Raton Pass on one leg of the Santa Fe Trail in 1866, and mountain man Uncle Dick Wootton charged tolls of every traveler "except Indians." But only one toll system was instigated in Colorado to pay for a major road system. The Denver-Boulder Turnpike, built in the mid-1950s, paid its $6.3 million in bonds and $2.3 million in interest in less than half its projected 30 years, and became a free road in 1967.

In 1956, Congress created the 40,000-mile interstate highway system—later extended to 42,500 miles—and Colorado's future as a transportation hub for the inner-western United States was sealed. Two of the great border-to-border interstate systems traversed Colorado and merged at Denver, and a third was joined at Denver through Nebraska to Chicago.

The north-south Interstate 25 from Cuidad Juarez, Mexico links Calgary, Canada in a direct route along the Rocky Mountains. In Wyoming it links with I-90 from Chicago, which terminates in Seattle, and I-80, which terminates in San Francisco. In New Mexico I-25 links with I-40 (East Coast to Los Angeles) and I-10 runs from Florida to Southern California. Interstate 25, an international highway, serves Colorado's Front Range cities of Trinidad, Pueblo, Colorado Springs, Denver, Longmont, and Fort Collins along a 299-mile super highway. It enters Colorado at Raton, New Mexico and Cheyenne, Wyoming.

The main east-west Interstate 70, originating in Washington, D.C. and terminating via Interstate 15 at Los Angeles and Interstate 80 at San Francisco, traverses nearly 450 miles in Colorado. I-70 is the super highway of the Colorado mountains, and its corridor in the central mountains links many of the mountain and ski resorts with Denver and Grand Junction. Entering Colorado from Kansas (the main route through Kansas City), I-70 directly serves the major Colorado cities and towns of Burlington, Limon, Metropolitan Denver, Idaho Springs and Georgetown, Frisco and Breckenridge, Eagle, Glenwood Springs, and Rifle before exiting the state on the Utah border west of Grand Junction.

An eastern spur, Interstate 76 from Denver, joins I-80 in Nebraska (the main route through Lincoln and Omaha) for direct routing to Chicago. This section in Colorado is

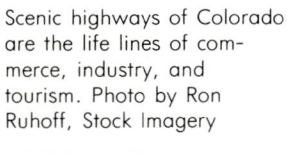

Scenic highways of Colorado are the life lines of commerce, industry, and tourism. Photo by Ron Ruhoff, Stock Imagery

PROFILE

Dixon Paper Company
Pioneering the Distribution Industry

Colorado's strategic geographic location has long made the state the ideal site to claim the role as the distribution center for much of the Rocky Mountain Region's business and industrial activity. A Colorado-founded enterprise, Dixon Paper Company has been a major contributor to establishing this important segment of the economy, and celebrated its 75th anniversary in 1986.

Established in 1911 by T.A. Dixon, who came to Colorado from Chicago, the company built its reputation as one of the first local distributors of paper products to the Rocky Mountain West.

Colorado, and particularly Denver, was becoming a distribution and wholesale center for the region when Dixon located its operations here. The early establishment of good surface transportation for the Rocky Mountain West made it a natural point for warehousing and supply operations.

Dixon Paper Company remained a small enterprise in the early days, because it was not until World War I that paper became an important part of the industrial and commercial segments of the economy. Gradually Colorado became the printing center for the region too, and Dixon was a pioneer company in supplying the new printing industry. Printing is now ranked as the largest single type of industry in the manufacturing sector of Colorado's economy in the total number of businesses operating. While many of the printing establishments are small in numbers of employees, the total employment in the industry is among the state's largest.

Today Dixon Paper Company, with 13 wholesale warehouses located in Colorado, West Texas, Montana, Idaho, Utah, Nevada, Arizona, and New Mexico, is a purely wholesale organization by definition. The company buys and owns all of its products prior to resale. The company also operates five retail, cash-and-carry stores in Colorado and Utah.

Dixon Paper Company's greatest growth began after World War II, and has continued as Colorado's position as a distribution center for the multistate region has expanded. Until 1961, Dixon Paper Company was a privately owned organization. In that year shareholders sold to Mead Corporation of Dayton, Ohio. Mead divested its ownership in 1972, and Dixon Paper once again became a privately owned wholesale distributor. Under private ownership, Dixon Paper Company has continued to expand in the Rocky Mountain area market, and successfully competes with larger distribution companies that have acquired competitors in Dixon's regional operating territory.

The Colorado-founded company is a primary supplier of printing papers used by commercial and noncommerical printers, graphics supplies, film, printing plates, inks, and other products used in the printing industry.

Dixon's industrial products line is extensive, with dominant products being packaging materials, sanitary products, and some food supplies. In recent years, it has expanded into technical products for the high-tech industry, and a large variety of items associated with computers and information processing equipment.

Since its early founding in this century, Dixon has purchased products from America's best known paper manufacturers, in addition to Mead. The company purchases from such notable American paper makers as Scott Paper, Kimberly Clark, Simpson Paper, Weyerhaeuser, Boise Cascade, and Georgia Pacific. Its other major product lines come from such companies as 3M Corporation, Kodak, and DuPont.

Since early in its history, Dixon Paper Company has helped establish Colorado as the wholesale and distribution center for the Rocky Mountain Region.

Mountain activity centers, such as Georgetown, were founded in the gold rush and remain as service centers for the diversified Colorado economy. Photo by Ron Ruhoff, Stock Imagery

184.14 miles and from Denver passes through Fort Morgan, Sterling, and Julesburg. Two other sections of interstate highway, I-225 and I-270, are bypass routes joining I-25 and I-70 east of Denver. A third bypass, I-470, scheduled to connect I-25 and I-70 west of Denver, was deleted by a gubernatorial veto in 1974 and set the stage for another of Colorado's "great highway debates."

The eastern spur was completed in 1986, after being downgraded from an interstate highway to a four-lane, controlled access state route. It was designated Colorado 470, instead of an interstate.

Most of the state's 976.45 miles of interstate highway have been completed. The one notable exception is a 12.5-mile stretch through scenic Glenwood Canyon. That piece of highway, finally under construction in 1985, was the subject of an often heated, very costly, decade-old debate between supporters and environmentalists. The Glenwood Canyon section, along with the Eisenhower Memorial Tunnel under the Continental Divide, may be among the most expensive pieces of highway ever built in the world.

But before the Glenwood Canyon debate was fully joined, Interstate Highway 70 had to cross the Great Divide. To drive a four-lane highway under a mountain required skills and equipment only perfected in the most modern times.

The splendid, scenic super highway had been completed to a point just west of Georgetown, and on the other side of the mountain to a point east of Dillon. This junction was achieved by a detour over one of Colorado's most beautiful, highest, and often most grueling passes—the 11,992 foot high Loveland Pass on U.S. 6. Traffic, even in summer, was a nightmare on the twisting, two-lane pass; and in winter was often impossible. The demand of traffic to justify tunneling beneath the Continental Divide can best be measured by the traffic using the first tunnel during the six months after it was completed in March 1973. In six months, two million cars had passed through the first two-lane bore.

The Eisenhower Memorial Tunnel, the world's highest auto tunnel, was the largest single federal aid highway contract ever awarded in the United States at the time it was completed. Mining of the tunnel on the west portal began on March 13, 1968 and took five years to complete. Building mountain tunnels for highways and railroads was not new in Colorado, but constructing a super highway through the heart of a mountain was new. It was just such a costly proposition that caused the early railroads to seek lower crossing of the transcontinental railroad a hundred years before.

After numerous studies, several changes forced by unstable conditions found during pilot borings, and several millions of dollars, the first boring began. The first bore was 8,941 feet (1.693 miles) long. Of that distance, 7,789 feet were bored through hard rock. The first bore was 48 feet high, pro-

Glenwood Canyon, one of Colorado's most scenic areas, is being crossed by the last segment of construction on I-70. Every care to protect the environment is being expended. Photo by Judith D. Morison

viding huge exhaust fans and a 16'4" clearance for vehicles. The bore was 40 feet wide, providing two drive lanes 13 feet wide, and a two-and-a-half-foot-wide walkway. Total cost of the 1.6 mile first bore was $109 million, plus about $7 million for ventilation, plazas, and the pilot bore.

The second two-lane bore, the east bound tunnel, was begun on August 18, 1975. At a tunneling cost exceeding $103 million, this additional two-lane, 1.6 mile tunnel was completed in 1979. This bore was dedicated to Edwin C. Johnson, a former governor. The four-lane tunnel, which is really two parallel tunnels, covering just over 1.5 miles, cost nearly a quarter billion dollars. But its value to the motoring public, the tourism industry, and the movement of goods in commerce cannot be calculated. Between three and four million vehicles use the tunnels each year.

But completing I-70 through this great natural barrier did not link the great highway, and even before the tunnel was completed another barrier had to be surpassed. In 1969, with much of the interstate system under construction across the nation, the U.S. Senate passed the National Environmental Policy Act. The act had its most profound impact on highway building in Colorado, because new roads that had taken about three years to bring under contract, were subject to intensive environmental study.

A 20-mile stretch of uncompleted I-70 beyond the tunnels was aimed along U.S. 6 through the wilderness area between Dotsero and Glenwood Springs. The first public hearing on that stretch was held in July 1963, and work was not to begin for 20 more years while debate raged and alternate routes were studied. Hundreds attended hearings, and finally 26 organizations went on record in favor of the canyon route with two organizations in opposition. In additional hearings, 40 organizations favored the Glenwood Canyon route and 11 were against it—several opposing all highway construction in general. More than $750,000 was spent on studies.

In 1983 work began on the 12.5 miles through the canyon, one of the only remaining links to be completed on the nation's interstate highway system. The project requires moving U.S. 6 slightly to the north to construct two eastbound lanes that will connect both ends of the completed I-70. Traffic will then be diverted to the newly constructed lanes while the two westbound lanes are built at an upper level. The upper level will be chiseled, sculpture-like, from the walls of the canyon. A bike lane will parallel the highway.

Preservation of the canyon's natural beauty along a roaring, whitewater stretch of the Colorado River, is a required element of the design. In order to maintain the visual appearance of the canyon and the recreational potential of a dam and lake in the area, two vehicular tunnels are included in the plan. The road building involves diverting a live stream around the work. The small stretch of highway is scheduled to be completed in 1993, 30 years after the debate began, at a cost of a projected $320 million or $2,560,000 per mile.

The highways and roads of Colorado, while expensive to build and often controversial, are not only vital to the movement of the citizens living within the state, but are the nerve system of much of the economy. Without good roads, the millions of driving tourists coming into the state would certainly not return. Highway investment is also vital to business because in Colorado most of the merchandise of commerce, and the goods manufactured in the state move by truck.

Motor freight, handled by special contract and private carriers, is a rapidly growing sector of the Colorado economy. Approximately 75 intrastate scheduled common carriers operate in the state. In addition, 180 call-and-demand carriers specialize in truckload shipments, and as many as 600 call-and-demand carriers offer specialized equipment to move commodities. There are approximately 2,000 common carriers contracting to specific firms, and some 30,000 commercial delivery carriers assisting in the flow of goods over Colorado highways and roads.

Heavily dependent on the road system are the approximately 6,500 wholesale and distribution companies operating in Colorado. These firms employ nearly 77,000 people, in addition to approximately 19,000 employed in trucking and warehousing.

The state's most sizable payroll is manufacturing, and without question the industries of Colorado depend totally on the state's interstate and international transportation systems. Colorado manufacturers, with the state's population in 1986 of about 3.25 million, obviously manufacture goods and commodities for markets much larger than those found within the state. Therefore, the excellence of the transportation system—air, rail, and highway—is one of the key ingredients in the success of this most rapidly expanding sector of the economy.

Colorado industry is dependent on good transportation, and the state has developed the man-made resource of transportation to support the other sectors of the economy. The Coloradans' innovative development of exceptionally good transportation systems, often in the face of great obstacles, has kept the state competitive as it strives to modernize its industrial base. Colorado's transportation advantages have been among the key factors to past successes in adapting to the new type of manufacturing firms locating here.

Crossing the Rockies took pioneers weeks. The Eisenhower Tunnel under the Continental Divide cut the trip to minutes. Photo by Ron Ruhoff, Stock Imagery

147

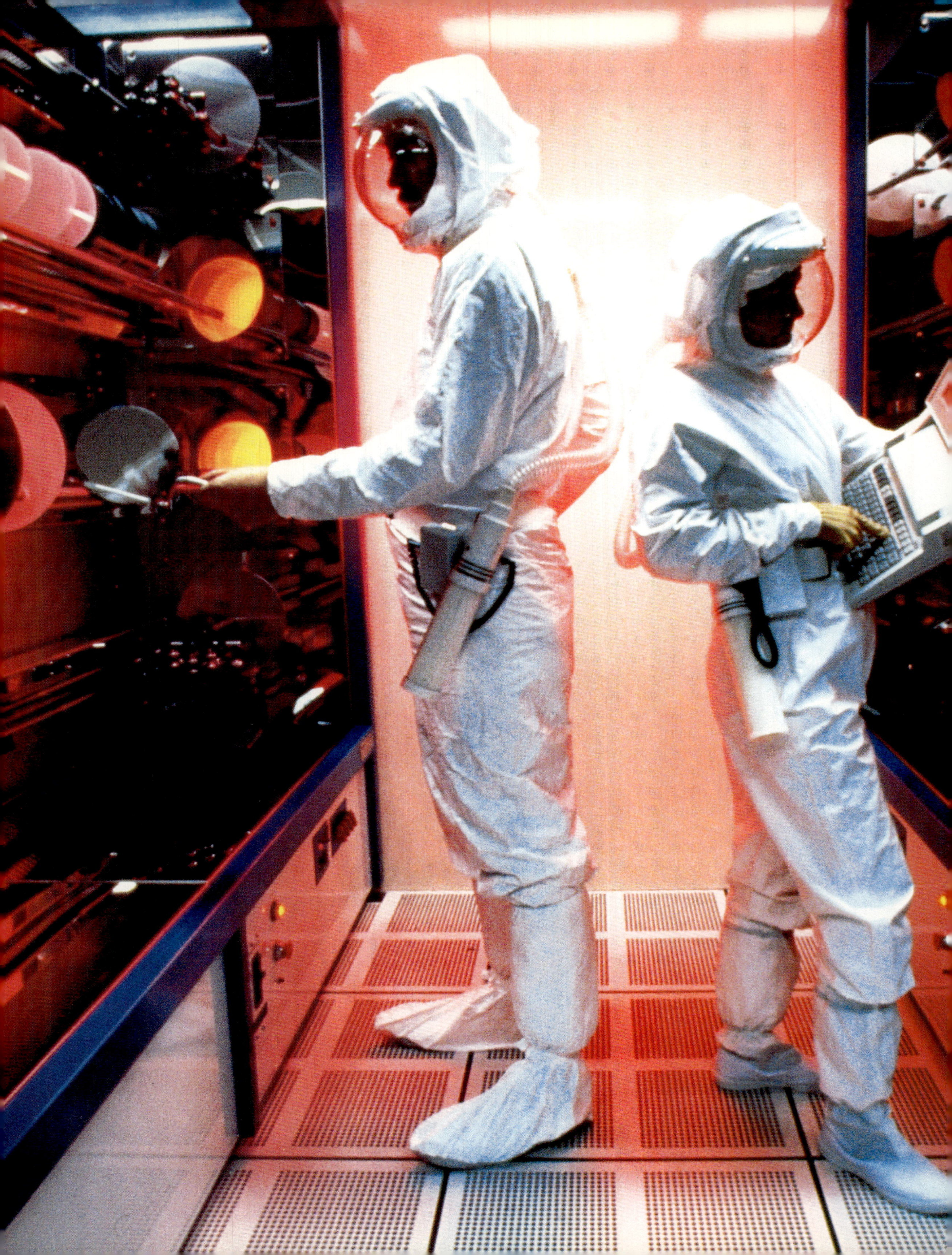

CHAPTER 7

People-Powered Industry
Manufacturing from Basics to High Tech

"Made in Colorado, U.S.A." If such a label was required on all products manufactured in Colorado, it would be found in some interesting and far-flung places—even on the planet Mars.

Products made in Colorado are literally orbiting the earth every day. The rising hum of high technology long ago drowned out the ring of the pioneering manufacturers' hammers and anvils. Now the state's factories hurl a highly diverse catalog of products toward the 21st century where not even the sky is the limit.

Whether making cans or computers, an intelligent labor force with a strong work ethic has made Colorado an advanced technology manufacturing leader among the industrial states. Despite its relatively small population, the state has become a manufacturing leader—not just in the development of better and more profitable ways to manufacture the basic products—but in aerospace, medical technology, electronics and instrumentation, and telecommunications. While Metropolitan Denver and the Front Range communities remain the industrial heart of the state, cities across the state are joining the Colorado industrial revolution as national pacesetters for futuristic industry.

Colorado's earliest manufacturers built plants to supply the incoming population; but today, Colorado is a manufacturing exporter to the U.S. and international markets, and even into outer space. The early territory developed, not because of its location on navigable rivers or sheltered deep seaports, but in support of those who came to develop the rich natural resources of the plains and mountains. Manufacturing followed for the same reasons—in support of natural resource production. Colorado established a broad manufacturing base early in its developmental history because of the distance from industrial centers of the East. This industry cadre remained even after transportation problems were solved.

The first territorial census of 1870 indicates that a solid base of manufacturers had already formed in the state, listing 232 blacksmiths, 114 brick and stone masons, 552 carpenters, 142 sawmill operators, and assorted clothing manufacturers, machinists, millers, and printers. The population of the whole territory at that time—six years before Colorado statehood—was 104,000.

Today, almost twice that number are employed in Colorado manufacturing alone, and most are employed in advanced technology industries. With nearly 200,000 persons employed in manufacturing jobs in the late 1980s, estimates are that as many as 120,000 of these jobs are in so-called "high technology" industries.

While manufacturing is the fourth largest sector of the state's economy in total numbers of jobs—trailing behind retail and wholesale trade, the service industry, and government—manufacturing employment produces the largest payroll, well exceeding $5 billion annually.

The multiplier effect or additional job creation in other sectors of the economy has the greatest impact on the overall economy. Economists value one manufacturing job two to three times higher than other types of jobs because the payroll of production workers creates the support positions in trade, service, and government.

Manufacturing jobs are also generally

Advance technology requires exacting standards of everyone, as this clean room environment built by a Colorado construction firm for Honeywell, Inc. shows. Photo by Paul Chesley/Aspen USA, courtesy of G.E. Johnson Construction Company

149

PROFILE

Ball Corporation
Innovations from Basic Industry to Aerospace

Products spanning the industrial spectrum—from containers for the food and beverage industry to advanced technology for America's space program—have established Ball Corporation as one of the stalwart manufacturers in Colorado.

The international corporation has not slowed its pace of growth and expansion in either facilities or product lines since acquiring a small Boulder firm in 1956. Colorado operations for the century-old Muncie, Indiana-based firm have grown from the original 10 employees 30 years ago to nearly 3,000. Its facilities in several Front Range communities employ the largest number of Ball Corporation workers in any of the 14 states and two foreign countries where the company operates research, development, and manufacturing facilities.

While the company is a historic leader in the food container industry, its modern manufacturing systems bring a degree of high technology to that industry. The Colorado facilities participate in many phases of Ball Corporation's diversified manufacturing interests, with plants in the state turning out products for packaging, industrial instrumentation, aerospace, and high technology markets.

The company's Colorado Office Center at Westminster is the headquarters for two operating groups—metal containers and technical products. That facility also houses the Ball Electronic Systems Division and several corporate staff functions.

The Edmund F. Ball Technical Center, also at Westminster, was opened as headquarters for several of Ball's Colorado-based research and new product development activities.

The metal container group, which manufactures lightweight, recyclable aluminum and steel containers for the beverage industry, includes con-

Ball Corporation has turned high technology into a practical consumer application with one of the nation's most advanced can manufacturing plants.

tainer plants in the United States as well as joint venture and technology relationships with companies in this country and overseas.

Ball Corporation's first metal container plant was built in Golden, Colorado, and has become a leading supplier of aluminum soft drink cans for the Rocky Mountain region. The Golden plant produces more than a billion cans and can ends each year.

The corporation's technical products group is composed of divisions engaged in high technology R&D and manufacturing for the nation's defense program, NASA, and other industries. Ball Aerospace Systems Division, located in Boulder, is the oldest and largest of the divisions. It is engaged in the production of spacecraft, satellite systems and subsystems, and space science instrumentation, including electro-optics and antennas for NASA and the Department of Defense.

Ball Electronic Systems Division is one of the country's leading producers of cathode ray tube data displays used by computer manufacturers. The division operates a contract manufacturing facility in Boulder, which produces electronic assemblies and subassemblies and printed circuit boards for some of the world's largest computer companies. A number of other Colorado companies are supplied and serviced by this contract manufacturing operation. R&D in industrial instrumentation conducted by this division is providing enhanced automated inspection processes for other manufacturers. The division develops vision and temperature gauging and inspection products.

Ball Corporation's commitment to research and development has been a major factor in the company's continued growth and expansion, and this commitment to technology advancement has been focused in new facilities in Colorado. Its new technical center at Westminster is the major R&D center for the container group, the hydrogen maser time and frequency standard program (atomic clocks), and research in industrial instrumentation, new corporate products, and corporate manufacturing systems productivity.

While Ball's products are found throughout the space program, including such well-known programs as Skylab and the Space Shuttle, its corporate feet are still solidly planted on earth in such products as canning jars, beverage cans, and zinc blanks for coins. Even in these common items, Ball Corporation has made significant technological breakthroughs, saving material, time, and money. While increasing the strength, stacking features, and production time of aluminum cans, Ball has reduced the weight of cans from 40 to 28 pounds per thousand cans.

Its contributions to the nation's defense program can be found in defense satellites, supersonic jet aircraft, submarines, aircraft carriers, helicopters, and numerous other systems. Its space contributions have been found in most of the better known NASA projects, and many of the earth and deep-space programs for study of the earth and stars. Ball also contracts for services in astronaut training, launch support, testing, and meteorology.

A catalog of Ball space products can be found in satellites from launch and propulsion systems to advanced astronomical sensors for planetary and interplanetary studies. Its special and scientific teams, employed in Colorado plants and laboratories, range in technologies from cryogenics, antenna systems, signal processing, optics, video systems and astronomy to a wide range of specialties in electronics, metals sciences, and hybrids.

With annual sales exceeding the $1 billion level, Ball Corporation has proven that U.S. manufacturers can continue to grow and expand in an everchanging world economy. The company that began as a manufacturer of glass "fruit jars" in Muncie, Indiana in 1888 is still making "fruit jars" today, while helping America reach into outer space.

The company has continued to seek "a better product" throughout its more than 100-year history. As its first products—wide-mouth Ball canning jars—continue to hold a leading spot in home canning, constantly improved products for the food packaging and beverage industry capture increasing shares of the worldwide market.

Ball Corporation also continues major capital investment in the future of Colorado, and the other states where its diverse operations are located. The Fortune 500 company devotes extensive R&D to making better glass for its first product lines and is pioneering in high barrier, coextruded plastics for its packaging business.

With its record for versatility and adapting to change, Ball Corporation can be expected to continue to write industrial history. Data from its Earth Radiation Budget Satellite (ERBS), which was launched in October 1984, is now providing NASA with weather and climate data for the nation's long-range weather forecasting program. Other Ball space programs are periodically launched from the Space Shuttle, with major satellites for exploration scheduled through the remainder of this decade.

Ball Corporation products, created and manufactured in its Colorado plants along the Front Range, can be found in the kitchens of America as well as on the edges of outer space.

On a given day in America, the average citizen popping a soft drink on the corner of Main Street, USA has a lot in common with the astronaut working in orbit around the earth—both are most likely using a Colorado-made Ball Corporation product.

Space-bound payloads developed at Ball Aerospace Systems are tested in a computer-operated vacuum chamber at one of the versatile company's Colorado plants.

Many components in the NASA space shuttle operations are contributed by Colorado manufacturers. As that program enters a new phase, Colorado firms' roles are expected to be extensive. Photo courtesy of Martin Marietta

classified as higher-skilled positions because of the nature of industry in Colorado. Nearly one-third of all manufacturing jobs in Colorado are in the production of computers and peripherals, electronics and components, aerospace products, and scientific and medical instrumentation. The national average of jobs in high technology production is only about 14 percent, compared to Colorado's approximate 33 percent. Geographic location and environmental factors, such as water use and industrial waste limits, demand that Colorado products be of high value-to-weight ratio. The state's requirements that new and emerging industry be "clean" has directed its industrial development toward the higher-valued products, such as instruments and computer components.

In the state's relatively short history of rapid industrialization, manufacturing has tended to locate in the urbanized Front Range area from Fort Collins on the north to Pueblo on the south.

Ten counties in Colorado have 85 percent of the manufacturing jobs, and the manufacturing heart of Colorado is centered in the Denver-Boulder Metropolitan Area, including the counties of Adams, Arapahoe, Denver, Boulder, and Jefferson. Within this thin corridor about 180 miles long, well over half of the approximately 4,500 manufacturing establishments in Colorado are located in five metropolitan area counties. Denver City and County, which has historically been the center of manufacturing activity in Colorado, remains the largest county in number of plants, with over one-quarter of all factories in the state. Boulder County is the state's second leading county in numbers of factories, but is closely followed by Jefferson, Arapahoe, and Adams Counties.

Fort Collins in Larimer County, Greeley in Weld County, and Sterling in Logan County all provide substantial numbers of production jobs in local factories.

Colorado Springs in El Paso County is in the same category with the Denver metropolitan counties, all exceeding 300 manufacturing establishments. Due to the location of the Consolidated Space Operations Command in Colorado Springs, the southern end of the Front Range is projected to be the fastest growing manufacturing area of Colorado.

Pueblo is also a historic center for manufacturing, and recent efforts to replace the jobs lost in its steel industry with higher technology manufacturing have enjoyed some success. Pueblo created the Business and Technology Center, a "business incubator" providing support services for new manufacturers, to encourage the growth of the local advance technology industry. This center was activated after Pueblo successfully attracted Sperry Corporation's new electronics plant. The location of Neoplan USA Corporation, a major transit bus assembly factory at Lamar, also expanded southeastern Colorado's industrial base away from a strictly agribusiness economy in the early 1980s.

A concentrated effort to diversify the economy on the Western Slope, particularly in the Grand Junction and Durango areas, has also met with success since the mid-1980s. Grand Junction further opened the high technology era on the Western Slope with the location of Sunstrand Corporation's new international instruments plant in 1985. Since that time, several new factories have located in Mesa County, partially offsetting job losses caused by reversals in oil shale development in that area.

In the southwestern part of the state, Durango has steadily diversified its manufacturing base with several new small manufacturers opening plants there since 1980. At nearby Mancos a traditional clothing factory is catering to non-traditional customers manufacturing space suits for NASA in a factory employing Native American Indians from reservations in the nearby Four Corners area.

In addition to these industrialized centers, several other counties have substantial manufacturing bases within the local economy. Other areas in Colorado with 25 or more manufacturing establishments include Delta, Douglas, Fremont, Garfield, Lake, Montezuma, Montrose, Morgan, and Otero Counties.

But even if an area has not been historically tied to manufacturing, a concentrated effort is being expended across the state to diversify the base of the economy by locating new factories in small towns. This effort to decentralize the industrial base is being led by the Division of Commerce and Development from Colorado's Department of Local Affairs in cooperation with a score of local economic development organizations. Communities that have historically been tied to bulk production of agricultural or mineral products are being urged to develop small local factories to process or enhance the value of natural resource products before shipping. An example is an intensive effort being made in the San Luis Valley, the state's major potato growing center, to attract a national food manufacturer to bring a potato processing and frozen food plant to the valley.

The fastest growing sector of the manufacturing economy of Colorado is in high technology, with some 1,100 manufacturing and research and development firms. Another 2,500 companies provide support for the state's fast-expanding, high-tech companies. But often the products of advanced technology are not what might be expected. For example, one of the world's most modern can manufacturing facilities is located in Colorado. Ball Corporation has applied high technology equipment to make almunium beverage cans in a faster and more efficient manufacturing process. High-technology output is not limited to spacecraft components and computer-like merchandise.

Colorado's manufacturing sector is highly diversified, and it is this diversification that has served the state well during economic downturns. Even massive layoffs in the early 1980s in some sectors of the state's computer technology industry did not dramatically affect the total manufacturing employment base of the state.

Colorado's industrial diversity is not only apparent in its wide assortment of products, but in the employment size of the individual manufacturers. While the state has about 65 plants in 27 communities that employ 1,000 or more production workers, the vast majori-

When U.S. astronauts walk in space to repair satellites they are wearing Colorado-made equipment. Photo courtesy of Martin Marietta

PROFILE

The Gates Corporation
Colorado Company Becomes International Leader

A Colorado company formed 75 years ago with an investment of a few thousand dollars has emerged into an international manufacturing leader doing more than a billion dollars a year in business on the world market.

The Gates Corporation, with its world headquarters in Denver, is a far different company than pioneer manufacturer Charles C. Gates Sr. might have envisioned when he and his brother, John, bought a troubled mail-order leather goods business in 1911. But the founders' successor Charles C. Gates Jr., who has guided the modern diversification of the company, believes that some basics of doing business from this central western state will never change.

The operations of the multinational company became so extensive that in 1982 a holding company, The Gates Corporation, was formed. Gates Rubber Company, which had been the primary corporation since the time when the automobile was introduced in the west, has grown from its original Denver plant to 19 manufacturing plants in the United States, and 11 additional plants in six other countries. The rubber company holds the position as the world's largest manufacturer of V-belts and hose products. It is the sixth largest producer of rubber products in America, even after the company stopped making vehicle tires in 1974. Around the world, Gates has 150,000 distributors, dealers, and sales specialists representing the company in 130 countries.

The company's products are used in almost every segment of industry in the United States, and in industrialized and developing nations throughout the world. Gates products, among them the V-belts and rubber hose equipment for vehicles that propelled the company into world markets, are found in transmitting mechanical and hydraulic power, moving materials, and numerous high technology applications. Gates parts, often found as components of other parts, are used on the farm, in the oil fields, at construction sites, in factories, offices, mine shafts, and under the sea.

A Colorado-founded company, Gates Corporation has grown to an international leader in its field. High technology is leading to new products.

The Gates Corporation's largest subsidiary remains its rubber products company, which employs about 10,000 workers around the world.

Other modern subsidiaries include Gates Learjet, manufacturers of executive jet aircraft, and Gates Learjet Aircraft Services Corporation, which provides general aviation maintenance and logistic support, and trains U.S. Air Force pilots at 16 U.S. and foreign locations. Gates Energy Products makes rechargeable, sealed, and lead-acid batteries. Gates Formed-Fibre Products makes molded fiber products. Gates Land Company is a residential land development organization, and A-Bar-A Ranches include a guest ranch and cattle raising operations along the Colorado-Wyoming border.

Charles C. Gates Jr., successor to the family-owned corporation, sees no reason to change those policies to remain competitive in a world-wide marketplace. The corporate headquarters location in Colorado continues to serve the world market too.

"With the majestic Colorado Rockies as a backdrop for our headquarters in this vibrant business community, we've found Denver to be an outstanding source of employees—both blue and white collar," says Gates, board chairman and CEO of the corporation. "In fact, our company has found this to be true for 75 years as we expanded our business from a local one into one with markets worldwide. We think good employees are the most important resource any company has. Our magnificent mountains nearby act as a magnet to attract people with a pioneer spirit embodying the work ethic that serves employers well. The invigorating climate helps to keep those people enthusiastic and inspired to do their best. Couple that with the Western flavor that is still alive and well in this community and you have an ideal place to live, work and play."

The Gates Foundation is one of Colorado's most outstanding contributors to educational, scientific, and cultural activities. It has contributed more than $31 million to the humanities, cultural and historic institutions, education, health, conservation and recreational programs, youth services, and public policy examination.

In 1985 alone 82 organizations throughout Colorado received substantial funding from the Gates Foundation, amounting to nearly $2.6 million in grants.

High technology not only produces sophisticated equipment for the space age, but better food and beverage products for everyday use. Photo courtesy of Adolph Coors Company

ty of Colorado manufacturers are classified as small business operations with fewer than 250 employees. More than 70 percent of the manufacturers employ 20 or fewer workers.

The diverse nature of manufacturing in Colorado is further seen in the fact that the state lists manufacturing operations in all 20 major Standard Industrial Classifications used to designate types of manufacturing jobs.

Diversified Industry Base

Despite its large high technology industry base, Colorado's historic position as an agricultural center makes its food and kindred products industry the largest single employment sector in the manufacturing category. In 1986 more than 26,000 workers were employed in plants processing foods and agriculture-based products. This industry sector is important because small factories and processing plants are located in virtually every area of the state, providing a solid base of employment in both large cities and small towns. Nearly 400 food products plants are operating in Colorado including meat packers poultry dressing plants, dairy processors, canneries, frozen and dehydrated fruit and vegetable plants flour and corn mills, pet food processors, bakeries, candy and confectionary plants, bottlers, brewers, wineries, and scores of other food preparers. An additional 3,100 workers are employed in textile industry jobs, many based on Colorado's wool production. Wool processors, apparel manufacturers, and a wide assortment of weavers, tanners, and other textile companies are also located in smaller towns and cities across the state.

Closely akin to the non-durable industries dependent on Colorado's natural resources are the durable products manufacturers in lumber, wood products, furniture, stone, clay, glass, and concrete. Plants, mills, and processing facilities in these categories employ more than 16,500 workers in the state. These plants are spread throughout the state, in small towns as well as the large cities.

Chemicals, natural resource derivatives, and other non-durable goods production account for another 17,000 workers.

Printing and publishing, which is classified as a manufacturing industry, was once rated as the largest manufacturing classification and is still sizable, with about 900 printing establishments listed in 1986. This sector, however, includes many small print shops and instant print houses, and a large percentage of the employment in this sector could better be classified as "service" related. However, some of the largest employers, such as the *Denver Post* and the *Rocky Mountain News*, are also listed in this category. In all, the printing and publishing industry employs nearly 22,000 Coloradans. Paper and allied products manufacturing, such as box and carton manufacturing, employ an additional 2,200.

155

PROFILE

Samsonite Corporation
International Markets Extend from Colorado

A pioneering venture in the manufacture of suitcases led a Colorado-based company into the ranks of America's multinational corporations and the international marketplace.

Samsonite Corporation, founded in Denver in 1910 to meet a local market need, is today the world's best-known manufacturer of travel-related products and business cases, with more than half its sales outside the United States. Its world headquarters remains in Colorado, even though its marketing strategy is global in scope.

Jesse Shwayder, 28 when he founded the company, could not have dreamed that his original capital investment of $3,500 would begin a chain of events propelling the Colorado company into a $300 million annual sales volume. The Shwayder Trunk Manufacturing Company started small, in a shop space measuring only 50 X 125 feet.

Today the successor manufacturing company operates from a 120,000 square foot world center and headquarters in Denver, with an additional 520,000 square foot assembly plant nearby. Samsonite also operates plants in Arizona, Belgium, France, Spain, and Canada. The Denver-based luggage giant has joint venture operations in Mexico and Italy and licensing agreements in Japan, Brazil, Argentina, and Pakistan.

Malcolm Candlish, president of Samsonite Corporation, says the key to success in the closing years of the 20th century has changed little since the formative years.

Executives and engineers do not design the jet age luggage or cases. "At Samsonite our customers design our products," Candlish says.

When a new line of travel products was recently being considered, more than 1,000 users were consulted. Every suggestion was computed before product design began.

The result of bringing the ultimate user into the design process was "The World's Greatest Garment Bag," and Samsonite could not manufacture the new product fast enough to meet its early acceptance.

"If U.S. industry is going to compete favorably with foreign manufacturers, it must be with higher quality products and a keener awareness of the changing needs of consumers. If our products cost a little more to manufacture they must clearly be worth the difference," Candlish asserts.

At Samsonite, business innovation reaches into every aspect of manufacturing—from the purchase of raw material to the incentives offered its highly skilled workforce. Even with the company's state-of-the-art industrial automation, employees are given a pride in workmanship through a manufacturing system that permits them to make the whole item from the molding to the finished product, instead of contributing only a part on an endless assembly line.

As a corporation within the Beatrice Companies, Inc. multinational operation, Samsonite still customizes its lines for specific markets. Beatrice, headquartered in Chicago, bought Samsonite in 1973 and added its international strength to the Colorado company.

Samsonite, a brand name that has become an international word for luggage, still serves its specific customers in diverse marketplaces. The company manufactures distinct products and maintains separate distribution channels for the specialty store trade, catalog showrooms, and national department stores. Its operational versatility permits manufacturing for export and import in both its U.S. and foreign plants.

Samsonite employs a workforce of more than 4,000 worldwide. Approximately 1,500 are located in the Denver manufacturing and marketing center.

Production supervisors John Hagen, left, and Bob Lattimore are part of the team who listen to the customer in the development of Samsonite products.

Whether it's high technology or exotic tea, Colorado's diversified manufacturing base is supported by skilled employees. Photo by McAllister of Denver

The second largest manufacturing sector is non-electrical machinery. With the exception of those companies now manufacturing aerospace equipment, this historic industry sector dates back to the pioneering days when foundries were the first big plants to open.

Machinery production is again a growing sector of the economy with new employment gains following the slumps caused by slow downs in the mining and energy development fields. Nearly 28,000 are employed in non-electrical machinery manufacturing in the state. A closely related manufacturing sector, fabricated and primary metals, is also enjoying small growth and expansion. Employment in primary and fabricated metals is over 15,000.

Industrial diversification is also taking place geographically throughout the state. From a new flute factory at Grand Junction to a metro transit bus assembly plant at Lamar, from space suits at Mancos to designer jeans at Sterling—factories without smokestacks are springing up in new places across the length and breadth of Colorado.

The late 1980s has seen a resurgence in the quest for diversification, similar to the massive community effort launched 20 years ago that set the stage for today's enviable high technology position. The biggest difference in today's drive for diversification is geographical. In the 1960s, Denver led the effort to broaden its industrial base. In the late 1980s the effort is to decentralize and bring manufacturing into additional areas of the state. While the central industrial section of the state continues to grow too, new light industry is being directed to all parts of Colorado.

One major contributor to a more diversified manufacturing base has been the introduction in recent years of specialty products, which are manufactured in small factories located in smaller cities and towns. The recreational assets of Colorado's great outdoors have spawned a relatively new industry—the manufacture of ski equipment and clothing, mountain climbing gear, camping gear, and survival gear. Small companies in Colorado are gaining world reputations for these specialty products.

Some of this recognition is the result of free advertising. The *Denver Post* examined the impact of national advertising on Colorado manufacturers in a recent study. The report noted that a dozen national companies used scenes of technical climbing—ascents on rock or ice so steep that it's wise to use ropes and other gear—in consumer and business-to-business advertising. These ads carried clearly visible labels of unique Colorado products. Big-name companies using Colorado climbing scenes (and merchandise) included Ford, Grape Nuts, Camel cigarettes, Sanka, Du-Pont, The Wall Street Journal, Lord Calvert whiskey, and Fiat. Colorado gear and equipment is frequently used because it is readily available and used by the Colorado technical climbers hired to appear in the ads. Many of the products being developed in Colorado are created by professional skiers and mountaineers residing in the state. They naturally locate their companies near the action.

This diversification, along with growth in long-established industries such as food processing and the recent explosive growth in high technology, is helping Colorado maintain a leading position as a manufacturing state. Colorado manufacturing jobs increased by 25 percent during the five-year period from 1977 to 1982. The 1982 Census of Manufacturers published in 1985 indicated that Colorado manufacturing jobs were increasing at a rate

PROFILE

Hach Company
High Technology Contributing to Better Life

The headquarters for the Hach Company is the site for emerging high technology that is being used in important testing and analysis around the world.

High technology is contributing to a better life quality and the efficiency of manufacturing is becoming one of the principal products of the emerging new economy of Colorado. Hach Company, with its world headquarters near the Fort Collins-Loveland area, is one of the state's pacesetters in this futuristic endeavor.

Combining a major commitment to advanced research and high technology manufacturing, the Hach Company has grown with Colorado's new Front Range industrial community to become a recognized leader in the field of analytical instruments and reagents. The company continues to apply its expertise in developing "systems of analysis" for new market areas such as food processing and electroplating. Its products are being used around the world to test the quality of foods, water, various industrial processes, and the environment. Hach testing systems are unique because they provide everything needed to perform a test in a simplified, step-by-step manner so that practically any literate person can obtain the required results. Simplification of testing systems for accuracy and purity has created the growing world market for Hach's many technical testing instruments, kits, and chemicals.

In addition to the Hach Company's world headquarters, Colorado facilities include a 150,000-square-foot research and development and instruments manufacturing plant. A 140,000-square-foot facility in Ames, Iowa, where the company was started in 1946, handles chemicals manufacturing operations and shipping. Hach Synthesis, Inc. produces chemicals in Casper, Wyoming, and the company has sales and distribution offices in five U.S. cities. Hach Europe, located in Namur, Belgium, handles international business in Europe, Africa, and the Near East.

Hach's decision to open the headquarters in Colorado was partially based on the availability of the scientists and technicians to be found in the communities around the Front Range higher-education and research institutions. The highly skilled and enthusiastic workforce available in Colorado is cited as another factor in the successful Colorado expansion.

Hach Company manufactures a broad range of precision testing equipment for the critical work of quality control analysts. The company's own research and development programs have pioneered in advanced technology in that important field. The company consistently develops improved methods, procedures, and equipment to save time, labor, and increase productivity in testing. At the same time, Hach Company has developed testing equipment and procedures which allow greater accuracy of measurements in a field where accuracy is most important—the processing of foods, beverages, and water for human use.

The company's rapid-test instruments and methods are designed to permit the food or beverage processor to conduct analysis and get immediate results. Because of the critical nature of analysis in the industry Hach Company serves, it has established a rigorous quality-control program for all its instruments and chemicals. In the last 35 years, Hach has evolved from a company primarily making chemical and test kits into a full-line supplier of laboratory and on-line process instruments, portable laboratories, test kits, and analytical chemicals.

Its procedures and instruments can monitor sterilization, disinfection, waste treatment, or dechlorination processes.

Monitoring by on-line instruments is provided by Hach products to assure quality control of both food and beverages during processing. Similar equipment can monitor the water used for boilers, cooling systems, and manufacturing processes, and the effluent hardness from industrial water softeners.

far greater than in most other states. These increases came during a period when the United States suffered a slight drop in the number of manufacturing jobs. Manufacturing jobs were on the increase throughout most of the western states during that period of time.

Although manufacturing in Colorado over the decade from the early 1970s to the early 1980s grew 50 percent, production workers in Colorado still account for only about one in eight workers, compared to the national average of one in five.

High Country High Tech

The rapid growth in Colorado manufacturing employment actually began three decades ago, when light, non-polluting industry began coming into the state to take advantage of the natural beauty to be found in the nearby mountains. Manufacturing was beginning to change across the nation following the end of World War II as high technology industries began to emerge. This type of industry had no historic roots, and its founders tended to look for locations that would attract the highly skilled and trained new scientists they needed. Among the early high-tech companies that came to the state are Stearns-Roger, IBM, Hewlett-Packard, Eastman Kodak, Honeywell, Ampex, Western Electric, Digital Equipment, and the home-grown Storage Technology.

Other national and international high-technology companies that found the Colorado work environment favorable for large operations are Rockwell International, Cobe Labs, ITT, Ford Aerospace, Texas Instruments, Honeywell, NCR, Data General Corp., MiniScribe, United Technologies, and a list that goes into all areas of advanced industry.

In defining what "high technology" really means, a number of major Colorado companies involved in production of basic products can and should be considered "high tech." If the broader definition of "using the fruits of high-tech products to increase efficiency" is applied, then Colorado manufacturers in virtually every category can be considered high technology companies. Because of the importance of high value-added products in shipping long distances to domestic and international markets, Colorado factories and manufacturing processes are generally modern and highly advanced.

By narrow definition, "high tech" includes manufacturers in aerospace, biotechnology, computers, "new materials," robotics, and telecommunications. Specialized medical and optical equipment is often added to the list.

Skilled workers have helped to diversify Colorado's industrial base as locally founded companies have grown to international operations. Photo courtesy of Samsonite Corporation

PROFILE

Martin Marietta Corporation
Launching Colorado into an Aerospace Future

A first step beyond traditional industry, taken from a site in the foothills of the Rocky Mountains near Denver in the mid-1950s, hurled Colorado into aerospace orbits and forever changed the character of manufacturing in the state.

That first giant step was taken in February 1956, when Martin Marietta Corporation began construction on its Denver Aerospace facilities. Since that time, Coloradans have been a part of nearly every major U.S. venture into space. Perhaps of more importance to the citizens of the state was the birth of a technological revolution in the manufacturing base of Colorado.

Today, Martin Marietta Denver Aerospace is one of the nation's largest and most active private space and defense centers, and the company is Colorado's largest industrial employer. The aerospace/high technology industry is growing and thriving across the length and breadth of Colorado.

Currently, Martin Marietta, with about 14,000 persons employed in the Denver and Front Range area, is working on more than 400 active contracts, with a highly diversified business base for NASA, the Department of Defense, other government agencies, and the private sector.

Denver Aerospace employees have worked on such world-changing projects as the Space Shuttle, Titan space boosters, the Viking missions to Mars, Manned Maneuvering Unit space propulsion backpacks for Shuttle astronauts, and Skylab.

Work being conducted in the half-billion-dollar Colorado space center continues to propel Colorado toward the stars. The company is involved in the development of complex computerized systems used in controlling operations that range from Space Shuttle launch preparations to unmanned exploration of distant planets. Assisting in the Free World's defense, the company has made contributions to the first Titan I ICBM program, to assembly and testing of the Peacekeeper (MX) and the Small ICBM, and to the development of military electronic systems.

Martin Marietta is working on projects that will increase access to space for commercial enterprises, and on the design of intelligent robots for future industrial uses. The company is also participating in many phases of the National Aeronautics and Space Administration's manned space station program, which has far-reaching industrial potential.

The Colorado complex, which has grown over the years to include more than 40 highly sophisticated laboratories, includes computerized engineering design, manufacturing, and administration facilities.

Martin Marietta Denver Aerospace serves as the base for several primary functions of the parent company, which is headquartered in Bethesda, Maryland. The corporation also has major aerospace operations at Orlando, New Orleans, and Baltimore. The principal functions headquartered in Denver include NASA and Military Space Systems, Space Systems, Strategic Systems, Space Launch Systems, Defense Systems, and the Space Station program. Also located in the Colorado complex is Martin Marietta Information & Communications Systems, formed in 1984 to design, build, and integrate advanced information processing and communications programs; and Martin Marietta Data Systems, which provides Martin Marietta's aerospace operations with a full range of computer services, and markets software products to commercial customers.

As the United States continues its program toward placing a permanent space station in orbit, Martin Marietta Denver Aerospace will continue to perform a major role. The design work done by Coloradans could become major features of the orbiting station, including laboratories and living areas. Another futuristic project under way at the Colorado complex is work on the Strategic Defense Initiative, popularly known as "Star Wars."

Its plant on the edge of the Rockies, Martin Marietta is a national aerospace center. The company has lead Colorado industry into the space age.

Martin Marietta recently opened a new laboratory to conduct simulations and actual tests of some elements of the space-based defense system. Called the Rapid Retargeting/Precision Pointing facility, this laboratory will also be used by researchers from other aerospace companies. Some of the work in the facility will involve the testing of systems for a new generation of non-nuclear weapons that can be used against large numbers of missiles. Such advanced technologies as systems for space-based laser beams and kinetic energy (non-explosive projectiles) are also the subject of studies.

The company's projects also span many areas of science and technology outside the aerospace and defense arena. Data Systems has contracts to assist a major county government in the management of data processing facilities for tax assessment, payroll, health and welfare benefits, and other information for an area of two million residents. Another project for the Department of the Interior calls for the expansion of a mineral management system to be used to facilitate the collection and distribution of revenues from mineral leases off-shore, and on federal and Indian lands.

Through its Information & Communication Systems group located in Colorado, the company is at the forefront of a burgeoning market for information management systems that combine software, hardware, data links, and technologies for man-machine interface. While some of the programs have applications in space and defense, they also serve business and communications industries. Some of its research focuses on creating computer programs that could coordinate and run a space-based defense system. One of its programs in the design, engineering, and integration of complex information systems is being jointly developed for air traffic control with applications in commercial and civilian aviation. The company is the systems engineering and integration contractor for a new National Airspace System Plan—a comprehensive blueprint for modernizing and restructuring the country's air traffic control, navigation, communications, and auxiliary systems. Work to win the program was conducted in Denver, but the program has since moved to Washington, D.C.

Many of the company's contributions to science are still in the laboratory stage. For example, Martin Marietta has been conducting research into zero-gravity fluid management for space systems for the past 25 years. Among other technologies being studied at the Colorado facility are robotics and artificial intelligence, advanced optics, radiation-hardened microelectronics, high speed integrated circuitry, and spacecraft guidance and control.

Martin Marietta's impact on other Colorado high technology and aerospace projects at smaller companies has been extensive throughout its history in the state. The company spends approximately $60 million annually on new construction and outfitting facilities, and has literally hundreds of subcontractors providing goods, services, and cooperative efforts on a portion of its more than $1 billion in annual contracts. The company works with the state's higher education institutions in a continuing quest to upgrade the technological training programs in the universities and colleges of the state.

Colorado has been given a place in the stars and a major role in the aerospace industry because Martin Marietta chose to take a first big step into the space frontier nearly 30 years ago.

As the industry in the state continues to advance into new fields of high technology and aerospace, the path will most likely continue to be explored by the state's first and largest space company.

When astronauts walk in space they wear equipment such as this Manned Maneuvering Unit. If the propulsion pack had a label it would read: Made in Colorado.

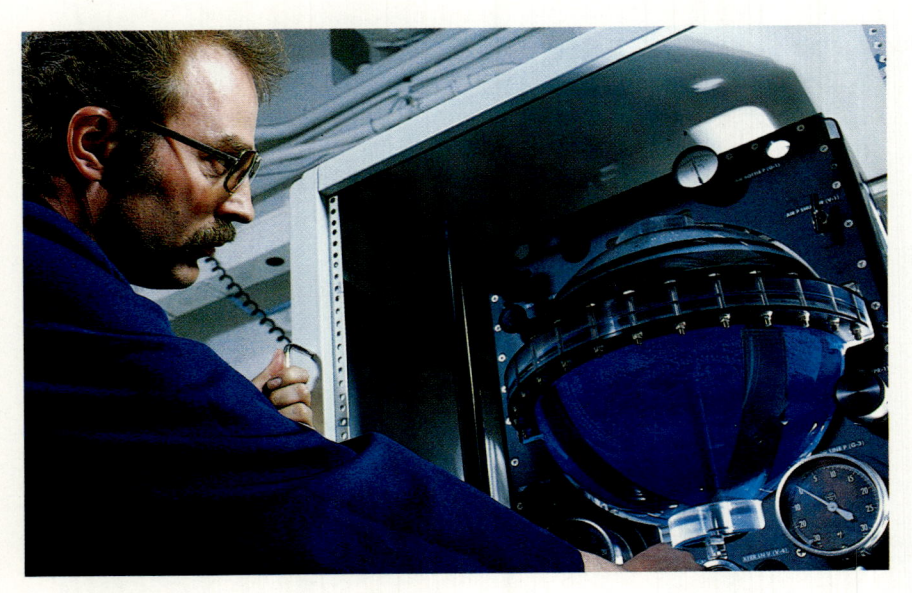

Colorado seems destined to become America's center for the new aerospace industry, and the sophistication in manufacturing and trained personnel is already in place to accept the challenge. Photo courtesy of Martin Marietta

A part of the equipment enabling NASA to take this photograph on the Planet Mars was manufactured in Colorado. Photo courtesy of Martin Marietta

Colorado's first truly high-tech industry was aerospace, and the first steps into the aerospace industry were taken in the late 1950s by two giants of Colorado's present day high-tech industry—Martin Marietta and Ball Corporation. These firms introduced a new kind of diversification of manufacturing into the state. Even before "high tech" became a popular buzz word in manufacturing, plants were beginning to announce locations along Colorado's Front Range to manufacture things nobody had ever heard of before.

Martin Marietta is the state's largest private employer and has greatly diversified its manufacturing base from its early days as a high technology manufacturer for the nation's aerospace program. However, because of such firms as Martin Marietta and Ball Aerospace, many subcontractors and high technology suppliers have been created in the aerospace sector of the economy.

Small factories to manufacture microelectronics, computers, precision instruments, space vehicle components, biomedical products, and scientific instruments began opening in office parks and campus-like industrial districts from one end of the Front Range to the other. So diversified was the technology and so small were most of the new plants, that the technology revolution changed the very character of manufacturing in Colorado before many realized what had happened.

The most notable characteristic differentiating Colorado manufacturing firms from other U.S. manufacturers may well be the size of the workforce in the individual firms. The average Colorado manufacturing firm employs 8.6 persons, ranking the state number one on the list in "smallest average number of employees." This compares with other high technology manufacturing states such as Delaware with an average of 51 employees per firm, Connecticut with 47 per firm, and Massachusetts with about 30 per firm. Colorado's small high technology companies are intensely "entrepreneurial," with the founders and owners working closely with their employees and very much involved in the day-to-day operations.

While Colorado's Front Range had not become a Silicon Valley overnight, it had, in less than two decades, become one of the top 10 states in America in the number of electronics firms. Despite some downturns in the computer industry, Colorado has seen steady and strong growth in high technology industrial employment from the very beginning of the 1960s. Even in the past five years, when the national computer industry has experienced serious employment problems, Colorado's electrical machinery, instruments and high-tech equipment, and transportation equipment sectors have steadily grown.

In 1986, more than 23,000 Coloradans worked in the production of electrical machinery, almost 17,000 in transportation equipment (including space vehicles), and more than 24,000 in instrumentation and scientific equipment.

The estimates of direct and indirect employment in various advanced technology, R&D, and support fields range as high as 120,000 workers. A comprehensive trends study conducted for industry, government, and educational institutions by Strategic

High technology is found everywhere in the manufacturing processes of Colorado. New plants and equipment are poised for a new age in advanced industry. Photo courtesy of Kodak Colorado

Assessments, Inc. in late 1985 indicated that as many as 1,200 Colorado firms, employing more than 119,000 workers, were involved in one or more advanced technology fields. Strategic Assessments, Inc., an advanced technology, electronic publishing, and information evaluation company located in Boulder, placed revenues of advanced technology firms in Colorado in excess of $11 billion in 1984.

The company's study indicated a mid-1980s annual growth rate of 17 percent for the combined industries within the advanced technology categories.

One difficulty in accurately estimating the impact of advanced technology on Colorado industries is the diversity of products.

Many of the founders of Colorado's high technology firms come out of other larger high-tech industries in the state or from the universities or major federal research centers. Much of the diversity in types of advanced technology can be traced to the long-term establishment of some of the world's leading research centers in Colorado. Federal research labs have attracted top scientists to the area to work in or near such facilities as the National Center for Atmospheric Research in Boulder, the Solar Energy Research Institute in Golden, the National Bureau of Standards in Boulder, and the newly created Consolidated Space Operations Command in Colorado Springs.

The growth rate in high technology industries was the highest during the late 1960s and early 1970s. But the rate continued to be among the highest in the nation into the early 1980s. Colorado experienced a 98.3 percent growth in high technology employment between 1975 and 1981, the second highest rate in the nation. The state was ninth, during that period, in actual number of new jobs in high technology, with 26,968 reported in the five-year period.

And it does not appear that this trend will change much in the coming years. A number of events seem to be moving the state into another realm of high technology.

Colorado is on the leading edge of the new "super computer" and exotic "super chips" era. Some truly amazing things are coming out of both the small and large high technology companies. As the computer industry in general reels from endless and often instantaneous change, Colorado keeps coming back with newer and better products, or new uses for products.

An example is Ford Motor Company's opening of a $33 million factory in Colorado Springs to mass produce new material for a whole new generation of semiconductors to be used in cars and by the military. The new material, gallium arsenide, which may someday replace silicon in many types of integrated circuits, introduces a new era to the world's computer industries. This new era has already been staged in Colorado. When the exotic new chip is manufactured it will be the first high-volume product made for sale on

PROFILE

Neoplan USA Corporation
Introducing Industrial Diversity

Neoplan has opened Colorado's Eastern Plains to advanced industry, and is supplying modern transportation, like this new Denver bus, to cities across America.

A modern version of the opening of a new frontier in Colorado offers all the glamour of a tale from the past with the success of Neoplan USA Corporation's establishment of a major new industry at Lamar. Situating the big plant on the historically agricultural Colorado Eastern Plains, the West German transit bus manufacturer has rapidly become one of the largest suppliers to the public transportation systems of the United States.

Neoplan, which employs between 600 and 700 Lamar-area residents, selected the Lamar site for its major manufacturing facility because the Colorado location met its needs for a readily trainable work force, in a smaller community with technical education and other support services available.

Neoplan is among the leading suppliers of public transit buses to cities across the United States, with its vehicles serving more than 50 American cities and towns. Its German parent company's international operations supply public transit vehicles to 47 countries, with an international work force of more than 3,000 employees. With the modernization of Denver's bus fleet by the Regional Transportation District, Neoplan is supplying as many as 250 new buses.

Neoplan's move into Colorado to open its sizable Lamar plant in 1981 in effect opened a new era for that section of the country. A number of satellite manufacturing plants and fabricators soon followed to further diversify the previously agribusiness economy. Among the new plants locating in the Lamar area as a direct result of Neoplan's pioneering effort include a bus air-conditioning company, a fiberglass housing fabricator, an air-conditioning compressor manufacturer, and other related suppliers.

In addition to the diversification of the jobs base, other indirect benefits of Neoplan's pioneering new industry are accruing to the Eastern Plains area. The educational and community infrastructure has been considerably strengthened, and because of the nature of the new industry an unusual community benefit has been offered.

Neoplan USA Corporation opened its double-line manufacturing plant in Lamar on May 22, 1981, and its position as one of the leading suppliers of modern transit equipment in America has continued to expand ever since.

President Bob Lee, who is technical director of the company's international group and has over two decades of experience in Neoplan bus technology, believes the decision to place a major plant in a community in rural Colorado was sound.

"The dedication of people raised in the farm-ranch tradition of working hard to achieve big results has brought about Neoplan USA's overwhelming gain in percentage of transit bus sales in America," says Neoplan President Lee. "Neoplan USA looks forward to seeing Neoplan buses operating in each of the 50 states someday."

Neoplan USA manufactures eight different models of public transit vehicles in its U.S. plants at Lamar and Honey Brook, Pennsylvania. In addition, the versatile manufacturer provides many options to meet the local conditions required of bus fleets in different geographical locations.

the open market. The plant will be operated by Ford's high technology arm, Ford Microelectronics. The gallium-arsenide market was placed at $75 million in 1983, and is expected to reach about $7 billion by 1990.

Beyond computers, components, and computer programs, Colorado is a national leader in the development and manufacture of optical disks and microelectronics. With the rapid advancements in computer technology, Colorado manufacturers have aggressively sought to remain on the leading edge in order to stay competitive. In one major area, small Colorado companies are leading the nation. Optical disk technology, which allows computer users to store enormous amounts of information on a small storage device, is expected to propel computer technology into the next era, and Colorado firms were the unchallenged leaders in this field in 1986. Explosive growth is expected in the optical disk field, with some sales estimates exceeding $4 billion annually by 1990. Most present disk storage technology is based on magnetic storage; optical disk technology is based on storage created by laser beam allowing vast amounts of information to be stored in very small amounts of space. This new technology is already being used by Colorado-based information companies in the services industry discussed in Chapter 5.

Total employment in this specialized classification, including production, fabrication, design, and assembly of electronic components, subassemblies and finished products, is about 22,000. Growth of jobs in this area is projected at about 15 to 20 percent a year.

High technology materials to support the local industry, including plastics, metals, and chemicals, are also processed and fabricated within the state. A number of firms using advanced materials in industrial processes have formed the Advanced Materials Institute (AMI) for the purpose of providing basic research materials and assuring a readily available local supply.

Telecommunications is yet another important segment of the high technology industry. The application of advanced telecommunications is discussed in Chapter 5, but it also provides the base for a major manufacturing industry. AT&T and Rolm both maintain sizable R&D programs and manufacturing operations in Colorado, and more than two dozen smaller companies operate production and R&D plants in the state.

Advanced medical technology and biotechnology are relative newcomers to the manufacturing base in Colorado, with notable exceptions such as Cobe Laboratories, Inc. But medical and biomedical firms are pioneering in everything from instrumentation to immunology, from new tissues and artificial limbs to diagnostics and dialysis controls.

Companies in Colorado, spinning off biotech research from the universities located in Colorado and elsewhere, are providing leading edge products in gene manipulation and reproduction. Products in these areas are benefiting human health as well as enhancing livestock quality.

High technology manufacturing activities are concentrated along the Front Range corridor from Fort Collins-Loveland-Greeley on

Colorado-produced equipment is used in this high technology government laboratory. Photo by Ron Phillips, Phillips Photographics

PROFILE

T.A. Pelsue Company
Creating a Safe Work Environment

Safety and improved working conditions are the hallmarks of the innovative equipment designed and manufactured by the Pelsue and Langdon companies.

The T.A. Pelsue Company, located in Englewood, germinated from the need to create a safe working environment for cable construction workers in the telecommunications industry. In the years following World War II, T. Allen Pelsue, the company's founder, capitalized on the new requirements to locate utility cables underground. He designed and patented specialized heaters, ventilators, and other auxiliary safety items for workers in manholes and other confined work spaces.

In 1962, the T.A. Pelsue Company was formed to manufacture other products needed by cable construction workers, including mobile power generation equipment, and equipment for work area protection, safety lighting, and shelters. Now in its second generation of family management, Pelsue Company continues to innovate and adapt to the needs of industry.

Additions to the product line include a patented line of tents developed by company Vice President Allan Beavers for use in aerial and underground construction. In 1978, a production facility was established to manufacture this Pelsue tent.

Today, T.A. Pelsue Company, with more than 45,000 square feet of manufacturing space in its Englewood plant, makes equipment predominantly for underground cable construction, and is one of the leading suppliers of equipment for cable placing, splicing, and cable maintenance in the United States and abroad. Pelsue also provides custom design and fabrication for a myriad of applications including mobile climate control, ground support, and monitoring equipment for NASA, and several aerospace companies. Always intrigued by the challenge of custom design, Pelsue has been called upon to develop special shelters for missile transportation systems.

Fiber optics has been the focus of recent Pelsue product development. Specialized winches for the placing of underground fiber optic cables and specialized splicing trailers are among the newest Pelsue products.

As the growing demand for the Pelsue tent forced continued expansion of the sewing facilities, a new firm was added to the Pelsue companies. In 1982, Langdon Manufacturing Company of Wichita, Kansas was acquired to increase production and to augment its line of specialty sewn products.

The Langdon Manufactuing Company, founded in 1886, was one of the largest manufacturers of custom sewn products such as tents, military specialties, and custom designed and sewn oil drilling rig shelters. Langdon maintains plants in Wichita and Englewood. A leader in custom shelters and sewn products, Langdon makes a wide range of items from specialized carrying cases to intricate insulated casings for NASA and jet engine covers.

Both Pelsue and Langdon are among the leading Colorado manufacturers exporting manufactured goods in foreign trade, and T.A. Pelsue Company was cited with the Governor's Award for Excellence in Exporting in 1981. Their products are shipped to the Middle East, Taiwan, the Philippines, Korea, Central and South America, and Europe. The company has a product assembly plant in Montreal, Quebec for its Canadian business.

Pelmark, the newest subsidiary of Langdon Company, is a marketing trade name to introduce Pelsue products to the public. Products include tents and shelters for family campers and backpackers. Special events shelters by Pelmark allow advertisers to offer their products under individualized shelters at outdoor events such as fairs, races, and outdoor athletic competitions. Because of easy set up, Pelmark shelters are used for mountain and outdoor search and rescue efforts, and are in use as decontamination shelters for hazardous spills.

In 1984, Bradley Pelsue, the current president of Pelsue, joined with several other Colorado businessmen to provide the initial investment for the Sentry Environmental Protection Systems Corporation, and Wastek of Colorado. Both firms are engaged in the treatment and recycling of hazardous waste.

Pelsue Company and its affiliates are providing an example of many of the emerging Colorado manufacturers that find innovative ways to answer the needs of a changing American society.

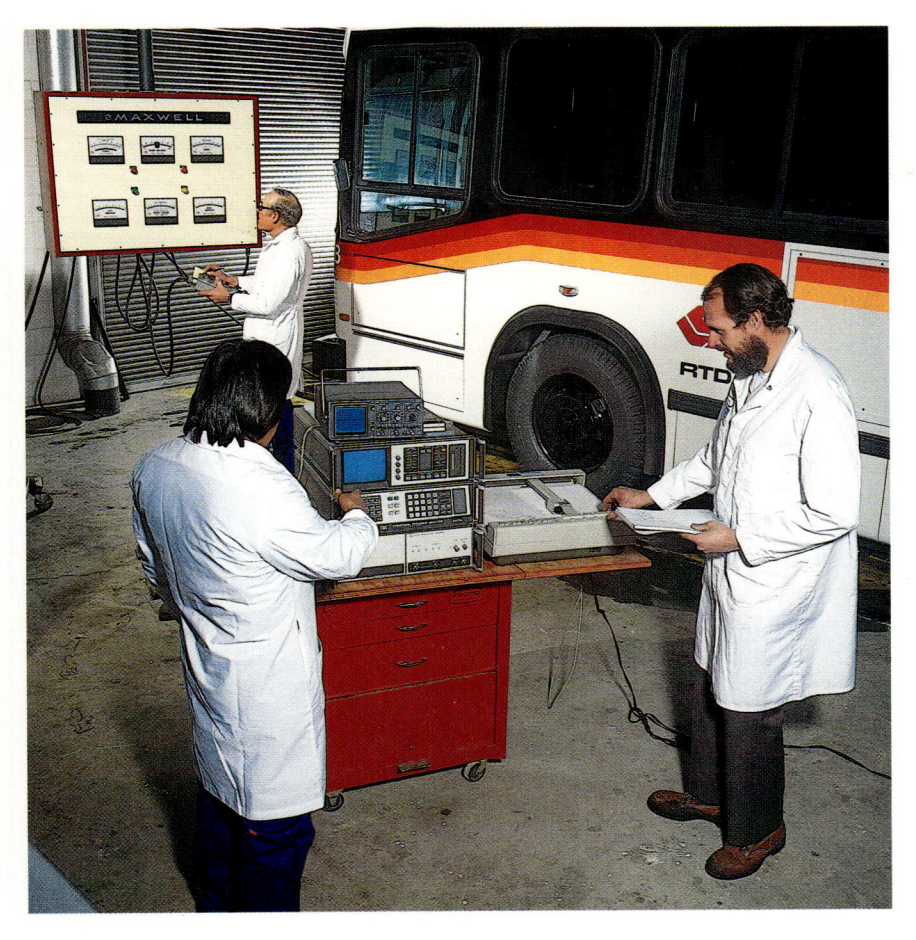

Neoplan makes the most modern buses available to the public transit industry in America from a new plant at Lamar. Photo by Ron Phillips, Phillips Photographics

the north, to Colorado Springs on the south. Aerospace activities are concentrated in the Denver-Boulder area, with manufacturing activities also located at Longmont and Colorado Springs. The top employment centers in numbers of high-tech jobs are Denver, Colorado Springs, Boulder, and Englewood, with strong and growing activities in Broomfield, Longmont, Aurora, and Fort Collins.

Biotechnology manufacturing activities are more broadly based around the state, with major activities in and around Fort Collins, Greeley, Boulder, Broomfield, throughout the metropolitan counties of Denver, Arapahoe, Jefferson, Adams, and Douglas, and in Colorado Springs and Pueblo.

Microelectronics manufacturing is also broadly based along the Front Range, with major manufacturing being in the Boulder-Longmont-Broomfield areas, throughout metropolitan Denver area counties, and in Colorado Springs.

Other high technology manufacturing in telecommunications, film, and various electronics, is concentrated in Denver, with both large and small factories also operating from Colorado Springs to Fort Collins.

But high technology, by its characteristics of being high value-added for the weight of the product, can be found in plants throughout the urbanized areas of Colorado. Other than the immediate Front Range counties, high technology plants are located in Cheyenne, Eagle, Fremont, Garfield, Mesa, Montrose, Pitkin, Routt, and San Miguel counties.

Support for High Tech

One of the primary reasons for the concentration of high-tech companies in the Front Range area has been the strong university support systems available at Denver, Boulder, Colorado Springs, Greeley, and Fort Collins. The University of Colorado's Office of Space Science has more than 50 NASA contracts for space-oriented research. Colorado State University specializes in materials processing and surface analysis as well as significant biotechnical research projects. The University of Colorado at Colorado Springs has special programs in processing and fabrication technology, with growing support systems for aerospace and microelectronics technology. The University of Colorado at Denver is a center for computer system architecture, microelectronics, and computer applications. Colorado School of Mines at Golden is adding computer-aided instrumentation to its already strong position in advanced metals research.

Colorado's 16 four-year colleges and universities, including the U.S. Air Force Academy, have a combined enrollment of over 120,000 students, and several universities and colleges have developed off-campus engineering and business technology programs in direct support of industry. In-plant educational programs are delivered to major industrial firms by area colleges. On-site college programs are also offered at locations within area industrial parks.

Four universities are offering graduate programs in sciences and engineering. The University of Colorado, with its major research programs, offers graduate science programs on-demand at campuses in Boulder, Denver, and Colorado Springs. Colorado State University at Fort Collins also offers graduate degree programs in several industrial sciences, and Colorado School of Mines is providing graduate work both on and off campus in chemical engineering, metallurgy, and other advanced sciences.

The University of Denver, the largest private university in the Rocky Mountain states, has tailored many of its advanced degrees to high technology industry needs in mathematics and the sciences.

Many of the graduate programs at these

PROFILE

Kodak Company of Colorado
Major Manufacturer Fits Colorado's Environment

One of Colorado's largest and most important manufacturing complexes sits nestled quietly and almost unobserved amid working farms, grazing cattle, and a wildlife sanctuary.

The placid environment surrounding this industrial giant did not occur by accident. Eastman Kodak Company planned it that way and applied the best technical know-how available in building the ultramodern Kodak Colorado facility in the late 1960s.

When Kodak decided they needed another manufacturing facility in the western United States, the world-famous photographic supplier deliberately sought a rural American environment. But because of the worldwide market to be served by the facility, a set of exacting prerequisites had to be met.

A plant of this magnitude required a parcel of land with room to grow; an adequate pure water supply for the sensitive photographic manufacturing processes; a good transportation and distribution network to serve the national and international markets; an intelligent and enthusiastic work force; nearby universities and vocational schools capable of filling the training needs for a high-tech future; and attractive residential communities offering culture, recreation, and scenic beauty.

There was no room for compromise, for it is a Kodak tradition that employees are the company's greatest asset and the work environment a key ingredient to business success. The selection of the 3,000-acre site near Windsor, Colorado was the culmination of a three-year search throughout the West and Midwest.

With production for international markets beginning in 1971, Kodak Colorado operates from one of the state's most sophisticated industrial plants at Windsor, Colorado in the

Kodak's modern Colorado plant shares sophisticated industrial space with surrounding wildlife areas and agricultural enterprise.

center of the Front Range communities of Fort Collins, Greeley, and Loveland. More than 2,500 employees bring space-age skills to the workplace, while living and working within sight of the towering Rocky Mountains and nearby wilderness.

Kodak Colorado uses only a fraction of its vast acreage for more than three million square feet of plant space. Most of the remaining land is leased for grazing livestock and raising crops. A 400-acre wildlife and migratory bird sanctuary is set aside on a parcel of the property. The wildlife and agrarian activity outside the nine plant structures exists undisturbed by the daily manufacturing activity inside.

The Colorado division is the company's primary producer of such products as medical X-ray film and lithographic printing plates. With more than 25 percent of these products sold overseas, Kodak Colorado is one of Colorado's largest exporters. Approximately 1,000 different products are manufactured in the facility, but the Colorado plant's primary products are used in the medical and health, color photography, and printing industries. The facility completes other Kodak products initially manufactured elsewhere, such as Kodacolor 110-format films used in pocket cameras, phototypesetting papers used in graphic arts production, negative microfilm for information storage and retrieval, and 16mm Eastman color print film used for mass distribution of motion pictures.

The complex also serves as one of two major U.S. distribution centers for other products of the Eastman Kodak Company. As part of the parent company's Distribution Division, the Colorado center is responsible for moving products manufactured here and elsewhere to regional distribution centers throughout the United States and to most countries around the world.

The Colorado employees are among Eastman Kodak's U.S. work force of over 80,000 and worldwide work force of more than 120,000. Availability of a highly motivated, skilled labor force was essential to the modern operations at Kodak Colorado.

"Positive work attitudes, a strong work ethic and modern training facilities in universities and technical programs are necessary to the success of an operation like ours," says Vernon A. Dyke, general manager of Kodak Colorado. "Much of the advanced technology we use is state-of-the-art, and the quality and precision of the finished product is critical."

The work environment inside the plant is laboratory-like, with many of the functions being performed in light- and moisture-controlled environments. To avoid intrusion of dust or foreign objects on highly sensitive film or plates, hospital-clean conditions are provided.

"Quality in product and packaging is mandatory," says Dyke. "Keep in mind that Kodak film was used by our astronauts to take the photographs on their moon walks. Medical and industrial dependence on Kodak quality is even more demanding.

High technology from Colorado is opening new international markets due to the industrial progress of such employers as Kodak Company of Colorado located at Windsor.

That's one reason our people are such an important part of our operation."

Kodak Colorado cooperates with the area's major universities, both in providing input and support for scientific curriculum development and in recruiting for its jobs at the local plant and around the world. Because of the proximity of campuses, Kodak works especially closely with the University of Colorado, Colorado State University, and the University of Northern Colorado. The company also participates in technical programs of local public schools and is a major sponsor of Junior Achievement activities.

Kodak Colorado interacts extensively with other Colorado businesses, purchasing over $18 million annually in goods and services within the state. It is also an active corporate participant in community betterment projects in the nearby towns and cities where its employees make their homes.

PROFILE

American Web Offset
Applying Technology to Communications

Applying the latest technology to the increasing demands of the emerging information age is placing Colorado in the forefront of the specialized publishing industry, and American Web Offset in Denver has become one of the recognized national leaders in this field.

Beginning in 1981, when three young printing professionals purchased an existing publications printing company, American Web Offset today is manufacturing magazines, catalogs, and other periodicals for small to medium size publishers from the East Coast to Alaska and Hawaii. Each month its state-of-the-art, high technology preprinting equipment, computerized presses, and bindery machines turn out hundreds of thousands of high quality, full-color magazines and periodicals for nearly 100 publishers. The Denver-based company expects to be printing 115 magazine titles next year.

As a publisher's printer tailoring its high technology printing operations to magazines in the circulation range from 10,000 to 100,000, American Web Offset's five years of growth and expansion in Colorado is nothing short of spectacular. Since Gary Hansen, senior vice president for administration and finance; Anthony White, senior vice president for sales and marketing; and Terry Choate, senior vice president for manufacturing operations, purchased the printing company they previously managed, sales have expanded nationwide. The company recently was cited in one of the nation's top industry journals among the top five percent of the growth companies in the printing industry. The company also is ranked in the top five percent of the U.S. printing companies in sales volume per employee.

"While we are committed to bringing the best advanced technology in the printing industry to Colorado and our nationwide customer base, we have, at the same time, assembled an outstanding quality of craftsmanship in our people," says White. "We have never met any craftsmen in this industry with a stronger work ethic, and a greater personal commitment to the company and the clients."

The ultramodern plant facility, which was purchased and doubled in size, is a showplace of computerized graphic arts equipment. The big color press, a five-unit Hantscho Mark VI, was installed two years ago. A second, larger computerized press, with faster and even more sophisticated features, is being installed late in 1986; and a third addition is planned for 1988.

American Web Offset's management counts its location in geographically centered Colorado as one of the reasons for the company soaring from an unlisted printing firm to the nation's 382nd largest in less than five years.

To these ingredients for success should be added the vision of its dynamic, entrepreneurial owners. They recognized the need for a specialized service in the fast-growing communications field in Colorado, as well as a void in the national market for printers to serve the expanding trade and special-interest publications industry. American Web Offset's three founders met that challenge by introducing the most cost-effective and high quality print manufacturing equipment, gathering a new generation of Colorado craftsmen eager to learn the new high technology, and expanding the marketing potential from a strategically excellent geographic location in Colorado to include the entire United States.

At American Web Offset the result has been a modern success story to equal those tales of early pioneer enterprise.

American Web Offset, with the most advanced equipment available, is helping make Colorado a national publishing center in the magazine industry. Photo by Harry Boyd

Aerospace technology is brought down to earth for many purposes to enhance the life styles of people around the world. Photo courtesy of Martin Marietta

universities are ranked among the top 50 schools in the nation in such fields as biological sciences, biochemistry, microbiology, electrical engineering, mechanical engineering, math and the physical sciences.

In addition to the big university programs and four-year and community college programs, Colorado's vocational and technical education program reaches into every section of the state to support expanding basic and high technology manufacturing. The state's vocational/technical education system is currently offering 486 post-secondary vocational training programs that produce over 5,000 skilled graduates each year. Community colleges and area vocational schools provide customized training for local business and industry in every large community in the state.

Area vocational schools include Aurora, Boulder, Delta-Montrose, Denver, Larimer County, San Juan Area, San Luis Valley Area, Arapahoe/Douglas County Area, Mesa County, and Jefferson County. In all, there are 21 such vocational schools and community colleges offering employer-tailored programs in electronics, welding, drafting and design, machining, civil engineering, environmental control, industrial maintenance, building crafts, data processing, and other industry-related subjects.

Some of the nation's leading federal research and development programs, mostly located at national institutions along the Front Range, are centered in Colorado. The area has one of the nation's largest concentrations of professional scientific personnel, with many working in the environmental sciences.

Boulder is headquarters for the Environmental Research Laboratories of the National Oceanic and Atmospheric Administration; the National Bureau of Standards of the U.S. Department of Commerce and its Institute for Telecommunications Sciences; the National Center for Atmospheric Research; the Joint Institute for Laboratory Astrophysics; and the Cooperative Institute for Research in Environmental Sciences. The University of Colorado at Boulder has the Laboratory for Atmospheric and Space Physics, an Engineering Research Center, and Bureaus of Economic and Business Research.

The United States Geological Survey in the Denver Federal Center employs over 1,600 technicians and support personnel working in earth sciences, fuels, and water research. Both the U.S. Bureau of Reclamation and Bureau of Mines have major research facilities in Denver.

Golden is headquarters for the Mines Research Institute at the Colorado School of Mines, the world's leading solar and alternative energy research lab at the Solar Energy Research Institute, and the state-supported Colorado Energy Research Institute. The U.S. Geological Survey's National Earthquake Information Service is also located in that Jefferson County seat.

At Fort Collins the Colorado State University hosts the Agricultural Experiment Station, with research programs primarily supporting the agribusiness industry. Also located on that campus is the Solar Energy Applications Lab, conducting research into remote sensing of atmospheric and ground phenomenon and the National Center for Nuclear Magnetic Resonance, which studies

PROFILE

Best Manufacturing Company
Diversifying Colorado's Industry

The advancing technology era is providing many companies an option to locate new and expanding facilities in places throughout Colorado where their executives and employees could once go only for vacations.

One example of this new trend is provided by Best Manufacturing Company, already a national leader in its industry, and now expanding its international markets from Montrose, in the heart of the mountain country.

In 1980 Best Manufacturing, which had been a leading manufacturer of business signage since after World War II, was in search of a location to expand its design and manufacturing facilites. The company was founded in Kansas City in 1924, and through the development of innovative new materials and manufacturing systems for a wide array of modern business and institutional signs had grown to an international operation.

A two-year search covering 60 communities in five states, led Best to select Montrose on the scenic Western Slope of the Colorado Rockies.

"The new home in Montrose has proven ideal for both the people and the firm," says Chairman Frank Newell. "Our employees are close to downhill and cross-country skiing, hunting, fishing, and other outdoor recreation; and our headquarters and manufacturing facility adjoins a community airport with commercial and executive air operations, and a U.S. highway system."

Colorado's strategic location in the most rapidly growing part of the United States provides the location the company requires for its national and international operations.

Best Manufacturing has a tradition of concern for its personnel, and a record for hiring and retaining the best specialists in the field. Employees in turn are expected to support the company's commitment to providing the highest quality in signs and sign systems, and supporting its obligations to customers and shareholders. Locating in Montrose has been a plus in employee development goals, and a profitable decision in its competitive field.

Best Manufacturing, one of the nation's leading industrial sign makers, introduced a new type of industry to Colorado in its move to the Western Slope.

Best Manufacturing moved into their state-of-the-art, energy efficient manufacturing plant in Montrose in 1984, and built expansion capabilities to provide a modern 100,000-square-foot industrial plant. The production plant and headquarters building provides the facilities for highly skilled craftsmen in the graphics, engraving of metals, and organic and synthetic materials fields.

The company, through its research and development program, pioneered the Graphic Blast (registered trademark) carving process. New designs in exterior sign systems have provided several "firsts" in the industry, including a vandalism-proof hidden fastening system. Earlier firsts in the sign and sign system industry included the first "pictorial directory," the first directory designed exclusively for health care facilities, and the first captive message type sign.

Their modern processes can produce signs in practically any building material available to industry from mirrored metals to marble. The company provides custom graphics that are used in decorative lobby artwork in every medium from 19th Century letter styling to ultra-modern pictorial backgrounds. Its products span the world of signage communications including large directories, pictorial directories, interior signage, room numbering, emergency indicators and direction instructions, personal identification systems, memorials, award plaques, control panels for industry, free-standing signage, health care directories, and traffic signs, to a complete range of exterior signage and directional systems from finely carved woods to futuristic metals in any sizes ordered by the customers. The company's products are marketed under the registered trade name BEST Sign Systems.

New materials, processes and graphic systems being developed at Best Manufacturing and the company's ability to match new materials to new designs are giving added freedom to designers and planners.

Best Manufacturing's story of locating its modern new plant in western Colorado truly is one of the best examples of how the technology age is opening new business opportunities throughout the state.

organic compounds. The U.S. Department of Agriculture's western center is home to the Rocky Mountain Forest and Range Experiment Station, the Regional Computation Center, the Soil and Water Engineering Center, and the Colorado Water Resource Research Institute.

The Denver Research Institute, associated with the University of Denver, is one of the region's foremost research facilities. Its employees work on sponsored research for government and industry in chemistry, electronics, mechanics, metallurgy, physics, mathematics, industrial and social economics, and technology transfer.

Voyagers in space still use sextants, but this modern version manufactured at Martin Marietta would astound ancient mariners. Photo by Gary R. Graf

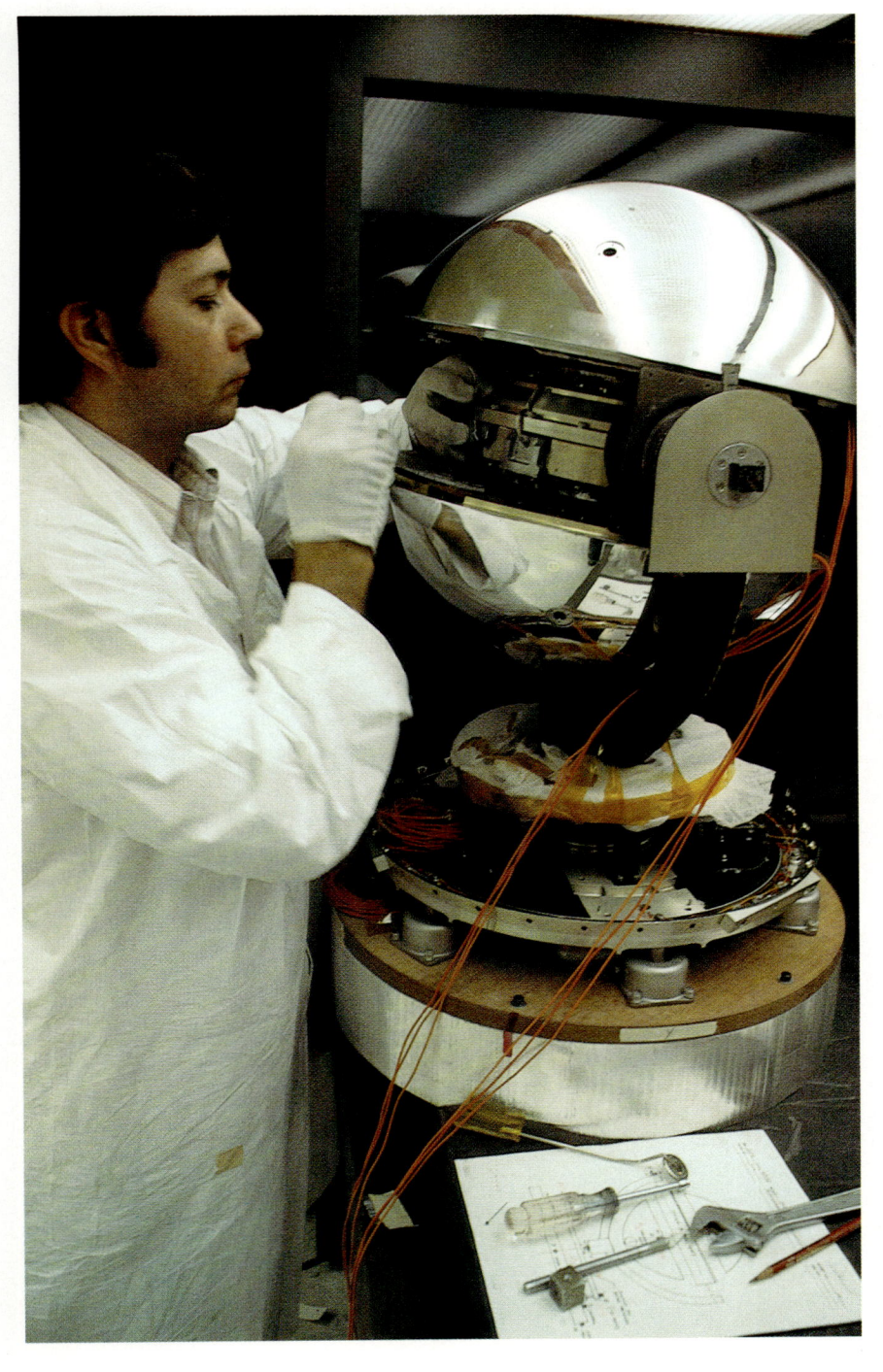

The Colorado Advanced Technology Institute (CATI) has been organized to coordinate the state's higher education and industrial research activities. This government/privately-funded organization is covered in more detail in Chapter 11.

These, and numerous private enterprise research projects, all provide a steady input for the creation of new products in the high technology field, and assure a continued expansion of Colorado's high technology industrial base.

Colorado manufacturing has undergone tremendous change from its early days when almost all products were made for the local economy, and in support of the basic mining and agricultural industries of the state. Today, Colorado's manufactured products, with the exception of some food processing, are exported across the nation and around the world. In recent years, international export trade has been the primary target of many of the state's manufacturers. The state established a special International Trade Division within the Colorado Department of Local Affairs to assist small manufacturers in establishing international contacts to sell Colorado products abroad.

In addition, foreign trade zones have been established in Colorado Springs and Denver, providing for the duty-free movement of materials and manufactured goods until products actually enter the U.S. marketplace.

Until recently, accurate records of Colorado-manufactured products going into international markets were not consolidated. Colorado has long been a major exporter of agricultural products such as grain and meat, but records of durable goods being exported were kept on an industry-by-industry basis. Colorado manufactured products going into foreign trade have been increasing during the 1980s, from under $1.5 billion in 1980 to an estimated $3 billion in 1986.

With a concentrated effort by state government to coordinate Colorado manufacturing activities toward foreign markets, the state's position as a center for emerging biotechnical and electronic products may soon make it a major international exporter.

Whether seeking new international markets or funding the development of new products from the laboratory to the marketplace, Colorado's continued economic expansion depends upon good sources of financing and underwriting. The important ingredient to future industrial development is financing, just as the capital investment of the past was critical to the development of the natural resources of the state.

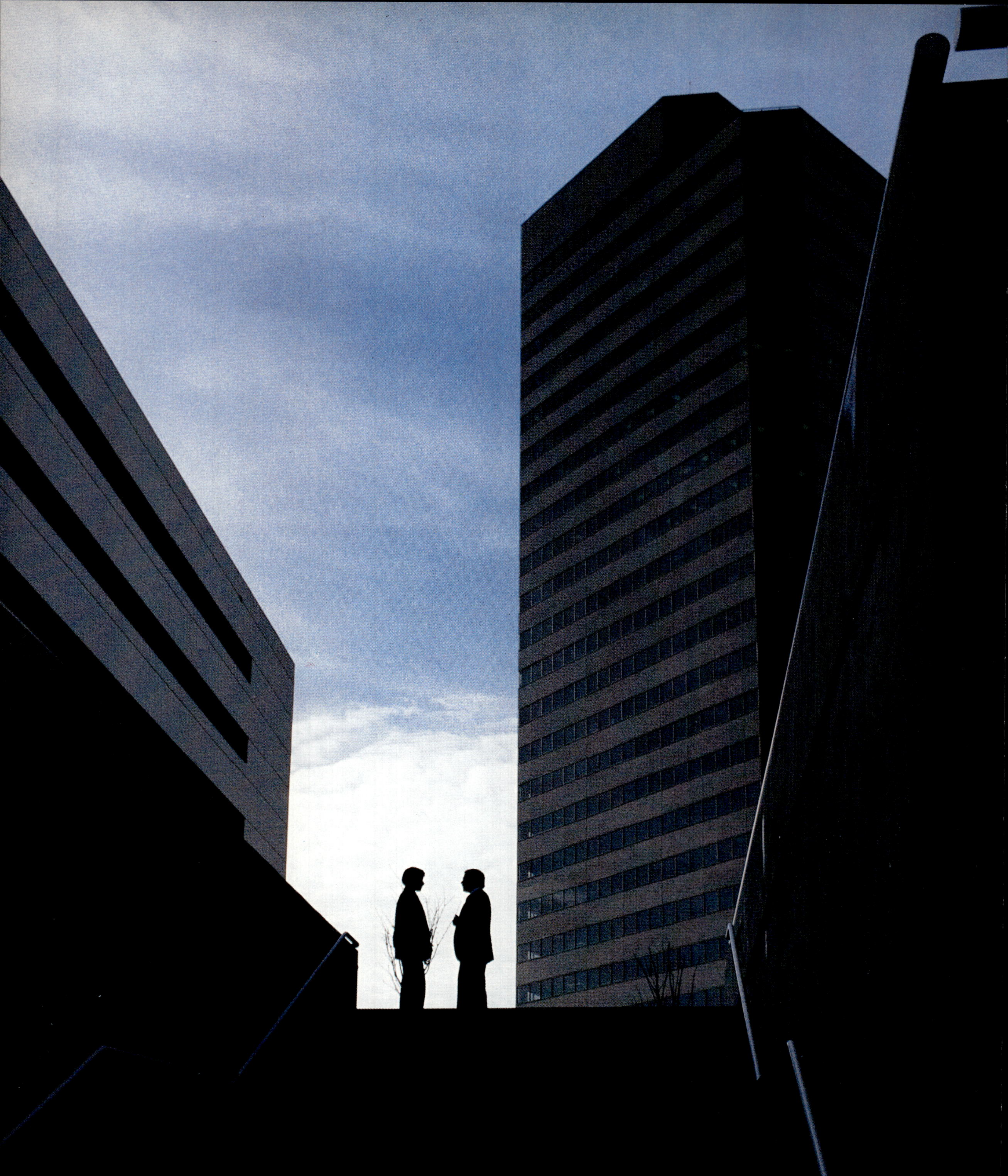

CHAPTER 8

Financing a Mile-High Empire
The Underwriters of Enterprise

Financial decisions made on Denver's 17th Street, the "Wall Street of the West," are developing the new West. Photo by Doug Wilson, Stock Imagery

When the great vault doors to the natural resources of the Rocky Mountains were finally opened, unlocking the hidden wealth in Colorado, the rush for development was begun on one of America's last frontiers. The gold booms lasted only long enough to reveal to the world the immense and diverse natural riches of the region, but they set the stage for a "rush" to capitalize on opportunity that has not abated in the century and a half since.

Gold discovery was the quickest and surest way to wealth in those founding days—a glittering magnet drawing the first settlers to the region. Since it was precious metal that started the economic development, it might be said that "finance" was the catalyst that created Colorado. Today it could just as accurately be said that "finance" is the fuel of Colorado's modern economic engine.

The financial institutions in Colorado, a state which has historically been starved for capital to develop its resources, have experienced a remarkable transformation during the 1980s. In the past decade a number of financial factors have combined to mature the state and bring its financial community of age as a regional business and financial center. Even though 17th Street in Denver has been known as the Wall Street of the West since the turn of the century, the most dramatic growth in the strength of Colorado's various financial institutions is just beginning.

Colorado's banks, savings and loan institutions, stocks and bonds brokerages, insurance companies, investment banking groups, and other credit agencies have grown rapidly in every category, from total assets and deposits to types of underwritings and loans. Modernization in financial systems and services to both individual and corporate clients has been the hallmark of all types of money managing agencies in Colorado, especially since the late 1970s.

A look at the past decade (1976 to 1986) of financial activities in Colorado tells the dramatic story. Commercial bank deposits nearly tripled from $8 billion to nearly $24 billion. Savings and loan association deposits nearly quadrupled, from more than $4 billion to almost $16 billion. Credit union deposits nearly quadrupled from less than $700 million to nearly $2.4 billion. Total life insurance sales soared, from $3.4 billion to $16.4 billion.

While considerable national and international investment money still flows to projects in Colorado, many of the development projects in the state and in other states of the Rocky Mountain West are being funded by Colorado financial institutions. Despite its regulations against regional interstate banking, the state's reputation as a member of the national financial community is gaining respect as more and more of the development projects of the West are funded by Coloradans.

A gold development in the early days might have been underwritten by investors in New York or London, and the first smelters paid for by Germans. But today's mining company is likely to be grubstaked by a Colorado brokerage firm, and a new, small, high-tech manufacturer by a group of Colorado investment bankers.

Financial resources range widely in Colorado. There are about 350 state-chartered commercial and industrial banks, and 145 national banks operating in the state. Denver alone has four banks with over a billion

175

PROFILE

First Interstate Bank of Denver
Bringing Capital to Western Enterprise

The first banking establishment formed in Colorado to bring financial management to a capital-starved mining frontier is today fulfilling a similar role on the economic frontier of Colorado and the Rockies. The difference, however, is gigantic in scope.

First Interstate Bank of Denver, with a banking service legacy of over 125 years, is matching capital to human and natural resource development through one of the largest financial bases in the United States. Its participation as one of the lead institutions in the First Interstate Bank 15-state system brings a $48 billion asset base to underwrite giant corporate projects and small business developments alike.

First Interstate Bank of Denver traces its origins to the Clark, Gruber & Company Bank and Mint, opening in a $5,000 building on January 18, 1860. The bank has continued to provide capital and financial support which has helped to write the mining-energy, manufacturing-distribution, transportation, and retail history in Colorado and the Rocky Mountain region.

It is still writing history, as domestic and international business changes. While First Interstate Bank of Denver joined the multistate First Interstate Bancorp system in 1983, it remains a uniquely Colorado institution, with a powerful local asset base of more than $2 billion and banking services designed to support the characteristics of the region's economy. The bank is organized to provide a full range of banking specialties—from an Enterprise Banking Group serving small Colorado businesses to an International Services Group with 36 offices around the world.

First Interstate of Denver provides a comprehensive range of banking services for both local and regional customers of all sizes and complexity, including a wide range of credit services, cash management assistance,

The artwork and architecture of First Interstate Bank has become a landmark proclaiming Denver's 17th Street as "The Wall Street of the West."

and investment services. It also offers financial teams with expertise in specific sectors of the Colorado economy.

Departments have been established to serve the unique financial needs of industries with a strong position in the Colorado economy—including agriculture, wholesale, energy, manufacturing, real estate, transportation, retailing, high technology, cable television, and service industries. The Denver bank also has experts available for employee benefit planning, trust operations, and correspondent banking.

Merging with First Interstate Bancorp, headquartered in Los Angeles, the big Denver bank joined in a partnership with some of the most powerful individual banks in the United States. The parent organization is one of the nation's 10 largest banking companies, with 1,100 full-service banking offices in 15 western states including Alaska, and in several major midwestern states as well. First Interstate Bancorp serves the fastest growing and most economically dynamic part of the United States, which includes Colorado, and its territory covers half the country's geographical area.

"The merger allows us to bring additional capital into Colorado to support many of the development opportunities existing here now, and those new opportunities maturing on the horizon," says Denver First Interstate President Robert J. Malone. "Within our own system we can provide the loan support required for almost any size project. This added strength can only enhance the economic development of the state we have served for more than 125 years."

First Interstate management believes that new technology and a new American and international business climate call for innovative new financial structures. With its Colorado banking affiliates as a part of this new structuring, First Interstate is positioning the company for the economic future rapidly expanding in the western United States.

Money is literally made in Colorado as the blanks at the Denver Mint prove. But the financial story of Colorado remains the investment opportunity in one of the nation's most dynamic regions. Photo by McAllister of Denver

dollars in assets. The state capital is home to a branch of the Federal Reserve Bank and the regional Clearing House Association. The U.S. Mint in Denver began producing the new Statue of Liberty half dollar in December 1985, and is a major supplier of the United States' coinage, including pennies, nickels, dimes, and quarters. Creative financing for development within the state is provided by about 40 non-profit industrial development corporations, which often provide land at cost, construction lease-back arrangements, and other incentives for new companies to move into their towns.

Since 1967, nearly a half billion dollars of industrial revenue bonds have been authorized in Colorado by cities and towns to bring new jobs into their communities. These revenue bonds have been issued to acquire and improve industrial and office parks, and to underwrite costs of constructing the needed buildings and equipment of new industry.

The state's savings and loan associations have become active leaders in financing major commercial and business land development projects, as well as financing the residential expansion of the communities of the state. Venture capital availability for new and expanding industry of the state has increased in Colorado more rapidly than in almost any part of the country.

Employment in the finance sector of Colorado has been a pacesetter for job growth in the state during this decade of financial expansion. In 1986 more than 71,000 persons were employed in the banks, credit agencies, and other financial institutions of Colorado.

The days when Colorado was almost totally dependent on outside investment for its development seem to be drawing to a close, with financial deregulation and its resulting better interest rates attracting more deposits from within the state. These stronger local deposits provide a base for a wider variety of business loans from the lending agencies across the state. Commercial bank, savings and loan, and credit union deposits have grown substantially since 1983 in Colorado, and the trend is expected to continue.

In 1986, with the deregulation of the industry, interest on savings accounts and deposits in commercial banks and savings and loans are expected to grow even stronger. The rapidly expanding credit union deposits category is also expected to continue to grow, as are deposits in the state's industrial banks. Despite the strong growth in assets and deposits in Colorado's financial institutions, critics of Colorado's banking regulations are seeking to liberalize interstate banking laws. Some see the state's restrictions on activities of out-of-state banks as a threat to Colorado's long-standing position as the financial center for the Rocky Mountain Region. In recent years, legislative battles have been waged to change the banking laws and open the state's borders to out-of-state and regional interstate banking.

The Banking Establishment

Combined deposits in Colorado banks are greater than combined total deposits in commercial banks in any of the eight Rocky Mountain states. There may not be a bank on every major street corner, but the approximately 425 commercial banks in the state provide banking service to almost every community in the state. Affiliates of large bank holding companies are also well represented

PROFILE

United Banks of Colorado
Financial Leadership to Expand the Economy

A bank can only be as strong as the community it serves.

That's an operating philosophy of United Banks of Colorado, Inc., one of the largest financial institutions in the Rocky Mountains. With this as a guideline, company executives and personnel throughout the organization devote their time, talent, and resources to helping improve the communities the company serves with more than 30 banks.

United Banks' position as Colorado's largest financial institution is obvious when traveling almost anywhere in the state. The United Bank emblem is proudly displayed on buildings in the heart of both small towns and large cities from Grand Junction on the Western Slope to Greeley on the high plains, and from Fort Collins in the north to Pueblo in the south.

The company's anchor bank is United Bank of Denver. It has more than $2.7 billion in assets, which makes it the largest commercial bank in Colorado. United Bank of Denver and its predecessors have served Coloradans for more than a century. Besides United Bank of Denver, the company has nearly 20 banks providing services throughout metropolitan Denver. Each carries the name of the city, town, or community it serves: Arvada, Aurora, Boulder, Lakewood, and Littleton, to name just a few of the other cities; and Cherry Creek, Skyline, and University Hills, to cite a few neighborhoods in Denver itself.

The company's focus is far more than metropolitan Denver, however. Its bankers serve bustling communities up and down the Front Range of the Rockies: Fort Collins, Greeley, and other communities to the north of Denver, and Colorado Springs and Pueblo to the south.

United Banks also has a strong presence in western Colorado. It serves resort towns like Steamboat Springs up near the Wyoming line; agricultural communities like Montrose in the Gunnison River country; and transportation and distribution centers like Grand Junction. One of its banks, United Bank of Ignacio, is on the Southern Ute Reservation.

"Our company can best serve communities in Colorado through local banks and local management," says N. Berne Hart, chairman and CEO. "United Banks is a strong system serving many diverse markets, but it can only be as strong as the communities it serves. For our individual banks to benefit both the individual and business customer, our local management must be involved in the community. That's the key to economic development and community improvement."

Although many of its individual banks can trace their origins back to the 19th century, United Banks of Colorado did not come into being until 1964, when it became one of the state's first bank holding companies. Originally called Denver U.S. Bancorporation, it was organized to provide a broad range of financial services to large customers, rapidly growing smaller businesses, and geographically diverse groups of consumers.

In 1970, after acquiring several additional banks, the company changed its name to United Banks of Colorado, Inc., and each individual bank incorporated United Bank in its own name. Since then, whenever the company has acquired a new bank, it has taken the name United. There are now 32 banks in the United Bank system, and together they have nearly $5 billion in assets, more than any other financial services organization in Colorado.

Throughout its history, United Banks of Colorado has kept in the vanguard of industry change. It was among the first organizations in

United Banks has become a regional financial leader with service professionals in all sectors of the economy, but its focus remains personal.

Colorado to offer banking by telephone, MasterCard and VISA, and a guaranteed check card. It was one of two founders of the MINIBANK Switch Network of automated teller machines, which provides service to customers 24 hours a day. Because that system is now part of CIRRUS, the nation's largest network of ATMs, United Bank customers have access to their accounts in more than 2,100 cities throughout North America.

Many of its banks have convenience centers that offer customers the utmost in speedy service through ATMs, and Touch-Me computers.

Its new headquarters building, One United Bank Center, located at the corner of 17th and Lincoln Streets in Denver, has become a fixture in the Denver skyline since the building topped out at 52 stories in 1982.

While United Banks has developed a broad array of products and services for consumers, it has also made every effort to meet the needs of business. Each United Bank is geared to serve the small and medium-sized enterprises that form the backbone of Colorado's economy. The strength and soundness of the United Bank organization is particularly important in serving those customers, because it allows them to benefit from a $5 billion organization.

The company serves its large customers principally through United Bank of Denver. With about 60 percent of the company's assets, it has the size necessary to provide the diverse loan, deposit, and cash management services required by major corporations.

To serve the credit needs of various customers, the bank has created a number of specialized groups, such as its oil and gas specialists who have worked in that industry for more than 35 years. The bank's Real Estate Banking group works with both commercial and residential developers by providing funds for development and construction. The group offers a full range of banking services to many of the largest real estate companies operating in the Rocky Mountain region.

The bank serves the needs of many Fortune 500 companies through the activities of its Corporate Banking Group. These bankers also work closely with the major savings and loan institutions, credit unions, and insurance companies, as well as the branches of national brokerage houses located in Colorado.

The Investment Services area meets the needs of corporations, institutional investors, and individuals seeking a high return from fixed income investments. The bank's Investment Banking area serves the needs of municipalities and corporations seeking to raise capital through the sale of taxable or tax-exempt securities.

Asset Management Services offers both traditional trust products such as the management of employee benefit plans, personal trusts, estate management, escrow agent, and bond trustee services, as well as other specialized services including investment management accounts and MiniTrust, a miniature trust agreement that provides access to their managed investment portfolios.

The company also offers trust services through some of its other banks, such as United Bank of Fort Collins and United Bank of Colorado Springs. Finally, the company offers a worldwide banking link through United Bank of Denver's International Banking Group, which has a network of 650 correspondent banks in many countries.

The company's goal is to deliver the most modern and comprehensive group of products in a way that combines state-of-the-art technology with superior service that will distinguish United Banks from the competition. In this age of less regulation and more intensified competition, quality service is good business. Customers deserve it, and United Banks intends to provide it.

Headquartered in one of the best-known landmark skyscrapers in the Rocky Mountains, United Banks provide service to all of Colorado. Photo by Bob Fader.

179

PROFILE

Colorado National Bankshares
Growing Through History with Colorado

One of Colorado's largest and most historic banking organizations has been a vital part of the underwriting of progress throughout the state since the earliest days of development. Colorado National Bankshares, the holding company for 23 Colorado bank subsidiaries, was formed under the leadership of Colorado National Bank of Denver in 1968.

Colorado National Bankshares has total assets nearing $3 billion. And while the individual banks within the organization maintain their local character and management, the combined resources provide additional strength and service to the individual local banks.

The group has enjoyed strong growth throughout the almost two decades since the creation of the holding company, and its combined resources make its members a part of one of the leading statewide banks in Colorado.

All its subsidiary banks include the name Colorado National Bank in their titles, to provide customers with a common identification. The local banks are able to serve the growing base of existing and emerging companies of Colorado with numerous financial services.

The lead bank in the holding company, Colorado National Bank of Denver was founded in 1862, and is the largest in the Colorado National Bankshares group, with assets of over $1.5 billion and deposits exceeding $1.1 billion.

The holding company has established a strong presence in the Front Range communities, where the most rapid growth in Colorado's high technology industry base is occurring. In the Denver area, subsidiaries include Colorado National Bank of Denver, Colorado National Bank—Northeast, Colorado National Bank—Boulevard, Colorado National Bank — South, Colorado National Bank—Aurora, Colorado National Bank—Tech Center, Colorado National Bank—Arapahoe, Colorado National Bank—Southwest, Colorado National Bank—Lakewood, Colorado National Bank—Arvada, Colorado National Bank—Golden, and Colorado National Bank—Evergreen.

Three banking subsidiaries are located in Boulder County, including Colorado National Bank—Boulder, Colorado National Bank—East Boulder, and Colorado National Bank—Longmont. In the northern part of the Front Range, Colorado National has banks in Fort Collins, Greeley, and Sterling.

In the central and southern section of the Front Range, the organization consists of Colorado National Bank—Exchange, Colorado National Bank—Belmont, and Colorado National Bank—Pueblo. Serving the central mountain region is Colorado National Bank—Glenwood and on the Western Slope is Colorado National Bank—Grand Junction.

Rocky Mountain BankCard System, a subsidiary of the Colorado National Bank of Denver, continues to be one of the largest card issuers in the nation. The system processes more than $1.5 billion in retail sales each year. The Plus System of nationwide Automatic Teller Machines (ATM) serves 1,400 banks in the United States, Canada, Great Britain, and Japan and is managed by the Rocky Mountain BankCard System. With more than 10,000 ATMs connected to the system, it is estimated that 65 million accounts will have access to this vast financial network.

Colorado National's expansion of the Plus System and Rocky Mountain BankCard System has positioned the big Colorado banking institution as a leader in the United States in providing technologically advanced financial services to it customers.

Colorado National Banks operate on the premise that while advances in technology are available to provide more efficient and cost-effective banking, the local bank must provide personal and friendly service that has been its tradition. The banks strive to combine the efficiency of financial technology with personalized, people-to-people service.

Colorado National Banks' role in the development of the state and the West has been extensive. Its motto applies to its development policies, stating, "We Make Big Ideas Happen."

Colorado National Bank has grown from its landmark facility, left, to expanded new skyscraper quarters as one of the state's leading financial centers.

Photo by David Williams

Denver's 17th Street has throughout modern history been known as the "Wall Street of the West" and that nickname has never been truer than today.

Photo by Joel Silverman

in each region, and in most towns in the state.

The growth rate in deposits in commercial banks exceeded 10 percent each year during the past decade, and 27 new banks were opened in the state in 1984. Since the banks are the major day-to-day business financiers in most Colorado communities, they are very much involved in the impact of change in the economy of the communities they serve. Some Colorado banks have suffered from depressed local economic conditions in the energy, mining, and agriculture industries of their regions, and there have been a few bank closures. But generally, the banks of Colorado have enjoyed record levels of deposits throughout the 1980s.

Of the 425 commercial banks in the state, 314 report 1985 deposits in excess of $10 million, and 32 had deposits exceeding $100 million. Four banks in Denver had deposits exceeding $1 billion, and two of these had deposits of about $2.5 billion.

Employment in the banking sector of the finance community has not grown proportionally with the rapid increase in deposits because of the high degree of modernization and computerization within the industry. In 1986 approximately 22,300 people were employed by the banks in the state, a level that has not substantially increased since the early 1980s.

However, in virtually every large community in the state, automatic banking service has been introduced, as management has modernized to remain competitive with other financial services also expanding into areas historically the preserve of the commercial bank. Even with interest rate ceilings being lifted on most types of savings accounts, banks have had to screen loan applications more carefully for higher quality accounts. Modernization has provided more services to bank customers, but banking management has had to use the efficiency of automation to sharpen their competitive position.

With other types of financial institutions, such as brokerage firms, savings and loan associations, and private credit agencies now extending credit card services, Colorado banks and bank holding institutions have also seen consumer lending become more competitive in Colorado as it has elsewhere in the country. But, at the same time, Colorado banks have recently entered into areas of finance formerly the domain of other types of financial agencies, such as cash management services and securities services.

Competition among the banks within the state has also increased in recent years, with many neighborhood banks and smaller city banks vying for a greater share of the growing deposits base in the state.

Colorado's bank holding companies are also providing centralized services to their banking affiliates outside the metropolitan areas, which are bringing a higher degree of automated services to bank customers in smaller communities and suburban areas. In Colorado, over 175 banks are affiliated with the top 15 Colorado bank holding companies. Five of these large holding companies have more than 20 affiliated banks each. These 15 bank holding companies and their affiliated banks account for more than half the total

PROFILE

Central Bancorporation, Inc.
Growing to Meet the Needs of an Expanding State

Modern banking within an atmosphere of traditional personal service has marked the expanding financial role of the Central banks throughout Colorado.

The changing needs of businesses and individuals demand financial institutions that can keep pace. This means providing a blend of the most advanced as well as trusted traditional financial services.

Central Bancorporation, Inc. and its 20 member banks located throughout Colorado, are meeting the challenge of providing sophisticated financial services while maintaining the personalized approach to their customer base.

The bank holding company has assets of more than $2.1 billion. Its lead bank, Central Bank of Denver, is the fourth largest bank in Colorado, with assets in excess of $1.3 billion and deposits of nearly a billion dollars. A highly innovative and efficient centralized system is ushering in a new era of expanded service to member banks with a broad mix of customers in a variety of strategic locations in the state.

Sophisticated data processing and bookkeeping operations, as well as customized services for different types of business and individual accounts, are enabling the bank corporation to deploy assets throughout the organization.

CBI's exceptionally strong capital base was further strengthened in 1984 by a major investment made through a limited partnership with AmeriTrust Corporation, a $7.8 billion bank holding company based in Cleveland. This capital strength enables CBI to meet the growing needs of its members and to take advantage of new product and expansion opportunities.

Central Bank of Denver, which recently purchased total control of the Park Central Building in Denver, also led the way for the development of one of Colorado's most innovative new concepts in automated banking. That bank's newly opened Automated Banking Center offers a number of time-saving automated services for greater customer convenience.

Other products and services have been added throughout the Central Bancorporation system. New drive-in facilities and additional automated tellers provide greater access and faster service. More convenient check cashing and credit capabilities; specialized investment, tax, and retirement planning information; improved corporate cash management services; and a variety of individual and business credit products, such as customized real estate financing have been added to traditional products at its facilities across the state.

Among the diverse capabilities offered are such areas as retirement planning, business and financial strategies, corporate cash management, automated business management services, personal and corporate trust services, and administration of employee benefit plans.

The banks are also offering extensive information programs on financial matters to assist individuals and businesses with their financial planning and management.

CBI banks have also taken active roles in promoting the development and prosperity of their communities. The banks focus not only on supporting community organizations and attracting participation for community programs and events, but also on providing valuable information to individuals and businesses in their regions.

Banks affiliated with Central Bancorporation include: Central Bank of Academy Boulevard, Central Bank of Aurora, Central Bank of Broomfield, Central Bank at Centennial, Central Bank of Chapel Hills, Central Bank of Chatfield, Central Bank of Colorado Springs, Central Bank of Denver, Central Bank of East Aurora, Central Bank of Garden of the Gods, Central Bank of Greeley, Central Bank of Inverness, Central Bank of North Denver, Central Bank of Pueblo, Central Bank of Westminster, First National Bank in Aspen, First National Bank in Craig, First National Bank in Glenwood Springs, First National Bank in Grand Junction, and Rocky Ford National Bank.

Offering an ever expanding, multifaceted line of products, and taking advantage of the latest in technology to provide efficiency and service, the member banks of Central Bancorporation live up to their slogan, "The Better Bankers."

deposits in all Colorado banks, with deposits exceeding $13 billion of the approximately $23.7 billion.

Seven of the 15 largest bank holding companies headquarter in Denver, with others headquartered in Boulder, Lakewood, Brush, Glenwood Springs, Westminster, and Colorado Springs. One holding company is affiliated with a huge regional system headquartered in Los Angeles. The six bank holding companies with total assets exceeding a billion dollars include United Banks of Colorado, First Interstate Bancorp, Colorado National Bankshares, Affiliated Bankshares of Colorado, Central Bancorporation, and Intra-West Financial Corporation.

Industrial banks are also among the financial institutions of Colorado that have enjoyed fast-paced growth in deposits during the past decade. Total deposits in these banks have soared from just over $202 million in 1976 to more than $633 million in 1986, and indications are that deposits in the industrials are growing at an annual rate exceeding seven percent.

European investment in Colorado and the Rocky Mountain region is almost as historic as the early pioneering development of the natural resources. Early mining, agricultural, and manufacturing development were aided by European investors. A number of European and Canadian banks maintain offices in Denver to serve the Rocky Mountain region, and these banking interests still bring investments into the state.

The major foreign banks with sizable lending programs in the region and offices in the Denver metro area include: Banque Paribas of Paris; Den Norske of Oslo; Lloyds Bank International, a subsidiary of the British Lloyds Bank; National Westminister USA, a subsidiary of National Westminister Bank of London; Royal Bank of Canada; Canadian Imperial Bank of Commerce; Bank of Montreal; Toronto Dominion Colorado Inc., a subsidary of the Toronto Dominion Bank; and Mercantile Bank of Canada Financial Services.

According to Gail L. Pitts, a leading business news writer for the *Denver Post*, these banks have shifted their investment interests from energy to a number of development activities. Among their major lending activities, in addition to oil and gas development, are commercial and major residential real estate development, agribusiness, cable TV, and general corporate finance.

Canadian banks have long been major lenders in the developing Front Range, heavily involved in energy development and representing clients in the purchase and development of some of the major office buildings and office parks in the Front Range area.

Another area of substantial growth in

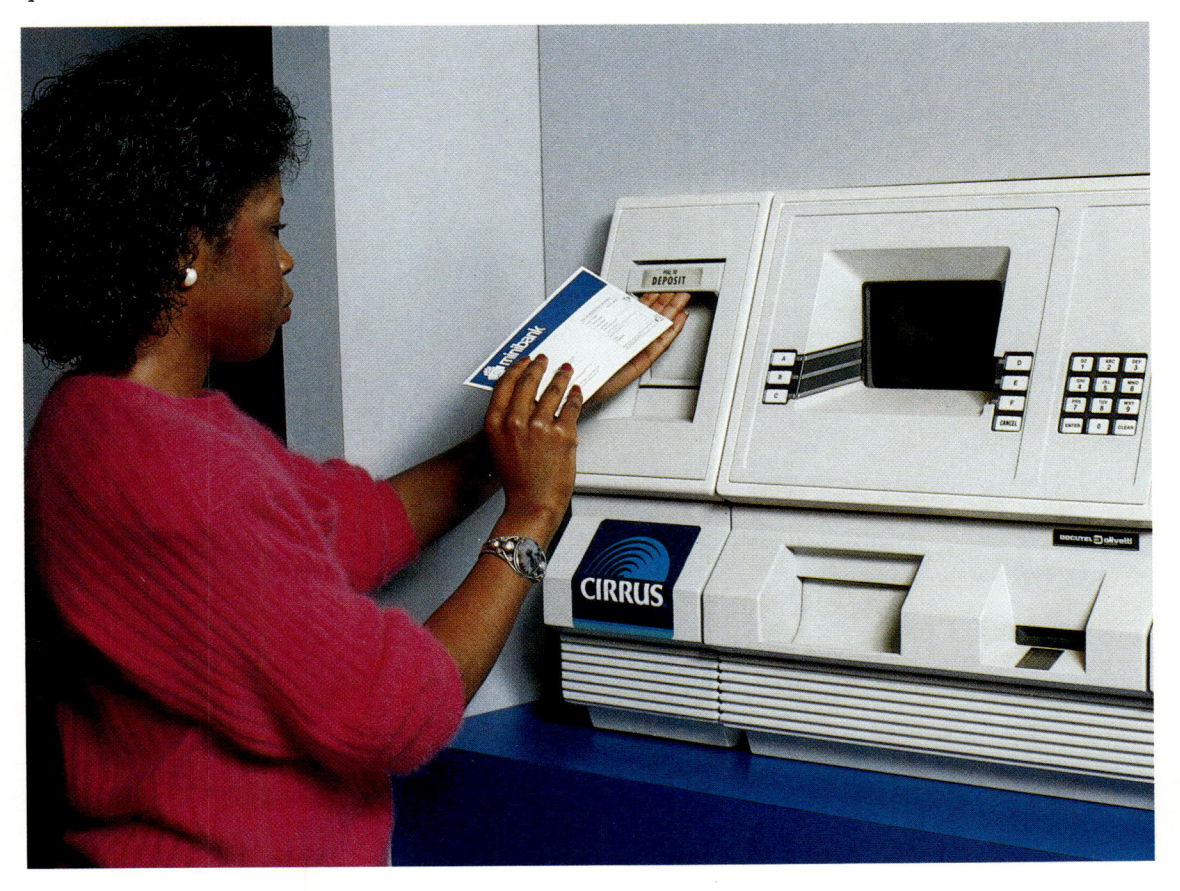

Even with high technology in banking, Colorado's financial institutions have maintained the practice of individual attention to the customers' needs. Photo courtesy of United Banks

183

PROFILE

American Federal Savings and Loan Association
Opening Financial Frontiers on the Front Range

Nationally ranked among the top performing savings and loan associations, American Federal Savings and Loan Association of Colorado has been a leader in innovative funding to finance real estate along the state's Front Range.

American Federal, which celebrated its half-century as a Colorado financial institution in 1984, is ranked as Colorado's seventh largest association with an asset base of nearly $600 million. Its loans finance projects for the purchase, construction, development, and improvement of properties in the most populated, fastest growing part of the state.

The savings and loan association has been Colorado Springs' leading real estate lender through the 1980s. American Federal maintains a major lending office in Denver, and has ten consumer deposit offices in Colorado, including three in Pueblo, six in Colorado Springs, and one in Canon City.

A well capitalized association, American Federal has a tangible net worth of nearly twice that required by the Federal Savings and Loan Insurance Corporation. Its stock, which is traded on the national market system of NASDAQ, is actively traded by 11 Wall Street firms. Ranked over a period of two and a half years with 31 major publicly traded thrifts in the country in 1985, American Federal was named by Salomon Brothers, Inc. of New York City as one of the top five performers in the nation. The Colorado-based company has earned that position by being consistently profitable, even during the difficult economic periods since it was converted to a capital stock association in 1980.

A major construction lender in the fast growing sectors of the Front Range economy, American Federal had a total loan volume of $322 million in 1985. The association, which concentrates its lending activities in the Front Range cities and not in the resort areas, specializes in loans for income-producing properties and acquisition and development. To service these loans, American Federal has developed a staff of highly experienced commercial real estate lenders, who are backed by credit and appraisal analysts, civil engineers, CPAs, and administrators. Its emphasis on funding income-producing properties has provided loans with higher yields and shorter maturities to more closely match its source of funds from depositors.

This concentration on performance-oriented business has led American Federal to develop professional administrators with the sophistication required to lend in the construction and commercial real estate field. The Association is strongly committed to "relationship-oriented lending," and dealing with development organizations with known capabilities and demonstrated success in the marketplace.

American Federal's funds acquisitions are principally from consumer checking and savings, and a large segment of its customers depend on interest as an important source of their income. For that reason, the association constantly develops innovative products and income protection programs for its depositors.

The key to American Federal's success in this area is quick response to perceived consumer needs. Consumer input from branch offices is constantly evaluated and used to design savings plans that meet needs and desires that are expressed: interest rate certainty, maturity dates that allow deferral of taxes, and other components that respond directly to customer Feedback. As a result, American Federal has led the industry in new product design, introducing several savings plans that have become prototypes for products offered by similar institutions across the nation.

As an active corporate member of the cities where it operates, American Federal has a long history of service to its communities in Colorado.

American Federal is leading the Colorado financial community in innovative new programs for its customers and investors from offices near Pikes Peak.

A new era in banking combines the best of high technology in finance, such as this downtown automation center filled with instant services, with a continued high level of personal service. Photo courtesy of Central Banks

Colorado's financial community in recent years has been in the membership-owned credit unions. Credit union deposits have increased rapidly since 1980, nearly doubling in five years and reaching approximately $2.5 billion in 1986. The growth rate of credit union deposits has been about 20 percent per year in the past five years.

While the individual company-based, employee-owned credit unions are generally smaller in size than the banks and savings associations, they are important lenders, especially in areas of consumer loans. In 1985, there were approximately 260 credit unions operating in the state, compared to 337 in 1980. But the size of these financial organizations has grown due to mergers and the influx of employee deposits. Their popularity has grown with employees because of the relative ease of obtaining short-term loans, favorable loan and deposit interest rates, and new bank-like services offered by many of the organizations. Credit unions account for about five percent of the savings on deposit in Colorado.

Most of the larger credit unions in the state have been formed by government and utility workers, but several of the top credit unions are formed within the state's larger companies. The combined membership in the top 25 credit unions in the state is over 455,000 employees, which represents more than a quarter of the entire employed workforce of Colorado. The credit unions themselves become major depositors in other savings and investment plans of banks, savings and loan associations, and other funds.

Being member-owned, and without having to manage loans outside their membership, the credit unions are not major employers in the state. But they do play an important and increasing role in the overall finance picture in Colorado.

Financing Development

From a financing point of view, a survey conducted by the University of Colorado's College of Business Administration in 1984 depicts strong growth in Colorado business and industry. The survey indicated that fully two-thirds of Colorado manufacturers—particularly in the so-called high technology areas—planned to expand their plant and office facilities by 1987.

New and growing Colorado companies have a broadening range of options for their financial underwriting. Some financial analysts believe that recent downturns in agriculture and energy development in the state are releasing funds for easier access by business and manufacturing firms seeking expansion funding. In addition, a study by the United Banks of Colorado reported that in 1984 a net total of 14,000 new businesses were formed, the second largest number of new firms started in a single year in the state's history. According to the bank's report,

PROFILE

Silverado Banking
Making an Impact with Service, Products and Performance

Silverado Banking, federally insured and one of the largest financial institutions in Colorado, has made an impact with its service, its products, and its interest in its customers' financial success.

The company's distinctive and highly visible headquarters are located at the intersection of I-25 and Colorado Boulevard, and are a landmark on the Denver skyline.

The company offers customers a tailored approach to financial services, utilizing a network of banking centers strategically located in key areas throughout the Front Range. The Silverado Banking Center network is complemented by a Consumer Investment Desk. . . . . 1-800-228-4754. . . . .bringing high performance products and services and immediate access to current rates to customers' homes and offices.

Staff members at Silverado are extraordinarily adept in financial services. They are top caliber, professional people who are knowledgeable about the company's innovative products and how they perform against other investment alternatives.

Silverado has implemented operational efficiencies so customers can enjoy the highest rates available, and the company is continually developing new ideas that result in attractive alternatives to traditional banking.

The people of Colorado have responded by making Silverado one of the state's premier financial institutions.

Colorado ranks 13th nationally in the number of new businesses incorporated.

Several methods of financing new enterprises are available until they can establish the credentials necessary to acquire traditional funding. Most companies begin with private equity and retained earnings before approaching investors or lenders. But when operational records are established, small firms find a number of available avenues open in the state for expansion of facilities and product.

Once a small manufacturer or other business entrepreneur has proven to have sound management and good market potential, venture capital is available in Colorado. In 1983, *Venture Capital Journal* ranked Colorado as a major national center for venture capital. The state was rated fifth in the nation in venture capital disbursements, with more than $134 million invested within the state. A score of venture capital funds in Colorado raised $100 million in 1984, almost four times the amount raised in the previous year. The magazine reported that much of that investment money was targeted to high technology, but also noted that a considerable amount of underwriting also went into high-growth markets for consumer products. These new and expanding businesses also attract investment from regional and national pension funds.

While the "technology" label alone no longer attracts immediate response from venture capital funds or stockbrokers in Colorado, the *Colorado Business & Technology Update* noted in a survey in late 1984 that "venture capital, which is becoming less available in other states, is starting to flow more strongly in Colorado." The publication noted that investors and lenders today are much more concerned with the quality of management than before, and "at the same time are demanding that markets for new products and service be demonstrated, if not clearly developed."

Colorado technological development is becoming more dependent on investment capital as young firms expand. The local securities market, which for many years was heavily targeted toward energy development, is now opening up to consumer and technology companies.

Nearly $300 million was raised in 1985 in new Colorado stock underwritings, and those stocks were stronger in 1986 than new issues coming forward on the local stock market in recent years. A total of 84 new issues for Colorado companies came to market in 1985 and unlike previous years, most were manufacturing companies. A majority of the new stock issues were in electronics, video, equipment, medical and biotechnical, and other high technology areas. The previous year, 98 new Colorado companies had been underwritten in the public market.

According to *Colorado Business & Technology Update*, the higher standards being set by investors could be beneficial.

"The outcome may be fewer players in the

Financial professionals in the banking institutions of Colorado offer expertise in every sector of the economy. Photo courtesy of United Banks

PROFILE

The Travelers Companies
A National Tradition in the Region

The insurance industry has played a large role in the financial progress of Colorado, since the earliest pioneering days. One such company is The Travelers, a leader in the insurance community, and a major investor in Colorado economic development projects and in community betterment programs.

With offices in Denver, Colorado Springs, Fort Collins, and Grand Junction, many of the nearly 300 employees located in the state take active roles in a variety of local community life and betterment programs. The Travelers Companies Foundation is active in Colorado Older American programs, job training and preparation, health and social services, higher education, and arts and culture programs. Travelers Real Estate Investment Department, located in Denver and Fort Collins, has placed more than $615 million in urban and agricultural development throughout the state.

The Travelers serves the large Colorado market with a wide range of services, fitting the needs of individuals, small businesses, and large corporations. As the financial sophistication of the region has developed over the years, The Travelers has tailored thousands of products to meet its customers specialized needs.

Because Colorado has an unusually large percentage of "small businesses," Travelers combined its expertise with the expertise of the independent agent and acquired a special knowledge of the unique needs of the small and emerging business in the state. The Travelers is heavily involved in both financial and insurance programs for retail establishment, service businesses, wholesalers, manufacturers, franchises, professional practices, and associations, to name but a few.

They also provide financial services to some of Colorado's largest firms and institutions, trade and professional associations, government units, and non-profit organizations. The Travelers is among the nation's top 10 pension fund managers, with over $20 billion in assets under management. Its Employee Benefits Department insures over 1,700 large group customers nationwide, with a total annual premium exceeding $4.6 billion. Combining that with the nearly 45,000 small- to medium-sized companies, the Employee Benefit Department's annual premiums exceed $5.3 billion.

The Travelers has become one of America's largest private mortgage lenders and structures long-term private placements for large- and medium-sized businesses. They are one of five members of the Municipal Bond Insurance Association, which insures tax-exempt securities, and one of the nation's largest writers of worker's compensation and disability insurance, bringing specialized knowledge to the requirements of compensation laws for Colorado and other Rocky Mountain states.

The Hartford, Connecticut-based company has its principal Colorado office in Denver. From here, Travelers Property-Casualty Department serves its commercial and personal lines customers, as do the Employee Benefits Department; Life, Health, and Financial Services; the Field Litigation Division of the Law Department; Engineering; and Surety & Claim. Their Property-Casualty insurance programs are designed to meet the needs of companies of all sizes in protection from personal hazard to buildings, fleets of vehicles, equipment, and inventory.

The Employee Benefits Department brings a highly trained staff of experts to Colorado, assisting local companies in the creation of health cost-containment programs designed to help control the rising costs of medical insurance and providing a number of innovative employee financial services for any size business or corporation.

By focusing on customer needs; offering a diversity of products, services, and investments; sustaining technological superiority in information processing and communications; and dedicating themselves to efficiency and professionalism in every aspect of their work, The Travelers will continue to be a premier underwriter of insurance and financial products in the state of Colorado and nationwide.

A leader in the insurance industry, The Travelers heavily invests its people and resources in economic development and community betterment in Colorado.

Denver serves the Rocky Mountain Region as the headquarters and financial center. Its financial services role has grown over the years as the economy has expanded. Photo by Ron Ruhoff, Stock Imagery

high-tech scramble, but fewer losers also. In short, the high-tech economy is maturing, and the long-haul consequences for Colorado can only be beneficial," the industry publication opined.

In 1981 the Colorado legislature authorized another potentially important source of financing for the expansion of small Colorado manufacturers. The Colorado Housing Finance Authority (CHFA) was charged with developing a "loans-to-lenders" program targeted at small business. Using tax-exempt bonds, this program could provide fixed-rate, long-term funding for plants, equipment, and real estate for small, but established, Colorado manufacturers. Through the issue of bonds, local lenders can provide up to 70 percent of the funding of an expansion project at low rates similar to those available to much larger companies. The balance of the projects, costs are usually funded by the participating lender at conventional rates.

Competition for investors among the banks, S&Ls, and stockbrokers has picked up in recent years in Colorado, with the brokerages offering services formally available only from banks. At the same time, a number of major banks are getting into brokerage services for their investing clients. Some major national brokerage firms were also offering their best customers business and real estate loans at low interest rates and with flexible repayment terms. Such loans are tied to the investors' stock portfolio values.

The Denver Metropolitan Area is home to several substantial regional securities firms, and regional offices for most of the big national firms are located in the area. In addition, other Colorado cities have branch offices of the major companies. Some of the smaller cities in resort areas, such as Aspen and Telluride, also have a good representation of licensed brokers and securities offices to serve the investment-minded residents who have homes and retreats in these mountain communities.

Mutual funds based in Colorado have also gained growing support in recent years. Several mutual funds based in Denver continue to show gains, and these longer-term investment opportunities remain an important part of the Colorado financial picture.

Another important field of finance for Colorado is the municipal bond market. In 1985 a record $6 billion in municipal bonds was sold to underwrite improvement in cities and public works projects. Financial firms dealing in Colorado municipal bonds offer tax-exempt issues to build Colorado airports, public housing, public sports, arts and recreation centers, parking facilities, and a wide assortment of projects to improve the lifestyle

PROFILE

Boettcher & Company
Investing in the Rocky Mountain West

Boettcher & Company is one of the leading underwriters of progress in the emerging West, with a tradition of supporting both public and private projects.

The story of the development of the West has always been tied to capital investment, and Boettcher & Company has played a large part in raising the funds necessary for many of the more notable projects in Colorado.

A full-service investment banking and stock brokerage firm that has grown up with the West, the company has developed a record of service and commitment to Colorado investors, municipalities, and businesses.

Founded and headquartered in Denver since 1910, Boettcher has become one of the largest and most respected investment firms in the West, with 22 offices in Colorado, Alaska, Arizona, New Mexico, Oregon, Texas, Utah, Washington, and Wyoming. Approximately 900 employees and partners are specialists in investments for the most rapidly growing section of the United States, and bring this first-hand knowledge to the underwriting of projects throughout the region.

One example of Boettcher's experience in the state was its capital underwriting of the now world-famous Vail resort area, which has become one of Colorado's leading new towns as well. But that project is only one of many; Boettcher has been involved in major Colorado and western U.S. projects throughout the region's history. The firm financed the Moffat Tunnel through the Rockies in 1924, and issued the first revenue bonds for Stapleton International Airport in 1939. It financed the Denver-Boulder Turnpike in 1948, which was paid off well ahead of schedule; and companies assisted by Boettcher financings are on the roster of Colorado's leading firms in most sectors of the economy.

The big investment firm, which has membership in the New York and American Stock Exchanges as well as all major exchanges and the Securities Investor Protection Corporation, believes the opportunities for investment abound in this region. Their corporate commitment notes that the "opportunities are as boundless as the vistas...people who live in the West are more inclined to invest than people who live in any other region of the country."

Boettcher believes this is true because "the West offers more new jobs, faster-growing incomes, world leadership in high technology, and a new leadership in launching and consumption of a wide range of new products."

Retail and institutional clients are served by 300 account executives with a vast support system. The more than 65,000 retail investment accounts can call on a wide variety of services from Boettcher Product Centers. These include financial services such as employee benefit plans, mutual funds, unit investment trusts, annuities, insurance, retirement plans, and financial planning. Other product centers are fixed income securities, managed accounts, research, and direct investments.

Boettcher & Company is one of the West's leading public project financiers. In the years 1981-1985, Boettcher managed or co-managed over $13 billion in tax-exempt financings for issuers in one-third of the United States. The company has the largest public finance staff located anywhere outside New York City, with more than 50 professionals located in six western states.

Corporate Finance offices in Denver and Seattle participate in both public and private offerings in research and development companies, oil and gas operations, communications, leasing, and venture capital firms. The total value of Boettcher's managed or co-managed corporate finance transactions exceeded a quarter billion dollars in 1985.

The company has been involved in real estate syndication activities since 1978, selling more than $125 million in both private and public property limited partnerships.

The firm was founded by the late Claude K. Boettcher, the son of one of Colorado's earliest immigrant families. Together with a partner, John Henry Porter, he launched the investment firm in the early boom days of this century. Today, 20 percent of the firm is owned by its partners, who operate the company as an independent and autonomous investment firm. Kemper Corporation, a diversified national financial services company, owns 80 percent of the company.

The skyline of Denver serves as a reminder that Colorado is the headquarters center for much of the Rockies. Photo courtesy of Central Banks

in the state.

Colorado has also historically been a leading state in the Rocky Mountain region in the insurance industry. The insurance industry has been both a major service sector of the economy, and a major investment industry. Many of the largest building projects in the state were underwritten by local and national insurance companies. That segment of the financial community of Colorado remains a strong growth industry. Total life insurance sales in 1986 are expected to be nearly $16.5 billion, a jump from just under $3.5 billion 10 years earlier.

The insurance industry is a sizable employer—both in headquarters and regional office employment, and in agents and support staff. More than 23,000 Coloradans are employed in the insurance sector. With premium prices for property and casualty coverage rising nationally as well as locally, this segment of the finance industry is expected to show improved profitability, and thus continued growth. The life insurance industry is introducing new interest-sensitive products in an effort to offer competitive investment opportunities for its clients.

Coloradans as individuals are well insured, compared to the national average. The average Colorado family has nearly $61,000 in life insurance in force, compared with $54,000 for the average American family. In 1983 Coloradans were insured for a total life insurance value of $80 billion, with 4.9 million policies in force in a state with a population of 3.2 million people.

An important member of the Colorado financial community is the savings and loan association industry, which underwrites most of the state's residential needs and a growing part of its commercial real estate development. This strong and vital financial sector includes 43 S&L associations in Colorado, the largest number in any of the Rocky Mountain states. Its depositor base has increased almost four-fold in the past decade, with deposits in S&Ls soaring from $4.6 billion in 1976 to almost $16 billion in 1986. The growth has been most rapid since 1980. Despite a soft real estate industry in the state, the so-called "thrifts" are reporting improved profits and assets as their services are expanded.

The savings and loan institutions, like the banks, provide offices and branches in cities and towns throughout the state, with expanding services now provided far beyond the traditional home loans. These institutions are extremely important in providing the support for the high quality of life and high standards of housing Colorado families enjoy.

Also of importance in the origination of mortgage credit in Colorado is the mortgage banking industry with more than 100 member firms in the state. Mortgage banking firms, which are not depositories like banks or S&Ls, are important loan originators for both residential and commercial properties. The mortgage bankers, serving as middle agencies for real estate transactions, arrange loans and then sell them to other lenders and investors within Colorado, the United States, and abroad.

The banks, savings and loan associations, insurance companies, and other financial institutions of Colorado are vital to the continued development of the state. They seem to weather the booms and slumps in the economy of their communities, and all are channels for investment dollars generated both from within the state and from their out-of-state networks.

Ultimately, the progress and continued growth of Colorado is dependent upon the financial community's support and underwriting.

Colorado's development—and particularly its goal to enjoy economic prosperity while maintaining the quality of its natural environment—to a large extent depends upon matching local and imported financial resources with ingenuity and enterprise.

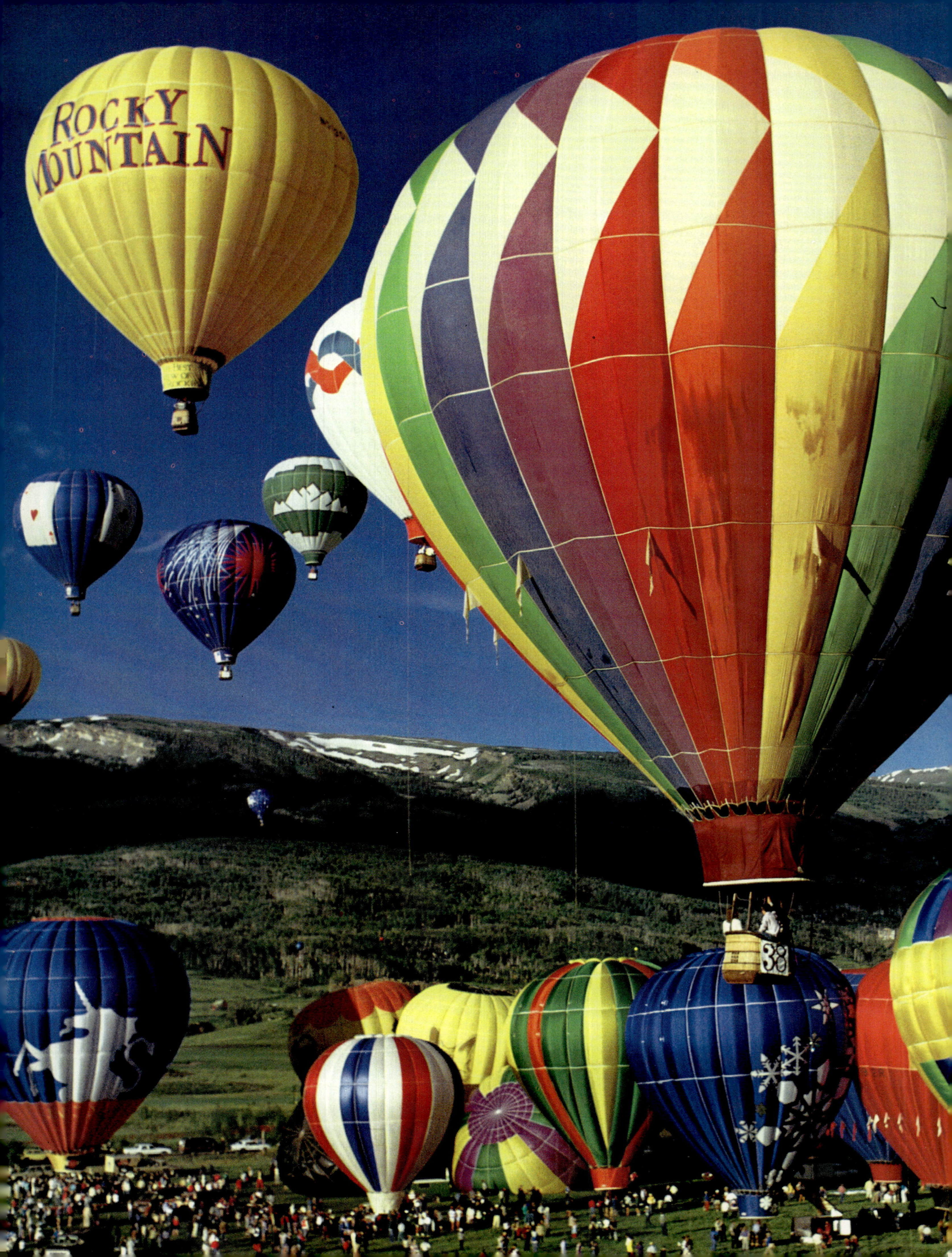
ROCKY MOUNTAIN
38

CHAPTER 9

High-Altitude Recreation
A Mountain Land for Vacations, Arts, and Culture

It's schussing down a snow-clad mountain in winter.

It's contemplating a cold, crystal brook in summer.

It's making human thunder in an orange-bathed football stadium on an autumn afternoon.

It's being inspired by Tchaikovsky on a spring evening, in the best concert hall in the West.

Colorado is the place where 20 million people each year recreate the best in themselves through an endless variety of vacations, amusements, festivals, and cultural activities.

Its seasonal and diverse offerings make Colorado most Americans' "dream vacation spot." In fact, there's proof it even beats out the vacation meccas of California and Florida. AT&T recently conducted an independent "Ideal American Vacation" survey, and Colorado ranked third behind only Hawaii and the Caribbean as this hemisphere's choice.

The recreational riches of the state provide more than enjoyment for Colorado residents—they attract a tourist trade that generates a substantial part of the state's financial wealth. In all seasons the visitor industry generates income that supports tens of thousands of Coloradans.

Travel and tourism are big, big business in nearly every geographical sector of the state, amounting to nearly $4.5 billion a year during the mid-1980s. The visitor industry directly employs more than 100,000 people, and many more are indirectly employed through visitor-generated retailing and support activities. Total economic impact of the industry has been estimated at more than $11 billion annually, when such factors as purchase of goods by visitors and businesses within the industry are calculated.

Why Colorado? It has historically been a visitor center. It earned the nickname "America's Alps" for its winter sports soon after the beginning of this century. It was the "Playground of America" to summer visitors who journeyed to the mountains for health and recuperation even before vacations became an innovation for working Americans.

The state is only now reaching its potential as a "place for all seasons," with the diversity of accommodations required to play hostess to the millions of Americans and foreign visitors wanting to share in Colorado's high-altitude, leisure-time pursuits.

Tourism, long a major sector of the economy of Colorado, has become increasingly strong throughout the state in recent years, because visitor centers are extending their seasons. Not only has mechanical snow-making extended the skiing season, but mountain resorts once open only for winter skiing have developed year-round programs. Popular summer camps are remaining open with new winter activities. Condominiums, originally built for alpine ski business, now advertise as summer lodges for white-water rafting, hiking, ballooning, horseback riding, or special summer business conferences. Guest ranches, once closed after the aspen leaves turned, now offer Nordic ski and cross-country ski programs, snowmobiling holidays, and other winter packages.

These expanded seasons and broader programs—along with organized national advertising campaigns conducted by the state, tourism associations, and private resorts—are paying big dividends in this booming industry. The Colorado Tourism Board has

"It couldn't be any higher" than greeting the Colorado morning at the Snowmass Balloon Competition. Photo by Patricia Barry Levy, Stockyard

193

White water challenges the skill and nerve whether kayaking or rafting the rivers of Colorado. Photo by Nathan Bilow

Rocky Mountain trout call to sportsmen in tiny voices that cause a summer migration of visitors to Colorado streams. Even missing the strike is fun. Photo by W.A. Hunt III, Phillips Photographics

reported steady increases in visitor-generated income, and from 1983 to 1984 noticed a whopping 30 percent increase in the number of travelers in Colorado. A recent study, conductd by the U.S. Travel Data Center in Washington, D.C., found that every one of Colorado's 63 counties benefits directly from some type of tourism.

While $2.8 billion of the nearly $4.5 billion dollars spent in the industry comes from out-of-state or foreign visitors, Coloradans spent the balance traveling within their own state to enjoy the bountiful local opportunities.

The visitor industry directly accounts for 7.5 percent of all of Colorado's non-agriculture employment. The more than 103,000 persons working in hotels, restaurants, visitor transportation, and amusements and support facilities account for a Colorado payroll exceeding $1.1 billion in salaries and wages. These statistics do not include day trips made by Coloradans of less than 100 miles from home, excluding 40 percent of the local ski lift tickets. Tourists spend more than $12 million per day in Colorado the year round— ranking the state 16th in the United States in vacation expenditures.

Denver County receives a large 43-percent share of the visitor expenditures, because of its position in the year-round convention business, its role as the transportation hub, and its own offering of historic, cultural, and western attractions. El Paso County with Colorado Springs is the second largest visitor center in the state, followed by Arapahoe County (Littleton and Englewood, both with

Many visitors are surprised to find that yachtsmen thrive in the high, thin air of Colorado, with ample mountain lakes for sailors. Photo by Ann Duncan, Tom Stack & Associates

facilities for year-round conventions and business conferences), and the mountain resort counties of Summit and Eagle.

Summertime in the Rockies

When most "out of staters" think of Colorado vacations, visions of brightly costumed ski bunnies dancing down the slopes in a winter wonderland come to mind. There are those, too, but the majority of visitors to Colorado come in the other seasons in station wagons—loaded with children. If skis mounted on car roofs is the most common sight of winter, the rod and reel or golf club is the true Colorado side arm most of the remaining part of the year. Campers, RVs, jeeps and sedans head into the state on highways originating from both coasts. They fly in on jets in camera-hung groups from all over the world. They come to play golf or tennis, to fish, hike, or climb mountains, to run wildly roaring rivers in rubber boats, to photograph forests and valleys full of native American wildlife, or just to gape in awe at one or more of Colorado's 54 peaks towering above 14,000 feet.

Literally from corner to corner, Colorado is a visitors' smorgasbord of natural and historic attractions. At the far northwest corner near Rangley is the Dinosaur National Monument. In the southwest corner near Durango-Cortez the Mesa Verde National Park is one of the state's oldest and most popular visitor stops. The deer and the antelope still play on the Comanche National Grassland near Springfield in the southeast corner, and on the Pawnee National Grassland near Sterling in the northeast corner. Within the state are six national monuments, three national parks, and two national recreation areas, along with a dozen national forests covering much of the state's geography. Colorado's spectacular gorges include the Black Canyon of the Gunnison River, and a system within the great mesa area at Grand Junction in the Colorado National Monument. Its Great Sand Dunes National Monument is 10 miles long, with the highest dunes in America.

Colorado is popular for its ghost towns, and these not only date back to the old gold camps but include the ancient cliff dwellings of Mesa Verde and the Hovenweep National Monument's prehistoric towers and pueblo ruins. The dozen or more gold-boom-era ghost towns can be reached by jeep trails or short hikes from all-weather roads, and feature the skeletons of wooden buildings, log houses, and the remains of the mines they once served. Fully restored historic districts (there are 23 historic towns and districts in the state) offer more appeal to visitors, and are found throughout Colorado.

Several entire towns have been declared historic districts, particularly in the mining centers of the Colorado Rockies. Complete restoration of the Victorian buildings, with up-to-date utilities, offers a real-life experience back into another era.

Since gold mining was done in the mountains, most of the historic mining towns preserved in an authentic Victorian atmo-

PROFILE

Winter Park Resort
Coloradans Share Year-round Recreation

In the early 1900s, when Coloradans were more interested in extracting gold from the mountains than enjoying their bountiful recreational opportunities, the city fathers of Denver were purchasing prime land miles from the city for future generations to use as parks.

Fortunately for modern Coloradans, the area that has come to be known as Winter Park Resort was one of these relatively close-by sites. Today a year-round mountain wonderland, including the Winter Park and Mary Jane ski areas, is high on the vacation and weekend recreation list of Colorado citizens and visitors alike.

The recreation area is approaching its half-century of public use, with the ski facilities dating to the earliest beginnings of Colorado's designation as the "American Alps." Broad use of the recreational area as a skiing location began as early 1940.

The Winter Park Resort surveys show Winter Park/Mary Jane as the first choice of Colorado's active skiers, many of whom take to the slopes for day trips or long weekends from the bustling Front Range urban areas.

In recent years, activities at the Winter Park Resort and nearby ranching communities have been expanded to all-year recreational activities. Combined with recent expansion of recreational real estate development and millions of dollars in improvements at the resort—such as new lifts and slopes—the decision of the early Coloradans to preserve the area as a public recreation area has proven prophetic.

Winter Park Resort completed total modernization of the ski facilities in 1980, with the opening of the $6 million West Portal Station. The popular Mary Jane ski area was completed in 1976, and improvements for the 1985-86 season raised the summit to 11,220 feet, with a vertical drop to 2,220 feet. New lifts and base area improvements were included.

Coloradans share the extraordinary ski slopes of Winter Park with visitors from across the United States. Photo by Grafton Marshall Smith

The nearby town of Winter Park expanded too, with 279 new condominium units and 67,000 square feet of commercial space available for the 1986 season. This private development expansion continues, as recreational activities for all seasons transform the area to a summer resort, as well as a favorite winter activity center.

A typical winter season sees more than a score of special ski events at Winter Park Resort, including the annual Winter Wild West Week and the Annual First Interstate Bank Cup, the longest running professional ski race in the world. The survey of Colorado skiers, conducted by the University of Colorado, Ski Country USA, and the Lucey Group in Denver, indicated that 34 percent of the visitors brought their families; and 38 percent came with friends. About 60 percent of the Colorado skiers regularly using the park were single, and 99 percent said they "would definitely come back to ski Winter Park."

The resort's 83 trails provide a full season of skiing, from its opening in mid-November through closing of the ski season late in April. Winter Park has invested $2 million in snow-making and snow-grooming equipment to assure a full season no matter how fickle the weather. The skier wakes up to a new mountain of smooth trails each morning.

In other seasons, those Colorado and out-of-state families with condominiums return to enjoy the invigorating mountain seasons offering such pastimes as trail riding, back packing, rock climbing, river rafting, and just relaxing, as Colorado's aspen trees green for the summer or turn the autumn mountainsides to gold.

Guest ranch events, mountain stream fishing, and sightseeing complete the all-season activities in this "very Colorado" recreation area at Winter Park Resort. Nearby Grand Lake, Shadow Mountain Lake, and the western entrance to the Rocky Mountain National Park have also made this recreation area one of the favorites of Coloradans and out-of-state vacationers.

Winter Park Resort Association is implementing a major, $60 million expansion program to maintain the resort area and assist the town of Winter Park, located two miles from the resort, as year-round center of activities. Among the improvements planned for the next several years are additional new lifts, new base facilities, new meeting and lodging facilities, improved access, and expanded ski terrain.

sphere sit amidst mountain panorama. Notable among these towns are Silverton, Ouray, Creede, Telluride, Lake City, and Westcliffe in the southern mountains; Cripple Creek, Leadville, Georgetown, Idaho Springs, Central City-Black Hawk, Empire, and Silver Plume in the central mountains; and the old towns at Steamboat Springs and Kremmling in the northern mountains. Many of the larger cities and towns of Colorado have major historical districts preserved in Victorian Era sections.

A number of frontier outposts for trade and military operations in the old west have been preserved. The restored Bent's Fort, eight miles east of La Junta, was one of the first outposts of Anglo-American development in the state, built in 1833 as a fur-trade center. Fort Garland, 26 miles east of Alamosa, is a restored adobe Army post once under the command of Kit Carson. Replicas of Fort Vasquez at Platteville (circa 1837), and Pike's Stockade (circa 1807), 25 miles south of Alamosa are reminders of the earliest era of settlement in the region.

Authentically restored buildings are still used as restaurants, hotels, and shops. In the urbanized areas from Trinidad to Denver, many still serve as executive offices. Victorian hotels, completely refurbished with four-poster beds and period furniture, are not just for sightseeing. Millions of dollars have been invested to bring them up to modern standards and reopen them for regular guests. Western lorists or Victorian furniture buffs can sleep in rooms that once hosted such notables as Teddy Roosevelt, Ulysses S. Grant, Tom Thumb, Mark Twain or Bat Masterson. More contemporary famed guests include Al Capone, Clark Gable, the Beatles, and several recent presidents.

Ten of the 15 frontier hotels in the membership of the Historic Hotels of the Rocky Mountain West are located in Colorado. The list includes: Peck House (1860) at Empire, the Golden Rose Hotel (1874) at Central City, the Hearthstone Inn (1885) at Colorado Springs, the Strater Hotel (1887) at Durango, the Oxford Hotel (1891) and the Brown Palace (1892) at Denver, the Hotel Colorado (1893) at Glenwood Springs, the Imperial Hotel (1896) at Cripple Creek, the Hotel Boulderado (1908) at Boulder, and the Stanley Hotel (1909) at Estes Park. All are listed in the National Registry of Historic Places.

Other historic hotels still accommodate guests around the state, and many are either being restored or have been refurbished with much of the Victorian flair of their early days in the West. The world-famed Broadmoor Resort Complex, in the shadows of Colorado's famous Pikes Peak, remains one of the state's primary visitor facilities.

Visitors to Colorado also find modern accommodations to suit almost any vacation

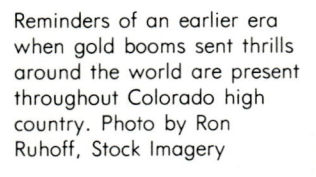

Reminders of an earlier era when gold booms sent thrills around the world are present throughout Colorado high country. Photo by Ron Ruhoff, Stock Imagery

Making the mountains safer and more enjoyable takes skill and training as the specialists in mountain rescue can attest. Photo by Howard M. Paul, courtesy of Alpine Rescue Team

budget. There are 928 hotels and motels in the state, 98 commercial recreational trailer parks, dozens of lodges, and scores of private homes—each offering its own bit of Western history—catering to the bed-and-breakfast seeker. Guest ranches, many with working ranch operations, are scattered along the streams and valleys from one end of the still agrarian countryside to the other. There's even modern lodging on the Southern Ute Indian reservation at Ignacio near the New Mexico border.

Those who bring their own housing, in the form of tents or recreational vehicles, find Colorado's federal lands, state parks, and private recreational parks offer 47 campgrounds with modern facilities, and scores of additional campsites in unimproved, isolated wilderness.

For the visitors with a yearning for learning, Colorado's towns and cities provide 112 major museums and zoos. Many museums have an Old West theme featuring pioneer farming and ranching, mining, railroad, or military history; but the major activity centers also offer museums of quality art, natural history, science, and industry. Both Denver and Colorado Springs have nationally recognized zoos.

While visitors enjoy excellent accommodations and outstanding recreational and cultural attractions in the cities and towns,

Historic hotels, such as the Broadmoor at Colorado Springs, offer the finest in modern facilities with a flair of heritage from the past. Photo by Ron Ruhoff, Stock Imagery

The contrasts seem limitless when exploring in Colorado. A trekker takes the peak of another type in Great Sand Dunes National Monument. Photo by Sharon Gerig, Tom Stack & Associates

the great landscape of mountains, canyons, forests, lakes, and rivers are the real national asset Colorado holds in trust for the nation. These wilderness areas offer the camping, fishing, hiking, horsepacking, hunting, and winter sports activities making the state a world-renowned visitor haven.

The national forests in the state contain more than 16 million acres of land with most of Colorado's campgrounds, peaks, winter sports areas, streams, and river headwaters located on federal lands. The national forests include Arapaho, Grand Mesa, Uncompahgre, Gunnison, Pike, Rio Grande, Roosevelt, Routt, San Isabel, San Juan, and White River. In addition to the numerous state parks in Colorado, two of the nation's most famous national parks are located in the state.

Rocky Mountain National Park, which covers a vast area on each side of the Continental Divide, is one of America's great wildlife preserves. Its 265,000 acres contain deer, elk, bighorn sheep, and many species of smaller animals. Over 200 kinds of birds and 700 varieties of flowers, including rare tundra vegetation, are found in the vast park only a short distance from major urbanized Front Range areas like Denver, Boulder, Longmont, Loveland, Fort Collins, and Greeley.

The second famous national park is Mesa Verde near Cortez and Durango. Archaeologists have excavated only a small portion of the vast ruins known to exist in this region settled by ancient agricultural Indians about 100 years after the death of Christ. The ruins, open to visitors, are the most extensive anywhere in North America.

Scenic national monuments are also preserved within the state. The Black Canyon National Monument 13 miles from Montrose includes 22 square miles of deep and dark canyon along 10 miles of the Gunnison River.

PROFILE

Keystone Resort
Summer and Winter Recreation Mecca

Winter sports are almost forgotten in this famous ski resort as summer attracts visitors for the mountain beauty. Keystone offers year-round recreation.

Located only 75 miles west of the bustling Denver Metropolitan Area, the Keystone Resort has evolved into one of Colorado's primary year-round recreational centers.

A full agenda of winter activities designed around three major ski areas is matched by a summer program filled with everything from executive seminars and conventions to family-oriented high-mountain vacations.

The versatile Keystone Resort program has been one of the pioneering enterprises turning Colorado's skiing and winter sports industry into a year-round service industry.

While hundreds of spring-summer-fall meetings and conventions share the year-round calendar with winter sports and actually outnumber the winter activities, Keystone owners and operators have consistently improved and expanded the ski facilities. Since 1978 advanced and diversified terrain has been added to the Keystone Mountain area through the purchase of Arapahoe Basin, five miles to the east, and most recently the world-famed advanced ski area at North Peak.

With three mountains to ski, Keystone brought a new innovation to Colorado and visiting skiers by opening some of its choice beginner and intermediate terrain to night skiing. Some 13 ski runs, offering 2,340 feet of vertical terrain were lighted for the increasingly popular new evening sport.

The investment in the development of world-class ski facilities at Keystone has resulted in competitors and coaches of the U.S. Ski Team choosing the North Peak mountain for intense training in preparation for World Cup races in Europe. The U.S. team's top slalom and giant slalom competitors chose the facilities for training during the 1985-86 season.

Another encounter with famed U.S. ski team members has further enhanced the reputation of Colorado's Keystone Resort as one of the nation's leading winter activity centers. Phil and Steve Mahre, Olympic medalists, and their former coach and the alpine director of the U.S. Ski Team, operate the Mahre Training Center at Keystone. The U.S. Olympians created the training center, not for the top competitors of the ski world, but to train "families for recreation—to show them how to learn and enjoy a sport that can be with them forever."

Such activities have earned Keystone a top national reputation in America's winter sports industry. In 1986 a grand total of 1.16 million skiers visited Keystone, retaining its number three position in popularity in a field of 630 U.S. ski areas.

But the Keystone story is far from told by winter activities alone. Summer convention facilities, when the lodges, condominiums and other facilities housing the skiers are turned over to summer visitors, have won Keystone the Gold Key Award for excellence in planned meetings. A summer agenda as full as the diverse winter program, including special summer rate packages for family vacationers, business groups, and study groups, utilizes the historic mountain country for such summer activities as trail riding, mountain hiking, rafting and kayaking, sailing, hot air ballooning, and just relaxing in the high, cool mountain air. Keystone's Tennis Center, with a dozen outdoor and two indoor courts, and its championship golf course, designed by Robert Trent Jones Jr. are recreational bonuses for visitors who come to perfect their skills in the valleys under Keystone's towering peaks.

Keystone's Science School provides summer programs for youth, including the Rocky Mountain Trek and Wildlife Discovery Program. The science school, opened at Keystone Center in 1976, is a non-profit, tax-exempt educational organization offering year-round programs.

200

Another famed Colorado canyon is the Royal Gorge located west of Canon City. Colorado National Monument west of Grand Junction features sheer canyons too, and is also noted for its towering monoliths and expansive views of rugged high mesas and desert.

Dinosaur National Monument, 60 miles west of Craig, is one of America's richest sites for fossils. Prehistoric animals roaming in the region 140 million years ago left ample evidence of their existence in the high, arid land. Another prehistoric burial ground, a long-vanished lake bed dating to 35 million years ago, is the Florissant Fossil Beds National Monument located 35 miles west of Colorado Springs. The Great Sand Dunes National Monument, northwest of Alamosa, is a shifting sandhill formation running for miles along the base of the Sangre de Cristo Mountains.

Despite the great variety of man-made and natural visitor attractions, it's still the mountains that are "Colorado" to tourist and resident alike. They are the true magnets drawing millions of people. Everywhere are mountains. Even coming from the great plains on the east, a traveler is not long into Colorado before sighting the first rim of the Rockies on the horizon. The chain of the Rockies, with its fingers of sub-ranges, is visible to the visitor arriving by air, car, or train from any point on the compass.

It is said of Coloradans that they quickly lose their bearing when they leave the state and cannot orient themselves to a mountain.

Winter on the Rim of the Continent

A golden autumn of changing aspen leaves tells the last of the summer visitors that the program is changing in Colorado. Colorado's visitor-industry hosts change the marquees, and an entirely different amusement machine begins purring to life in the crisp mountain air. Visitor shops in the towns replace the fishing license signs with signs for ski rentals. Hotels, motels, lodges, and resorts stock up with firewood. Local radio stations in dozens of towns broadcast job openings at the big ski resorts, as the recreational service industry prepares to move indoors for the season. The weather reports are like an-

Mountain country can be just for viewing enjoyment during the turning of the aspen.
Ron Phillips, Phillips Photographics

Only half the trip is uphill when biking Colorado high country, and the glide down the other side is unusually spectacular. Photo by Nathan Bilow

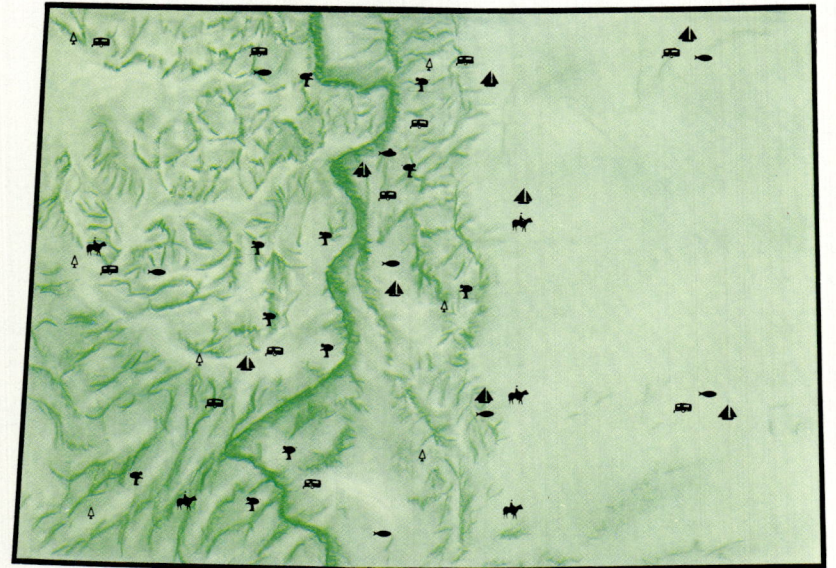

⌂ National Parks/Monuments
⛵ Boating
🐟 Fishing
🚐 Camping
⛷ Winter Sports
🐎 Dude Ranches

Recreation in Colorado—Events for all seasons, whether man-made or natural, await the visitor to Colorado. The figures indicate the approximate general location of some of these sports centers.

nouncements that gold has been discovered, because the season's success can be enhanced by early snow.

Probably no other place on earth finds more people "praying" for snow than in the Colorado mountains in October.

Approximately 45,000 people work directly in the ski industry. Skiers, while fewer in number than visitors in other seasons, spend a higher proportion of the tourism dollars coming into the state.

Colorado, with its 34 first class resorts and major ski facilities, is the nation's unchallenged winter sports leader. Its reputation as a ski locale is international and competition is now global.

Investment in the ski facilities and support resort accommodations is tremendous, and continues to be one of the most important parts of the state's construction industry. The state's ski resort association, Colorado Ski Country USA, noted that construction for the 1985-86 season exceeded $128 million in ski facilities and resort building. This investment did not include millions more spent in new private facilities at ski locations, including condominiums, hotels, and private businesses.

It did include the addition of 27 new lifts, bringing the state's total at the 34 ski areas to 241 lifts and tows, and over 1,000 acres of new ski slopes, which brings that total to more than 16,000 acres. Snowmaking has greatly expanded in recent years, assuring an early start to the Colorado ski season— usually around Thanksgiving. In 1985, 235 additional acres covered by snowmaking equipment brought the state's total to more than 3,000 acres.

In addition to the 34 ski resorts in operation in 1986, eight new areas were under construction and scheduled for completion before the end of the decade.

Virtually no part of Colorado is more than a short drive from a major ski area, and the resorts extend along the Colorado Rockies from near the Wyoming border to the border of New Mexico. Nearly 10 million lift tickets are issued in a typical year, and about a third of these are purchased by Coloradans.

Whole new Colorado towns have been sired by the ski industry, and many dead or almost-ghost towns have been brought back to life. Wherever a ski resort has been built, the financial welfare of the local area has vastly improved, with new jobs, added tax values, and general enhancement of the economy.

Despite considerable concern for the environmental impact of construction on ski runs and support facilities, most ski areas fit

Riding the crest of a snow-covered ridge can set the spirit soaring—if the skier is as expert as this one. Photo by Nathan Bilow

almost unnoticed into the mountainous countryside. One reason for the compatibility of the ski resorts with the surrounding wilderness, mining, or agrarian neighborhoods, is the great care developers have taken in the type of building allowed within the resorts. Most ski resorts feature Alpine or rustic, natural architecture blending with the environment. Where Victorian buildings of historic significance existed in the community near the resort, that theme is usually continued in new construction.

Many of the ski areas advertise themselves as Western resorts, and skiers wearing cowboy hats are the style in some areas. One can almost always tell a ski resort is nearby when the familiar farming or mining pickup trucks traveling the mountain roads become outnumbered by Mercedes.

Downhill skiing is by far the largest winter sport, but most of the resort areas also feature cross-country skiing facilities. In addition, a dozen independent centers for Nordic skiing are found within the state, and several guest ranches now offer cross-country skiing as well. The sport is becoming more popular,

The moon somehow seems larger when cross country skiing near the top of the Continental Divide in Colorado. Photo by Nathan Bilow

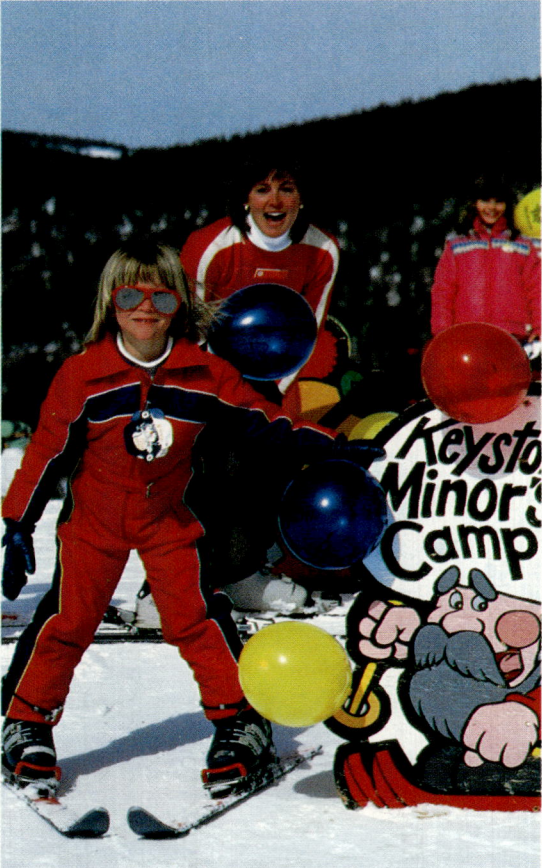

A lot of the fun and games of winter sports take place off the slopes when families gather to enjoy Colorado's resorts. Photo courtesy of Keystone Resort

particularly for residents of the state. Cross-country skiing affords the best opportunity to observe wildlife in the mountains during winter.

Several winter resort centers and ranches also sponsor vacations, camping trips, and snowshoeing into the winter wilderness.

For the even more adventurous skier, helicopter skiing has been introduced in several areas of Colorado. To participate in this popular sport helicopters lift the skiers high into untouched terrain for the thrill of breaking trails on distant mountain slopes of untouched powder.

Most of the major ski resorts now have ice skating facilities and many feature night skiing facilities. All have extensive entertainment programs for "after the lifts close" each evening, with apres ski as the main event of the sport for some.

Many visitors coming to the state to ski arrive by air, although during ski season out-of-state license plates may seem to outnumber cars with Colorado plates at the resorts. Denver's Stapleton International Airport is the primary hub of arriving ski parties, and a visit to the busy terminal might lead one to believe every passenger is lugging a set of skis and poles.

Other airports in the state also service the ski visitors, including Walker Field in Grand Junction, Colorado Springs Airport, Sardy Field in Aspen, Avon Stolport, Gunnison Airport, Montrose Airport, La Plata Airport in Durango, Steamboat Airport in Steamboat Springs, the new Telluride Airport, Pueblo Airport, Alamosa Airport and Cortez Airport. All are served by commercial service directly from out-of-state or via connections at Stapleton. The impact of the ski industry has prompted American Airlines to inaugurate regular seasonal service to Gunnison Airport to serve the Crested Butte ski area from Dallas/Fort Worth, Houston, Chicago, and Los Angeles. Because of the close proximity to ski areas on the Western Slope and the Interstate 70 highway corridor, many out-of-state skiers, particularly from the West Coast, are entering Colorado at the modern Walker Field in Grand Junction.

Good all-season highways now link ski resorts from all parts of the state, with high mountain roads and passes cleared for travel during all but the briefest periods after a winter storm.

In northern Colorado the ski areas include Steamboat at Steamboat Springs, Ski Estes Park at Estes Park, Sharktooth near Greeley, Silver Creek between Georgetown and Kremmling, Eldora near Boulder, Winter Park/Mary Jane and Ski Idlewild at Winter Park, and Berthoud off I-70 near Winter Park.

Interstate Highway 70, which crosses Colorado east to west, is virtually a ski belt across the state, with 10 major ski areas almost abutting the super highway. These include St. Mary's Glacier near Idaho Springs, Loveland Basin near Georgetown, Arapahoe Basin-North Peak-Keystone at Keystone, Breckenridge at Breckenridge, Copper Mountain at Copper Mountain, Vail at Vail, Beaver Creek at Avon, Sunlight at Glenwood Springs, and Ski Cooper at Leadville.

The most extensive expansion in the Colorado ski industry has occurred in recent years in southern Colorado, with several new ski resorts recently completed. These ski areas include Powderhorn at Mesa, Snowmass, Buttermilk, Aspen Highlands and Aspen Mountain at Aspen, Geneva Basin at Grant, Crested Butte near Gunnison, Monarch at Garfield, Conquistador at Westcliffe, Telluride at Telluride, Purgatory at Durango, Wolf Creek at Pagosa Springs, and Cuchara Valley Resort near Walsenburg and Trinidad.

The hundreds of millions of dollars invested in permanent resort facilities at ski areas have spawned another major year-round income for the visitor industry. Businessmen visiting the state on winter vacations are returning home to tell of the facilities in Colorado. More and more conferences and conventions are coming to the state. Many of the ski resorts, and the hotels locating to support them, have become major sites for conferences, seminars, business and training meetings, and small to medium-size conventions. Several national and international institutes hold annual sessions during summer and non-ski season at resorts at Aspen, Vail, Telluride, and other centers, first built to accommodate winter sports.

In cities and towns across Colorado, more than 60 facilities are now equipped with rooms large enough to accommodate conventions, conferences, or meetings that require seating for more than 500 people. Approximately 125 facilities offer major exhibit space for trade shows. The Denver Metropolitan Area and Colorado Springs have long been among the nation's most popular convention cities. In more recent years the attractions of the Colorado mountains combined with the building of new meeting facilities are turning the whole state into a vast convention and conference center. Denver alone attracts almost a half million convention delegates each year.

Racing downhill on a fast slope at one of Colorado's world-class ski resorts helps maintain the state's nickname as the "Switzerland of America." Photo by Nathan Bilow

PROFILE

Breckenridge Ski Area
Preservation with Progress in Vacationland

When the gaslights were installed in the Victorian mining town of Breckenridge 128 years ago, the pioneering city fathers could not know they were lighting the streets for what would someday be one of North America's largest and most popular ski resorts.

The lights have been converted to electricity and many of the 354 Victorian-era homes and buildings listed on the National Historic Registry have been refurbished with modern amenities, but the authenticity of the turn-of-the-century village has been maintained alongside millions of dollars in modern development. Breckenridge's three mountains, where gold and silver once was the chief source of income, now provide more than 50 miles of ski trails and 110 runs with some of North America's most challenging expert slopes, as well as enjoyable terrain for the family and the beginner.

Breckenridge has been careful to maintain this mix of the historic and modern because it is Colorado's only authentic Victorian mining town/ski resort. It is the oldest continuously occupied mining town on Colorado's Western Slope, and century-old buildings now house hundreds of shops, galleries, and restaurants. At the same time, tens of millions of dollars have been invested in new resort housing, with $60 million in permits issued for construction to expand the 1985-86 season alone. New and modern hotel and condominium construction is carefully planned to preserve the environment of the historic sections of the town, and yet provide the convenience of being within walking distance of many of the ski slopes. The community has expanded accommodations for winter guests to comfortably handle 21,000 visitors at a time.

The resort area offers one of the Rocky Mountain's largest conference facilities, seating 1,200 guests at one event, and provides Colorado's largest Nordic Center. Its 14 lift systems can easily accommodate 22,000 skiers per hour, journeying up the Summit County mountains to elevations as high as 12,213 feet above sea level to enjoy the 1,460 acres of ski terrain. Modern snowmaking and grooming equipment assure a full season for winter sportsmen.

The Breckenridge Ski Area hosts the events and has developed the features that earned Colorado the leading role as America's winter recreation center. Every ski season Breckenridge hosts the World Cup Freestyle Skiing competition, which is scheduled to be a major new event for Winter Olympics. The Ullr Festival (old man winter rites), the Telemark Returns, and season-long community events turn this resort 85 miles west of Denver into a continual celebration of Colorado's role as the North American Alps.

While Breckenridge has concentrated on providing the best available winter recreational activities, the resort facilities provide an increasingly important resource to Colorado's summer and fall visitor industry. Its careful preservation of historic assets makes it one of the state's most important summer visitor centers. Breckenridge becomes a headquarters for all the white water, mountain trailing activities offered by the Rockies in the summer.

The Breckenridge Outdoor Education Center is an increasingly important Colorado resource offering challenging activities, and group support to develop self-esteem and independent living skills for people with varying abilities, disabilities, and special needs.

Culturally, Breckenridge is an arts center, with the Breckenridge Music Institute offering a Festival of Music at the Summit during July. In autumn the Breckenridge Festival of Film attracts both film lovers and film stars to four days of presentations.

Breckenridge is keeping alive a valuable part of Colorado's heritage while providing the facilities and services to support the state's modern role as America's recreation center.

Breckenridge has maintained its historic town charm while becoming one of the most modern vacation resorts in Colorado. New peaks are open for winter sports.

The world of fine art is opened to the minds and hearts of residents in the Rockies through Denver's Museum of Fine Arts. Photo by David Williams

Mountain Mecca of Arts and Culture

There has always been a communion between artists and nature, and Colorado's wilderness seems to either attract creative talents to the state or inspire creativity in those who live here. Artists and artisans from every discipline can be found in communities across the state. Professional and amateur painters, sculptors, writers, photographers, actors, singers and musicians, dancers, potters, weavers, metalsmiths, and a host of angels supporting their arts flourish in the rarified Colorado atmosphere.

Cultural centers in cities, towns, and rural areas are developed around this unusually high population of creative people. A glance at a recent audit of fine arts organizations, albeit partial, is impressive. Some 60 Colorado communities have performing or fine arts councils or programs. The state has 31 theatre groups, 33 not-for-profit art galleries, and 22 dance groups. Symphony, concert, and opera groups are not only sponsored in the largest cities, but are found is some very unexpected places.

Weavers, potters, and other artisans form a sizable industry in the state. A surprising number of full-time artists including painters, creative photographers, and musicians make a living at their chosen arts. The community colleges, private and public colleges, and universities attract some of the top creative talents in each of the arts, and these institutions share their cultural assets with the communities which host them.

While Denver is the undisputed cultural center of the state in terms of the variety of arts represented, many other cities host complete programs in support of the performing arts. Boulder and nearby Longmont have 26 recognized dance, musical, theatre, graphic arts, prose and poetry, and fine arts organizations. Aspen supports 14 arts organizations, including such internationally noted organizations as the Aspen Institute. Colorado Springs is home to 15 arts groups, including symphony, ballet, and opera. With strong university support, Fort Collins with 14 and Greeley with 11 fine arts and performing arts groups are cultural centers for northern Colordo.

Mountain resort areas also attract sizable numbers of creative artists, despite small populations which would not usually be expected to support the arts.

Among those mountain communities sponsoring diverse cultural programs are: Breckenridge with music, theatre, and film festivals; Carbondale, through the Colorado Rocky Mountain School and its council on arts and humanities; Crested Butte and Gunnison with dance, theatre, and a consortium of fine arts; Canon City and Central City, with a full range of arts programs; Creede's notable repertory theatre; the Delta/Montrose concert program; Eagle, with a fine arts council; and Estes Park and Glenwood Springs, with councils of fine arts.

Fort Garland is the home of several fine arts programs at Sangre de Cristo Ranches;

The curtain is always up on some major cultural offering in Colorado's fine arts community. Cities and towns across the state support the arts on a grand scale. Photo courtesy of the Denver Center for the Performing Arts

Idaho Springs has a council on fine arts; Leadville has a theatre and an arts council; Loveland supports a museum, art gallery, and arts council; Lake City has a council on arts and humanities; Ouray has its own music festival; Salida has a region-wide fine arts association; Steamboat Springs has an arts and crafts community and a council on arts and humanities; Silverton has two groups supporting fine arts; Snowmass Village offers facilities drawing well-known performers for summer theatre; Vail has both performing and fine arts groups; and Westcliffe hosts an area-wide council on arts.

Telluride is home to a bluegrass music festival, film festival, writers guild, dance festival, and fine arts council. John Naisbitt, forecaster and bestselling author, was instrumental in the formation of the Telluride Institute, which is a new futuristic planning organization.

Durango in southwestern Colorado is the cultural center for the Four Corners area where the Colorado, New Mexico, Arizona, and Utah borders touch. With the visitor industry at the top of its economic scale, cultural activities far exceed what would be expected in such a city of its population. Four Corners Opera attracts performers from the New York Metropolitan Opera during off-season, and the community supports dance, chorale, and a large artist and writer community. Like the Aspen area, Durango also supports a sizable cottage industry in art pottery, weaving, and other arts and crafts.

The mountains do not have a monopoly on fine arts and performing arts programs. Holyoke, located in the far northeast corner of the state in Colorado's wheat belt, supports a museum association, community concert program, and fine arts council. Other communities on Colorado's Eastern Plains sponsoring fine arts and performing arts programs include Fort Morgan, La Junta (children's theatre, concert group, and literary guild), Lamar, and Sterling.

On the Western Slope, Grand Junction is a focal point for cultural activities with a symphony program, concert band, Western culture museum, arts center, and a council on fine arts. Other communities in the western part of the state with active arts programs are Craig, Hotchkiss, Nucla, Rangley, and Rifle.

Southern Colorado has active fine arts organizations at Alamosa, Pueblo and Trinidad. Pueblo supports symphony, theatre, a handweavers guild, the Sangre de Cristo Center, and an arts council.

The Denver Metropolitan Area has fine arts and performing arts programs spanning all the disciplines, and most cities in the urbanized area have organizations supporting all the major arts. Private and public colleges and universities also contribute programs that are enjoyed by the local communities as well as the student bodies.

The Arvada Center is one of the leading arts support facilities in the state, with a community-funded fine arts and theatre building and extensive year-round programs. Aurora citizens support theatre, ballet, a wind ensemble, and a broad program of arts and humanities. Englewood is host to symphony, theatre, the Fiddler's Green amphitheater, and the nearby Greenwood Village arts council. The near mountain city of Evergreen has a choral program and an arts center, as well as the Colorado Philharmonic. Golden also sponsors symphony, the Foothills Art Center, and a community college art gallery. Littleton is home to a fine arts guild, weavers group, and fine arts center. Lakewood supports a weavers guild, museum group, chamber choir, and arts center. Northglenn has an active arts council, and Lafayette is home to an organists guild.

Denver with its nine dance groups, 12 major music programs, and nine theatre groups is also headquarters for many of the fine arts and performing arts associations working in the state. Fine arts and performing arts councils are headquartered here, and many of the large fine arts organizations provide programs for communities throughout the state While many of the state performing arts ballet, music, and arts groups are located in Denver they are state organizations. Denver is Colorado's cultural treasure house, and citizens from all over the state and visitors from the Rocky Mountain region draw upon the cultural resources. Its superb museums literally serve the entire state and most of the Rocky Mountain States, as well as provide a major base for the tourism industry. Among these cultural centers with high national ratings are the Colorado Heritage Center, Denver Botanic Gardens, Denver Museum of Natural History and Charles C. Gates Planetarium, Denver Art Museum, and the Denver Zoo.

The metropolitan area also serves as headquarters for a number of national artists and writers groups, such as the National Writer's Club with a national professional writers membership of 5,000, headquartered in Aurora. Several top-name writers headquarter in Colorado including Leon Uris in Aspen, Clive Cussler in Golden, and Louis L'Amour in Durango.

One of the leading cultural institutions in the Rocky Mountain states is the Denver Center for the Performing Arts (DCPA). Its programs in the performing arts, and the huge complex it supports bring some of the nation's top cultural and arts events to the Rockies. The Denver Center is a non-profit organization concentrating the area's efforts in the performing arts. It is also a complex of outstanding facilities that include the Helen Bonfils Theatre Complex, Boettcher Concert Hall, and the Denver Auditorium Theatre and Arena. The administration center houses an advanced recording and research facility and the National Theatre Conservatory. The DCPA represents a public/private investment in the arts in excess of $100 million in facilities and operating costs, and continues an ambitious expansion program in both operations and buildings.

The DCPA is host to the Denver Center Theatre Company, a professional repertory acting company; the Denver Center Cinema, a classic and contemporary films theatre; Robert Garner/Center Attractions, a series of touring Broadway shows; and Denver Center Productions, a revival of classic plays and musicals and production of new works.

Coloradans love their cultural events as much as they enjoy the natural resources of the great outdoors. Photo courtesy of the Denver Center for the Performing Arts

Colorado is bike country for the casual rider or the serious competitor, and the Coors Bicycle Classic is becoming one of the nation's top sports events. Photo by Nathan Bilow

Colorado's western heritage has spawned an enthusiastic following of rodeo cowboys. Nearly every weekend in summer pro-am cowboys are competing somewhere in the state for fun or prizes. Photo by Nathan Bilow

The National Theatre Conservatory, with 200 students from across the nation in residence, is truly national in scope. The national theatre school was established by Congressional Charter, and after being licensed by the American National Theatre and Academy, admitted its first class in 1984. A division of the Denver Center Theatre Company, the Conservatory has a full class of first- and second-year acting students. It is adding courses in theatre design and technology, directing, play writing, management, and media arts.

The DCPA program and facilities are drawing more and more national attention, as a recent commentary in the *San Francisco Chronicle* indicates:

". . .Here in this fast-growing metropolis in the middle of the Rockies, one finds a healthy, growing representative of the new American theatre. . .The Denver Center Theatre Company, with three performing spaces in this architecturally impressive performing arts center, established itself as a comer right from the start. . ."

Another facility and program generating national interest is the DCPA's Recording and Research Center. *Smithsonian Magazine* called the center a "lively and unique" voice-research facility devoted to vocal production. It is one of the only research centers in the world directly connected to a working theatre and theatre school.

The facility offers more than a pioneering research program into bettering the quality and life of actors and singers. It is also seeking solutions to voice and throat-related problems for all professionals dependent upon speaking in their careers. The research center is studying voice loss due to aging, air pollution, and other causes.

The only facility in the world of its kind, it has also brought state-of-the-art audio and video recording equipment to Colorado. The world-class studio allows the quality of Denver Center productions to be taped on audio and video recordings for release nationwide. The Recording and Research Center has opened the way for the Denver Center for the Performing Arts to participate in cooperative projects with organizations like Washington, D.C.'s Kennedy Center, the Public Broadcasting System, major television networks, and cable outlets.

Cultural activities in Colorado have become a sizable industry and Coloradans are increasingly supporting the arts on a great scale. A survey of non-profit cultural activities in the state, completed in 1986 by the Colorado Council on Arts and Humanities revealed the arts are a multimillion-dollar economic factor.

Man's ancient dreams of soaring with the eagles come true for a hang glider who challenges the very roof of the planet. Photo by Nathan Bilow

Non-profit cultural activity expenditures are approaching $60 million a year in the state, and almost seven million tickets to fine arts and performing arts events are purchased each year. The not-for-profit arts sector of the state's economy employs almost 2,500 persons on a full-time basis, and the more than 14,000 volunteers in 97 audited organizations contribute more than 600,000 hours of free labor each year. The arts also pay a great portion of their own expenses with total revenue through ticket sales of $55.5 million per year.

Another important sector of the recreation industry in Colorado is spectator sports. The Denver Broncos, Colorado's American Football Conference team, have drawn sellout crowds for every home game for the past dozen years, and each season more than 750,000 fans pack the Mile High Stadium.

Another Colorado pro team, based in Denver, is the always-winning Denver Nuggets of the National Basketball Association. Home court for the team is McNichols Arena in Denver. Colorado, with the Zephyrs minor league baseball team, is high on the list for a national team.

Across the state one of the best attended spectator sports is rodeo. Its western heritage, and the fact that Colorado is in the heart of America's cattle country, makes rodeo the leading spectator sport in professional athletic events. In 1986 more than 400,000 spectators attended the granddaddy of them all, The 80th National Western Stock Show and Rodeo in Denver. The rodeo portion of this world-class event is historically sold out during all competitions.

The varsity teams in the colleges and universities show well in all sports in national and regional competition, and even in losing seasons are supported by loyal alumni and local fans alike.

As a place to relax or to exercise, Colorado has few real peers in the world, because of its extraordinary diversity and the development of access to its natural wonders. The variety is nearly endless.

But the best feature of visiting the attractions might be the Colorado people themselves. They clearly know the importance of the visitor industry to their own families, and welcome strangers with open arms and friendly smiles.

A badge found on lapels in all parts of the state, says simply: "Smile, You're In Colorado." It's more than a motto. It's a way of life.

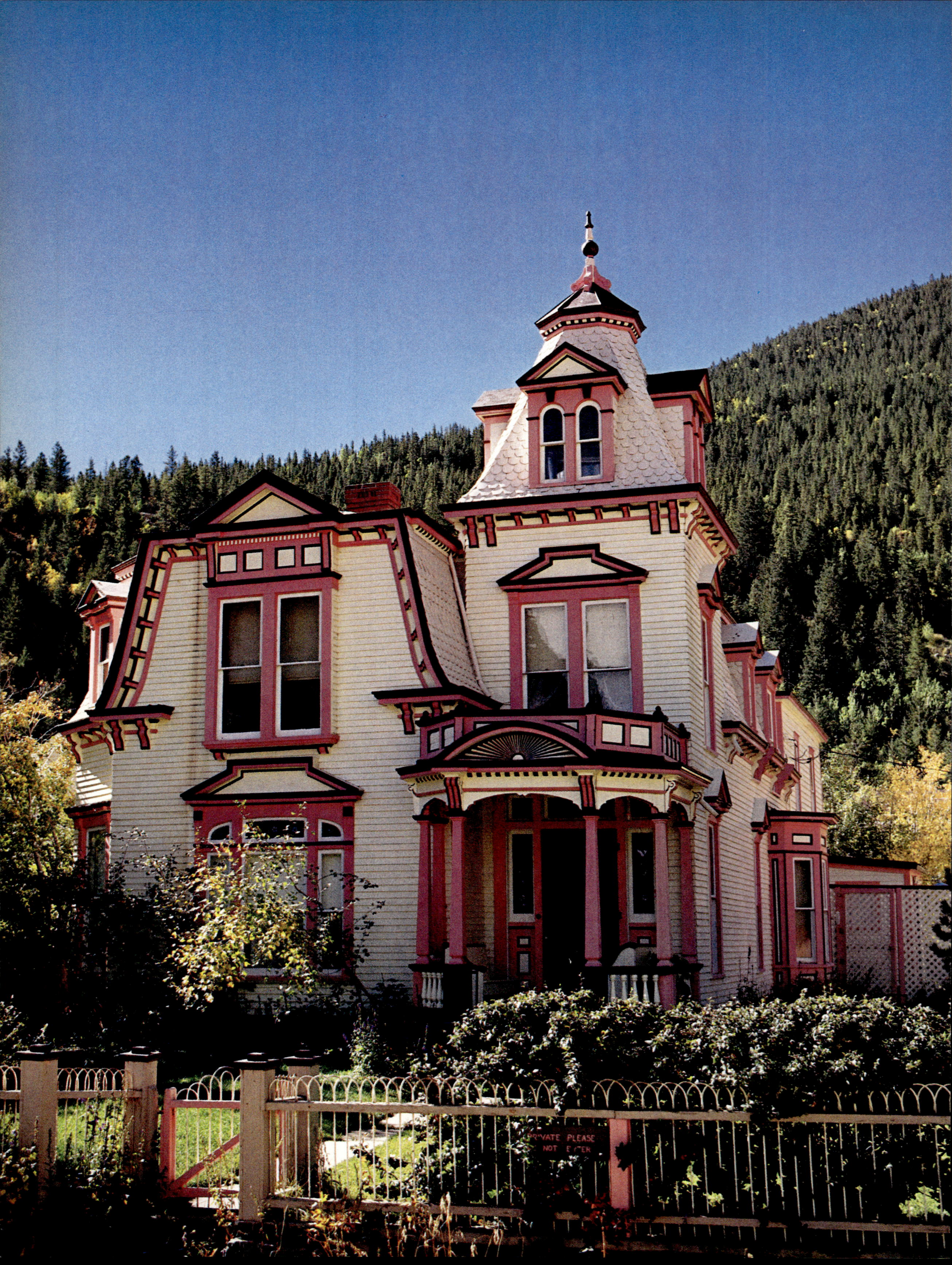
PLEASE
NOT

CHAPTER 10

Managing for the Future
The Land and Its Uses

When the uses of the land are discussed, the words "progress" and "preservation" are synonymous to the modern Coloradan. Environmental and ecological values are of personal concern to almost every Colorado citizen, whether homeowner or industrial park developer.

Beneath the facade of a strong, massive mountain chain lies a sometimes fragile ecology of thin, high-altitude vegetation on a semi-arid terrain. The natural beauty of the region and the abundance of delicate flora and fauna remain to a great extent as they have since human development began, and Coloradans, for the most part, want it preserved.

Colorado's population growth since the 1960s has been among the fastest of any state in the country, and this urban expansion has created an environmental awareness unmatched, perhaps, by any other place on earth. Members of zero growth factions, city elders, state legislators, federal protection agents, builders and developers, and citizens from all walks of life are not only aware of the importance of maintaining the ecological balance, but are directly involved in trying to guarantee that it happens.

The job of implementing the public policy of "preservation" and meeting the challenges of "progress" falls on no single group of citizens or public officials as heavily as on the men and women in the development and real estate industry of the state.

It is safe to say that those who would develop the land in Colorado, whether by choice and personal commitment or by competitive reality, are de facto guardians of the land. A developer who ignores the aesthetics of his development cannot compete anywhere in the state, because business leaders and residents alike demand a quality environment in the places they live and work.

This is not to say that excesses of the past—pollution by miners, industrialists, the military, cities, and citizens—have not left many problems of misuse in the environment. And it does not mean an ecological utopia exists. But today, let one barrel of industrial waste dump into a Colorado stream, either by accident or intent, and the furor becomes frontpage news in any part of the state.

The concern of Coloradans for their living and working environment pays off, too. Most first-time visitors to the state are impressed by the beauty that abounds in the parks and out-of-doors, the pristine waters, the shining cleanliness of the modern cities and towns. Old towns of the state are filled with restored Victorian homes and businesses, and literally glow with fresh paint on the structures. New neighborhoods display a striking resemblance to the natural environment, with open space and lawns greener than the countryside. Campus-like industrial parks and office districts are hardly distinguishable from the state's arbored universities and colleges. Only the height of the newly planted trees and architectural design in all types of development distinguish old Colorado places from new Colorado places.

Because the homes and workplaces of about 80 percent of the population are located between Pueblo and Fort Collins, the pressures to preserve and protect the land are greatest on the Front Range and the mountains nearest the urbanized areas. But in no part of the state—from the highest mountain communities, to the prairie towns, to the growing cities—is the proper use of the land

Coloradans believe in the preservation of their heritage even as they build one of the nation's most modern new life styles. Photo by Arthur Bilsten, Stock Imagery

213

PROFILE

The Schuck Corporation
Extending the Environment in Development

The Pikes Peak region along Colorado's Front Range of the Rocky Mountains is among the nation's most rapidly developing high technology and aerospace business centers. Yet the area retains its role as one of the leading recreational centers because of the beauty of its natural environment.

A leading Colorado commercial, industrial, and investment real estate corporation has played a strong role in maintaining this balance between economic development and environmental quality. The Schuck Corporation, headquartered in Colorado Springs, is the largest full-service real estate firm in the Pikes Peak region.

The corporation is characterized by its diversity of talents brought to the region in four aggressive, independent subsidiaries. The companies are The Schuck Land Management Corporation; The Schuck Development Corporation; Schuck Property Management, Inc.; and Schuck Financial Services, Inc. A former subsidiary, The Schuck Commercial Brokerage Company, was acquired by Grubb & Ellis in 1985, and its operations in the Pikes Peak area have been continued by that national real estate services firm.

The Schuck Corporation is a full-service developer of the wholesale and retail levels of all types of commercial, industrial and investment real estate. In addition to its operations in the burgeoning Colorado Springs area, The Schuck Corporation has other development programs in the metropolitan areas of Denver as well as Phoenix, Arizona. The corporation also acts as general partner and operational manager for numerous private investor groups, partnerships and joint ventures with real estate holdings exceeding $150 million.

Stephen M. Schuck, who founded the corporation in 1969, actively serves in a number of leadership positions with organizations fostering orderly expansion of the Colorado economy, coupled with environmental protection.

President and Chief Executive Officer at The Schuck Corporation, Gerald W. Ricker, shares the goals and working practices established by the founder.

"I think there are many challenges in growth, but I see most of them as positive, and ones that can be overcome." says Ricker. "The types of people who are attracted by the high-tech industries and the space center are very involved with their community. These people have the commitment and capability to solve problems and to make sure that in 10 or 15 years we have the same benefits that we enjoy today."

The Schuck Land Management Corporation converts raw ground to finished sites ready for construction. In Schuck developments, wide avenues, parkways, and recreational facilities such as picnic grounds, are designed as an integral part of the commercial or industrial park or business center.

The operating companies are involved in all phases of development, finance, and marketing of commercial properties. The Schuck Development Corporation produces custom-designed facilities for specific users as well as speculative structures in anticipation of market needs. These developments include office buildings, retail space, and research and development facilities.

Funding for the acquisition, construction, development financing, and refinancing of real estate projects is secured by Schuck Financial Services. This group's financial experts stay current on financial trends in the market that can make the difference between the success and failure of a real estate investment.

All of the Schuck companies are active participants in community activities, and executives in these companies are afforded time to serve in voluntary community betterment projects with more than a score of agencies.

Schuck Corporation is setting the pace for high quality development, like the Foster Technology Center, in the emerging aerospace community at Colorado Springs.

Entire new communities have been built in recent years among the valleys and foothills of the Front Range. Photo by W.A. Hunt III, Phillips Photographics

left off the agenda of the local planning authorities. Consideration for a permit to dig a well in a rural mountain valley is just as intense as the review for a new subdivision in suburban Denver.

The relationship between quality of life and economic development has long been accepted as a matter of public policy in Colorado, as an official guideline for the state's future noted in 1981:

"To function, modern society must have housing, power, surface and air transportation and a variety of other investments," stated the Governor's Blue Ribbon Panel on Colorado's future. "Whether financed by private capital or not, the quality of those investments and the ability of the private sector to provide them are matters of public concern."

The report, entitled "Colorado: Investing in the Future," clearly focused on the important role of land development in maintaining Colorado's high standard of living, stating: "Longer-term, major initiatives are needed with regard to housing. This forecast indicates that the entire housing stock of the state will need to be doubled in the next 20 years."

It also addressed related public issues important to the use of the land and preservation of the natural ecology, such as the need to continue the development of water and sewage treatment facilities, solid waste disposal methods, and expanded utilities.

The extensive study noted that Colorado in the past 20 years had outpaced the nation in both population and economic growth and that the growth would continue, even if at a slower pace.

So the real estate and construction industry, in fields of commercial, industrial, residential, and public facilities development, has been given a critical responsibility and an important role in shaping the future direction of the state.

Preserved Open Spaces

If Coloradans have one characteristic in common, it is their love for open spaces. Whether a native of the state, who has come to take the vistas for granted, or a newcomer, who moved into Colorado because of them, few people are offered such a continuous fare of wide open panoramic sights. From one edge of the state to the other, at home or at work, the Coloradan has a view of either splendid mountains and high mesas or sweeping seas of prairie.

No town or city in Colorado is without landscaped parks and playgrounds, or natural areas set aside for public use. Within the state are nearly eight million acres of national forests, and an additional 234,000 acres available for public use under municipal or state ownership. The national parks and monuments, with millions of additional acres available to the public, are a national treasure discussed in the preceding chapter.

The open spaces most used by local Coloradans are the state parks, which provide

PROFILE

The Writer Corporation
Pacesetter for Quality Environmental Life Style

Coloradans' demand for alternative life styles with a high degree of environmental quality in the places they live and work has been matched by one of the state's leading developers of residential and mixed-use commercial properties.

The Writer Corporation, with communities located throughout the metropolitan Front Range area, was among Colorado's first major real estate developers to bring the environment into urban residential planning. As a pioneer of comprehensively planned, environmentally sound communities, Writer has set the pace that has challenged many builders to remember the fragile ecology as the state has grown.

The Writer Corporation's operating philosophy states the case for balancing economic growth and environmental quality.

"In the years ahead, only those developers who creatively confront challenges will merit a place in the vanguard of the building industry in Colorado," says George S. Writer Jr., chairman and chief executive officer of the Writer Corporation.

The company has practiced this philosophy in more than a dozen of the best-known real estate projects in Colorado, ranging from planned communities, to a modern downtown Denver landmark development on the 16th Street Mall, to the new suburban commercial center along Littleton's Platte River front.

The corporation also heeds the changes occurring in the dynamic Colorado economy. "The social revolution has greatly increased life style alternatives, creating the need for new and different types of housing," according to President William E. Nollsch, who serves as the chief operating officer for Writer. He cites family mobility, and the environmental considerations of land use, water, traffic, and clean air as factors that a modern Colorado builder must now consider a part of every new project.

All these factors have been considered and incorporated in the many major projects bearing The Writer Corporation signature, beginning with its novel Aurora development, which paved the way for a new type of real estate venture in the late 1960s. The Dam, the first "Planned Unit Development" in Colorado, replaced the usual grid pattern of single family housing with a new blend of cul-de-sacs, open space, and dramatic architecture. Since that time Writer communities have set an example for environmentally aware real estate developers across the nation.

The Writer Corporation has also diversified from its basic business of building residential communities through the development of multipurpose centers. Writer Square, located in Denver's emerging lower downtown residential and commercial district, is a community within a community-featuring restaurants,

Writer developed the exciting Riverfront Festival Center along the Platte River bringing a new standard of commercial development to Colorado.

retail shops, office space, townhomes, and condominiums. Located on the 16th Street Mall between the Tabor Center and Larimer Square, the project brought new vitality to an area that is becoming Colorado's best example of core-area redevelopment.

A second major project in downtown Littleton, the seat of rapidly growing Arapahoe County, has won acclaim throughout the West. The Writer Corporation opened the Riverfront Festival Center on the banks of the South Platte River in 1986. This mixed-use retail, commercial and entertainment complex brings a new activity center to the rapidly growing southwest part of the Denver metropolitan area.

Writer Corporation is also constructing Willow Creek Center, a 150,000-square-foot shopping complex in the south suburban area, which in both design and concept goes far beyond the traditional neighborhood shopping center to become a 21st century retail facility. It will feature upscale retail and commercial space and restaurants to befit the neighborhood where Writer has built over 1,500 executive homes.

The veteran development company has brought executive communities to points around the compass since its pioneering residential community project. Southpark, located in Littleton, offers several living options from executive single-family homes to mid-priced townhomes. More than 40 percent of the 176-acre community, which features all amenities of modern living, is dedicated to greenbelts.

In the north part of the Denver metropolitan area, Writer has developed the Northpark residential community in Westminster, offering a blend of townhomes and single-family residences in a wide range of prices available to young families and established executives. This community is conveniently located to serve the high technology companies headquartered in the Broomfield-to-Boulder and Westminster-to-Denver corridors.

Writer has purchased ground for 906 residences in the Castle Pines development in Douglas County. Luxury homes for this community of the future will be built for executive families moving into this corridor between Denver and Colorado Springs.

The Writer Corporation is building Country Meadows at the Green Valley Ranch, a planned community that will include schools, shopping centers, a medical clinic, and recreational facilities. This development is located on the eastern side of the metro area near I-70 and Tower Road.

Two of the distinctive communities at the spectacular Ken Caryl Ranch, southwest of the metropolitan area near the Front Range of mountains are projects of the Writer Corporation.

Chambers Ridge in Aurora likewise offers the Colorado style of living in townhomes for young professionals and first-time homebuyers.

The Vista at Piney Creek, a master-planned community in Arapahoe County, offers executive homes. Willow Creek, Writer's largest planned community to date, sold out in 1984. Meadowglen, another single-family community built by Writer was completed in 1984.

Greenbrook is Writer's newest addition in Aurora, offering large townhomes situated with only 12 units per acre. This configuration provides for large open space and recreational areas.

Quincy Hill also in Aurora offers panoramic mountain views from townhomes located near the popular Cherry Creek Reservoir. It is a complete community offering easy access to Stapleton International Airport, the Denver Technological Center, and downtown from an affordable two- and three-bedroom townhouse community with exclusive recreational features.

Recently Writer Corporation moved its planned community concepts to Colorado Springs, home for the new Consolidated Aerospace Command Center. Meadow Ridge at Briargate is part of a planned community aimed at providing modern homes for discerning first-time buyers. Cottonwood Creek is a new townhome community located along the peaceful creek for which the development is named. Like most Writer communities, it too offers recreational amenities and maximum use of natural open space.

As The Writer Corporation continues to develop prime residential communities and new commercial properties to serve Colorado, its determination to preserve the natural environment is certain to continue its place as a pacesetter for the real estate industry. This resolve is not just a motto at Writer Corporation, it is a part of the company's master-plan for the future, and its legacy to the 21st century.

The Writer Corporation has been a leader in Colorado's quest to balance a good life style with preservation of the environment. Its homes set a pace for quality.

PROFILE

John Madden Company
Making Fine Art of Development

Madden's Greenwood Plaza is a museum of outdoor sculptures; and the architecture, such as the Tuscany facility, is a tribute to modern development.

Towering Rocky Mountains along Colorado's Front Range form the backdrop for buildings and grounds that can truly be described as "works of art" in a unique modern museum of commerce and industry.

The John Madden Company's Greenwood Plaza is a working collection of imported statuary, art in architecture, and office buildings made from Carrara and travertine marble, similar to the beautiful rock Italian renaissance artists used for shaping some of the world's most noted sculptures.

The company's founder, John W. Madden Jr., explained his motivation for combining art and architecture in his development at a recent ceremony dedicating The Tuscany, one of the most extraordinary office buildings ever constructed in the West.

"Actually, I'm just taking a fresh approach toward some fairly traditional goals: to create office environments of unsurpassed beauty and efficiency, to offer distinctive designs that capture the eye and the imagination, and to make a lasting contribution to Denver's business community."

The 20-year-old John Madden Company, a privately owned real estate development company headquartered in Englewood, provides completely integrated development services including property acquisition/disposition, financing project management leasing tenant finish, and property management In 1970 the company began the 283-acre parcel along Interstate 25 in the Front Range high technology corridor just south of Denver. Their commitment to excellence in architecture and artistry soon gained the project a reputation for long-term investment value, and major regional and national corporations began headquartering operations at the site.

The Greenwood Plaza office park is a commercial community, but with far greater impact on the environmental quality of the region than its utilitarian function. Over the years, John Madden has invested in the community through acquisition and placement of sculpture located throughout the office park, and built facilities of lasting value to the whole community. The office park, and outdoor museum of sculptures, includes the 20,000-seat Fiddler's Green Amphitheatre, a new fitness and wellness center, the University Center at Greenwood Plaza, the Metropolitan Club, and the Greenwood Plaza Child Care Center.

The University Center at Greenwood Plaza is a new concept in Colorado, bringing a partnership between the business community and the University of Colorado into focus. The facility within the office park offers graduate programs and extensive executive education for the southwest corridor of metropolitan Denver.

Greenwood Plaza Athletic Club, which offers wellness and fitness programs through a joint venture with St. Joseph's Hospital as well as recreational opportunities, is a preventive medicine clinic and traditional athletic club.

A new concept in service to the working community is the Greenwood Plaza Child Care Center. A partnership among the businesses in the office park, the center offers Montessori child care and educational programming to children of employees in the office park.

The John Madden Company has gone beyond the concept of preserving the environment in its projects to the creation of art through economic development in a people-oriented place.

160,000 acres of recreational land. Denver is unique among American cities because its founding fathers went far beyond the city limits to establish a chain of mountain parks.

But the public lands are by no means the only open spaces. Practically every major land development for any purpose—commercial or residential—has its own open spaces built into the project. In many industrial parks and residential subdivisions more land is set aside for open space than is used for buildings and homes. Most of the major new companies building facilities in Colorado in the past two decades have situated their plants amidst expansive greenbelts or preserved natural surroundings. The added development costs are obvious, but the results provide a living and working environment second to none in the United States.

Commercial Development

Colorado has built an infrastructure of industrial, commercial, public, and residential real estate, which through the remainder of the decade of the 1980s, places it in a favorable competitive position for economic expansion. The energy boom years of the late 1970s and early 1980s saw the state's construction activities at record levels in all types of building and modernization activities. Towering office buildings in downtown and near downtown Denver, office and manufacturing parks in metropolitan suburbs, and new and expanded executive and middle-income family residences were developed in anticipation of a rapid expansion of the economy due to energy development throughout the Rocky Mountain region.

When the threats of a world energy crisis subsided, much of the building was in place, creating a temporary surplus of all types of modern commercial and residential property. Instead of rapid boom, Colorado began to experience long-term, steady growth. The result of overbuilding, while the emphasis should certainly be placed on the word "temporary," has positioned Colorado cities and towns with structures in place for room to grow. From downtown Denver, throughout all the metropolitan cities, all along the Front Range from Colorado Springs to Greeley and Fort Collins, and onto the Western Slope at Grand Junction, outstanding real estate values await new companies and new residents.

Downtown Denver and the near downtown areas feature the highest concentration of new commercial property. Denver's ultramodern Central Business District has 125 office buildings, and an additional 57 are located in midtown areas. A large percentage of Denver's skyscrapers are less than a decade old, and many of the older structures have been modernized. Even the turn-of-the-century buildings have been completely refurbished, maintaining the charm of the Victorian era and incorporating the comfort and efficiency of this century.

Spreading from the downtown Denver area

Coloradans are building for a future with promise in the new eras of high technology, aerospace, and telecommunications. Photo by Hull & Kangas Photographers

PROFILE

Mission Viejo Realty Group
Environmentally Sound New Town Rises on Front Range

The first town builders moving under the shadows of the Rocky Mountains came with a vision to create a new way of life. Modern Colorado town builders have much the same dream, and Mission Viejo Realty Group's Highlands Ranch project near Denver is such a dream realized.

Sometime in the early part of the 21st century, the state will boast a new city of approximately 90,000 residents, complete with schools, medical and recreational facilities, retail establishments, and business/industry parks. Already the 12,000-acre community has substantially taken shape along the northern boundary of Douglas County.

Its comprehensive master plan, which makes it the largest new town development in Colorado, features a prime business center in Colorado's most rapidly growing business/industrial corridor.

More than 1,400 acres of the project have been set aside for corporate, research and development, distribution, office, and other business uses. The site is strategically located in south metropolitan Denver along the newly opened Centennial Freeway (C-470) between Interstate 25 and U.S. 85.

In addition to the business park and office parks, Highlands Ranch offers housing options from entry-level townhomes to executive estates. The new community is supported by elementary and junior/senior high schools within the project; an on-site recreation center; a medical care center; and its own municipal services, including water and sanitation districts, post office, and metropolitan districts for fire and other municipal services.

Its own business centers, Ridgeline Business Park, Centennial Office Park, and Highlands Ranch Corporate Center, will offer complete business services. Ridgeline Business Park is planned to accommodate a variety of site sizes for garden offices, office/warehouse, and warehouse/distribution facilities on 76 acres.

Centennial Office Park is situated at the major intersection of Broadway and Centennial Freeway and is designed for users seeking high visibility.

Highlands Ranch Corporate Center is particularly suited for corporate users seeking a low density, campus-like environment. A full range of retail and support services—including restaurants, hotel, and health club—are planned to serve businesses and employees.

The historic 22,000-acre Highlands Ranch, which was purchased by Mission Viejo's parent company, the multinational Philip Morris Companies Inc., features a 12,000-acre planned community with more than 10,000 acres of the rolling, foothills property set aside for non-urban uses.

Construction of the new community began in 1980, after one of the most exhaustive master planning efforts in the history of new development in Colorado was completed. Planning included the water supply, sanitation and sewage handling, parks and recreation, fire protection, and streets. Streets are designed in a circular pattern that helps prevent and control air pollution by reducing miles and trips required to reach points within the community. Throughout the residential and commercial areas, greenbelts and natural areas will create an enjoyable, park-like environment.

The nearby foothills and Rocky Mountain peaks form the background to the west of Highlands Ranch, and the developing area has clear vistas of metropolitan Denver on its northern horizon. The Chatfield State Recreation Area is minutes away, offering residents boating, swimming, camping, fishing, and horseback riding.

In addition to the Mission Viejo Realty Group, Philip Morris Companies Inc. owns such companies as Miller Brewing Company, General Foods, and Philip Morris International. The multinational company has annual sales of nearly $23 billion.

The hills are alive over Mission Viejo, an environmentally planned Colorado "new town" on the Front Range. The project offers homes and high-tech space.

Office parks are carefully landscaped to capture the best of Colorado's natural beauty. Photo by Hull & Kangas Photographers

into the bustling surrounding cities, some of America's finest and most modern office and industrial parks have risen during the past decade.

The best known are three of the state's largest and most modern industrial parks: the Denver Technological Center (DTC), Greenwood Plaza, and Inverness. These parks, along the Interstate 25 corridor from Denver through Englewood and Littleton into Douglas County, are extensive mixed-use properties that offer all the amenities for commercial, R&D, and light industrial activities to be found in complete cities. Their location at junctions of major highway networks—I-25, I-225, and C-470—make them attractive for many business and industry headquarters.

They feature easy access to airports, such as the large executive Centennial Airport, and to Stapleton International. Onsite support services such as restaurants and international hotels, health and fitness centers, and even advanced university programs, are a part of these complexes. Nearby executive residential areas and major regional shopping centers complete the infrastructure and give these developments all the characteristics of substantial "business cities."

Other substantial office and industrial parks, well integrated into the cities of Arvada, Aurora, Boulder, Broomfield, Golden, Lakewood, and Northglenn, round out the industrial and business communities available in the immediate Denver Metropolitan Area, and provide ample commercial real estate opportunities for the new or expanding company.

The Denver Metro area, including Boulder, had approximately 80 million square feet of new office space built or near completion in 1985, and with a relatively high vacancy rate, offered a wide range of options in types of space and prices. While commercial real estate transactions have not been as numerous or as large as in the recent building boom, substantial real estate trades continue to make headlines in the metropolitan area. Major national real estate firms, along with real estate investors from Canada, England, and other foreign countries, are prominent in local real estate transactions in the metro area.

But growth along the Front Range is not limited to this metropolitan center.

Greeley at the north end of the fast growing Front Range has made great strides since 1985 to develop additional high technology office and industrial areas, and Colorado Springs, with the new Consolidated Aerospace Center, is emerging as one of the nation's fastest developing high technology

PROFILE

Denver Technological Center/ Meridian Business Center
Pioneering New Concepts in Economic Development

The emergence of Colorado into a lead role as a national center for technological and aerospace industries might well have had its beginning almost by accident only a little over two decades ago. Land use planners for a small engineering firm drew up a bold blueprint for the development of 40 acres in prairielands southeast of Denver.

George M. Wallace, P.E., a mechanical engineer who had purchased the property, wanted his small parcel developed for modest plant space to house emerging technology companies. His designer mapped out an unusual plan that would leave nearly half the property as park-like open space. That was in 1962, and today The Denver Technological Center, over 750 acres, is a model for international developers wishing to capture its ambience and environmental quality in modern, urban high-tech centers across the nation and the around the world.

Conceived by Wallace as a suburban office park, the DTC has evolved into one of the most notable urban centers in America. The supporting infrastructure of streets and utilities are hardly noticed, yet the efficiency built into the center continues to draw the cream of Colorado's business and industry to make corporate homes on the southeast Denver site.

Open, treeless prairies have been turned into tree-covered, lake-dotted parks. A mixed-use community has evolved, with balanced land use combining offices, retail, hotels, restaurants, shops, and extensive open space. Landscaping at the Denver Tech Center is blended with commanding architecture and efficient design to create a working environment more like a botanical garden than an industrial district.

With more than 600 companies, many of which are regional headquarters for members of the Fortune 500, the Denver Technological Center has succeeded in proving that economic development and ecological preservation can thrive side by side. The key element guiding the inception and the continuing evolution of the Tech Center's development is a philosophy that the working environment should be centered around man.

An extension on this success story is the newly developing Meridian International Business Center, opening several miles south of the Denver Technological Center. The new 1,200-acre development is a business community that totally integrates commercial, office, research, health, and recreational facilities with the beauty of the land. Meridian's centerpiece is an 18-hole golf course designed by Jack Nicklaus.

Both the Denver Technological Center and the new Meridian International Business Center are located in the fastest growing technological corridor in the Rocky Mountain West. The centers are directly served by the major I-25 network with quick access to the region's best highway and air transportation services.

The high technology centers are also situated in easy proximity to the beautiful southeastern Denver area executive residential neighborhoods. Modern schools, parks, recreational facilities, the region's largest shopping centers, and advanced educational facilities are all within a short distance of these centers.

The Denver Tech Center and Meridian have set the pace for progressive land use planning techniques, fine architecture, and implementation of such new technological amenities as fiber optic communications systems. Beauty and efficiency are designed to work together, and both centers are assured of continued dedication to these principles by strict protective covenants and design guidelines.

The Tech Center pioneered quality environments for high technology, and this park-like environment has been carried forward in the new Meridian Center.

The building of Colorado today is a carefully planned process. As a leading state in the emerging West the balance between progress and preservation is important. Photo by Stewart M. Green

office park centers. The competition for new corporate tenants is sharp in these areas, furthering the availability of first-class property at favorable rates to new and expanding companies.

On the Western Slope, particularly in the Grand Junction area, commercial property built for the expected boom in the oil shale industry is also in place to attract new companies. And national firms have been discovering this area of the state, with several new plants announcing openings since 1985.

This expansion both within the Front Range and in other parts of the state from Lamar to Durango, and from Craig to Fort Morgan, is gradually bringing a more diverse commercialization to Colorado. The Front Range will likely remain the most active growth area in Colorado for the future, but options are beginning to appear all across the state.

The most active sector of the commercial real estate industry in Colorado is in retail properties, and strong growth in the retail sector of the economy promises continued high activity in most parts of Colorado. In the Denver metropolitan area alone, nearly four million square feet of retail space was absorbed in 1983 and 1984. An additional three million square feet was built in the Front Range Counties around Denver in 1984.

The Grubb & Ellis Commecial Brokerage Group issued a report on the brisk activity in retail-type real estate transactions, and noted that 20 neighborhood/community shopping centers had been sold during 1984 in the Denver Metro Area. The important role of the shopping center and the retail establishment to the commercial life of Colorado is detailed in Chapter 2. The dynamic retail sector of the economy is also one of the major generators of real estate activity in the state.

Homes on the Edge of the Sky

As with much of the commercial development in Colorado, great effort is expended to match the residential areas throughout the cities, towns, and rural communities of the state with the splendor of the natural environment. And like the life style of Coloradans, their homes often reflect the wide range of alternatives available.

In the 1980 Census there were 1,194,000 housing units counted in the state, and the housing was generally newer and more modern than in most states. Only in Alaska, Arizona, Florida, Nevada, and Wyoming were the average ages of houses newer than in Colorado, where nearly 40 percent of the homes in the state had been built since 1970. Almost a quarter of the residences in the state were multi-family units (condominiums and apartments), and nearly 70 percent of all residential structures were owner-occupied. Coloradans also invest more in their homes than residents of most states, with the 1980 median value of Colorado residences placed at $64,100, the sixth highest median value in the United States.

The wide diversity of housing available in the state can accommodate almost any life style, taste, or budget. However, as in most western states, a shortage of low income housing is beginning to pose a problem, as most new structures are targeted for the middle-to-upper income consumer. The greatest options for housing to suit different life styles are found along the Front Range urbanized area, where mountain communities are within an easy drive to most of the state's workplaces.

In this area, residential subdivisions and housing offer a wide contrast. The most sophisticated urbanite can easily find high-rise apartments and condominiums in the heart of the cities, or the outdoor types can find ample property within minutes of work to raise

PROFILE

Phelps, Inc.
Building the West for the Future

The building of the West continues into modern times at a faster pace than ever before in history, proving that the region is still very much America's last frontier.

A leading construction corporation, which has been a part of this new frontier development for nearly half a century, remains a pacesetter as Colorado and the western United States prepare for economic leadership roles in the 21st century.

Phelps, Inc. and its operating companies, Hensel Phelps Construction Co. and Clearwater Constructors, Inc., are literally changing the skyline of the cities and towns of the Rockies. The Phelps contribution to architectural and construction quality has helped set the high standards to assure that the region can balance development with environmental quality.

Hensel Phelps Construction Co., the flagship company of Phelps Inc., was named for its founder, who in 1937 formed what was to become one of the largest construction firms in the West. Clearwater Constructors of Colorado, formed in 1981, has already left its mark of excellence throughout the region. A national, multimillion-dollar corporation, Phelps construction firms have built industrial and institutional facilities, commercial buildings and skyscrapers, treatment plants, bridges, and dams from Maryland to Dutch Harbor in Alaska.

Headquartered, along with the corporate offices, at Greeley, Colorado, Hensel Phelps Construction has earned a reputation throughout the vast western region for completing major projects on time, on budget, and with a consistent standard of quality.

In 1985, management of the construction companies passed to the fourth generation of leadership with the naming of Jerry L. Morgensen, president of Hensel Phelps, and Harold G. Evans, president of Clearwater. Following the tradition of leadership set by its founder, and continued by his son, Joseph Phelps, and by Bob Tointon (both of whom served as president), the corporation's management has remained in the hands of working construction experts.

Phelps Construction is noted throughout the United States for its high standards of construction. This skyscraper was built around a historic chapel.

The projects completed and underway by the Phelps construction companies read like a directory of economic development in this fastest growing region of America.

Hensel Phelps' presence is strongly evident on the "Main Street of the Rockies," Denver's 16th Street pedestrian/transitway mall. The anchoring facility to the commercial end of that mile-long mall is the Tabor Center, a mixed-use complex of office, hotel, and futuristic retail facilities.

Another project in downtown Denver demonstrates the precision and expertise of this major construction company. When a skyscraper was to be built immediately behind Denver's historic Holy Ghost Catholic Church, the giant structure literally had to share the block with the tiny sanctuary. Phelps constructed the $55 million, 43-story 1999 Broadway office building without damage to the church, and the massive glass building seems to provide a sheltering frame for the small historic building.

Clearwater's latest contributions to the fine and functional architecture of Colorado include the new $20-million Grande Butte Hotel at Crested Butte, and Littleton's new Riverfront Festival Center in south metropolitan Denver.

Among a few of the other noteworthy Colorado structures erected by this locally founded firm are the Alamo Plaza and Writers Square in downtown Denver; the Racquet World's massive sports center in Englewood; the Sheraton at Steamboat Springs; mountain recreation centers at Vail, Breckenridge, and Copper Mountain; industrial plants for Eastman Kodak at Windsor, Hewlett-Packard at Greeley, and scores of others in Colorado; and hospitals at Greeley and Denver.

a garden or even livestock. "Horse property," the common name for a house with acreage and proper zoning for animals, is available less than 30 minutes drive from Denver's Central Business District, as are an endless variety of housing options from prairie land subdivisions to mountain villages tucked out of sight of the major arterials.

Old Victorian neighborhoods that have been completely restored vie with modern earth-tone subdivisions in cities and towns all over the state. Whole new towns have been built and are under construction all along the Front Range, high in the mountains, and on the high mesas of the Western Slope. Modern manufacturing companies, situating new plants where wheat fields once prevailed, draw modern new residential and commercial communities, and restore fading farm towns.

In the mid-1980s there was a residential surplus in some areas of the state, where building in anticipation of rapid energy development exceeded the resulting reality. While residential vacancy rates along the Front Range were not as great as office space vacancy rates, housing prices for middle income and executive homes stabilized from boom costs of the 1970s.

Over most of the state, the combination of slower growth rates and heavy building activity generated by an expected energy boom, has made residential real estate a "buyer's market" during the mid-1980s. Coupled with the lowest mortgage interest rates in years, which prevailed in 1986, excellent opportunities exist for first-home buyers, families upgrading their space and living conditions, or newcomers to Colorado.

The real estate industry has added nearly 2,000 employees to its workforce since 1984, and has leveled off at approximately 26,200 workers. In the mid-1980s there were nearly 40,000 licensed real estate brokers in the state, but fewer than half were employed full-time in the industry. The state had about 3,000 registered real estate offices, but many were branch offices of major real estate companies.

Despite the leveling off of growth in this sector of the economy, jobs in real estate have increased substantially over the past decade, rising from just over 15,000 employees in 1976. The largest growth in this sector was during 1978 and 1979, when real estate development took a huge leap. The higher level of activity has been maintained, despite

Life styles of Coloradans blend into the natural environment in new developments in rapidly growing Douglas County. Photo courtesy of South Metro Denver

PROFILE

Upland Industries Corporation
Pioneer Company Building for the Future

Upland Industries Corporation has not only pioneered industrial real estate development along Union Pacific's rail system throughout the Rocky Mountains, but in more recent times has expanded its historic role to become a prime developer in the mixed use industrial, office, hotel, and rapidly expanding high technology and research and development industries. Its Colorado light-industry and advanced-technology properties, in addition to having exceptional rail service, are situated on the leading highway and air transportation networks.

Upland, the real estate subsidiary of Union Pacific Corporation, is one of the nation's largest developers of prime industrial and commercial property. The company has major programs underway in states across the West, throughout the Rockies, and on Colorado's rapidly growing Front Range. Upland has four established sites located in Fort Collins, Denver, Aurora, and Adams County, north of Denver.

Prospect Business Park in Fort Collins, adjacent to Union Pacific Railroad, is only a mile from the Fort Collins Airport and two miles from Interstate Highway 25, the main north-south highway of the Rocky Mountain Region. Consistent with its historic commitment to quality in real estate development, Upland Industries maintains protective covenants to enhance and protect property values and assure the type of long-term environmental quality demanded by ecology-minded Coloradans.

The Fort Collins property is situated near the leading businesses in this university city, where a number of leading Colorado high-tech companies are located.

Upland's largest developments in Colorado are located in Denver and Aurora near Stapleton International, the world's sixth busiest commercial airport. In the Denver/Aurora area, Upland Industries has developed or marketed more than 2,200 acres of prime business properties especially suited for light or high-technology manufacturing and distribution facilities, and for commercial usage such as office buildings, retailing, and related service industries. The properties are located just east of the major commercial air hub, and are bisected by Interstate 70, the major east-west highway through Colorado. Two of the properties are adjacent to Interstate 225, which provides direct freeway access to other industrial and commercial properties and the rapidly expanding south corridor off Interstate 25.

Upland also has an industrial site north of the airport in Adams County, adjacent to Interstate 76, Colorado's main link to Nebraska and the midwestern states.

Upland Industries Corporation markets its properties and developments in 22 southern, central, and western states. Properties in or near major and secondary metropolitan areas total more than 21,000 acres.

The company is involved in all phases of planned business real estate development. Their business parks offer a mix of large and small office buildings; showrooms; research and development buildings; and service, retail, and hotel facilities. Upland's industrial parks are dedicated to light manufacturing, assembly, and warehousing. The industrial districts are designed for large manufacturing and warehousing operations. Upland also develops stand-alone office buildings, hotels, and special projects such as single-site mixes of buildings for offices, hotels, retail, and government.

Upland Industries offers new office parks on the Front Range in keeping with its historic development role as part of Union Pacific. Photo by Roger Whitacre

Careful development practices have made Keystone Resort one of the world's most famous recreation areas, with full programs for both winter and summer. Photo by Ron Ruhoff, Stock Imagery

what many in the industry describe as a "flat real estate market."

Colorado's housing inventory remained relatively high, with about 26,000 single and multifamily residential units on the market at the beginning of 1986. With sales running close to 2,000 units per month, the inventory of residential units would mean almost a year's supply of houses on the market. But with the average price of homes declining for the first time in 20 years and interest rates hovering around 10 percent, sales in this market are expected to eliminate any real surplus.

High Country Builders

Because of the overbuilding in commercial and private structures, the state's once-booming construction industry leveled off at just over 86,000 workers in 1986. It should be noted that construction employment still remained at a high plateau of near-record employment levels. Only a decade ago the construction industry accounted for fewer than 56,000 jobs. Record employment in construction was reached in 1984 and 1985 at about 88,000 workers.

Construction is still one of the largest industries in the state, averaging well over $4 billion a year since the beginning of the 1980s.

F.W. Dodge Company, which closely follows building trends, notes that the construction industry in Colorado has grown from under $2 billion annually to well over $4 billion in the past decade.

Residential construction remains the largest single part of the building industry in the state. In 1986 residential construction was estimated at $2 billion, with about 33,000 housing units under construction in Colorado. Even though construction has slowed since 1984, the level of employment and value in total construction remained well above the 10-year average of approximately 77,500 employees.

An area of residential construction that is enjoying some expansion is manufactured housing. Rising building costs for custom homes and subdivision housing is leading a growing number of Coloradans to opt for homes either partially or wholly prefabricated before being placed on their lots and acreage. Prefab or manufactured homes have long been popular in mountain communities where

227

PROFILE

G.E. Johnson Construction Company
Building a Lasting Future in Quality Construction

Millennium One at Greenwood Village is an example of the diversified projects being built by G.E. Johnson for the high-tech era. Photo by Jay S. Simon

Colorado's rapid emergence as one of the nation's leaders in the field of high technology has challenged the state's construction industry to produce the often highly sophisticated facilities to match the complexity of advanced science.

One of Colorado's leading construction companies has been meeting the challenges for the nearly two decades of the "technology revolution," and its landmark buildings are found throughout the state's institutions, industrial parks, and higher-quality commercial projects.

G.E. Johnson Construction Company, Inc., a Colorado founded and operated design/build/construction management firm, bases its operations solely in the state. Headquartered in Colorado Springs, the company list of huge projects is extensive, with more than $100 million in annual sales volume in Colorado. More than half is comprised of repeat business.

G.E. Johnson Construction Company has also earned an outstanding reputation for its careful cost management and timely completion of complex projects for business, industry, and institutions of the state. Projects range from highly technical spaces for the high technology, defense, and aerospace industry to power generating plants. The company has built functional, comfortable learning centers from elementary schools to college and university facilities. Added to these construction management achievements are maximum security correctional facilities, concert halls, intricate hospital centers, industrial plants, printing plants, water treatment plants, inspiring traditional churches, and bustling jet-age airports.

Founded in 1967, G.E. Johnson Construction Company employs over 450 skilled professionals and tradesmen. The company is employee-owned and performs a substantial part of its work with its own staff.

"We feel that we are able to attract the most qualified employees due to the growth opportunities which are presented both within our firm and in the state," says Gilbert E. Johnson, president. "The general environment of Colorado makes this a very attractive location for raising a family. Colorado is an extremely competitive market; but for those who accept this challenge, the opportunities are very rewarding."

G.E. Johnson Construction, which has won numerous awards for design and construction, is noted for its contribution to a broad range of projects. In commercial construction the company has built such noted facilities as the Millennium Office Building for US West, MIS Headquarters, Broadmoor West Hotel, and the Tamarac Plaza/Texaco Building.

Notable among its industrial projects are the Colorado Springs Gazette-Telegraph, R.D. Nixon Power Plant, IBM Industrial Waste Treatment Facility, and the Fountain Valley Water Treatment Plant. The company has built some of the state's most recognized public projects such as the Centennial Correction Facility, Ordway Medium Security Prison, the University of Colorado at Colorado Springs Engineering Building, and the Colorado Springs Airport. Their construction management work includes the Pikes Peak Community College, and the impressive Pikes Peak Center, one of the state's finest performing arts facilities.

The facilities it has built for high technology companies, including highly complicated clean rooms and research and development centers, reads like a directory of the high-tech companies in Colorado: Digital Equipment Corporation, Hewlett-Packard, UTMC, Ford Microelectronics, Martin Marietta, Ball Aerospace, Honeywell, Litton Industries, TRW, and NCR.

As a Colorado-based company, G.E. Johnson Construction's key personnel are active in volunteer leadership roles, both within the construction industry associations and in community and statewide development organizations.

they were initially introduced as second homes or vacation homes. Mobile or prefabricated houses are also popular in communities where rapid growth in the past, created by energy booms, has created a demand for quick construction. These homes are also seen throughout the farming and ranching areas of the state.

However, improvements in the quality and size of manufactured housing are making them a popular alternative for first-time homebuyers, and for retired persons settling in a growing number of Colorado retirement communities.

The Manufactured Housing Industry, the trade association for this group, reported in 1986 that over 87,000 mobile homes housed nearly 220,000 Coloradans. Over half these homes are located on the owner's property and the remainder in designated park developments.

Five Colorado companies were manufacturing prefabricated homes in 1986. Each year these firms deliver nearly 1,000 homes that meet standards set by the Housing and Urban Development code.

Average total value of construction remained at high levels through the mid-1980s. Residential real estate construction totaled $674 million in 1976, compared with about $2 billion in 1986. The average annual value of construction over the past 10 years has been $1.6 billion. Non-residential construction was estimated at $1.78 billion in 1986, up from $444 million in 1976 and a half-billion dollars above the yearly average for the past 10 years. Non-building construction in the state was placed at $735 million in 1986, compared with a yearly average for the past decade of $623 million. So while some declines have been experienced due to overbuilding, activity levels remain near historic highs in the construction industry.

With a one-year oversupply in residential property in the state and an estimated two-year oversupply in high-rise building space, new construction starts are expected to stabilize while the market absorbs the surplus housing and commercial space. However, continued growth, even at a slower pace, will soon absorb this space surplus in most areas of the state.

One exception to the slow construction activity has been in the construction of ski-area facilities. Heavy investments continue to be made in expanded and improved facilities at ski areas all over the state. While the big expenditures in virtually every resort area seen in the 1985-86 period may slow somewhat, expansion in that sector of the economy is expected to continue to meet the rapidly growing popularity of Colorado's outdoor recreational attractions.

Utilities to Support Growth

Colorado is located in a region of the United States that benefits directly from locally available fuel resources providing the power for relatively inexpensive utilities. Coal to generate electricity, natural gas for direct use, and the facilities to generate and transport power are well developed in the state. Colorado is an exporter of both electricity and natural gas to other sections of the United States.

Pride in workmanship and a strong sense of preserving the quality of life in Colorado are primary motivators behind the state's development. Photo by Stewart M. Green

PROFILE

Stonegate–Mobil Development Corp.
Building a City of the Future

A city of the future is being built today by the Mobil Land Development Corporation in Colorado's emerging new advanced technology corridor between Denver and Colorado Springs.

Stonegate, a truly complete new-town concept, has been designed as a self-contained community where its citizens could live, work, and rear families in a quality environment not totally oriented to the automobile. Significantly, the new community, which was under construction in 1986, is being sponsored by one of America's largest oil companies.

Stonegate Development Inc., an affiliate of Mobil Land Development Corporation, has master planned a small city which, upon completion in the 1990s, will include its own infrastructure of water treatment and waste recycling, internal community schools, complete office and light industry park, shopping center, recreational facilities, and a wide choice of residential communities. The 1,450-acre Stonegate will literally offer the total life style environment of a sizable town.

The multifaceted urban center, located three miles east of I-25 in north Douglas County, will have secluded neighborhood enclaves of about 2,500 single and multifamily homes, a campus-style business center with seven million square feet of office and light industry space, a retail village, and extensive recreational facilities, greenbelts, and avenue-like streets.

Stonegate, which has its own water supply and treatment system, treats all its own wastewater and, after recycling, uses the water to irrigate its landscaped green areas. The site, crossed by a stream, was rugged, treeless grazing land when Stonegate Development Inc. purchased it five years ago. Already more than 1,500 mature trees have been planted as progress is ongoing in the new development.

"Every phase of the project exemplifies the development philosophy of Mobil Land Development Corporation," according to Rawleigh Warner Jr., chairman of the board of Mobil. "The company will utilize long-range, creative planning to provide attractive living and recreation areas consistent with protection of the environment."

The community is designed to offer its corporate and residential citizens a high degree of independence from the automobile. The center will be served directly by such outstanding highway arterials as a newly improved Lincoln Avenue, the major east-west feeder between I-25 and Parker Road, and the planned new E-470, a proposed connection tying the south corridor directly to the new international regional airport and the western route (C-470) to the mountains.

Patterned after Mobil's internationally recognized "new town" of Reston, Virginia, located between Washington, D.C. and Dulles International Airport, the Stonegate project has been designed in close cooperation between the Mobil Land Development Colorado staff, expert consultants, and regional and local government planners. It is one of 19 major projects of Mobil Land Development in Colorado and seven other states.

"We're addressing Colorado's concerns of enhancing the natural beauty of the state, and offering a high quality project that maintains the ambience of the Colorado life style," concludes Warner.

Attention to the fine details of life quality is making Stonegate a new community in Colorado's future. A master stone cutter works on the village logo.

Planned communities throughout Colorado strive to maintain a high quality of life style. Photo by William Swartz

The state has well-developed generating capacity, and some of the facilities are the largest and most modern in North America. Many of the huge electric generating plants are located immediately adjacent to long-term supplies of coal. In 1986 the state had over 6,000 megawatts in electric generating capacity, enough for its own needs in the immediate future and for continued export of electricity. Low-sulphur coal, supplied within the state or in Wyoming, is the primary fuel for generating electricity, with smaller contributions from hydro-electric plants and the Rocky Mountain area's one nuclear generating station at St. Vrain in northern Colorado.

Approximately 70 percent of Colorado's electricity is supplied by the Public Service Company of Colorado, with 30 municipal systems, 29 rural electric cooperatives, and one other private company providing the balance. Public Service serves the Denver Metropolitan Area and cities across the state from Sterling and Brush on the eastern plains to Grand Junction on the Western Slope, and in the south to Alamosa. Home Light and Power, a subsidiary of Public Service Company of Colorado, provides service in the Greeley area; and Public Service also sells wholesale electricity to several other utility companies in the state.

Pueblo and the Arkansas Valley from Canon City to Rocky Ford is supplied by the Southern Colorado Power Division of the Central Telephone and Utilities Corporation. Municipal systems serve a number of cities in the state, including a large system at Colorado Springs. In the north central area of the state, the Platte River Power Authority, a wholesale power consortium, provides service to city systems in Fort Collins, Loveland, Longmont, and Estes Park. A similar consortium, the Arkansas River Power Authority, has been created to supply municipal systems at LaJunta, Las Animas, Lamar, Trinidad, Walsenburg, and Raton, New Mexico.

Rural electric cooperatives serve most of the state's non-urban areas, and are supplying some new development areas on the Front Range. The Bureau of Reclamation hydro plants provide some of this electricity, but there are also two major wholesale associations providing power to the rural electrification cooperatives. The large associations are Colorado-Ute Electric Association, serving the western and southern part of the state, and Tri-State Generation and Transmission

PROFILE

Metro Brokers, Inc.
Realtors Combine for High Standards of Service

Independent realtors have formed an alliance in Metro Brokers, Inc. to bring better service and high professional standards to Colorado homebuyers.

A decade ago a group of independent real estate brokers formed Metro Brokers, Inc., an organization that has become one of the most important forces in Colorado real estate.

Operating much like a trade association, the group has united its efforts in providing a strong network for improving quality in the industry, applying a unified high standard of ethics, combining advertising efforts to provide a stronger network of companies.

Metro Brokers, Inc. was formed in 1976 by six brokers and the organization rapidly expanded its member/shareholder base to its present 300-broker company association.

The association provides some similarities in the way it operates to other large brokerage offices. Members of each office share in showing listings, make weekly visits to new listings, and share on-call floor duty assignments. A member who has a phone call while away from the office is assured that the call will be handled in a capable manner by another experienced broker in the office.

Through the state organization, Metro Brokers, Inc. members can offer professional relocation assistance and information to individuals and families moving into Colorado.

Combined annual sales of its members exceed one-half billion dollars, and Metro Broker companies account for a significant volume of the real estate sales in Denver and Colorado Springs.

With 28 offices along the Front Range, Metro Brokers, Inc. is one of the fastest growing real estate organizations in Colorado. The association is unlike other organizations of independent brokers because its members own equal shares in the corporation. Each member is a real estate broker who is the owner and manager of his or her own real estate business and receives all commissions generated by the individual office. At the same time, the broker-owner remains a member of the group through membership fees entitling the independent member to be an equal voting member of Metro Brokers, Inc. Approximately 65 percent of the income of Metro Brokers, Inc. is allocated to advertising, and the remainder of the fee structure is dedicated to the administrative expenses of the organization.

Three of the Metro Brokers, Inc. offices specialize in commercial real estate, investments, and leasing, while all other offices offer a complete range of residential real estate services.

Operated like a trade association, Metro Brokers, Inc. members elect its own board of directors and officers; and committees comprised of volunteer members address such issues as approval of applications for new membership, advertising programs, ethics standards, continuing education and certification practices, and out-of-state office relations.

A membership committee carefully reviews applications of new broker members to assure high grade, top quality Colorado brokers meet the high standards of ethics set by the group. The organization combines its resources to assure the home or property buyer is given efficient service and dependable results.

Association, serving northeastern Colorado and parts of Nebraska and Wyoming.

With abundant natural gas available in Colorado fields, this inexpensive energy is available to 90 percent of Colorado's population. Colorado Interstate Gas Company is the largest pipeline operation, providing natural gas to many of the local utility companies that also provide electricity. Independent companies also provide natural gas supplies to large industrial users under direct contract in many parts of the state.

While Colorado's location near the energy sources promises a good supply of some of the least expensive electricity and natural gas in the nation, the state's historically inexpensive water and waste treatment utilities are not assured without major investments in facilities.

Water is in such surplus within the state from the Rocky Mountain snowmelt that much of the fresh water in the western United States originates in Colorado. But storage and treatment facilities in some rapidly growing parts of the state are not keeping up with the demands. The state's water future is discussed in greater detail in the next chapter.

Sewage treatment facilities in the urbanized areas of the state are also requiring the attention of officials in both the public and private sectors.

The federal government spends about $32 million a year to assist Colorado cities in building and expanding waste-water treatment facilities, but major local investments are projected in the remaining years of this century.

The largest treatment network in the state is located in Denver, and serves 20 local municipalities and 22 special sanitation districts along the Front Range. This system, Metropolitan Denver Sewage Disposal District No. 1, is constantly upgrading its systems and services.

Water treatment and waste disposal are two issues most directly affecting the continued orderly growth and development of Colorado. Further land-use planning and sound management of the expected continued growth in the state depend upon these and other factors discussed in Chapter 11.

Coloradans want to see the state grow and prosper. To assure the preservation of the natural wonders that provide a high quality life style, the state faces a challenging agenda for the future. This agenda is being addressed by citizens and leaders from all walks of life in both the public and private sectors of the economy.

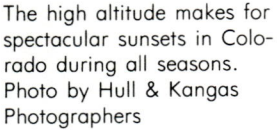

The high altitude makes for spectacular sunsets in Colorado during all seasons. Photo by Hull & Kangas Photographers

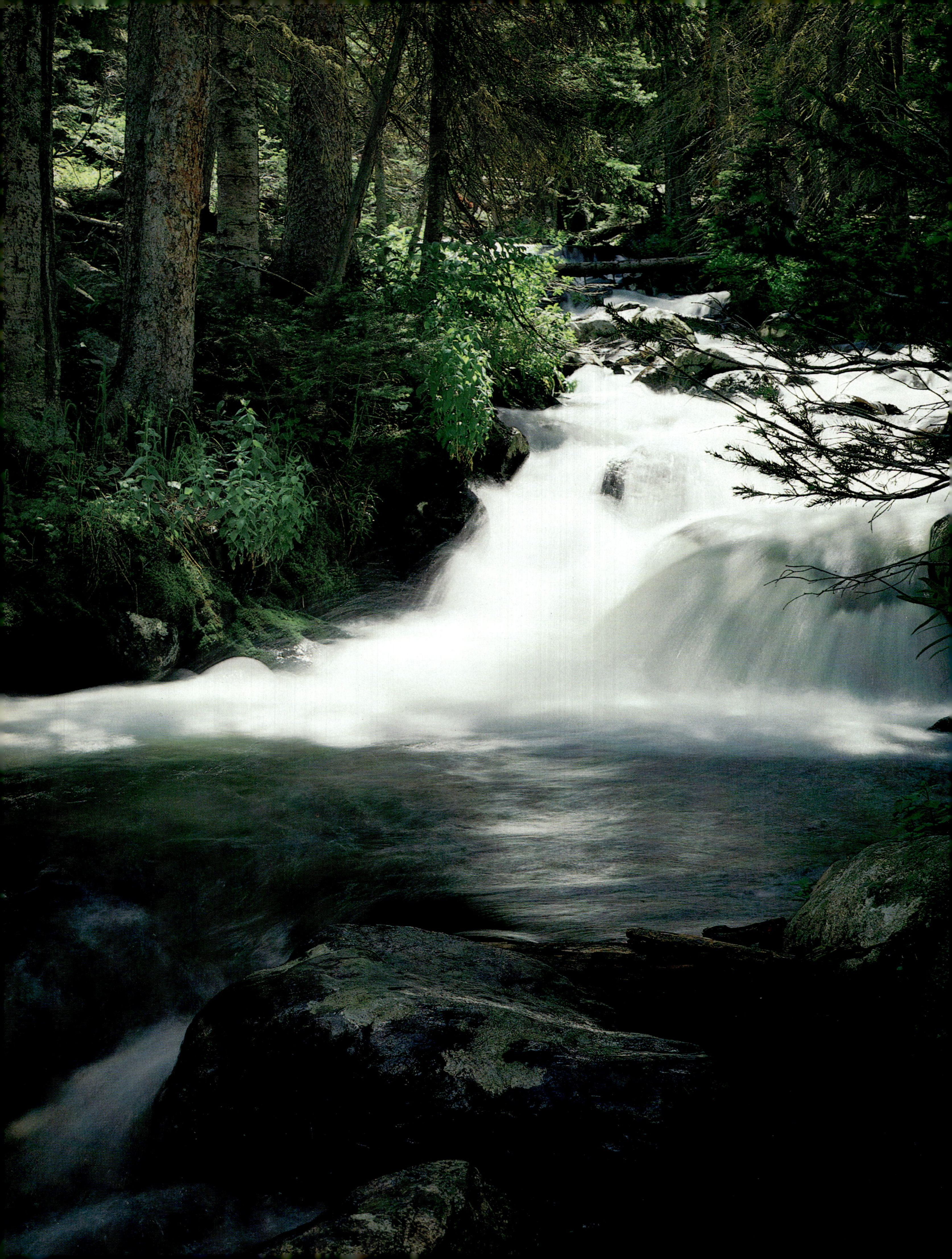

CHAPTER 11

A Future Challenge
The Delicate Balance

The diversity of its natural and human resources has provided Colorado with a cornucopia of choices in life style and careers.

The economy of the state has been in relatively rapid transition during the past decade. This process of change will accelerate in the final few years of this century. If Colorado is to continue to enjoy the luxury of offering "alternatives" in the ways its citizens live and work, changing global realities will have to be measured and tailored to local conditions.

Colorado's changing economic base is more and more affected by events outside the control of Coloradans, but only local citizens can determine how they will deal with these changes. Clearly, Colorado can no longer rely solely on its historic strong economy tied to the land.

Traditional agricultural methods, centered around the family farm, could become as much a dinosaur industry in middle America as the smokestack industries are becoming in the American East. U.S. agricultural economists predict that in the next decade one million more family farms, of the 2.4 million American farms in existence in the 1980s, will disappear. If Colorado loses its share of these, it would mean that the state's 27,000 farms would be reduced by another 40 percent, to fewer than 16,000 farms.

A state with one of the nation's fastest growing populations cannot depend on the periodic booms and busts of mineral and energy economies dictated by foreign markets and international cartels.

These basic natural resource industries can remain an asset to the state for years to come, and the natural environment of the state's forests and mountains will still be among its greatest economic factors. The natural environment invites visitors—a strong and growing industry in Colorado—as well as permanent new business firms to the state.

Just as external factors have impacted the natural resource industries that built the state, Colorado's economy of the future will vie for a share of the markets with the rest of the nation and, increasingly, with foreign competitors.

It is for that reason that the solid foundation of economic diversification on which the state's economy has been built becomes more important. The infrastructure in the Colorado community, whether large Front Range city or mountain village, becomes a key factor in this economic competition. None of the blessings of Colorado's bountiful natural environment can be fully enjoyed without the income from the jobs offered in the workplace. Poverty in a scenic mountain hamlet is no less painful than poverty in an urban ghetto. Declining employment in a rising population could prove more damaging to the quality of life than any of the environmental issues facing Coloradans. The lack of adequate job growth would force Colorado's young people to leave their homes and undermine the community structures and institutions.

So Coloradans are faced with the challenge of accommodating economic change and at the same time maintaining the good environment which now gives the state such a strong competitive edge.

Providing progress and prosperity, and preserving the environment and life quality surely requires attaining a delicate balance. And it is that challenge which engrosses Coloradans and their organizations as they face the coming of the 21st century.

Colorado streams literally water the western United States, originating in the high mountains to provide the source for the big rivers. Photo by Ron Phillips, Phillips Photographics

Celebrating its 100th anniversary in 1976, the Centennial State is young and vigorous in its leadership role. Photo by Stewart M. Green

Growth and Diversification

Based on birth, death, and immigration rates, forecasters project a steady expansion of the population in Colorado to more than 4.3 million people by the year 2000. If that growth rate is realized, it will represent an increase in population of more than 34 percent in less than 15 years, or more than a million additional Coloradans joining the approximately 3.25 million living here now.

A sustained growth rate is likely even without any major new "boom" in the economy, and at much slower immigration rates than Colorado experienced in the 1970s. From 1980 to 1985 Colorado was the seventh fastest growing state in the United States. That growth was largely attributed to net gains in population within the state through an increased birthrate and increasing longevity, not from people moving in from other states.

Projections made by the Demographic Section of the Colorado Division of Local Government showed population growth exceeding 34 percent in the Front Range counties, where 80 percent of the population already lives and works. The growth rate by the year 2000 is expected to be even higher on the Western Slope. Projections for that area show the population gain at nearly 50 percent, increasing from about 340,000 in 1986 to more than 508,000 by the year 2000. Rapid expansion of the winter and summer resort industry, coupled with concentrated efforts to diversify the agribusiness industry and introduce advanced technology manufacturing in the cities and towns of the Western Slope, could make these projections low.

"We are already built for the future," says Bill Cleary, president of the Western Slope's consolidated economic development organization called Club 20. "The oil shale boom did not materialize as expected, but it left us with an outstanding infrastructure in place."

Cleary says the cities and towns, particularly in the center of the expected oil shale boom that fizzled, are built up with modern water and sewer treatment, transportation, educational programs, schools and public buildings, and are prepared for industrial diversification. He says the whole Western Slope from Craig to Durango is "turning it around; we're doing it ourselves."

The Eastern Mountains area of Colorado, which abuts the urbanized Front Range, is expected to grow in population by nearly 30 percent during the next 15 years, from over 102,000 to more than 133,000.

Only on the Eastern Plains and in the San Luis Valley is population growth expected to remain at about current levels. Presently, both those sub-regions are heavily dependent on agriculture, but economic diversification could change these projections too.

For example, a gigantic national physics research project is being discussed for possible location on Colorado's northeastern plains. While still very much in the talking stage, the construction of a 100-mile underground atomic super collider somewhere between Limon and Brush could create 12,000 construction jobs and radically alter any current population projections. That futuristic device could be mankind's next source of renewable energy.

"We are looking for the right kind of manufacturing facilities to diversify the economy, particularly ways to enhance the crops or process more of what is grown in this region," says Randy Sunderland, co-publisher of the *Limon Leader* and president of the Limon Chamber of Commerce. "The mood is definitely to supplement the historic agricultural base with modern industry. But we want to retain this important natural resource base in agriculture too."

Sunderland thinks the atomic super collider, which would create a 21st century medical and super high-tech research industry, is likely to happen in his part of the state, but not in the near future. Even without something as dramatic as the large research project, population will increase in the area. Current projections place growth in the Eastern Plains counties at just over 7,200 persons, an increase to about 149,000; with a gain of about 3,000 in the San Luis Valley, to a population of about 43,000 by the turn of the century.

Front Range population projections for the region between Pueblo and Fort Collins call for nearly a million more people, bringing total population to 3.5 million by the end of this century. It is in this densely populated corridor that the momentum of gains from births alone is almost certain to cause the heaviest impacts.

A single county in this region, Douglas County on the southern edge of the Denver Metropolitan Area, is expected to grow in population from about 39,000 in 1986 to more than 122,000 by the year 2000, a jump of nearly 215 percent. Douglas County at present is almost totally a rural county, with a sizable agriculture base. In 15 years, if projections are realized, the county would be an advanced technology manufacturing and urbanized area.

These urbanization and transitional changes in the economy of Colorado have citizens and institutions alike refocusing considerable energy and money into future planning. The impacts and implications of such population growth justify the concerns.

Three-term governor Richard Lamm (1974-86) cited one priority for the late 1980s: "The challenge is to diversify the economy statewide.

"Given western Colorado's attractiveness as a place to live, vast mineral resources, and the nation's need for energy, we are truly in the hinge of history. We must recognize that energy supply and development considerations will compound every public economic development decision we face in the future."

Lamm warned against a continued laissez-faire or reactive posture toward economic development and diversity in all parts of the state, noting that such attitudes would continue to leave the vast western part of the state in "boom and bust" cycles. He called for a planned and aggressive economic development program that could create "the grist for the mill of economic diversity."

With general population increases expected on the Front Range, on the Western Slope, and in the Eastern Mountain regions, expansion will be required in existing programs for highways and roads, hospitals and health centers, water treatment and waste disposal plants, schools, parks, and other community support facilities. Services provided by private

On a clear evening in Colorado's high altitude environment, the city lights seem to become a part of the night sky. Photo by Hull & Kangas Photographers

enterprise in every sector of the economy can also be expected to expand to meet increasing demand. The present surplus in existing housing and office space can be expected to disappear.

Since local government revenues in Colorado, as in every other state, are declining under federal cost-cutting programs, more of the costs to provide service to Colorado's growing population will be borne by local and state sources and by the private sector. Business and industry expansion will be required to generate these new local revenues, since government produces revenue only from taxing its employed citizens and profitable businesses.

If the quality of life in Colorado is to continue at a high level, it is thus imperative that a healthy growing economy, providing new jobs and new capital investment, underwrite the state's expansion.

The challenge becomes whether Colorado's business expansion and the resulting new jobs can keep pace with the population growth already in motion within the state.

Economy in Transition

Two important changes affecting the future of the economy of Colorado have been gaining momentum since the early 1980s. The depressed agriculture and energy industries of the state have caused citizens, economic developers, and government leaders to look closely at the state's job future.

Business and government leaders from across the state have moved forward with programs to further diversify and enhance existing business and industry through adding value to traditional products and finding export markets both within the United States and abroad. There is also an effort to decentralize or at least share the growth with areas of the state outside the immediate Front Range. This effort is being supported by organizations in both the public and private sectors.

The efforts to upgrade raw products, such as livestock and crops from the farms and ranches, are evidenced in efforts by local business leaders in agriculture areas to locate plants to process fruit and vegetable crops now being shipped as produce. Juice plants, potato processing and freezing operations, and all kinds of vegetable processing and packaging operations are being underwritten by private industry and associations.

Renewed efforts to locate manufacturing plants outside the immediate Front Range area have already been successful in Alamosa in the San Luis Valley, Pueblo at the extreme southern end of the Front Range, Lamar on the Eastern Plains, Durango in southwestern Colorado, and Grand Junction on the Western Slope.

The Colorado Division of Commerce and Development in the Department of Local Affairs has mounted a major campaign, including the opening of regional development offices, to direct the attention of prospective new business and industry to the assets available in cities and towns throughout the state. Of course, the large and well-organized development groups on the Front Range, both associations and private developers, remain in the strongest position to extoll the features of the established and emerging industrial and business parks in the Front Range.

Colorado is already considered to be among the top four leading states in space research and development—behind only California, Florida, and Texas—and is also among the top 10 states in other high technology industries. Thus, the state's future as an advanced technology leader seems assured.

That position is further assured by the state's selection as headquarters for the Consolidated Space Operations Center (CSOC). The first facilities of the Department of Defense consolidated space center opened in Colorado Springs in January 1986 on a huge tract of land near Peterson Air Force Base. It is surrounded by private industrial and research park developments that could amount to $3 billion in construction over the next 30 years. The center will be headed by the new Unified Space Command, which will oversee space operations for all branches of the military. The command was scheduled to take over operations by the end of 1986, with military space shuttle flights expected by the early 1990s.

While the exact impact on the state's economy continues to be a matter of speculation, the fact that the command center is located in Colorado has already begun to attract new space-related and other high technology industry into the state. Colorado already has over 75 aerospace companies from the giant Martin Marietta in Denver, to small subcontracting plants spread out along the Front Range from Pueblo to Greeley.

The more optimistic forecasters believe the Consolidated Space Operations Center will make Colorado the world's new space center. But even if this does not happen in the short term, the advanced technology industry beginning to locate new branch offices along the Front Range to take advantage of early contacts with the program are already a fact.

Colorado is indeed a land of contrast with sunshine warming the snow-covered fields on the Western Slope. Photo by Iris Photography

Joining a substantial high technology computer, biomedical, telecommunications, and already existing aerospace industry on the Front Range, the area is already being called the "Silcon Mountains"—a predicted competitor to California's Silcon Valley.

Joseph B. Verrengia, science writer for the *Rocky Mountain News*, predicts that Colorado is assured a place in the stars, regardless of the outcome of the Defense Department's schedule to implement the "Star Wars" program.

In a special report on the future of the aerospace industry in Colorado, Verrengia wrote, "From university laboratories in Boulder to the military installations around Colorado Springs, the countdown has started for space research to launch the state into a new era of high-tech prosperity and prominence."

With military space and NASA spending in Colorado already approaching the $3 billion level in 1986, the new Colorado-based space center is expected to raise that spending level to $4 billion annually before 1990.

Basic industry in the state is not fading away. Colorado has never had much "smokestack industry," with the exception of the once huge steel operations around Pueblo. Basic industries manufacturing lighter consumer products, food, and electronics remain competitive, and plants are generally modern.

Jeff Coors, fourth generation president of Adolph Coors Company, thinks Colorado's companies are among the most resilient in America, and that basic industry in the state has always handled change easier than have the more traditional Eastern companies.

Coors, who was elected to serve as chairman of the Colorado Association of Commerce and Industry (CACI) for 1986-87, notes that Colorado's basic industries are "on the leading edge of technology" and not saddled with old equipment, old products, or old systems.

"Our industrial base is in an area of the economy that typically will have a higher rate of growth," Coors says. "We are going through an adjustment and some realignment in some sectors of the economy."

But Coors does not believe such important basic sectors of the economy as agriculture and energy are the dinosaurs of the West.

"Agriculture—despite its problems—and energy are going to remain a strong part of the Nation's and Colorado's economy for years to come," says Coors, whose company is not only a leading U.S. beer manufacturer,

Pure mountain water is one of Colorado's most valued resources, and is critical to the development of the economy. Photo courtesy of Adolph Coors Company

but directly involved in many phases of agribusiness and energy development. "Technology, just as it is rapidly developing in Colorado's manufacturing base, will play an increasing role in agriculture in this state."

Coors says Colorado is "primed for growth," but believes it must be carefully guided by "the right environmental considerations."

Educational Support for Change

In support of advanced technology industries, most of the state's 50 public and private colleges, universities, and vocational education schools at the post-secondary level have geared their programs to provide most of the needed skills for advanced technicians and scientists. The major universities have tailored programs to provide continuing educational opportunities as technology changes. And several of the area universities have moved specific programs onto industrial sites for advanced training programs requested by industry.

The University of Colorado at its Boulder campus, and at campuses in Denver and Colorado Springs, is already participating in advanced research projects connected to the aerospace program. CU has actively been recruiting top space scientists for the past several years, and has created an Office of Space Science Technology to coordinate its expanding research program. CU's campus at Colorado Springs is expected to become a leading space educational center as the CSOC program is implemented. Colorado School of Mines, already one of the world's leading research centers in metallurgy, has begun work on advanced metals research for the nation's future space program, and other space science curriculum is being added at other universities in the state.

Colorado, which until recent years lagged behind other states in spending programs for higher education, is calling on the private sector to assist in improving the higher education system's ability to provide the needed training and research programs to compete with other high-tech centers of the country.

The Colorado Advanced Technology Institute (CATI), created by the state in 1983 to foster economic development through the support of advanced technology research and education in Colorado, works with both the private and public sector. In its first year of operations, CATI generated $900,000 in private sector industrial and federal research support to augment the $300,000 seed money provided by the state.

CATI has three major missions, including the improvement of research capabilities at Colorado's existing universities, attracting and retaining superior faculty members, and attracting private industry investment to multiply state investment in advanced technology education, research, and development.

The organization is working on three specific advanced technology projects that have already begun operations. The Advanced Materials Institute, under the leadership provided at Colorado School of Mines, also involves work being done at Colorado State University, the University of Colorado, and the University of Denver.

CATI's second project, now underway, is the establishment of a supercomputer network using existing resources of the universities and private industries. The organization's primary role is to identify and organize resources, such as hardware and software, equipment and libraries, into a centralized network. Centered around CSU's Cyber 205 supercomputer at Fort Collins, the network already connects CSU and CU at Boulder. It will soon include CU at Denver, Metro State, CU at Colorado Springs, and the School of Mines. The network plans to expand to colleges in the southern and western areas of the state at Pueblo, Durango, Grand Junction, and Gunnison.

A longer-range coordinating role for CATI is the state's competition for the U.S. Department of Energy's Superconducting Super Collider project. Only a few states have the open terrain of Colorado's Eastern Plains that can accommodate a giant facility of this type. The high-energy physics facility at CU has made preliminary assessments of potential Colorado sites for such a project, and CATI is spearheading a joint public/private campaign to secure the location of the project in Colorado at some time in the future. But the competition with other states is fierce, and many believe Colorado businesses and government are not investing enough money in the bid to compete with other states.

CATI also is working with universities and private industry to foster microelectronic, biotechnical, and other advanced scientific educational projects in existing colleges and universities around the state.

Much of the challenge to improve the state's higher education systems to be more competitive for a role in the nation's aerospace and advanced technology industry of the future will fall on the state's higher education systems at a time when budgetary cuts are being made by the Colorado Legislature.

A Changing Society

As Colorado manufacturing continues to expand into next-century technology, the role of general business and commerce also expands in various other sectors of the economy.

Colorado's increasingly important position in high technology and aerospace programs will almost certainly be matched by an expanding role as the service and supply center for the Rocky Mountain Region. The service industry sector of the economy is projected to continue growing at a faster pace than any other part of the economy.

This sector supplies not only the support services for the local economy, but to a great degree for the dozen other states in the region. Employment in the various service and support firms has been projected as high as 457,000 by 1995, an increase of more than 100,000 jobs in the next decade. The service sector, including the visitor industry, business services, health services, and other professional services, supports a region far greater than just Colorado.

Already, projections for growth in the visitor industry, which reached record levels in 1985 and 1986, are being exceeded by actual numbers of visitors to the state. Huge new investments in ski and summer recreation facilities continue to be announced, and greatly reduced gasoline prices for the next

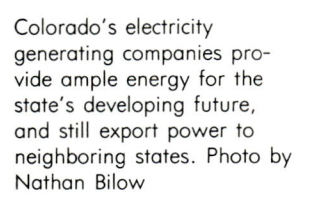

Colorado's electricity generating companies provide ample energy for the state's developing future, and still export power to neighboring states. Photo by Nathan Bilow

Even though much of the nation's natural energy reserves are locked in the Rocky Mountains, Colorado is a pacesetter state in the development of renewable energy sources such as wind generation. Photo by Stewart M. Green, Tom Stack & Associates

several years promise new records in that sector.

Retail and wholesale trade, transportation, utilities, financial services, and other support sectors of Colorado's economy can all be expected to continue to grow steadily over the next decade.

"We Coloradans cannot ignore what is happening to our neighbors. The citizens of the other Rocky Mountain states look to Colorado for every kind of support service," notes Denver economist Tucker Hart Adams. "We are already in an economy based on service. A big part of our restructuring now is only a matter of rethinking what we already have in place."

The diversification of the state's economy, a long-time goal of many of the state's business and civic leaders, seems to have been accomplished in the past two decades. Colorado is no longer as subject to the vagaries of "boom or bust" in a single sector of the economy. It still faces ups and downs in every sector, but modern Colorado is more likely to be affected by national and international trends than by a chance "gold strike" or some modern day equivalent.

N. Berne Hart, chairman of the Colorado Association of Commerce and Industry (CACI) in 1985-86, believes the Colorado economy has attained the enviable position of a truly diversified economy in a modern international arena.

As president of the United Banks of Colorado he notes that international investment in local economy is extensive. Stock in institutions like his are internationally held.

"We are continually asked by international investors about the state of the economy in Colorado and the western region, questions about energy or agriculture cycles," says Hart. "One of the things we preach and point out is the diversity of the Colorado economy. This diversity is unique to Colorado."

He says that while the headlines emphasize the cycles in agriculture and mining, including energy development, "the biggest single story is in the broad sector called service." Hart, who believes agriculture has made a full circle and that solid Colorado farming families will now begin to make progress, notes that the strength of diversity in Colorado extends to the high technology-aerospace-telecommunications industry, the visitor industry, and the huge Colorado service industry.

Impacts of Growth

An expanding economy, with a steadily growing population, exacts demands on the sometimes fragile environment of Colorado. Even when the primary cause of expansion does not rely on extracting minerals or consuming water, the environmental and ecological impacts on the land must be taken into consideration. Quite simply, more people require more of everything from the natural environment—more land for housing and workplaces; more surface and air space for transportation; more schools, hospitals, public services, and safety. Coloradans, particularly on the Front Range, may discourage the introduction of new water-dependent industry, but the added population created by any new industry requires more water collection, treatment and distribution, and more sewer and solid waste disposal.

In 1980, 5,512 gallons of water per day were required by every man, woman, and child living in Colorado. Of course, each individual did not consume that much water, but for all requirements, including irrigation, industrial use, lawn watering, sanitation, and

A spring electrical storm over Colorado seems to be competing with a power station to produce the most energy. Photo by Jason Winter

consumption, the state drew about 16 billion gallons of water each day from the rivers, lakes, and wells of the state. Colorado's per capita consumption of water, while not the highest in the nation, is more than twice the U.S. average daily consumption of just under 2,000 gallons per day. The western agricultural states, heavily dependent on irrigation, are the greatest water consumers. In New York state, for example, the average daily per capita withdrawal of water is only 967 gallons, five times less than Colorado's requirement.

Water, in a semi-arid climate with about 14 inches of new surface moisture from rain and snow annually, becomes a serious consideration if economic growth is to permit a continued high quality of life.

Despite the semi-arid climate, much raw water exists within the state. The Colorado mountains receive massive amounts of water in the form of snowfall each winter, and the gradual melting of this snow waters much of the western United States and portions of northern Mexico. Colorado's Eastern Plains are also on the edge of a giant underground fresh-water sea called the Ogallala Aquifer, which provides near surface water from Texas to Nebraska. Other subsurface aquifers are found throughout the state.

So why should water be a problem for continued population and industrial growth?

The problem is twofold. First, water rights are a factor, and, second, raw water must be gathered, treated, and delivered to the end user.

Water rights in the west are fiercely guarded, and many of these rights were established in the 1880s. The water fight has not stopped since that time. Today it is waged between municipal users, Indians, farmers and ranchers, mineral developers, industrial developers, recreational interests, and preservationists. The fight is waged between cities, and between the Front Range and Western Slope within the state, between states of the region, and between the United States and Mexico. Everyone has a vested interest in water, and it has been said that the fees for a majority of all water rights attorneys in America flow from headwaters in the Colorado Rockies.

In some parts of the state water exists in abundance, particularly on the less-developed Western Slope. The Denver Water Department, the state's largest developer of water for human consumption, notes that less than two percent of the streamflow in Colorado is used for human consumption, implying that 98 percent flows out of the state to California, Arizona, New Mexico, and Mexico. By prior rights, Colorado has claim to about a quarter of the giant Colorado and Rio Grande River flows.

Adding to the problem, the once-believed

It all begins with a trickle from melting snow, but the tiny stream will turn to a roaring river as it feeds the thirsty West. Photo by Tom Myers, Tom Stack & Associates

The Flatirons along the Front Range don a stark winter coat in a land marked by distinct seasons of the year. Photo by Ann Duncan, Tom Stack & Associates

inexhaustible Ogallala Aquifer, the giant subsurface source of irrigation for the Great Plains, is gradually being depleted. During the mid-1980s there were more than 109,000 water wells drawing on the aquifers of Colorado. More than 62,000 of these wells were for household or domestic uses, such as lawn and garden watering, 12,500 for livestock watering tanks, and 21,000 for crop irrigation. The depleting subsurface water table not only requires drilling ever deeper water wells, but it also increases competition for surface water between farm and city, and the various water-dependent states of the West. Water from the Platte and Arkansas Rivers flowing to the plains from Colorado is in greater dispute.

Since the availability of water directly affects all types of development through the control of the number of water taps for new structures, water is one of the impacts most affecting future expansion.

Water resources for most of the urbanized centers are assured, at least through the remainder of this century. Major new water-development projects, such as the new Two Forks dam and reservoir to be built by the Denver Water Department, will provide adequate storage for Denver and many of the cities and towns in the immediate Denver Metropolitan Area. The Two Forks project, at its completion, would create a 25-mile-long lake with a storage capacity of 1.1 million acre-feet of water. In addition to supplying the City of Denver, the Denver Water Department is the principal supplier of 44 communities with membership in an organization called the Metropolitan Water Providers.

A number of other major water development projects affecting the state also assure adequate water for all parts of the state well beyond the end of this century. Some of these new projects include the huge Dolores Project and McPhee Dam near Cortez; the Dallas Creek Water Project in the Uncompahgre Valley near Montrose; the Animas-La Plata Project near Durango; a Poudre River dam above Fort Collins; Homestake II storage project for Aurora and Colorado Springs; a Clear Creek dam project providing water for Arvada, Broomfield, and several private water companies and local industries; the Turkey Creek project for water development in the Pagosa Springs area; and a Palisade-Grand Junction-area hydroelectric and water development project.

In the longer term, Colorado still has water rights to river flow which have yet to be exercised. Competition for these rights is the subject of controversy throughout much of the western section of the United States.

The disposition of waste water and sewage, and the ongoing solutions to the use of solid waste from urban development faced by all major developing areas is also of concern to Colorado planners and developers. Present facilities are adequate for growth in most areas of the state, but the continued major public and private investment in expanded and more modern systems for treating urban and industrial waste are subject to financing strategy at all levels of local and state government.

Future Mobility

Surface and air transportation are vital to the state's ability to continue to keep pace with population growth and economic expansion. State and local governments are making large strides toward assuring that highways and airports are modernized to handle this expansion. Practically all of the state's surface transportation will continue to be tied to the highway and road system, since no public mass-transit options are likely to be offered, even in the most densely populated urban areas, in the next decade.

The state legislature took major steps to address the needs of highway transportation improvements, including the repair and upgrading of roads and bridges, with the passage of an additional fuels tax in 1986. The Colorado Department of Highways had estimated a $10.2 billion shortfall for the state's total needs in highway, city street, county road, and other surface systems by the year 2000. While making the state's gasoline tax one of the highest in the United States, passage of the added fuel tax is expected to assure that the roads and highways necessary to such important industries as tourism and trade will be maintained.

No relief from the dependency on streets and highways—even in the more congested Front Range transit corridors—is expected from mass rail transportation. The state's largest transit authority, the six-county Regional Transportation District, has spent nearly $5 million on mass transit studies since its inception in 1972, and continues to study transit needs. A special bus corridor is under consideration for the northern part of the district, centered in Denver; and a southeast mass transit corridor from downtown Denver to the major industrial parks is still a candidate for possible rail transit in the future.

The Denver area's continuing problem with air pollution, primarily caused by automobile exhaust fumes in the high, thin air, is of growing concern as an increasing number of citizens join the traveling work force. With no public transit option except more buses, which are also air polluters, officials seem to be casting about in vain for answers.

Nine public transportation systems, including the RTD, all have expanded bus transit plans to provide some local service, but the state, like most western states, is likely to continue its reliance on the automobile for

The sun rises over Rocky Mountain National Park, symbolic of the dawning of a new era in Colorado. Photo by John Shaw, Tom Stack & Associates

much of its surface transportation during the remainder of this century.

No major new highways, other than those under construction in 1986, are planned for the state. But Colorado is seeing a greater cooperative effort in highway and road building between private developers and the state, counties, and cities. Most of the major interchanges under development in the rapidly expanding southeast corridor of Metropolitan Denver, and others in the Colorado Springs area, feature heavy private investment.

One of the leading Colorado organizations behind this futuristic approach to building needed transportation systems is the Joint Southeast Public Improvement Association (JSPIA). A consortium of the largest private industrial developers in the southern Denver Metro Area, the group is actively engaged in building needed highway interchanges, coordinating highway building both within its properties and in adjoining Douglas County, and in developing a plan for a future rapid-transit system in the metropolitan area.

George M. Wallace, chairman of JSPIA and the founder of Denver Technological Center, says that good public transportation is one area where every competitor for new business can agree. The private organization has already invested $30 million in public highway improvements in the I-25 corridor south of Denver.

"I am convinced that if we do the job of development right we will come out better, both financially and in the quality of life for the future," says the veteran of 40 years in engineering and industrial park development.

Modern Coloradans are looking to the future with optimism from a land blessed with abundant natural resources. Photo by Hull & Kangas Photographers

"The growth in Colorado is going to happen; there is too much impetus to stop it. We are in a position to make it happen the way it should so that both the economy and the environment benefit."

Air transportation improvements for Colorado, an essential part of the infrastructure assuring economic growth, is much more advanced in both planning and implementation than either new highway or new public transit development. Progressive municipal officials and local leaders are building and expanding airports in all sectors of the state, led by a massive new $2 to $3 billion super-international Denver airport to serve the entire Rocky Mountain West.

Denver's Stapleton International Airport, truly a regional hub airport for the entire Rockies, served approximately 28 million boarding and deplaning passengers in 1984, with over a half million aircraft takeoffs and landings. Obviously, the airport serves far more than the state's population of just over 3 million, because Stapleton passenger trips outnumber the local citizenry by 9 to 1.

The giant new airport, to be built with revenue bonds and paid off by users, is scheduled for completion by 1995 at a site on the Denver and Adams County lines east of the present airport. Airport authorities have said the new airport could be used by as many as 100 million passengers each year by the year 2010. Located on a 15,000-acre site, the big port would feature eight runways with a high-speed subway moving passengers to and between planes. Plans call for the new airport to be modeled after the Atlanta Hartsfield International Airport, with huge open spaces, 40-foot escalators leading to underground trains, and other ultramodern conveniences and safety features for airlines and passengers.

Denver is not the state's only center for air activity, with expansion projects planned at airports in Aspen, Colorado Springs, Gunnison, Telluride, Durango, Grand Junction, Arapahoe County (Centennial), Jefferson County, and a dozen other commercial and general aviation centers. In 1986, Telluride opened the highest commercial airport in America, at an altitude of 9,100 feet. Gunnison, also a mountain recreation center, plans to expand its runways to 10,000 feet in length.

Investment in the future of aviation brings almost certain returns to Colorado, where growth in the visitor industry is outstripping all projections. Visitors, particularly skiers, are heavy users of Colorado's modern air services. And the rapidly growing advanced

The history of the development of the West was tied to rail transportation, and the future is dependant upon outstanding air service. Photo by Kevin C. Beebe, Stockyard

technology industry demands excellence in air transportation.

Preservation Incentives

The rapid population and industrial growth along Colorado's Front Range in the 1970s led many citizens and government officials to predict an urban megalopolis of sprawl and ultimate decay in the high quality life style of the state. While the steadier, controlled growth of the 1980s has allayed some of these fears, the cry that a sprawling, Los Angeles-type urban area is building from Denver to Colorado Springs can still be heard.

Development along the interstate between the cities is occurring at a rapid pace, but county planners and the larger developers are cooperating to assure a high degree of protection and preservation of the environment.

The developer of one of the largest and best-planned projects along that corridor does not see Colorado taking the same course as southern California. Philip J. Reilly, president and CEO of Mission Viejo Realty Group, Inc., the developers of the 22,000-acre Highlands Ranch residential and commercial project, has good reason to know. He was a leading developer involved in some of the projects in southern California and served on the board of the Metropolitan Water District of southern California. That district served the water needs of 11 million people, and Reilly also served on the "Little Hoover" Commission on Governmental Efficiency for the State of California.

"Conditions for development today and in the 1960s are completely different," says Reilly. "Colorado's citizens and developers have had the advantage of learning from the mistakes of other states, and we are making progress. What makes me think Colorado will move ahead in an orderly fashion is a viable private/public partnership. We are developing a better methodology for development."

Reilly, who has seen an about-face even in southern California's development patterns, thinks the mistakes of the 1960s could not be made in the 1980s in Colorado.

"The Californians had a problem. There was no sense of place. A series of little towns grew up independently and never had enough space to be creative and build a base," Reilly states from first-hand experience. "That is not true in Colorado. We have an institutional infrastructure to build upon. Future development in Colorado can even be guided by mistakes made years ago in Denver. I do not think you will see sprawl because the marketplace is demanding quality development."

He notes that every major project underway along the Front Range requires designs that include good easements; areas set aside for open space and natural grounds; and provisions for adequate roads, water, and other amenities.

"Colorado, and particularly the Front Range, has all the elements to support growth and a fine life style," he says, in comparing this area with southern California. "This area's cultural and institutional assets are more like those of a San Francisco or Manhattan than a southern California."

Reilly's belief that the communities of Colorado will maintain a higher quality of life style, both because of that "sense of place," and because of private/public partnership, is supported by the large number of both private and public organizations working for a balance between economic development and preservation.

The Progress/Preservation Groups

Practically any agenda of economic development programs drawn up by the various public/private organizations in Colorado is balanced by two factors—economic development and conservation of all the elements of the natural environment.

All organizations charged with improvement of the economy, from the state's Division of Commerce and Development to the smallest county unit of government or chamber of commerce, the work programs all contain goals of equal importance. Too much of the economic health of the state depends directly on the preservation of the natural environment to be ignored. If thoughtless development occurred in some segments of the economy in the past, such practices have had to be abandoned in the face of economic realities. Modern Colorado literally depends on its natural beauty for whatever competitive advantage it has over other states in attracting both paying visitors and new high-tech companies.

A stronger sense of "sharing the wealth" prevails in Colorado today than even two decades ago. Citizens now realize that the economic health of the communities of the Eastern Plains impacts the well-being of the cities of the Front Range.

George Dibble, president of the Colorado Association of Commerce and Industry, sees inter-regional rivalries being put aside for the advancement of common state goals in economic development. He also believes that the various government entities, beginning at the governor's office and the state legislature, are finally joining the business community to help create a progressive environment for the future.

"Colorado must compete with other parts of the nation for new investment and retention of investment," says Dibble. "The economic development of the future will have a greater incentive because we are building the economy to provide future jobs for our own people. Inter-area rivalries are being put aside so that we can combine our resources to address mutual problems of water, highways, air transportation, education. As a result, Colorado is emerging as a strong regional force in the United States."

The state organization president believes that the greatest single challenge facing the public/private sector is "joint long-range action," not long-range planning.

"Joint cooperation on state financing, beyond a year-by-year budget, is essential," says Dibble. "Business and government, at all levels, must now look at the long-term needs and put aside partisan and regional politics if we are to reach our common goals. There is a strong awareness that if Coloradans are to continue to enjoy the good environment there must be a solid economic base to pay for it."

This type of inter-city, inter-regional problem solving is also high on the agenda of local governments and local chambers of commerce. While a specific city's development organization may work hard to present its best features in a highly competitive bid for a new plant, that organization will be found working shoulder-to-shoulder with its peer group from the next community to solve a regional issue. That cooperative mood, in many cases, will extend across state lines, because serious ecological or economic problems in any one area tend to affect the whole area.

Rex Jennings, president of the state's largest business association for the past two decades, has seen a new spirit of cooperation in problem solving evolve. The Denver Chamber of Commerce's chief executive thinks Colorado's emergence into the mainstream of national and world commerce has wiped out many of the vestiges of parochialism that once pitted city against city, and region against region.

"Colorado has matured in recent years," says the veteran organizational manager. "We have seen a breakthrough in the late 1980s. Our governmental entities are beginning to work together, and on the common issues we are becoming a family of communities."

Jennings thinks the rapid growth period of the late 1960s and 1970s provided a "great maturing experience" and left a legacy of strong and diverse economy upon which to build for the future.

"As we begin the next stage of development— and we are surely approaching another significant round of growth and development far more significant than the last—we start from a much stronger base, with new enthusiasm and a new kind of leadership," Jennings says. "We are now on the cutting edge of

With over 50 peaks towering above 14,000 feet in elevation, Colorado is a land of splendid contrasts. Photo by W.A. Hunt III, Phillips Photographics

the most advanced technological industries in the world. Our position in high technology, aerospace, telecommunications, and biomedical technology is solid. Within a few years we will have the world's most advanced airport."

He said the challenge of the late 1980s will be whether or not Colorado wants to spend the money to manage the future properly.

"We are either going to hang together or seize the opportunity to project this community into something uniquely special," says Jennings. "Our Colorado cities and towns can be the best places to live in the world. Despite the fact that we have 20 million tourists and visitors a year, we are still America's best kept secret."

But Jennings cautions that the task of maintaining the good environment and the sound economy has just begun.

This mood for more cooperation in assuring a strong economic and highquality life style is apparent in conversations and written programs of local chambers of commerce and allied economic development organizations across the state. The private sector/public sector cooperation is also clear within the communities between the business-oriented chambers and local governments. At the state level such inter-regional cooperation is being fostered by the leading private organization, the Colorado Association of Commerce and Industry, formed by the merger of the state chamber and state association of manufacturers.

There is no denying that Colorado faces many challenges in an increasingly competitive and rapidly changing national economy. Intensive efforts to enter its produce and products in national and international export markets are demanding some of the changes.

The fact that the nation is looking to the state for leadership in aerospace and other advanced industries, as well as its historic contributions from agribusiness and minerals, is increasing Colorado's national responsibility. As guardian of a large part of the nation's natural wilderness treasury, and host to millions of visitors seeking to enjoy these bountiful treasures, Coloradans are increasingly aware of both their good fortune and their obligation to make sure these resources remain available for generations to come.

The proposition on the ballot for the state's future is not "progress" vs "preservation." On the subject of living and working in Colorado, a good quality of life and a progressive workplace are synonymous. Coloradans, whether relative newcomers or native-born, are practicing one of the greatest legacies of the American West as they write their destinies and the futures of their children. As participants in writing the history of the New West at a time when this region of the nation is the most rapidly developing, the alternatives and options seem almost limitless.

Maintaining the delicate balance between environmental quality and economic prosperity becomes every Coloradan's challenge for the future.

Bibliography

Books

Adams, Eugene H., Dorsett, Lyle W., and Pulcipher, Robert S., *The Pioneer Western Bank: 1st of Denver 1860 - 1980.* Denver: First Interstate Bank of Denver and The State Historical Society of Colorado, 1984.

Athearn, Frederic J. *An Isolated Empire: A History of Northwestern Colorado.* Cultural Resources Series No. 2. U.S. Bureau of Land Management, 1982.

Boyd, LeRoy. *Fort Lyon, Colorado: One Hundred Years of Service.* Colorado Springs: H.& H. Printing Co. Inc., 1982.

Chorlton, Windsor. *Ice Ages, Planet Earth Series.* Alexandria, Virginia: TIME-LIFE Books, 1983.

Chronic, Halka. *Roadside Geology of Colorado.* Missoula, Montana: Mountain Press Publishing Co., 1980.

Delaney, Robert W., Jefferson, James, Thompson, Gregory C., and O'Neal, Floyd A., ed., *The Southern Utes: A Tribal History.* Salt Lake City, Utah: University of Utah Press, 1972.

Fehrenbach, T.R. *Lone Star.* New York, New York: Collier Books, a division of Macmillan Publishing Co., 1968.

Naisbitt, John. *Megatrends.* New York, New York: Warner Books, Inc., 1984.

Noel, Thomas J., *DENVER: Rocky Mountain Gold.* Tulsa: Continental Heritage Press, 1980.

Rochlin, Harriet and Fred. *Pioneer Jews: A New Life in the Far West.* Boston: Houghton Mifflin Company, 1984.

Sprague, Marshall. *Colorado, A History.* New York, New York and London, England: W.W. Norton & Co., 1984.

Walton, Roger A. *Colorado: A Practical Guide to its Government and Politics.* Fort Collins: Publishers' Consultants, 1977.

Wood, Myron and Nancy. *COLORADO: Big Mountain Country.* Garden City, N.Y.: Doubleday & Co., 1969.

Journals and Periodicals

Brown, Judy Steinbach. A Real Butte. *American Way* magazine. American Airlines. October-November, 1985.

CATI Catalyst, various issues. Denver: Colorado Advanced Technology Institute, 1984-85-86.

Colorado Business Magazine, various editions. Littleton, CO.: Wiesner, Inc., 1985-86.

Colorado Business & Technology Update, various editions. Englewood, CO: Colorado Information Associates, 1984.

Colorado Computing & Telecommunications Magazine. Boulder, CO.: Wells Communications, Winter 1985-86.

Colorado Ski Country USA Magazine, 1985-86 Season. Denver: Colorado Ski Country USA Inc., 1985.

Denver Post, various editions, Denver: The Denver Post Corporation, 1985-86.

Denver Business Magazine, various editions. Denver: General Communications, Inc., 1985-86.

Denver Magazine, various editions. Denver: General Communications, Inc., 1985-86.

Edwards, Mike. Colorado Dreaming. *National Geographic.* Washington, D.C.: National Geographic Society, August, 1984.

Rocky Mountain News, various editions, Denver: Scripps Howard-The Denver Publishing Co., 1985-86.

Rocky Mountain American Automobile Association. *Where to Vacation in Colorado, 1985.* Denver: Rocky Mountain AAA Auto Club, 1985.

Summer Guide to Salida, Poncha Springs, Buena Vista, Leadville. Salida, CO., 1985.

Top of the Rockies, Leadville, Buena Vista, Salida. Fort Collins: Holiday Publishing, Co., 1985.

The Mineral County Miner, Winter on the Rio Grande. Creede, CO: The South Fork Times, 1985.

———*Autumn on the Rio Grande.* Creede, CO: The South Fork Times, 1985.

The Conventioneer. Fall 1985. Denver: Denver Conventioneer Inc., 1985.

Travel & Recreation. Special Glenwood Springs Centennial Edition. Glenwood Springs: Eagle Publishing Co. Ltd., 1985.

Telluride Magazine. Winter 1984-Summer 1985. Telluride Publishing Co., 1984.

Telluride Annual Blue Grass Festival, 12th Annual Edition, 1985. Western Investor Magazine, Fall 1985 Edition. Portland, OR.: The Willamette Publishing Co., 1985.

U.S. and Colorado Government Reports and Publications

State of Colorado

———*Biotechnology in Colorado*, Governor's High Technology Cabinet Council, Colorado Association of Commerce and Industry, Colorado Commission on Higher Education, and Colorado State University, 1984.

———*Colorado Advanced Technology Institute*, Annual Report. 1984-1985

———*Colorado Agricultural Statistics, 1984.* Colorado Department of Agriculture, July, 1985.

———*Colorado Agricultural Trade Directory.* Division of Markets, Colorado Department of Agriculture, 1984.

———*Colorado Investing in the Future (1981-2001)*, The Final Report of the Governor's Blue Ribbon Panel, July 1981.

———*Colorado Education Directory, 1985-86.* Colorado Department of Education, 1986.

———*Colorado Executive Budget, 1986-87.* Budget Recommendations of Governor Richard D. Lamm, 1986.

———*Colorado Farm Fresh: A Guide to U-Pick Farms & Orchards, Roadside Stands, and Farm Markets.* Colorado Department of Agriculture/News Center 4, 1985.

———*Colorado Fruit Tree Survey, 1985.* Colorado Crop & Livestock Reporting Service, July 1985.

———*Colorado Labor Force Review.* Department of Labor and Employment, Division of Employment and Training, October 1985.

———*Colorado Population Projections*, Demographics Sections, Colorado Division of Local Governments, 1986.
County Economics Series
County Profile Data Base
Population and Percentage of Change for Colorado Counties
Population Projections 1985-2010

———*Colorado: The Ultimate Fringe Benefit.* Office of Business Development and Training, Colorado Division of Commerce and Development, Department of Local Affairs, May 1982.

———*Five Year Capital Investment Plan FY 1985-1989.* Office of State Planning and Budget, 1985.

_____High Tech in Colorado: Maintaining Our Competitive Edge. Governor's High Technology Cabinet Council, May 1985.
_____The High Road, Bicentennial Project of the Division of Highways, State Department of Highways, 1976.
_____Highway Department Annual Reports. State Department of Highways, various issues, 1980s.
_____Higher Education Directory, Academic Year 1985-86. Colorado Commission on Higher Education, 1986.
_____Oil & Gas Production Statistics by Counties. Colorado Oil & Gas Commission, 1986.
_____Orientation Handbook for Board Members and Commissioners. Department of Regulatory Agencies, 1984.
_____Summary of Mineral Industry Activities in Colorado 1970 to 1980. Colorado Division of Mines, Department of Natural Resources, 1981.
_____U.S. Farm Export Sales from the State of Colorado, 1971-1986. Colorado Department of Agriculture, 1986.

U.S. Government

Bureau of the Census
  Statistical Abstract of the United States: 1985 (105th Edition.) Washington, DC, 1984.
  Census of Territory of Colorado 1870-1878. U.S. Census Bureau, 1879.
  County Business Patterns 1983, Colorado. Washington, DC: U.S. Department of Commerce, 1985.
  1982 Census of Manufacturers, Colorado. Washington, DC: U.S. Department of Commerce, 1985.
  1982 Census of Service Industries, Colorado. Washington, DC: U.S. Department of Commerce, 1984.
  1982 Census of Wholesale Trade, Colorado. Washington, DC: U.S. Department of Commerce, 1984.
  1982 Census of Retail Trade, Colorado. Washington, DC: U.S. Department of Commerce, 1984.
  1982 Census of Agriculture, Colorado. Washington, DC: U.S. Department of Commerce, 1984.
  Number of Inhabitants, 1980 Census of Population. Washington, DC: U.S Department of Commerce, 1981.
Colorado, Montana, Wyoming, Directory of Federal Offices. Washington, DC: Office of Information Resources Management, U.S. General Services Administration, 1986.
Dolores Project/McPhee Dam. Bureau of Reclamation, U.S. Department of Interior, 1985.
Your Fragile Legacy. Bureau of Land Management, U.S. Department of Interior, 1982.
Users Guide to Outdoor Recreation and Public Lands in Colorado. U.S. Department of Interior, 1980.
Promise of the Land, U S. Department of Interior Washington, DC: U.S. Government Printing Office, 1983.
Wildlife on the Public Lands. U.S. Department of Interior. Washington, DC: U.S. Government Printing Office.

Universities and Colleges Publications

Business/Economic Outlook Forum, 21st Annual Colorado. Denver: College of Business and Administration, University of Colorado, and the Division of Commerce and Development, Colorado Department of Local Affairs, 1985.
CSM Resource List, Colorado School of Mines Office of Special Programs and Continuing Education. Golden: CSM Public Information Office, 1983.
Directory of Colorado Manufacturers. Boulder: University of Colorado Research Division, College of Business and Administration, 1985.
Much More Than Its Name. Colorado School of Mines. Golden: Colorado School of Mines Public Information Office, 1983.
Quality through Diversity. Annual Report of the University of Colorado. Boulder: University of Colorado, 1985.
Special Report: University of Denver Interaction with Business. Denver: University of Denver, 1985.

Business Studies/Special Reports

Annual Reports, Class I Railroads Serving Colorado
_____Atchison Topeka & Santa Fe, 1985.
_____Burlington Northern, 1985.
_____Denver & Rio Grande Western, 1985.
_____Union Pacific, 1985.
_____Missouri Pacific, 1985.
Careers in Mortgage Banking. Research and Educational Trust Fund of the Mortgage Bankers Assn. of America, (Undated)
Colorado Business Facilities. Colorado the Ultimate Fringe Benefit (booklet). Colorado Division of Commerce and Development, 1985.
Economic Forecast for 1986. Denver: United Banks of Colorado, Economics Department, 1985.
Foundation for Change. Colorado Hospital Association, 1985.
First Colorado Advanced Technology Trend Report. Boulder: Strategic Assessments, Inc., Fall 1985.
Flight Guide to Stapleton International Airport. Denver: Department of Public Works, City and County of Denver, 1986.
Healthcare in Colorado, A Matter of Facts. Colorado Hospital Association, 1983.
Metropolitan Denver Sewage Disposal District No. 1., *Annual Report.* Denver: 1985.
New Airport Master Plan: Forecast of Aviation. Denver: City and County of Denver, January 1986.
Newborn Country USA, Clinics in Perinatology. Denver: Children's Hospital, September, 1976.
Overall Economic Development Plan, Region 8. Alamosa, CO: San Luis Valley Regional Development & Planning Commission, 1984.
RTD Quarterly Reports. Denver: Regional Transportation District, 1985-86.
Solar Research for a Brighter Future. Golden, CO: Solar Energy Research Institute, 1983.
Vanguard of the Printing Industry. Arlington, VA: Printing Industries of America Inc., 1981.

Chambers of Commerce/ Economic Development Council Publications

Demographic Fact Sheets and Economic Development Brochures from 41 local chambers were provided the author.
Economic Development Manuals from 10 Colorado county or multi-county economic develop organizations were provided the author.
Denver Facts Book. Denver: The Denver Chamber of Commerce, 1986.
Legislative Guide. Denver: The Denver Chamber of Commerce, 1985.

Other Resources Including Private and Public Files and Data Banks

Special Research Data Was Provided by the Following Individuals:
_____Abrams, Stephen L., Director, Office of Business Development, Colorado Division of Commerce and Development.
_____Adams, Tucker Hart, Economist, United Banks of Colorado.
_____Andrade, Stephan, Business Developer, Advanced Technologies, Division of Commerce and Development, State of Colorado.
_____Anderson, Shirley, Executive Director, Cortez Chamber of Commerce.
_____Bailey, Janet, Manager, Pagosa Springs Chamber of Commerce.
_____Ballantine, Morley, Publisher, Durango Herald.
_____Boos, Frankie, Executive Director, Alamosa Chamber of Commerce.
_____Cannalte, Don, Public Relations Director, University of Colorado.
_____Cleary, Bill, Executive Director, Club 20.
_____Dean, Stebbins, President, Glen-

____wood Springs Chamber of Commerce.
____Ezzard, Shelly, Colorado Council on Arts & Humanities.
____Frayser, Stephen, Director, Greeley/Weld County Economic Development.
____Goodman, Jackie, Office Manager, Stapleton International Airport.
____Hawks, Douglas, Asst. Director, Public Relations, University of Denver.
____Holloway, J. Hunter, President, Colorado Search & Rescue Board.
____Hayes, Roger, President, Durango Tourism Board.
____Kiesinger, Carol D., Public Relations Director, Aspen Resort Assn.
____King, Gordon W., Analyst, Colorado Public Utilities Commission.
____Larsen, Timothy J., Marketing Specialist, Colorado Department of Agriculture.
____Leech, Richard G., President, Mesa County Economic Development Council.
____Logan, Linda, Manager, Montrose Chamber of Commerce.
____Lorenz, Marianne, Education Director, Colorado Historical Society.
____Madsen, Leslie, Foreign Trade Office, State of Colorado.
____Mallinen, Vernon J., Marketing Manager, Rocky Mountain News.
____Means, Lawrence C., Executive Director, Gunnison Country Chamber of Commerce.
____Moebius, Mark, DM Realtors, Snowmass Village.
____Mitchell, Diane, Public Relations Manager, Denver Metro Convention & Visitors Bureau.
____Morlan, Ed, Economic Development Manager, Southern Ute Indian Tribe.
____Murphy, Kristin L., Public Relations Director, Colorado Tourism Board.
____Murphy, Shirley, Manager, Durango Chamber of Commerce.
____O'Brien, Charlotte, Manager, LaJunta Chamber of Commerce.
____Parker, B. Stephens, President, Durango Economic Development Council.
____Parks, Shirley, Supervisor, Aspen Visitor Center.
____Reynolds, Reid T., State Demographer, Colorado Department of Local Affairs.
____Riley, Judy, Administrator, Heart of the Rockies Chamber of Commerce (Salida).
____Robbins, Scott, Manager, Office of Business Development, Colorado Division of Commerce and Development.
____Shaw, Jim, Executive Director, Grand Junction Chamber of Commerce.
____Smith, Karol W., Director, Colorado Motion Picture/TV Advisory Commission.
____Sorrentino, Carl T., Public Information Officer, Colorado Department of Highways.
____Steinhauser, Jan, Public Relations Director, Denver Center for the Performing Arts.
____Stephens, Betsy, Administrative Asst., Durango Tourism Board.
____Sunderland, Randy, President, Limon Chamber of Commerce.
____Uhrich, Amy, Manager, Monte Vista Chamber of Commerce.
____Ward, Gary, President, Rifle Chamber of Commerce.
____Webb, O.L. (Olie), Environmental Affairs Director, Colorado Association of Commerce and Industry.
____Weiszbrod, Judy, Executive Director, Delta Chamber of Commerce.
____Weston, Delores C., Office Manager, Craig Chamber of Commerce.
____Wheeler, Blanche, Manager, Rocky Ford Chamber of Commerce.

Index

A
Adams, Tucker Hart 102, 242.
Adams County *Profile* 34; 39, 41, 90, 91, 102, 111, 123, 152, 167, 246.
Advanced Materials Institute 165, 240.
Advertising 125, 157
Aerospace Industry 43, 152, 162, 167, 238, 239, 240
Affiliated Bankshares of Colorado 183
Agriculture 18, 19, 23, 25, 26, 27, 28, 33, 35, 49, 85, 86, 87, 90, 91, 93, 95, 97, 98, 153, 155, 183, 235, 238, 239
Air Travel 131, 135, 136, 137, 140, 221, 246
Akron 35, 97, 111
Alamosa 49, 51, 67, 111, 137, 197, 204, 208
Alamosa County 51, 91, 93
'America The Beautiful' 47
American Color *Profile* 122
American Federal Savings *Profile* 184
American Web Offset *Profile* 170
Anasazi 17
Antonito 51, 133
Applewood 43
Arapahoe Basin-North Peak-Keystone 205
Arapahoe County 39, 41, 91, 111, 123, 140, 152, 167, 171, 194, 246
Archuleta County 57, 101
Arkansas River 14, 25, 33, 244
Arthur Andersen & Co. *Profile* 108
Arts 207, 208, 209, 210, 211
Arvada 43, 208, 221
Aspen 16, 55, 61, 111, 123, 137, 142, 189, 204, 205, 207, 209, 246
Aspen Airways 137, 140
Aspen Highlands 205
Aspen Skiwear 67
AT&T *Profile* 124; 165
Atchison, Topeka, and Santa Fe Railroad 133
Auraria Higher Education Center 70, 73, 118
Aurora 41, 111, 123, 167, 171, 208, 209, 221
Austin 97
Avon 205

B
Baca County 35, 91, 93
Ball Corporation *Profile* 150, 151; 153, 162
Banks and Banking 175, 177, 181 183, 189, 191
  Affiliated Bankshares of Colorado 183; American Federal Savings *Profile* 184; Central Bankcorporation *Profile* 182; 183; Colorado National Bankshares *Profile* 180; 183; First Interstate Bankcorp *Profile* 176; 183; Intrawest Financial Corp. 183; Silverado Banking *Profile* 186; United Banks of Colorado *Profile* 178, 179; 183, 185, 242
Bates, Katharine Lee 47
Beaver Creek 205
Bench-Ad *Profile* 134
Bent County 35, 91
Bent's Fort 20, 197
Berthoud 41, 205
Best Manufacturing *Profile* 172
Biotechnology 73, 97, 165, 167
Black Canyon National Monument 57, 195, 199
Black Hawk 47, 197
Blacks 23
Blue Cross & Blue Shield *Profile* 68, 69
Boettcher & Co. *Profile* 68, 69
Boulder 24, 37, 39, 41, 73, 111, 129, 167, 171, 183, 197, 205, 207, 221
Boulder County 39, 41, 111, 123, 152

Breckenridge *Profile* 206; 55, 61, 123, 205, 207
Brighton 39, 41
Broadmoor Resort Complex 197
Broomfield *Profile* 42; 41, 43, 167, 221
Brush 35, 183, 236
Buena Vista 47, 83
Buffalo 23, 33
Burlington 35
Burlington Northern 133
Business and Industry 83, 118, 119, 125, 185, 187, 205, 238, 248
Business and Technology Center-Pueblo 152
Business Outlook Conference 118
BusinessWire 125
Buttermilk 205

C
Cache la Poudre 14, 24
Camp Hale 26
Canals 24
Canon City 12, 13, 14, 24, 47, 83, 101, 111, 118, 140, 207
Carbondale 55, 207
Caribou 24
Carson, Kit 21, 197
Castle Rock 43
Cederedge 57
Celsius Energy Corp. 102
Centennial State 25
Center 51, 97
Central Bankcorporation *Profile* 182; 183
Central City 16, 24, 47, 135, 197, 207
Chaffee County 47
Cherry Hill Village 41
Cheyenne County 35, 91, 93, 167
Cheyenne Wells 35
Children's Hospital 79
Cities and Towns
Akron 35, 97, 111; Alamosa 49, 51, 67, 111, 137, 197, 204, 208; Antonito 51, 133; Applewood 43; Arvada 43, 208, 221; Aspen 16, 55, 61, 111, 123, 137, 142, 189, 204, 205, 207, 209, 246; Aurora 41, 111, 123, 167, 171, 208, 209, 221; Austin 97; Avon 205; Berthoud 41, 205; Black Hawk 47, 197; Boulder 24, 37, 39, 41, 73, 111, 129, 167, 171, 183, 197, 205, 207, 221; Breckenridge *Profile* 206; 55, 61, 123, 205, 207; Brighton 39, 41; Broomfield *Profile* 42; 41, 43, 167, 221; Brush 35, 183, 236; Buena Vista 47, 83; Burlington 35; Canon City 12, 13, 14, 24, 47, 83, 101, 111, 118, 140, 207; Carbondale 55, 207; Caribou 24; Castle Rock 43; Cederedge 57; Center 51, 97; Central City 16, 24, 47, 135, 197, 207; Cherry Hills Village 41; Cheyenne Wells 35; Colorado Springs 24, 37, 39, 43, 47, 61, 73, 111, 123, 129, 132, 133, 137, 140, 149, 167, 183, 194, 197, 198, 204, 207, 221, 238, 246; Columbine 43; Commerce City 41; Conifer 43; Cortez 53, 57, 97, 111, 137, 195, 204; Costilla 51; Craig *Profile* 48; 53, 55, 87, 111, 137, 140, 208, 223; Creede 16, 51, 99, 197, 207; Crested Butte 57, 205, 207; Cripple Creek 16, 47, 135, 197; Dacona 41; Del Norte 24, 49, 51; Delta 57, 83, 123, 171, 207; Denver *Profile* 52; 11, 14, 15, 21, 22, 24, 37, 39, 41, 43, 64, 70, 71, 73, 79, 111, 123, 131, 132, 133, 140, 149, 167, 171, 177, 183, 189, 197, 198, 207, 208, 209, 219, 221, 244, 246; Dillon 55; Dinosaur 111; Dolores 57; Dotsero 146; Dove Creek 57; Durango *Profile* 46; 53, 57, 71, 111, 118, 123, 133, 137, 152, 195, 197,
204, 205, 208, 209, 223, 246; Eads 35; Eagle 55, 111, 140, 207; Eaton 133; Edgewater 43; Empire 197; Englewood 41, 123, 167, 194, 208, 221; Estes Park 41, 111, 197, 205, 207; Evans 24; Evans City 41; Evergreen 43, 208; Fairplay 13, 47, 111; Florence 13, 47; Florissant 111; Fort Collins 25, 37, 39, 41, 61, 73, 97, 111, 123, 133, 140, 152, 165, 167, 171, 207; Fort Garland 197, 207; Fort Lupton 20, 41; Fort Morgan 35, 97, 123, 208, 223; Franktown 43; Frisco 55; Fruita 53, 97, 111; Georgetown 24, 47, 133, 197, 205, 207; Gilman 16; Glenwood Springs 55, 111, 123, 131, 146, 183, 197, 205, 207; Golden 22, 24, 39, 43, 73, 83, 103, 105, 111, 171, 208, 209, 221; Granada 24; Grand Junction 53, 67, 71, 95, 97, 111, 123, 131, 132, 137, 152, 157, 195, 204, 205, 208, 223, 246; Grant 205; Greeley *Profile* 40; 24, 37, 39, 41, 61, 73, 87, 90, 97, 111, 123, 152, 165, 167, 205, 207, 221; Greenwood Village 41; Gunbarrel 43; Gunnison 57, 71, 97, 111, 137, 204, 205, 207, 246; Hayden 55; Holyoke 35, 208; Hot Sulphur Springs 13, 55; Hotchkiss 208; Hugo 35; Idaho Springs 16, 47, 197, 205, 208; Ignacio 18, 57, 198; Julesburg 35, 132; Ken Caryl 43; Kiowa 35; Kit Carson 35; Kremmling 55, 197, 205; La Junta 20, 35, 111, 123, 132, 141, 197, 208; Lafayette/Louisville 41, 208; Lake City 16, 57, 197, 208; Lakewood 43, 111, 183, 208, 221; Lamar 35, 67, 137, 152, 157, 208, 223; Larkspur 43; Las Animas 24, 35, 123; Leadville 16, 26, 47, 111, 140, 197, 205, 208; Limon 35, 111, 133, 236; Littleton 39, 41, 61, 123, 194, 208, 221; Longmont 24, 25, 41, 111, 133, 167, 207; Loveland 41, 111, 133, 165, 208; Lyons 41; Manassa 25; Mancos 57, 152, 157; Manitou Springs 45; Meeker 55, 111; Mesa 205; Mesa Verde 17, 57, 111, 195; Mission Viejo 43; Monte Vista 49, 51; Montezuma 57; Montrose *Profile* 44; 57, 67, 111, 123, 137, 171, 204, 207; Morrison 43; Mosca 111; Nederland 41; Northglenn 41, 208, 221; Nucla 208; Orchard City 57; Ordway 35, 83; Ouray 57, 141, 197, 208; Pagosa Springs 57, 205; Palisade 53; Paonia 5; Parachutte 103; Parker 43, 111; Platteville 197; Pueblo 24, 37, 39, 45, 61, 73, 111, 123, 132, 133, 137, 152, 167, 204, 208; Rangley 53, 55, 195, 208; Rifle 53, 55, 83, 208; Rocky Ford 25, 35, 97, 123; Saguache 51; Salida 47, 111, 140, 208; San Luis 21; Sanford 25; Sedalia 43; Sheridan 43; Silver Plume 197; Silverton 16, 57, 133, 141, 197, 208; Snowmass Village 55, 205, 208; Southfork 51; Southglenn 41; Springfield 35, 97, 111, 195; Steamboat Springs 55, 137, 197, 204, 205, 208; Sterling 25, 35, 67, 123, 140, 152, 157, 195, 208; Telluride 57, 137, 189, 197, 204, 205, 208, 246; Thornton 41; Towaoc 18, 57; Trinidad 13, 24, 49, 111, 132, 133, 205, 208; Vail 55, 61, 137, 205, 208; Walden 13, 55; Walsenburg 13, 97, 208; Walsh 97; Westcliffe 47, 197, 205, 208; Westminster 41, 183; Wheat Ridge 41, 43; Windsor 35; Winter Park *Profile* 196; 55, 205; Woodland Park 47; Wray 35
Clear Creek County 47

Clearing House Association 177
Climate 11, 14, 15, 243
Club 20 236
Coal 13, 98, 99, 101, 132, 229, 231
Cobe Laboratories 165
Colleges and Universities 65, 67, 70, 71, 73, 75, 118, 211, 240, 241
Adams State College, San Luis Valley 71; Baptist Bible College, Broomfield 73; Colorado Christian College, Denver 73; Colorado College, Colorado Springs 73; Colorado School of Mines, Golden 73, 105, 167, 171, 240, 241; Colorado State University, Fort Collins 41, 73, 97, 167, 171, 240, 241; Colorado Technical College, Colorado Springs 73; Denver Conservative Baptist Seminary, Denver 73; Fort Lewis College, Durango 71; Iliff School of Theology, Denver 73; Loretto Heights College, Denver 71; Mesa College, Grand Junction 71; Naropa Institute, Boulder 73; Nazarene Bible College, Colorado Springs 73; Parks College, Denver 73; Regis College, Denver, Colorado Springs, Sterling *Profile* 72; 71, 118; St. Thomas Seminary, Denver 73; U.S. Air Force Academy, Colorado Springs 43, 73, 111, 167; University of Colorado, Boulder, Colorado Springs, Denver 41, 73, 75, 79, 118, 119, 167, 171, 185, 240, 241; University of Denver, Denver 73, 118, 119, 167, 173, 240; University of Northern Colorado, Greeley 41, 73; University of Southern Colorado, Pueblo 73; Western State College, Gunnison 71; Yeshiva Toras Chaim Talmudical Seminary, Denver 73
Colorado Advanced Technology Institute 173, 240, 241
Colorado Agricultural Experiment Station 97
Colorado Association of Commerce and Industry 239, 242, 248, 249
Colorado Business and Technology Update 187
Colorado Council on the Arts and Humanities 210, 211
Colorado Department of Agriculture 97, 115
Colorado Division of Commerce and Development *Profile* 36; 118, 153, 238
Colorado Housing Finance Authority 189
Colorado International Trade Division 173
Colorado: Investing in the Future 215
Colorado National Bankshares *Profile* 180; 183
Colorado National Monument 195, 201
Colorado Plains, Inc. 35
Colorado River 14, 33, 51, 146
Colorado School of Mines 73, 105, 167, 171, 240, 241
Colorado Ski Country USA 202
Colorado Springs 24, 37, 39, 43, 47, 61, 73, 111, 123, 129, 132, 133, 137, 140, 152, 167, 183, 194, 197, 198, 204, 207, 221, 238, 246
Colorado State University 41, 73, 97, 167, 171, 240, 241
Colorado-Ute Electric Association *Profile* 82; 231
Columbine 43
Comanche National Grassland 195
Commerce City 41

Computer Industry 121, 123, 127, 129, 162, 163, 165, 240

253

Conejos County 51, 91, 93
Conifer 43
Conquistador 205
Consolidated Space Operations Center (CSOC) 43, 152, 163, 221, 238
Continental Airlines 135
Continental Divide 31, 51, 199
Conventions 205
Coopers and Lybrand *Profile* 110
Coors, Adolph Co. *Profile* 88, 89; 239
Copper Mountain 205
Cortez 53, 57, 97, 111, 123, 137, 195, 204
Costilla 51
Costilla County 51, 91, 93
Counties
  Adams Co. *Profile* 34; 39, 41, 90, 91, 102, 111, 123, 152, 167, 246; Alamosa Co. 51, 91, 93; Arapahoe Co. 39, 41, 91, 111, 123, 140, 152, 167, 171, 194, 246; Archuleta Co. 57, 101; Baca Co. 35, 91, 93; Bent Co. 35, 91; Boulder Co. 39, 41, 111, 123, 152; Chaffee Co. 47; Cheyenne Co. 35, 91, 93, 167; Clear Creek Co. 47; Conejos Co. 51, 91, 93; Costilla Co. 51, 91, 93; Crowley Co. 35; Custer Co. 47; Delta Co. 57, 93, 101, 153; Denver Co. 39, 152, 167, 194, 246; Dolores Co. 57, 91, 93; Douglas Co. *Profile* 38; 43, 153, 167, 171, 221, 237, 246; Eagle Co. 55, 167, 195; El Paso Co. 43, 111, 194; Elbert Co. 35, 91; Fremont Co. 47, 93, 101, 153, 167; Garfield Co. 55, 101, 103, 153, 167, 205; Gilpin Co. 47; Grand Co. 55; Gunnison Co. 57, 101; Hinsdale Co. 57; Huerfano Co. 47, 101; Jackson Co. 55, 101, 102; Jefferson Co. 37, 39, 43, 64, 111, 123, 140, 152, 167, 171, 246; Kiowa Co. 35, 91, 93, 102; Kit Carson Co. 35, 87, 91, 93; La Plata Co. 57, 101, 102; Lake Co. 47, 153; Larimer Co. 41, 91, 102, 111, 171; Las Animas Co. 49, 101; Lincoln Co. 35, 91; Logan Co. 35, 87, 90, 91, 102; Mesa Co. 55, 93, 95, 101, 103, 111, 152, 167, 171; Mineral Co. 51; Moffat Co. 55, 87, 91, 101, 102; Montezuma Co. 93, 153; Montrose Co. 57, 87, 93, 153, 167; Morgan Co. 35, 87, 90, 91, 93, 102, 153; Otero Co. 35, 153; Ouray Co. 57; Park Co. 47; Phillips Co. 35, 91, 93; Pitkin Co. 55, 101, 167; Prowers Co. 35, 87, 91, 93; Pueblo Co. 45, 111; Rio Blanco Co. 55, 87, 101, 102, 103; Rio Grande Co. 51, 91, 93; Routt Co. 55, 87, 101, 167; Saguache Co. 51, 91, 93; San Juan Co. 57, 171; San Miguel Co. 57, 87, 167; Sedgwick Co. 35, 91; Summit Co. 55, 195; Teller Co. 47; Washington Co. 35, 91, 93, 102; Weld Co. 39, 41, 87, 90, 91, 93, 101, 102, 111; Yuma Co. 35, 87, 90, 91, 93
Craig *Profile* 48; 53, 55, 87, 111, 137, 140, 208, 223
Credit Unions 177, 185
Creede 16, 51, 99, 197, 207
Crested Butte 57, 205, 207
Cripple Creek 16, 47, 135, 197
Crowley County 35
Cuchara Valley Resort 205
Cussler, Clive 209
Custer County 47

D
Dacona 41
Dams 244
Del Norte 24, 49, 51
Delta 57, 83, 123, 171, 207
Delta County 57, 93, 101, 153
Denver *Profile* 52; 11, 14, 15, 21, 22, 24, 37, 39, 41, 43, 64, 70, 71, 73, 79, 111, 123, 131, 132, 133, 140, 149, 167, 171, 177, 183, 189, 197, 198, 207, 208, 209, 219, 221, 244, 246
Denver and Rio Grande Western Railroad 132
Denver Business 127

Denver Center for the Performing Arts 209, 210
Denver Chamber of Commerce 248
Denver County 39, 152, 167, 194, 246
Denver Merchandise Mart *Profile* 116, 117
Denver Post 75, 155, 183
Denver Regional Council of Governments 43
Denver Research Institute 119, 173
Denver Technological Center *Profile* 222; 221, 246
Dibble, George 248
Dillon 55
Dinosaur 111
Dinosaur National Monument 195, 201
Dinosaurs 12, 201
Diversification 35, 51, 152, 153, 155, 157, 162, 235, 236, 237, 238, 242
Dixon Paper *Profile* 144
Dolores 57
Dolores County 57, 91, 93
Dolores River 17, 57
Dotsero 146
Douglas County *Profile* 38; 43, 153, 167, 171, 221, 237, 246
Dove Creek 57
Durango *Profile* 46; 53, 57, 71, 111, 118, 123, 133, 137, 152, 195, 197, 204, 205, 208, 209, 223, 246

E
Eads 35
Eagle 55, 111, 140, 207
Eagle County 55, 167, 195
Eastern Mountains 33, 45, 47, 70, 236
Eastern Plains 33, 35, 70, 91, 236, 237
Eastman Kodak *Profile* 168, 169; 37
Eaton 133
Economics 97, 98, 99, 101, 149, 163, 165, 175, 181, 183, 185, 187, 191, 193, 211, 227, 229, 239, 240
Edgewater 43
Education 27, 63, 64, 65, 67, 70, 71, 73, 75, 118, 167, 171, 173, 240, 241
Eisenhower Memorial Tunnel 145, 146
El Paso County 43, 111, 194
Elbert County 35, 91
Eldora 205
Emily Griffith Opportunity School 67
Empire 197
Employment 23, 25, 26, 28, 59, 65, 77, 79, 81, 86, 87, 98, 99, 102, 107, 111, 115, 118, 123, 127, 131, 147, 149, 152, 153, 155, 157, 162, 163, 165, 177, 181, 185, 191, 193, 194, 202, 211, 225, 227, 235, 241
Englewood, 41, 123, 167, 194, 208, 221
Environment 213, 215, 219, 247, 248
Estes Park 41, 111, 197, 205, 207
Evans 24
Evans City 41
Evergreen 43, 208
Exports 86, 91, 93, 95, 115, 149, 173, 229

F
Fairplay 13, 47, 111
Falcon Air Force Station 43
Farming See Ranching, Agriculture
Federal Government 29, 109, 111, 163, 171
Federal Reserve Bank 177
Film Industry 115, 118
Finance 29, 175, 177, 181, 183, 185, 187, 189, 191
Fire Departments See Police
First Interstate Bankcorp *Profile* 176; 183
Fitzsimons Army Medical Center 79
Florence 13, 47
Florissant 111
Florissant Fossil Beds National Monument 201
Flower Industry 95
Ford Motor Company 163, 165
Fort Carson 43, 111
Fort Collins 25, 37, 39, 41, 61, 73, 97, 111, 123, 133, 140, 152, 165, 167, 171, 207
Fort Garland 197, 207
Fort Lupton 20, 41

Fort Morgan 35, 97, 123, 208, 223
Fort St. Vrain 20
Fort Vasquez 197
Four Corners 53, 123, 152, 208
Franktown 43
Fremont, John 21
Fremont County 47, 93, 101, 153, 167
Frisco 55
Front Range 11, 13, 32, 37, 70, 152, 162, 213, 223, 236, 237, 238
Frontier Airline *Profile* 138, 139; 135
Fruit and Vegetable Production 86, 87, 91, 93, 95, 97
Fruita 53, 97, 111

G
Garfield County 55, 101, 103, 153, 167, 205
Gates Corp. *Profile* 154
General Communications, Inc. *Profile* 126
Geneva Basin 205
Geography 11, 13, 15, 16, 31, 32, 37, 39
Geology 12, 13
Georgetown 24, 47, 133, 197, 205
Gerry Division, Outdoor Sports Inc. 67
Gilman 16
Gilpin County 47
Glaciers 14, 16
Glenwood Canyon 145, 146
Glenwood Springs 55, 111, 123, 131, 146, 183, 197, 205, 207
Gold and Silver 16, 19, 21, 22, 47, 98, 99, 132, 175, 195
Golden 22, 24, 39, 43, 73, 83, 103, 105, 111, 171, 208, 209, 221
Goodnight - Loving Trail 25
Gore Range 37
Governor's Blue Ribbon Panel on Colorado 215
Governor's High-tech Cabinet Council 64
Grain Production 86, 87, 91, 93
Granada 24
Grand County 55
Grand Junction 53, 67, 71, 95, 97, 111, 123, 131, 132, 137, 152, 157, 195, 204, 205, 208, 223, 246
Grant 205
Great Sand Dunes National Monument 195, 201
Great Western Railway Co. 133
Greeley *Profile* 40; 24, 37, 39, 41, 61, 73, 87, 90, 111, 123, 152, 165, 167, 205, 207, 221
Greeley, Horace 8, 24
Greenwood Plaza 221
Greenwood Village 41
Gunbarrel 41
Gunnison 57, 71, 97, 111, 137, 204, 205, 207, 246
Gunnison County 57, 101
Gunnison River 195

H
Hach Co. *Profile* 158
Hansen, A.S. Inc. *Profile* 114
Hart, N. Berne 242
Hayden 55
High Technology 26, 41, 123, 127, 129, 149, 152, 153, 157, 159, 162, 163, 165, 167, 173, 185, 187, 238, 239
Highways 131, 140, 141, 142, 143, 145, 146, 147, 245, 246
Hinsdale County 57
Hispanic Culture 19, 49
Historic Buildings and Districts 195, 197
History 16-25, 141, 149
Holyoke 35, 208
Hospitals and Health Care 75, 77, 79
Hot Sulphur Springs 13, 55
Hotchkiss 208
Hotels 197, 198
  Brown Palace, Denver 197; Golden Rose Hotel, Central City 197; Hearth Stone Inn, Colorado Springs 197; Hotel Boulderado, Boulder 197; Hotel Colorado, Glenwood Springs 197; Imperial Hotel, Cripple Creek 197; Oxford Hotel, Denver 197; Peck House, Empire

197; Stanley Hotel, Estes Park 197; Strater Hotel, Durango 197
Hovenweep National Monument 195
Huerfano County 47, 101
Hugo 35

I
Idaho Springs 16, 47, 197, 205, 208
Ignacio 18, 57, 198
Image Corp *Profile* 128
Income 28, 59, 83, 86, 118, 194
Independence Pass 141
Indians 17, 18, 19, 22, 23, 152
Insurance 29, 191
Intrawest Financial Corp. 183
Inverness 221

J
Jackson County 55, 101, 102
Jefferson County 37, 39, 43, 64, 111, 123, 140, 152, 167, 171, 246
Jennings, Rex 248, 249
Johnson, G.E. Construction *Profile* 228
Joint Southeast Public Improvement Association 246
Julesburg 35, 132

K
KCNC Newscenter 4 97
KRMA - TV Channel 6 67
Ken Caryl 43
Keystone *Profile* 200; 55, 205
King Soopers *Profile* 92
Kiowa 35
Kiowa County 35, 91, 93, 102
Kit Carson 35
Kit Carson County 35, 87, 91, 93
Kremmling 55, 197, 205

L
La Junta 20, 35, 111, 123, 132, 141, 197, 208
La Plata County 57, 101, 102
Lafayette/Louisville 41, 208
Lake City 16, 57, 197, 208
Lake County 47, 153
Lakewood 43, 111, 183, 208, 221
Lamar 35, 67, 137, 152, 157, 208, 223
Lamm, Richard (Governor 1974-1986) 237
L'Amour, Louis 209
Land Use 32, 39, 202, 213, 215, 219, 242, 247
Larimer County 41, 91, 102, 111, 171
Larkspur 43
Las Animas 24, 35, 123
Las Animas County 49, 101
Law 83, 127
Leadville 16, 26, 47, 111, 140, 197, 205, 208
Legislature 81
Limon 35, 111, 133, 236
Lincoln County 35, 91
Littleton 39, 41, 61, 123, 194, 208, 221
Local Government See State and Local Government
Logan County 35, 87, 90, 91, 102
Long, Stephen H. 20
Longmont 24, 25, 41, 111, 133, 167, 207
Long's Peak 39
Lorton, Howard Galleries *Profile* 58
Loveland 41, 111, 133, 165, 208
Loveland Basin 205
Lumber Industry 95, 97
Lyons 41

M
MCI 129
Madden, John Co. *Profile* 218
Manassa 25
Mancos 57, 152, 157
Manitou Springs 45
Manufacturing 23, 25, 28, 35, 86, 90, 98, 149, 152, 153, 155, 157, 159, 173, 183, 185, 187, 189, 225, 238
Manville Corporation 37, 43
Martin Marietta *Profile* 160, 161; 26, 37, 162, 238
May D&F *Profile* 60
McIntosh, John 19
Medicine Bow Mountains 37
Meeker 55, 111
Megatrends 8

254

Mesa 205
Mesa County 55, 93, 95, 101, 103, 111, 152, 167, 171
Mesa Verde 17, 57, 111, 195
Mesa Verde National Park 195, 199
Metro Brokers *Profile* 232
Metropolitan State College 70
Miller Stockman *Profile* 94; 67
Million Dollar Highway 141
Mineral County 51
Mining and Minerals 13, 16, 22, 23, 25, 28, 45, 47, 51, 57, 98, 99, 101, 183, 195, 197
Mission Viejo 43
Mission Viejo Realty Group *Profile* 220; 247
Mix, Tom 118
Mobil Corporation 102
Moffat County 55, 87, 91, 101, 102
Molybdenum 98, 101
Monarch 205
Monfort of Colorado 87, 90
Monte Vista 49, 51
Montezuma 57
Montezuma County 93, 153
Montrose *Profile* 44; 57, 67, 111, 123, 137, 171, 204, 207
Montrose County 57, 87, 93, 153, 167
Morgan County 35, 87, 90, 91, 93, 102, 153
Mormons 20, 25
Morrison 43
Mosca 111
Mt. Elbert 12
Mt. Evans 39, 140
Mountain Bell 129
Mountain Rescue Association 83
Museums 198, 209

N
Naisbitt, John 8, 208
National Earthquake Information Service 105, 171
National Bureau of Standards 163, 171
National Center for Atmospheric Research 163, 171
National Jewish Center for Immunology and Respiratory Medicine 79
National Oceanic and Atmospheric Administration 171
National Parks, Monuments, Forests 198, 199, 201, 215, 219
  Arapaho National Forest 199; Black Canyon National Monument 57, 195, 199; Colorado National Monument 195, 201; Dinosaur National Monument 57; Florissant Fossil Beds National Monument 201; Grand Mesa National Forest 199; Great Sand Dunes National Monument 195, 201; Gunnison National Forest 199; Hovenweep National Monument 195; Mesa Verde National Park 195, 199; Pike National Forest 199; Rio Grande National Forest 199; Rocky Mountain National Park 41, 140, 199; Roosevelt National Forest 199; Routt National Forest 199; Royal Gorge 132, 135, 201; San Isabel National Forest 199; San Juan National Forest 199; Uncompahgre National Forest 199; White River National Forest 199
National Theatre Conservatory 210
National Western Stock Show and Rodeo 211
National Writer's Club 209
Nederland 41
Neoplan USA Corp. *Profile* 164; 35, 67, 152
Newspaper and Magazine Industry 75
North American Aerospace Defense Command (NORAD) 43, 111
North Park 13
Northglenn 41, 208, 221
Nucla 208

O
Oil and Gas Industry 55, 98, 99, 101, 102, 103, 183, 229, 239
Oil Shale 13, 53, 55, 103, 236
Optical Disk Technology 129, 165

Orchard City 57
Ordway 35, 83
Otero County 35, 153
Ouray 57, 141, 197, 208
Ouray County 57

P
Pagosa Springs 57, 205
Palisade 53
Paonia 57
Parachute 103
Park County 47
Parker 43, 111
Pawnee National Grassland 195
Pelsue, T.A. Co. *Profile* 166
Penrose Hospital *Profile* 78
Peterson Air Force Base 111
Phelps, Inc. *Profile* 224
Phillips County 35, 91, 93
Pike, Zebulon 20
Pikes Peak 20, 21, 22, 39, 43, 47, 135, 197
Pike's Stockade 197
Pitkin County 55, 101, 167
Platte River 14, 244
Platteville 197
Police and Fire Departments 81
Pollution 39, 245
Population 11, 22-27, 37, 41, 43, 53, 149, 236, 237
Powderhorn 205
Prowers County 35, 87, 91, 93
Public/Private Partnership 64, 247, 248, 249
Public Service Co. of Colorado *Profile* 66; 231
Public Utilities 29, 229, 231, 233
Pueblo 24, 37, 39, 45, 61, 73, 111, 123, 132, 133, 137, 152, 167, 204, 208
Pueblo County 45, 111
Pueblo Ordinance Depot 45
Purgatory 205

R
Radio 75
Railroads 24, 131, 132, 133, 135
Ranching and Farming 25, 27, 86, 87, 90, 91, 235
Rangely 53, 55, 195, 208
Real Estate 29, 183, 191, 215, 219, 221, 223, 225, 227, 229, 247
Recording and Research Center (DCPA) 210
Recreation 157, 193, 195, 199, 201, 211
Regional Transportation District 115, 245
Regis College *Profile* 72; 71, 118
Reilly, Philip J. 247, 248
Religion 81
Retail Industry 29, 59, 61, 223
Rifle 53, 55, 83, 208
Rio Blanco County 55, 87, 101, 102, 103
Rio Grande County 51, 91, 93
Rio Grande River 14, 51
Rivers 11, 14, 16, 24, 33
Robinson Dairy *Profile* 96
Rocky Ford 25, 35, 97, 123
Rocky Mountain Airways 137, 140
Rocky Mountain National Park 41, 140, 199
Rocky Mountain News, *Profile* 74; 75, 155, 239
Rocky Mountains 12, 13, 14, 45-49, 195, 199, 201
Rodeo 211
Rolm 165
Routt County 55, 87, 101, 167
Royal Gorge 132, 135, 201
Russell Stover Candy 67

S
Saguache 51
Saguache County 51, 91, 93
Saint Joseph Hospital *Profile* 76
St. Mary's Glacier 205
St. Vrain 231
Salida 47, 111, 140, 208
Samsonite Corp. *Profile* 156
San Juan County 57, 171
San Juan Mountains 12, 13, 57
San Luis 21
San Luis Valley *Profiles* 50, 104; 25,

49, 51, 71, 86, 91, 93, 132, 153, 171, 236, 237
San Miguel County 57, 87, 167
Sanford 25
Sangre de Christo Mountains 37, 47, 201
Santa Fe Trail 141, 143
Savings and Loan Associations 175, 177, 189, 191
Sawatch Range 47
Schmid, Fred Appliances & T.V. *Profile* 56
Schuck Corp. *Profile* 214
Sedalia 43
Sedgwick County 35, 91
Service Industry 28, 107, 109, 115, 121, 123, 125, 127, 129, 241, 242
17th Street 175
Sharktooth 205
Sheridan 43
Silver See Gold
Silver Creek 205
Silver Plume 197
Silverado Banking *Profile* 186
Silverton 16, 57, 133, 141, 197, 208
16th Street Mall 41, 61
Ski Cooper 205
Ski Idlewild 205
Ski Industry 26, 53, 55, 135, 137, 193, 194, 201, 203, 204, 205, 229
Snowmass Village 55, 205, 208
Social Services 81
Solar Energy 103
Solar Energy Research Institute 103, 105, 163, 171
South Fork 51
South Park 13, 47
South Platte River 33
Southglenn 41
Sperry Corporation 152
Sports 211
Springfield 35, 97, 111, 195
Stapleton International Airport 135, 136, 204, 221, 246
State and Local Government 81, 83, 111
Statehood 24, 25
Steamboat Springs 55, 137, 197, 204, 205, 208
Sterling 25, 35, 67, 123, 140, 152, 157, 195, 208
Stocks and Bonds 175, 177, 187, 189
Stonegate Developments *Profile* 230
Strategic Assessments, Inc. 162, 163
Summit County 55, 195
Summit Group, Inc. *Profile* 120
Sunlight 205
Sunstrand Corp. 67, 152

T
Technology See High Technology
Telecommunications 121, 123, 127, 129, 165
Television 67, 75, 121, 123, 183
Teller County 47
Telluride 57, 137, 189, 197, 204, 205, 208, 246
Territory of Colorado 19-22
Thornton 41
Tivoli Denver *Profile* 54
Toll Roads 143
Topography 11, 13, 31, 32, 39
Tourism 41, 132, 133, 135, 193, 194, 202, 241
Towoac 18, 57
Transpoation 28, 29, 131-133, 135, 137, 140-143, 145, 146, 147, 152, 245, 246
Travelers *Profile* 188
Trinidad 13, 24, 49, 111, 132, 133, 205, 208
Trucking 146, 147

U
Ultimate Foods, Inc. *Profile* 100
Uncompahgre Valley 97
Union Oil Company 103
Union Pacific Railroad 132, 133
United Airlines 135
United Banks of Colorado *Profile* 178, 179; 183, 185, 242
U.S. Air Force Academy 43, 73, 111, 167
U.S. Bureau of Land Management 111

U.S. Bureau of Mines 171
U.S. Bureau of Reclamation 111, 171, 231
U.S. Department of Agriculture 111, 173
U.S. Department of Transpoation 45, 135
U.S. Forest Service 111
U.S. Geological Survey 105, 111, 171
U.S. Immigration and Naturalization Service 111
U.S. Mint 177
U.S. National Park Service 111
U.S. Social Security Administration 111
U.S. Synthetic Fuels Corp. 103
US West *Profile* 112, 113; 127
University of Colorado 41, 73, 75, 79, 118, 119, 167, 171, 185, 240, 241
University of Denver 73, 118, 119, 167, 173, 240
University of Northern Colorado 41, 73
University of Southern Colorado 73
Upland Industries *Profile* 226
Uris, Leon 209
Ute Indians 17, 18, 22, 23, 57, 198

V
Vail 55, 61, 137, 205, 208
Vocational Education 67, 70, 171
  Aims Community College, Greeley 70; Arapahoe Community College, Littleton 70; Arapahoe/Douglas Area Vocational School, Mesa College, Grand Junction 67; Aurora Technical Center, Aurora 67; Boulder Valley Technical Center, Boulder 67; Colorado Mountain College, Glenwood Springs, Steamboat Springs, Leadville 70; Colorado Northwestern Community College, Rangely 20; Community College of Aurora, Aurora 70; Community College of Denver, Denver 70; Delta/Montrose Technical School, Delta 67; Emily Griffith Opportunity School, Denver 67; Front Range Community College, Westminster 70; Lamar Community College, Lamar 70; Larimer County Vocational Technical Center, Fort Collins 67; Morgan Community College, Fort Morgan 70; Northeastern Jr. College, Sterling 70; Otero Jr. College, La Junta 80; Pikes Peak Community College, Colorado Springs 70; Pueblo Community College, Pueblo 80; Red Rocks Community College, Golden 70; San Juan Basin Area Vocational School, Cortez 67 San Luis Valley Area Vocational School, Alamosa 67; Trinidad State Jr. College, Trinidad 70

W
Walden 13, 55
Wall Street of the West 175
Wallace, George M. 246
Walsenburg 13, 47, 205
Walsh 97
Washington County 35, 91, 93, 102
Waste Management *Profile* 80
Water Resources 11, 14, 24, 25, 49, 55, 91, 233, 242-245
Weld County *Profile* 40; 39, 41, 87, 90, 91, 93, 101, 102, 111
Westcliffe 47, 197, 205, 208
Western Slope 13, 15, 31, 51, 53, 55, 57, 103, 152, 223, 236
Westminster 41, 183
Wheat Ridge 41, 43
Windsor 41
Winter Park *Profile* 196; 55, 205
Wolf Creek 205
Woodland Park 47
Wray 35
Writer Corp. *Profile* 216, 217

Y
Yuma County 35, 87, 90, 91, 93

Z
Zoos 198, 209

255